ANNUALS & PERENNIALS

Golden Hands Books

Marshall Cavendish
London and New York

Edited by Maggi McCormick

Published by Marshall Cavendish Publications
Limited, 58 Old Compton Street,
London W1V 5PA

© Marshall Cavendish Limited 1968-68-70-73
This material was first published by
Marshall Cavendish Limited in
Encyclopedia of Gardening

This volume first published 1975

Printed in Great Britain

ISBN 0 85685 099 3

Picture Credits

A-Z Tourist Photo Library, pages 11, 57, 68,
111, 148, 169, 173
Bernard Alfieri, pages 166, 167
H. R. Allen, pages 166, 188
Alpine Garden Society, page 133
D. C. Arminson, pages 51, 53, 54, 57, 61, 62,
63, 66, 71, 72, 73, 74, 77, 88, 89, 116, 191
Barnaby's Picture Library, pages 27, 34
K. A. Beckett, pages 167, 172
Carlo Bevilacqua, pages 56, 60, 86, 173
Antony Birks, pages 63, 164
Blackmore & Langdon, pages 41, 132
D. V. Blogg, page 61
Arthur Boarder, page 139
P, Booth, page 64
R. J. Corbin, pages 8, 9, 10, 51, 52, 61, 72, 88,
89, 102, 103, 120, 122, 123, 124, 125, 126,
127, 128, 150, 153, 159, 166, 171, 175, 176,
177, 178, 181, 184
J. K. D. Cowley, page 86
A. F. Derrick, page 51
Gordon Douglas, pages 43, 48, 81
J. E. Downward, pages 18, 41, 50, 59, 62, 79,
80, 82, 84, 109, 112, 142, 149
Valerie Finnis, pages 16, 17, 23, 24, 49, 55, 65,
77, 82, 85, 94, 110, 111, 112, 114, 115, 121,
133, 137, 138, 143, 146, 147, 150, 155, 159,
162, 165, 167, 168, 176, 179, 186, 192
Paul Genereux, pages 45, 47
A. P. Hamilton, pages 54, 161
Iris Hardwick, pages 42, 107, 118, 186
Ron Hatfield, page 120
H. R. Hood, page 40
Peter Hunt, pages 7, 12, 15, 19, 34, 36, 51, 66,
97, 98, 105, 106, 113, 115, 118, 119, 141, 142,
143, 149, 151, 152, 153, 159, 183
A. J. Huxley, pages 51, 71, 75, 79, 81, 149, 191
George E. Hyde, pages 26, 33, 44, 59, 66, 69,
116, 160, 169, 187
Leslie Johns, pages 19, 33, 39, 104, 114, 118,
163
Reginald Kaye, pages 72, 163
N. Kelly, page 66
D. J. Kesby, pages 76, 85
Edna Knowles, page 174
John Markham, pages 135, 156, 172, 195
Elsa Megson, pages 153, 165, 166, 171, 184,
185, 186, 192
Ministry of Agriculture, page 11
H. Alan Morrison, page 70
Frank Naylor, page 87
Opera Mundi, pages 40, 136
Ronald Parrett, pages 55, 96, 130, 131, 159
Picturepoint, page 22
Ray Proctor, page 160
Christopher Reynolds, pages 50, 69
Peter Russell, page 155
Ruth Rutter, page 76
D. Smith, page 50
Harry Smith, pages 7, 10, 12, 13, 14, 15, 16, 17,
20, 21, 23, 24, 25, 26, 29, 30, 31, 32, 35, 37, 38,
40, 42, 44, 46, 48, 49, 54, 55, 56, 58, 60, 65, 67,
68, 70, 77, 78, 83, 84, 86, 87, 88, 89, 92, 93, 98,
106, 108, 117, 129, 134, 135, 136, 139, 140,
141, 142, 143, 144, 145, 146, 147, 148, 152,
153, 154, 157, 158, 160, 161, 162, 164, 165,
166, 167, 169, 173, 174, 178, 179, 180, 183,
185, 187, 188, 189, 190, 193, 194
Violet Stevenson, page 68
A. Twiner, page 113
D. S. Whicker, page 170
D. Wildridge, pages 91, 193
C. Williams, page 67
Henry Wood, pages 172, 173
Dennis Woodland, pages 64, 70, 72, 156, 183

Introduction

Annual and perennial flowering plants are known and grown in gardens throughout the world. *Annuals and Perennials* introduces the most popular of them, from the tiny, delicate *Ageratum* to the bright and brassy *Zinnia*. There is information about the planting of, and caring for, annuals and perennials, what species to grow where and how each is cultivated. There are special flowers for rock gardens, alpine sites, shady spots and hot houses. There are plants that climb and others that provide garden colour in the dull, drab winter months or startling foliage effects in the summer.

Whether your garden is large or small, shady or sunny, rocky or sandy – *Annuals and Perennials* contains a large and beautiful selection of favourite flowering plants that will suit your requirements.

Contents

Godetia 'Dwarf Double Mixture'

Eschscholtzia 'Double Hybrid'

ANNUALS

Hardy annuals are easy to grow and will give a quick and brilliant display provided they are grown in an open, sunny position in any good garden soil. Many annuals are tender and easily killed by frost, so these kinds are sown under glass in the spring and planted out when all danger of frost is over. Some hardy and half-hardy kinds make excellent pot plants for the greenhouse and there are others that need greenhouse cultivation entirely.

Some, such as the nasturtium, flower better if grown on rather poor soil. Most annuals will make too much leaf growth if grown in soil that is too rich or in shady places. Their rapid growth makes them invaluable for the new garden when flowers are wanted the first year, or for filling gaps in newly-planted herbaceous borders. Some, such as trail-

1 Nemesia strumosa, a half-hardy annual, has flowers in many colours.
2 'Yellow Pygmy' with double flowers is a useful variety of the tall annual Sunflower, Helianthus annuus.
3 Papaver somniferum, the Opium Poppy, is a hardy annual with single or fully double flowers.
4 The half-hardy Venidio-arctotis 'Tangerine' is one of the brightly-coloured varieties of this hybrid.
5 Linum grandiflorum, a hardy annual Flax, has flowers in scarlet, red or rose.
6 Thelesperma burridgeanum, a hardy annual from Texas, has yellow blooms with reddish-brown centres.

ing lobelias, dwarf nasturtiums and petunias are useful plants for hanging baskets. Many are useful for providing colour in urns, terrace pots, window

boxes, tubs and other plant containers. Certain low-growing annuals find a place in carpet bedding schemes such as are still found in public parks. Although the purist may frown upon their use in this way, a few annuals are suitable for the rock garden.

A number of annuals have very fragrant flowers. Some have flowers or seed heads which may be dried for winter decoration indoors (see Everlasting flowers).

Some annuals, including a number of those used for carpet bedding, are grown for the sake of their colourful foliage.

Apart from removing faded flowers, keeping them weeded and staking the taller kinds of annuals need little attention, and they are a quick and inexpensive way to provide masses of summer colour, especially in a new garden.

7

Planting

Of all the operations that contribute to successful gardening, correct planting procedure is one of the most important. Digging a hole, pushing in the plant and hoping is not enough. Any gardener who does just this is doomed to constant disappointments.

Before the actual planting is carried out, careful preparation of the site is necessary, whether the project involved is an extensive border, the planting of a bedding scheme, or the tiniest pocket for an alpine plant. Beds, borders or planting holes should be deeply dug before planting. As far as beds and borders are concerned, full-scale trenching is best although nowadays, most busy gardeners settle for double-digging, or bastard trenching as it is sometimes called.

The surface soil must be broken down to a tilth of a fineness appropriate to the size of the specimens which are to be planted. Obviously, the ground for trees and shrubs will not require such careful preparation as it will for annual bedding plants or alpines.

As well as being thoroughly broken down, the soil should be in good heart. This means that it must contain enough humus and plant foods for the initial requirements of whatever is being planted. This can be achieved by digging in adequate quantities of humus-rich materials such as peat, leafmould, well-rotted garden compost, or animal manures.

These can be supplemented by a dressing of a slow-acting organic fertiliser such as bonemeal or steamed bone flour, forked into the topsoil a week or

1 Peat is spread over the soil to a depth of 2 inches before planting begins.
2 The peat is forked lightly into the top few inches of soil.
3 Thorough raking is carried out before planting to prepare a fine tilth and remove stones. This is particularly important before small seedlings are set out, since the tender young roots need a minimum of resistance.

two in advance of planting or, where individual plantings are concerned, sprinkled into the holes.

Different kinds of plants will obviously need different planting procedures. The smaller they are, the more carefully should the operation be carried out. Appearances, however, can sometimes be deceptive. Nothing could look more delicate and vulnerable than a seedling

that has just made its first pair of true leaves. And yet, at this stage—the best stage for planting out most seedlings—they can be surprisingly tough, perhaps because transplanting causes less damage to their rudimentary root system provided that they are transferred, without undue delay, from seed pans into boxes or nursery beds.

Seedlings should be handled gently, yet firmly, easing them carefully out of the seed compost and grasping them firmly by the leaves between thumb and forefinger as you plant them out in their new soil.

After this operation, particular attention should be paid to watering. Little and often is the rule to follow. Over-watering can cause damping-off, but seedlings should never be allowed to dry out completely; this can prove equally disastrous.

Planting annuals and bedding plants It is important to success when planting annuals, to ensure that they receive as little check as possible; they will then start into active growth again almost immediately. Whether plants come out of boxes, pots or nursery beds, it is always better to wait for a day when the soil is moist (but not soggy) after rain and when the atmosphere is humid. In these conditions, the plants will lose little moisture through transpiration.

If planting out time should coincide with a long dry spell, the only course is to soak both plants and planting holes with water a few hours in advance. The water should be allowed to drain away from the holes before the plants go in. As soon as the soil is friable and the

weather favourable, hardy annuals should be sown where the plants are to flower. These quick growing plants are excellent for 'gapping' in a new herbaceous border where the perennials are still small. If the ground was not prepared last month, the area to be sown should be marked off with short sticks at once, the soil forked over and plenty of damp horticultural peat added to the top 2 or 3 inches. Soil for seed sowing needs to be very fine for good germination.

So the surface should be well raked down to a sand-like tilth before scattering the seed thinly, broadcast or in drills, just covered with soil. Twiggy sticks placed over the newly sown area will deter birds and prevent cats using the soil as a scratching ground.

Bedding plants should never be out of the ground for any length of time. They can suffer a serious check if they are left lying in the sun or in drying winds. The ideal course is to get them straight from box to bed. This is a difficulty that does not arise with plants that are set out from pots.

When planting from seed boxes, the roots of each individual plant should, if possible, be carefully disentangled from those of its neighbours. This will minimise damage and enable the plants to get away again quickly.

Some hardy annuals may be sown in August or September to flower early the following summer. As soon as the seedlings are large enough to handle they should be thinned. With autumn-sown annuals leave the final thinning until the following spring. Distances apart vary considerably, depending on the ultimate height of the annual, but as a general guide dwarf-growing annuals should be thinned to 4–6 inches apart. Those that grow to 15–18 inches tall should be thinned to 9–12 inches and taller kinds should be thinned to 1–2 feet apart.

If seed is wanted for sowing again next year it is best to mark a few good plants early in the summer. The seed-heads should not be gathered until they are fully ripe.

Half-hardy annuals Some annuals and a few perennials treated as annuals will not stand frost, so they are sown under glass in pots, pans or seed boxes, using seed compost or a soil-less seed compost. Sow the seeds thinly and cover and then place a sheet of glass and a piece of brown paper over the pot or box. Turn the glass daily to prevent condensation drips from falling on to the soil. Remove the paper as soon as the seeds germinate but leave the glass on for a further few days, tilting it slightly to admit some air.

When the seedlings are large enough prick them out into boxes of potting compost or a soil-less potting compost and shade them for a day or two from strong sunlight.

When watering seed boxes it is best to immerse them in water up to their rims until all the compost is thoroughly damp. i.e., when the surface has darkened. This method is preferable to watering overhead. Where a soilless seed compost based on peat and sand is used the initial watering usually suffices.

It is essential to harden the plants off well before they are planted out into their flowering positions at the end of May or the beginning of June. Transfer the boxes to a cold frame and gradually increase the ventilation, eventually leaving the lights off altogether except on nights when frost is likely. If a frame is not available, gradually increase the greenhouse ventilation, finally leaving doors and vents open day and night.

It is a great mistake to sow too early under glass as this simply means that the plants receive a severe check by becoming over-crowded in their boxes while waiting to be planted out into their permanent positions.

The damping-off disease at the seedling stage can be troublesome but it can be controlled to a very large extent by using sterilized or soil-less composts and by watering with Cheshunt compound.

It is also possible to sow half-hardy annuals in the open ground in May or early June and, flowering later, they extend the flowering season.

Greenhouse annuals Many hardy, half-hardy and tender annuals make colourful plants for the cool greenhouse. They may also be grown in this way for cut flowers; or the pots, when in flower, may be taken into the house.

Seed is sown as for half-hardy annuals in pans, pots or boxes and the seedlings are potted up when they are large enough to handle. Pot-on as soon as the roots fill the pot. Some annuals resent being transplanted so it is best to sow these straight into their flowering pots and thin out the seedlings later.

The great advantage of a greenhouse for annuals is that flowers may be had throughout the year by sowing at different times. The temperature when sowing should be about 65°F (18°C), but it is not necessary to maintain this high temperature afterwards, provided the greenhouse is completely frost free. Many of the greenhouse annuals will need their growing points pinched out to encourage bushy plants and some will need staking. Water liberally in the summer months but moderately in the winter, and feed the plants with weak liquid manure at regular intervals.

Many seeds of annuals can be sown directly into patio pots to give vivid colour later in the year and spring is the time to sow them. Seed is generally so inexpensive and readily available that a few failures are of no major significance. Alyssum, candytuft, nigella, campanula, mignonette, Virginian stock, wallflowers, forget-me-nots, pansies, *Anemone japonica*, London pride, armeria, arabis and many others

1 For planting in restricted spaces, for example between stones in a dry wall, a narrow two-pronged fork is useful.
2 The best tool to use for preparing holes for small plants is the trowel. The use of a dibber is not recommended, as the roots may get caught in a pocket of air.
3 Firming every plant gently after transplanting is very important. Do not push too hard, as young roots are easily damaged, but ensure that no air pockets are trapped below the surface.

are suitable and effective.

Choose low-growing plants rather than tall and make sure always that they do not get too dry at the roots.

As in the open garden, the greatest

effect is to be obtained by planting colours in concentrated blocks rather than scattering them indiscriminately like confetti. Annuals are cheap and instantly effective, so here, according to colour groupings, are brief selections of low growing annuals suited to window-boxes as well as container plantings on patio, balcony and roof garden. Some flowers, of course, come in several different colours, so may be listed more than once.

White: alyssum, begonia, daisy, candytuft, *Celosia nana*, dianthus, echium, eschscholzia, forget-me-not, gazania, linaria, lobelia, mignonette, nemesia, nemophila, pansy, petunia, *Phlox drummondii*, polyanthus, portulaca, Virginian stock, verbena.

Yellow: *Celosia nana*, eschscholzia, gazania, leptosiphon, limnanthes, nasturtium, nemesia, pansy, polyanthus, *Tagetes signata*, wallflower.

Red: anagallis, begonia, *Dianthus sinensis*, eschscholzia, leptosiphon, mignonette, nasturtium, nemesia, petunia, *Phlox drummondii*, polyanthus, portulaca, *Silene pendula*, Virginian stock, verbena, wallflower.

Blue: anagallis, anchusa, echium, forget-me-not, lobelia, nemesia, nemophila, pansy, petunia, phacelia, polyanthus, Virginian stock, verbena, viscaria.

Choose boxes of plants which are showing colour but which also have many buds waiting to open. Inspect them carefully to ensure that there is no disease present and that the soil is moist. When you get them home keep them in a cool and shady spot until you are ready to plant them.

Have your containers ready with soil, either potting compost or one of the proprietary no-soil mixtures. Water the boxes of plants again a few minutes before planting and then lift each plant out carefully with a good ball of soil adhering to the roots. Plant with a trowel, spreading the roots well and firming the soil over them. Water again thoroughly until water begins to trickle from the drainage holes. Leave the newly planted containers in shade for a day or two before bringing them to their final positions.

Once the plants are growing away well, examine them each day for disease, water regularly and pick off all dead flowers to ensure a continuity of bloom. Any plant that dies should be removed at once, both for the appearance of the container and in case the dead or dying plant spreads its infection to its neighbours.

Cloches

There are certain flowers which are particularly suited to cloche cultivation. These can be brought into bloom several weeks earlier and the quality of the flower is often much better. Hardy annuals, in particular, are ideal plants for cloche protection during the early

1

2

1 In a window box planted for summer flowering, purple and white Petunias are used with deep scarlet Pelargoniums and white Oxeye Daisies. Trails of yellow Lysimachia nummularia hang down to cover the box.
2 For the best effect in boxes and pots, use summer flowering plants that are just coming into bloom, taking care not to injure the roots during transplanting.

6 inches apart in the rows. Cloches must be placed over the rows as soon as the seed is sown in the north. Southern sowings need not be covered until early October.

As soon as the plants are a few inches high, they should be provided with pieces of brushwood, through which they will grow. If large flowers are required, plants should be grown in the cordon system. Only the strongest sidegrowth is allowed to grow on after the initial stopping, and this growth should be trained up a strong cane. Plenty of water is required during the summer. There are so many beautiful, reliable varieties that a selection should be made from a specialist's catalogue.

Other hardy annuals Those suitable for cloche work and autumn sowing include

stages of their growth. The most important of these are sweet peas.
Sweet Peas Sowing time for sweet peas in the north and south is late September. Seed can also be sown in March. The strip of ground should be deeply worked and plenty of organic matter incorporated in the form of peat, old manure or composted vegetable waste. Seed is sown one row per small cloche and two under the larger types. Space the seeds

calendula, candytuft, cornflower, scabious, viscaria, sweet sultan and nigella. For spring sowing the following are recommended: godetia, mignonette and clarkia. Seed is sown in groups as thinly as possible or in single rows. Large cloches can accommodate two rows.

Half-hardy annuals These benefit considerably from early covering after they have been sown in early April. Seed is sown thinly in single or double rows according to the size of the cloche. Final thinning is from 8-12 inches apart. Suitable varieties include zinnias, schizanthus, nemesia, nicotiana, petunia, and dimorphotheca.

Fragrant annuals

Those in search of fragrance are more likely to find it among the annuals and biennials than among the hardy perennials, for it is a quality possessed by many of the plants that are raised from seed sown in the spring, either under glass or in the open ground. Of these undoubtedly the most popular are the delightfully fragrant sweet peas, varieties of *Lathyrus odoratus*. As with other plants the fragrance varies a good deal but a good seedsman's list will make a point of describing those which possess it more strongly than others. Among other annuals and biennials which have it are Sweet Alison (*Lobularia maritima*), wallflowers (*cheiranthus*), snapdragons (*antirrhinum*), ten-week, Brompton and East Lothian stocks (*Matthiola incana*), night-scented stock (*Matthiola bicornis*), marigolds (*calendula*), nasturtiums (*tropaeolum*), mignonette (*Reseda odorata*), Sweet Sultan (*Centaurea moschata*), the sweet-scented tobacco plant (*nicotiana*), sweet scabious (*Scabiosa atropurpurea*), annual lupins and the biennial evening primrose (*Oenothera odorata*). All of these are popular with most gardeners, but less well known, perhaps, is the Marvel of Peru (*Mirabilis jalapa*), a half-hardy annual with small trumpet-shaped flowers in various colours, their fragrance identical with that of the sweet-scented tobacco plant. *Cleome spinosa*, the spider flower is another less common annual, 3 feet or so tall, with spidery-petalled pink or white flowers which add fragrance to their other attractions.

Bedding out

This term, in use by gardeners, describes a form of gardening in which plants raised elsewhere in a nursery garden or greenhouse are planted in a previously prepared bed.

The description bedding plant is not an exact one and only means that the plant is grown elsewhere in some quantity and then planted out as a temporary occupant of the bed; this being known as 'bedding out'.

The bedding plant in private gardens has, in general, had its day, since this style of gardening entails much expertise.

In public gardens and for certain formal occasions the bedding plant still has its uses.

Summer bedding Bedding plants for summer planting must be raised in early spring under glass. The skill of the operation is proved when a good uniform crop of plants is ready and hardened-off.

1 Cloche protection, given here to Polyanthus, insures speedy germination and improves the quality of the blooms. It also prevents damage by birds.
2 The fragrant flowers of the annual Evening Primrose open in the late afternoon and early evening and fill the garden with lovely scent.

11

Borders

There is no strict definition of the somewhat loose gardening feature known as a border, and there may, on occasions, become confusion between beds and borders. However, for the sake of convenience, a border may be looked upon as a bed which is considerably longer than it is wide. True beds are normally round, oval, square or rectangular, or of some other geometric shape in which the length is not much more than, perhaps, two or three times greater than the width, although even this cannot be considered to be an exact definition since a bed, say, 2 feet wide and 6–8 feet long would be better described as a bed rather than a border; longer than this it may be considered as a narrow border, sometimes described as a 'ribbon' border.

Two kinds of border which are occasionally seen, more often in large gardens than in small ones, are those devoted to one kind of plant and to plants of one colour. These can make pleasant features, but the drawback to a border devoted to one kind of plant is that its season is a short one. Thus a border planted up entirely with, say, lupins, paeonies, or delphiniums will be effective for not much more than three to four weeks. This may be tolerated in the large garden but is wasteful of space in smaller gardens. The one-colour border can be planned to have a much longer life, probably throughout much of the summer, but it is not easy to design to give continuity without awkward gaps appearing as plants go out of flower.

Another kind of border is the annual border, consisting entirely of hardy and half-hardy annuals. It is not too easy to plan a successful annual border, but properly planned and looked after it can be one of the most colourful features for many weeks during the summer and early autumn. When preparing the plan, which should be done on paper first, it is essential to take into consideration the differing heights of the plants to obtain a satisfactory overall effect, and their colours to avoid colour clashes, particularly as many of the more popular annuals tend to have bright colours, not all of which associate well together. The unfortunate visual effect which can be produced by grouping orange and the brighter reds together, can usually be avoided by separating these colours with patches of white-flowered plants or with grey-leaved annuals.

To prolong the flowering period as much as possible it is essential to dead-head the plants as soon as the flowers fade, otherwise they will run to seed and cease to flower. Regular feeding with weak liquid fertilizer will also help to make the plants flower longer.

The range of plants which may be grown is wide, with great variation in height and colour. It includes a fair number of plants grown for their colourful foliage. A pleasant effect, especially in a long, narrow border, may be obtained by using dwarf annuals only, those up to about 9 inches tall.

Another way of filling bare patches during the summer particularly, is to plunge pots of plants in flower into the ground, to their rims. Such plants as dahlias and early-flowering chrysanthemums may also be used to provide extra colour. The imaginative gardener will find still more variations of planting up the mixed border to provide a satisfactory and colourful feature.

All borders need extremely careful planning, and maintenance must be fairly consistent to keep the border at an optimum level of enjoyment. A complete overhaul is necessary during the dormant season, the time when the ground is dug thoroughly and fertilizer applied in preparation for the following year's blooming season. The annual border is a great advantage here; in other kinds of borders, mixed or devoted entirely to shrubs, bulbs or herbaceous plants, the plants remain in the ground and must be worked round with enormous care, which can be a time-consuming process.

1 Cladanthus arabicus, a plant from the western Mediterranean region, has yellow daisy-like flowers.
2 Tropaeolum majus is the well-known and deservedly popular Nasturtium.
3 A double-flowered form of the Pot Marigold, Calendula officinalis.
4 and 5 Two forms of the Californian Poppy, Eschscholzia californica, a hardy annual available in a wide choice of colours.

BIENNIALS

Biennials are a valuable division of garden plants for by the biennial habit of storing up in the first season a reserve which is expended wholly in the second season, a much greater quantity of blossom is possible than with either the annual or perennial habit of growth.

Where a new garden is being made annual and biennial plants will be of great service for it generally takes from three to five years to achieve a garden furnished satisfactorily with perennials and shrubs; and even then biennials will still be needed.

The chief drawback to the cultivation of biennials is the space which must be given to them in the reserve garden or frame, since they are not moved into their final stations until they are large, healthy plants.

The term *biennial* is not used too strictly by the gardener and some short-lived perennials, some monocarpic plants, and certain annuals also are sometimes given biennial treatment.

As with annuals, biennial plants are sub-divided into hardy and half-hardy biennials.

Cultivation Biennials may be sown in spring in a frame or cold greenhouse or outdoors from May onwards.

If seeds are sown in drills instead of broadcast it will be easier to keep them free from weeds by running the hoe between the rows from time to time.

After a severe thinning seedlings should be pushed on with adequate feeding until by October they will be large leafy plants, which may then be put into their final stations in the flower border. If the weather is dry when the time comes to transplant give the bed a thorough watering. Careful lifting, using a trowel, will minimize root disturbance, and subsequent checks to growth.

If it is intended to treat hardy annuals as biennials (and this gives excellent results) the only way in which the operation differs from that described above is in the time of the seed sowing, which should be at the end of the summer or even in early autumn, but do not sow too early or the plants will flower in their first year. Given this biennial treatment, annuals will make much larger plants than when grown in the normal way and this must be allowed for when they are planted out in their final positions.

Half-hardy biennials will need overwintering in frost-free conditions in a frame or a cold greenhouse. They are not an important section and one may well do without them, devoting precious greenhouse space to other things.

The following are biennials, or are often treated as biennial: adlumia, althaea (hollyhock), antirrhinum (snapdragon), *Campanula medium* (Canterbury bell), cheiranthus (wallflower), cnicus (fishbone thistle), *Dianthus barbatus* (Sweet William), *Digitalis purpurea* (foxglove), *Erysimum arkansanum*, *Hedysarum coronarium* (French honeysuckle), *Humea elegans* (half-hardy), hunnemannia, lunaria (honesty), matthiola (Brompton, Nice and Intermediate stock), some meconopsis, myosotis, *Oenothera biennis* (evening primrose), onopordon (cotton thistle), *Papaver nudicaule* (Iceland poppy), verbascum (mullein).

1 Dianthus barbatus, the well-known Sweet William, and 2, Lunaria biennis, the Honesty, are two of the many plants known as biennials, sown one year to flower the next.

Nigella 'Persian Jewels'

Ageratum (aj-er-a-tum)

From the Greek *a*, not, *geras*, old, a reference to the non-fading flowers (*Compositae*). Floss flower. Half-hardy compact annuals from Mexico. Useful for summer bedding schemes, carpeting, edging and window boxes. The English name floss flower well describes the blue-mauve tassel-like flowers borne in fluffy heads, which last well.

Species cultivated *A. houstonianum* (syn. *A. mexicanum*) 1½ feet when grown naturally. Heart-shaped leaves in rosette formation. Cultivars include 'Florist Blue', 'Little Dorrit' azure blue, 'Mexican White', 'Fairy Pink', 'Blue Ball'.

Cultivation Ageratums like a sunny spot and need to be planted not less than 6 inches apart to be effective. Propagation is by seed sown in pans in March in a temperature of 55°F (13°C). Prick off, and about ten days later pinch out the tips of the shoots to ensure branched and compact specimens. Harden off and plant out in late May or early June. The flowering season will be prolonged if the dead flower-heads are removed from time to time. When a really good colour is obtained cuttings may be taken in spring from a plant that has been potted up in the late summer and flower-buds removed. Pot up and harden off once the cuttings have rooted and plant out in May.

Alonsoa (al-on-so-a)

Named after a Spanish official, Alonzo Zanoni (*Scrophulariaceae*). Mask Flower. Half-hardy shrubby perennials with racemes of flowers. Grown as annuals outside or as perennials under glass.

Species cultivated *A. acutifolia* 1½–2 feet, bushy in habit, scarlet flowers; var. *alba*, white June outside or winter under glass. Both good as greenhouse pot plants or as half-hardy annuals. *A. incisifolia*, 1–2 feet, shrubby, for greenhouse cultivation, scarlet flowers, summer. *A. linearis*, to 2 feet, shrubby, grown as annual or greenhouse perennial, scarlet flowers, May–October; var. *gracilis*, more slender. *A. meridionalis* (syn. *A. mutisii*), 1 foot, flowers dull orange, summer.

Cultivation Recommended compost: 2 parts of loam, 1 of leaf mould and 1 of coarse sand. Plants require a sunny position under glass or outside and only moderate watering. Pot in March. Minimum winter temperature: 50°F (10°C). Propagation is by seed sown in March at 60°F (16°C), or by cuttings in August.

Alyssum

From the Greek *a*, not, and *lyssa*, madness: once thought to cure madness or rage (*Cruciferae*). Madwort. The dwarf perennial species in cultivation, mostly with grey foliage and yellow flowers, are chiefly confined to the rock garden; the taller-growing kinds are best in borders. The popular sweet alyssum or sweet Alison, is now cor-rectly called *Lobularia maritima*.

Species cultivated *A. alpestre*, 3 inches, of tufted habit, flowering in June. *A. argenteum*, to 18 inches, becomes woody at the base. Deep yellow flowers in clustered heads, May–July. *A. flexicaule*, 3 inches, tufts of fragrant yellow flowers, spring. *A. idaeum*, of trailing habit, soft yellow flowers, May–June. *A. moellendorfianum*, 6 inches, silvery plant, flowers in long racemes. *A. montanum*, to 10 inches, usually much lower, fragrant flowers, bright yellow, in loose racemes. *A. pyrenaicum*, 8–10 inches, dwarf shrubby growth, white velvety leaves, white flowers, summer. *A. saxatile*, gold dust, to 12 inches, spreading habit, numerous heads of golden-yellow flowers, April–June, vars. *citrinum*, lemon-yellow, *compactum*, 4–6 inches, 'Dudley Neville', 6–9 inches, biscuit yellow, *plenum*, double flowers, dwarf, 'Tom Thumb', *variegatum*, variegated foliage, yellow and green. *A. wulfenianum*, 3 inches, round, thick, silver leaves, pale yellow flowers in large, loose heads borne in summer.

Cultivation Alyssums require only ordinary, well-drained soils in the open. *A. saxatile* is often grown vertically in walls or on banks. It should be trimmed back after flowering to prevent it from straggling unduly. Young plants are occasionally used in spring bedding schemes. Propagation is by seed, division or by 2–3 inch long cuttings taken in early summer and rooted in shade.

Amaranthus (am-a-ran-thus)

So named (from the Greek *a*, not, and *maraino*, to fade) because of the lasting qualities of the flowers (*Amaranthaceae*). Half-hardy annuals grown in sub-tropical bedding schemes, some for their coloured foliage, in shades of red, crimson and green. They are good for pot culture under glass. *A. caudatus*, love-lies-bleeding, and *A. hypochondriacus*, prince's feather, are two of the hardiest and can be treated as hardy annuals in warmer areas.

Species cultivated *A. caudatus*, 2–3 feet, long, red, drooping tail-like flowers, August; vars. *albiflorus*, greenish white, *atropurpureus*, blood red. *A. gibbosus*, dwarf, slender flowers in red clusters. *A. hypochondriacus*, 4–5 feet, flowers in dense spikes, deep crimson, July, purplish green foliage; vars. *atropurpureus*, dark, *sanguineus*, blood red throughout, *sanguineus nanus*, dwarf form, *splendens*, good crimson foliage. *A. melancholicus*, 1–3 feet, grown chiefly for its variable coloured foliage; vars. *ruber*, leaves crimson, *bicolor*, leaves green streaked yellow, *tricolor*, Joseph's coat, 18 inches, purple and green leaves, yellow stalks, *salicifolius*, 3 feet, narrow, brightly coloured leaves, bronze-green with orange and crimson markings. Cultivars: 'Fire King', 'Molten Torch', 'Pygmy Torch'.

1 *Ageratum houstonianum is a half-hardy annual used for summer bedding.*
2 *Alonsoa meridionalis, the Mask Flower, is a half-hardy shrubby perennial usually grown as an annual in the open garden.*

Cultivation Plant out in June in sunny beds. Propagate by seed sown in a temperature of 55–60°F (13–16°C) in March. Harden off young plants carefully before planting out.

Amellus (a-mel-us)

From the name given by Virgil to a similar flower growing by the River Mella (*Compositae*). A small genus of annual or perennial plants from South Africa, easily grown, requiring no special care. They have single daisy-like flowers.

Species cultivated *A. annuus* (syn. *Kaulfussia amelloides*), 6 inches, yellow-centred blue flowers about 3–4 inches across, summer. An annual. *A. lychnitis*, 6 inches, an evergreen trailing plant with violet flower heads.

Cultivation *A. annuus* is grown as a hardy annual, propagated by seed sown in spring. *A. lychnitis* is a greenhouse perennial pot plant, increased by division or by cuttings from new growth in spring.

Ammobium (am-o-be-um)

Derived from Greek words *ammos*, sand and *bio*, to live, describing its sandy habitat (*Compositae*). Everlasting sand flower. The single species available is particularly useful as an 'everlasting' cut flower. It is normally grown as a half-hardy annual, though September-sown seedlings can be raised in a cool greenhouse. *A. alatum* grows 18–24 inches tall and its flower-heads are

1 The lemon-yellow Alyssum saxatile citrinum are excellent plants for a dry wall or a sunny bank.
2 Amaranthus 'Molten Torch' and 3 Amaranthus caudatus, Love-lies-Bleeding, are two half-hardy annuals used in sub-tropical bedding schemes.

silvery-white and yellow, about 1 inch across, var. *grandiflorum* has larger flowerheads, 2 inches across, summer.

Cultivation Seed is usually raised under glass in a temperature of 50–55°F (10–15°C), in early spring. Plant out in May at 6 inches apart in rich, light soil in a warm spot. Alternatively seed may be sown outside direct into borders in May; or, as above, in September to obtain larger plants. Flowers will remain their true silver-white colour if cut before they are fully expanded and hung up-sidedown in an airy building in shade.

Anagallis (an-a-gal-is)
From the Greek *anagelao*, meaning delightful (*Primulaceae*). Pimpernel. Though some species are naturally perennials, it is usual to treat all as annuals in cultivation. As such they are a delight at the front of the annual border, as they are usually low or even trailing in habit. *A. tenella* may be used to great advantage in a moist or boggy spot.

Species cultivated *A. arvensis* (poor man's weather glass), of prostrate growth, flowers $\frac{1}{4}$ inch wide, variable shades between scarlet and white, late summer; vars. *caerulea*, blue; *phoenicea*, red; *latifolia*, blue. *A. linifolia*, 12 inches, flowers blue, red undersides, $\frac{1}{2}$ inch wide, July; vars. *breweri*, red, *collina*, flowers rosy purple; *lilacina*, lilac; *monellii*, flowers larger than the species; *phillipsii*, deep gentian-blue. *A. tenella* (bog pimpernel), 2–4 inches, bell-shaped flowers, $\frac{1}{2}$ inch across, pink with darker veins, summer.

Cultivation A sunny spot suits these charming plants, in ordinary garden soil; a moist place for *A. tenella*. Seed may either be sown in heat in March and planted out in June, or sown direct into flowering positions in April. *A. linifolia* may be propagated by division in March if kept as a perennial.

Antirrhinum (an-tir-i-num)
From the Greek, *anti*, like, *rhinos*, snout, a reference to the curiously shaped flowers (*Scrophulariaceae*). The most important of these nearly hardy perennials is the snapdragon, *Antirrhinum majus*, which is grown extensively as a half-hardy annual for bedding purposes. In some districts it will prove hardy and remain perennial but as the plants are inclined to become straggly after the first year they are nearly always treated as annuals, although plants are sometimes naturalised in the crannies of old walls. *A. majus* originally came from the Mediterranean region where it grows to 3 feet in height. It has been considerably developed for bedding purposes by plant breeders. Species suitable for the rock garden are *A. asarina* and *A. glutinosum*, but like *A. majus* they are not reliably hardy.

Species cultivated *A. asarina*, a trailing plant with yellow flowers, from June to

1 *Anagallis linifolia is one of the best of the blue-flowered annuals.*
2 *Antirrhinum 'Sentinel Sunlight'.*
3 *The South African Amellus annuus has blue flowers with yellow centres.*

17

September. *A. glutinosum*, low growing with yellow and cream flowers in summer. *A. majus*, 3 feet, the well-known snapdragon. Flowers pink in the species. Many garden forms have developed from this species by natural variation. It has also been hybridized to produce plants in a wide range of colours and of various heights including dwarf spreading plants. Plants remain in flower over a long period, through summer and autumn.

Some good cultivars *Tall* (3–4 feet): 'Cloth of Gold', golden yellow. 'Giant Ruffled Tetra' strain mixed colours, large. 'Rocket Hybrids', mixed large flowers, vigorous plants. *Intermediate* (1½ feet): 'Dazzler' brilliant scarlet. 'Eldorado', deep, rich golden yellow. 'Fire King', orange and white. 'Malmaison', silver pink, dark foliage, 'Orange Glow', deep orange, cerise throat, 'Purity' white. Regal Rose', an F.1 rust-resistant hybrid; rich rose red. *Dwarf* (9 inches); 'Floral Carpet' Mixed F.1 Hybrids, extremely colourful. 'Magic Carpet Strain' mixed colours. 'Tom Thumb', 9 inches, available in various colours or mixed. *Rust resistant:* 'Amber Monarch', golden amber. 'Orange Glow', deep orange, cerise throat. 'Rust Resistant Roselight', rich glowing salmon, 'Toreador', deep crimson. 'Victory', buff pink, suffused orange. 'Wisley Golden Fleece', yellow. Seedsmen list many more and new ones appear regularly.

Cultivation The low growing species, *A. asarina* and *A. glutinosum*, need plenty of sun and good drainage and may be planted in April in any ordinary soil. It is wise to take cuttings in August, inserting them in sandy soil in a pot in case the parent plants are killed by frost in the winter. The garden forms of *A. majus* grown as half-hardy annuals, are sown in March in a temperature of 70°F (21°C); the seedlings are pricked out into boxes and then hardened off and planted out in May or the beginning of June. They may be used to fill gaps in borders but look best when planted in drifts in the garden or in bedding displays in public parks. Seed may also be sown outdoors in April. Plants may also be grown in pots in the cool greenhouse for spring display, for which purpose seed is sown in August. Plenty of ventilation should be given at all times. The height of these snapdragons varies a great deal, from the 9 inches of the dwarf kinds to the 4 feet of the tall varieties. Under glass, in pots, the latter may, by careful feeding and attention to watering, be induced to grow even taller.

A great deal of hybridizing has been carried out with these popular bedding plants and there are now tetraploid cultivars which have larger flowers on robust plants.

Antirrhinum rust is a troublesome disease of cultivated snapdragons caused by the attack of one of the rust fungi known as *Puccinia antirrhini*. It

Antirrhinum majus 'Fiery Red' is a tall growing perennial usually cultivated as an annual.

shows first as light brown pustules on the under surface of the leaves and later there appear dark brown ones on leaves and stems. Even small seedlings can be infected. Spraying may be useful if repeated often, but the only real remedy is to grow resistant varieties.

Arctotis (ark-to-tis)

From *arktos*, a bear in Greek and *ous*, an ear, probably referring to the shaggy fruits of this annual (*Compositae*). Decorative half-hardy annuals and perennials, mostly from South Africa, that flower from July to September and like being baked in the sun on a warm sunny bank.

Annual species cultivated *A. breviscapa*, 6 inches, orange. *A. grandis*, 1½ feet, silvery flowers with blue reverse. *A. laevis*, 8 inches, flowers brownish, suffused red. *A. stoechadifolia*, 2 feet, flowers white, blue reverse.

Parennial species cultivated *A. acaulis*, 6 inches, orange-carmine.

Hybrids There are large-flowered hybrids, half-hardy annuals listed as *A.* × *hybrida*, in a wide colour range, including yellows, oranges, reds, crimsons, purples and whites. All are about 1–1½ feet tall. 'Crane Hill', 2 feet, has white flowers with a blue centre and a yellow zone (see also Venidio-Arctotis).

Cultivation Sow seeds in heat in March, prick out the seedlings and harden them off before planting them out 1 foot apart when frosts are over. They make excellent plants for the unheated greenhouse in pots containing loam and leafmoud

in equal parts, plus a little sharp sand. These should start in a sunny place and should be watered moderately from October to March, freely at other times. Cuttings may be taken in early summer and rooted and overwintered in a frame or greenhouse, but propagation by seed is the usual method. *A. acaulis* needs cloche or frame protection in winter.

Argemone (ar-gem-o-ne)
From the Greek *argemos*, meaning a white spot, referring to a cataract on the eye which this plant was said to cure (*Papaveraceae*). A small genus of hardy summer-flowering perennial plants from America with poppy-like flowers, usually grown as annuals.

Species cultivated *A. grandiflora*, 3 feet, flowers large, up to 4 inches across, white, satiny lustre, leaves thistle-like, white-veined; var. *lutea*, yellow flowers. *A. mexicana*, prickly poppy, devil's fig, 2 feet, annual with spiny foliage, flowers 2½ inches across, lemon-yellow or orange. *A. platyceras*, 1–4 feet, white or purple flowers.

Cultivation The argemones do well in sandy soils and sunny situations. Sow the seeds in April thinly, where they are to flower, and thin later, spacing the plants 9 inches apart. They may also be grown from seed sown under glass in spring. The seedlings are pricked off into individual small pots and planted out in the open in May after they have been hardened off.

Arnebia (ar-ne-be-a)
Arneb, the Arabic name for one of the species gives this genus its name (*Boraninaceae*). Annuals and perennials that have been introduced from Turkey and Armenia, among them the prophet flower.

Species cultivated *A. cornuta*, 1½–2 feet, an annual, flowers yellow with purplish-brown spots in summer. *A. echioides*, 1 foot, the prophet flower, yellow flowers in summer, marked with brownish-purple spots, a perennial.

Cultivation Plant the perennial species in autumn or spring and propagate by seeds or division in spring. Sow seeds of the annuals in a frame or cool greenhouse in March and plant out seedlings in May. They all like an open, well-drained position and are not particular as to soil.

Asperula (as-per-u-la)
From the Greek *asper*, rough, as the leaves are rough to touch (*Rubiaceae*). A genus of herbaceous perennials and annuals, and a few shrubs, for the rock and woodland garden.

Species cultivated *A. arcadiensis*, low growing, deep pink tubular flowers, spring, needs protection against damp in winter. *A. gussonii*, 1 inch, forms low cushions and has shell-pink flowers in spring. *A. hexaphylla*, 1 foot, white flowers in summer. *A. lilaciflora caespitosa*,

prostrate form, pink flowers, a plant for the scree. *A. odorata*, the native woodruff, 9 inches, white, very fragrant flowers in spring, does well in shade. *A. orientalis*, 1 foot, annual with very fragrant blue flowers, summer. *A. suberosa*, makes an extensive 3 inch high mound smothered with pink flowers in summer, needs winter protection against damp, a good plant for the alpine house. *A. tinctoria*, prostrate, white flowers, summer.

Cultivation The perennial species, except where indicated, need well-drained soil and sunny positions. All may be propagated by seed and some of the perennial species will divide quite easily although *A. suberosa* and *A. arcadiensis* are more difficult. The annual *A. orientalis* thrives in a moist, shady position.

1 The blue flowers of Asperula orientalis are very fragrant.
2 An Arctotis hybrid.
3 A flower of Arctotis grandis.

1

2

3

Begonia (be-go-ne-a)

Commemorating Michel Bégon, 1638–1710, Governor of Canada, patron of botany (*Begoniaceae*). These half-hardy herbaceous and sub-shrubby plants are natives of moist tropical countries, apart from Australia. They need greenhouse treatment, though a large number are now used in summer bedding schemes.

The genus begonia is usually divided into two groups; those species with fibrous roots and those with tubers. Other classifications give special treatment to the winter-flowering forms, and to those grown exclusively for the interest of their leaves. A notable feature of begonias is their oblique, lop-sided leaves.

There has been so much hybridising in this genus that the naming has become quite complicated, and the custom of giving Latin specific names has not made matters easier.

The begonia, unlike the majority of plants, has, instead of hermaphrodite blooms, separate male and female blossoms on the same plant; the female flowers are generally removed as not being of much interest, though if seed is required,

1 and 2 Two excellent examples of large-flowered double begonia hybrids.
3 'Flamingo' is one of a number of Begonia semperflorens often used for summer bedding.
4 The Rex Begonias are grown for their colourful leaves.

they must, of course, be retained. The seed is dust-fine and needs no covering of soil, in fact the raising of begonias from seed has something in common with the art of raising ferns from spores.

Species cultivated The best-known begonias are the hybrids of the tuberous species: *B. boliviensis, B. clarkei, B. cinnabarina, B. davisii, B. pearcei.*

Another important group consists of the hybrids and varieties of *B. rex*, a plant from Assam with most interesting, colourful foliage. The winter-flowering and fibrous-rooted varieties derived from *B.* 'Gloire de Lorraine', a variety originally raised in France in 1891 by the plant breeder Victor Lemoine, who crossed *B. socotrana* and *B. dregei*, form a most valuable group as they furnish the greenhouse at a difficult time of the year.

Fibrous-rooted species include: *B. acutifolia*, white, spring. *B. angularis*, white-veined leaves. *B. coccinea*, scarlet, winter. *B. evansiana*, pink, almost hardy (possibly hardy in the south-west). *B. fuchsioides*, scarlet, winter. *B. froebelli*, scarlet, winter. *B. foliosa*, white and rose, summer. *B. glaucophylla*, pink and pendulous, winter. *B. haageana*, pink, autumn. *B. hydrocotylifolia*, pink, summer. *B. incarnata*, rose, winter. *B. manicata*, pink, winter. *B. scharffiana*, white, winter. *B. semperflorens*, rose (has important large-flowered vars.). *B. socotrana*, pink, winter.

Nurserymen's catalogues contain long lists of hybrids of the above, too numerous to mention here, but in various shades of pink, red, cream and white with enormous double flowers in a number of different forms.

Species with ornamental leaves include: *B. albo-picta, B. argenteo-guttata*, white and pink speckled leaves. *B. heracleifolia*, leaves deeply lobed. *B. imperialis*, velvety-green leaves. *B. boeringiana*, foliage purplish and green. *B. maculata*, foliage spotted white. *B. masoniana*, ('Iron Cross'), leaves green with a prominent dark 'iron cross' marking, popular as a houseplant. *B. metallica*, foliage has metallic lustre. *B. olbia*, bronze leaves spotted white. *B. rex*, foliage metallic silver and purple. *B. ricinifolia*, bronze leaves. *B. sanguinea*, leaves blood-red beneath. There are, in addition to the species given, many hybrids with beautiful leaves, especially named garden hybrids derived from *B. rex* and its varieties and other species, all known as Rex begonias.

Cultivation The fibrous-rooted begonias are usually obtained from seed, which should be sown in January in a temperature of 60°F (16°C). It is also possible to root growths from the base of the plant. The sub-shrubby perennial forms will

1 Begonia fuchsioides produces its scarlet flowers in winter in the greenhouse.
2 'Lady Roberts' is a large-flowered hybrid which blooms in winter.

come easily from normal cuttings, or all begonias may be raised by leaf cuttings. Leaf cuttings are single leaves which are pegged down in sandy compost, the undersides of all the main veins having been nicked with a razor blade. The temperature should be around 60–70°F (16–21°C). Little plants should form where veins were cut, and these may later be detached and potted-on separately. Most begonias need a winter temperature of about 60°F (16°C). The ornamental Rex type must not be exposed to full sunlight, and many of the other classes will be happy with much less light than suits other greenhouse plants.

The tuberous begonias may, of course, be grown from tubers. These are usually started into growth by placing them in shallow boxes of peat or leafmould in February or March, hollow side uppermost, in a temperature of 60–70°F (16–21°C). After roots have formed the tubers are potted up in small pots and later moved into larger ones. A compost of equal parts of loam, leafmould, well-rotted manure and silver sand is suitable. Do not start to feed these tuberous plants till they have formed roots, or they will decay, but after they are rooted a bi-weekly dose of liquid manure is helpful. The tuberous begonias may also

1 'Mrs Heal' is another winter-flowering Begonia.
2 Brachycome 'Purple King' is a striking hybrid of the Swan River Daisy.
3 Browallia speciosa is a handsome pot plant or annual bedding plant.

be raised from seed, and if this is sown in February plants may flower from July to October. These seed-raised plants are popular for summer bedding.

Tuberous begonias when their season is over must be gradually dried out. They may be left in their pots in a frost-proof shed, or knocked-out and stored in clean dry sand.

Brachycome (brak-e-ko-me)
From the Greek *brachys*, short, *comus*, hair (*Compositae*). A genus of half-hardy Australian annual or perennial herbs. The species usually cultivated is *B. iberidifolia*, the Swan River daisy, which grows 9–12 inches tall and has 1 inch wide daisy flowers in shades of blue, pink and white in summer. Named hybrids in separate colours are available, including: 'Little Blue Star', 'Purple King' and 'Red Star'.
Cultivation These plants are easily grown in a dry, sunny bed. Sow seed under glass in March in boxes of light soil and plant out in May, or sow in the

open in early May where the plants are to flower. When sown under glass in August or September they will make good pot plants for early spring display under glass.

Browallia (brow-al-le-a)
Commemorating either Johan Browallius, Bishop of Abs, or Dr John Browall of Sweden (*Solanaceae*). Annual and perennial plants from South America, usually grown as greenhouse plants. In a sheltered garden the annual species may be bedded out in early June.
Species cultivated *B. americana* (syn. *B.*

demissa, *B. elata*), 1–1½ feet, soft violet-blue, June to October, annual. *B. grandiflora*, 2 feet, blue with yellow tube, July, annual, Peru. *B. speciosa*, 1½–2 feet, blue, violet or white, perennial greenhouse plant usually grown as an annual, Colombia. *B. viscosa*, 1–1½ feet, violet-blue, white centre, summer, perennial in the greenhouse.

Cultivation Sow the seed in March in finely sifted soil, only just covering it, and germinate in a temperature of 55–65°F (13–18°C). When large enough to handle transplant three or four seedlings to a 5 inch pot and stand the pots on the greenhouse shelf. Give weak manure; water during May and June. Pinch plants back to make them bushy. They will flower from July onwards. Seedlings for planting outdoors must be well hardened off before planting in June.

Calandrinia (kal-an-drin-e-a)

Commemorating J. L. Calandrini, a Swiss botanist (*Portulacaceae*). Some of the species of the rock purslane are perennial in their South American and Californian habitats but are usually treated as half-hardy annuals. They are useful for the rock garden or for sunny crevices. The colours are dazzling.

Species cultivated *C. grandiflora*, 1–1½ feet, rosy-red, July to October, fleshy foliage. *C. menziesii* (syn. *C. speciosa*), 6–9 inches, ruby-crimson, June to September. There is also a white variety. *C. umbellata*, 6 inches, magenta, July to September, leaves dark green, narrow. In mild areas this Peruvian species may survive outdoors for two or three years.

Cultivation Sow the seed in boxes in March at a temperature of 55–60°F (13–16°C). The soil should be light and well-drained. Transplant seedlings into small pots when large enough to handle and plant out in the open in June. The seed may also be sown out of doors in April where plants are to flower. The plants must have a sunny position, for the flowers need sun to open fully.

Calceolaria (kal-see-o-lair-e-a)

From the Latin *calceolus*, a slipper or little shoe, referring to the curious shape of the flower (*Scrophulariaceae*). Half-hardy and greenhouse plants, shrubby, herbaceous and rock garden plants. They are mostly natives of Chile and Peru.

Herbaceous species cultivated *C. amplexicaulis*, 1–2 feet, yellow, summer. *C. arachnoidea*, 9–12 inches, purple, June to September. *C. corymbosa*, 1–1½ feet, yellow and purple, May to October. *C. pavonii*, 3–5 feet, deep yellow and brown,

1 The dwarf Peruvian Calandrinia umbellata reaches 6 inches in height and flowers in late summer.
2 Callistephus chinensis, the China Aster, are half-hardy and will flourish in most soils in open, sunny positions.

summer. *C. purpurea*, 1–2 feet, reddish-violet, July to September.

Hardy *C. acutifolia*, often confused with *C. polyrrhiza*, creeping, large yellow flowers with red dots, June. *C. biflora* (syn. *C. plantaginea*), 1 foot, yellow, July. *C. darwinii*, 3 inches, yellow with large brown spots on lip, June and July, rock garden or in a large pot in a cold frame; a difficult plant. *C. fothergillii*, 6 inches, sulphur-yellow, red spots, July. *C. tenella*, 3 inches, golden-yellow, crimson spots, June.

Cultivation: Herbaceous varieties Sow seed in July on the surface of fine soil in well-drained pans or shallow boxes. Cover with a sheet of glass and stand in a cold frame or under a bell-glass and keep moist and shaded. Transplant seedlings in August. In September pot singly into 2 inch pots in a compost of 2

Calendulas, sometimes called Mari-golds, are hardy annuals growing 12 to 15 inches in height.

1 'Geisha Girl' is a cultivar with incurved blooms.

2 'Art Shades' is a double strain vastly superior to those with single blooms.

parts of sandy loam, 1 part of leaf-mould, old manure and sharp sand. The winter temperature should be about 50°F (10°C). Discard the plants after they have flowered.

Hardy varieties Plant in March or September in soil enriched with leafmould and in partially shaded places on the rock garden. Water freely during dry weather in summer. Seed of annual varieties may be sown in the open during March and April.

Propagation of shrubby varieties is by

cuttings 3 inches long inserted in sandy soil in a shaded cold frame in September or October, or in a cool greenhouse; hardy varieties by division of the roots in March, or by seed sown in pans in February or March and only very lightly covered with sifted soil. Place in a cold greenhouse or frame.

Calendula (kal-en-du-la)
From the Latin *calendae*, the first day of the month, probably referring to the fact that some species flower almost perpetually (*Compositae*). Natives of Europe. One species only is widely grown, *C. officinalis*, the English, or pot marigold; the latter name is derived from its use in the past as a herb for flavouring soups etc. The specific name *officinalis* also means it was once considered to have medicinal properties. A hardy annual, the species grows 12–15 inches tall and bears single, orange, daisy-like flowers on branching stems. Through hybridization there are now many attractive cultivars from cream to deep orange, double, semi-double and quilled, mainly taller than the type, reaching about 2 feet, and blooming continuously throughout the summer and early autumn.

Cultivars 'Art Shades', a strain in apricot, orange, cream, etc.; 'Campfire', deep orange, long stems; 'Crested mixed', various colours; 'Flame Beauty'; 'Geisha Girl', like an incurved chrysanthemum; 'Indian Maid', pale orange, maroon centre; 'Pacific Beauty mixed', large flowers, various shades; 'Radio', quilled; 'Rays of Sunshine', various colours; 'Twilight', cream.

Cultivation Any ordinary soil which is not too rich is suitable and though plants will bloom in the shade, they tend to become leggy, and a sunny site is best. Seed is sown thinly out of doors in March or April where plants are to flower and the seedlings thinned to 9 inches apart. Seed may also be sown in September, slightly more thickly. The seedlings are then left to stand the winter and thinned in the spring. Losses occur more through wet and cold winds than hard frosts, so choose a sheltered site and well-drained soil. Grown this way plants are useful for cloching if wished.

Callistephus (kal-is-tef-us)
From the Greek *kallistos*, most beautiful *stephos*, a crown, a reference to the flower (*Compositae*). A genus of a single species, introduced from China by a Jesuit missionary in 1731. This is *C. chinensis*, commonly known as the China or annual aster, a half-hardy annual. The original plants had single purple flowers on 2 foot stems but *C. chinensis* has been greatly hybridised to give a wide variety of flower form, in which the petals may be quilled, shaggy, plumed or neat. Colours range from white through pinks and reds to purples and blues and recently yellow has been introduced; heights vary from 6 inches to 2½ feet.

Among the most important are the wilt-resistant strains. These flowers may be used for exhibition, bedding, cut-flowers and some strains make useful pot plants.
Cultivation China asters grow on a wide range of soils provided they have been well cultivated and manured and the lime content maintained. Open sunny sites give best results. Seed is sown in March in a temperature of 55°F (13°C), and the seedlings subsequently pricked out and hardened off, for planting out in May. Seed may also be sown as late as April in the cold frame. Plant out 6–12 inches apart according to the height of the variety. When flower buds show, give a feed of weak liquid manure. Never allow the plants to receive a check in any way. When raising plants keep them growing the whole time.

Many new cultivars may be bought in separate colours, and several are wilt-resistant. A good seedsman's catalogue should be consulted.

Named strains, in mixed colours include:

Single flowered, all 2–2½ feet: 'Southcote Beauty', long petals; 'Super Chinensis', good for cutting; 'Upright Rainbow', attractive mixture of colours.

. Semi-double and double, dwarf: 'Bedder' series, 6 inches; 'Feather Cushion', 6 inches; 'Thousand Wonders', 6 inches; 'Dwarf Cartmel', wilt-resistant, 10 inches; 'Dwarf Chrysanthemum-Flowered', 12 inches; 'Dwarf Queen', 12 inches; 'Dwarf Waldersee', carpet effect, semi-double, wilt-resistant; 'Lilliput', 15 inches, cut-flower.

Early-flowering: 'Early Burpeeana', 18 inches; 'Early Curlylocks', 18 inches, ostrich plume type; 'Early Wonder', 15 inches, comet type; 'Queen of the Market', 2 feet, cut-flower.

From 2–3 feet: 'Bouquet Powderpuff', densely petalled, centre quilled; 'Californian Giants', good for exhibition; 'Comet', mid season, curling petals; 'Crego', branching, long-stemmed, fluffy appearance; 'Duchesse', American introduction, vigorous, inward curving like a chrysanthemum, includes yellow; 'Mammoth Victoria', bedding and cutting; 'Ostrich Plume', old favourite, now with wilt-resistant varieties; 'Paeony-flowered', incurved, pale colours; 'Rayonantha', new, quilled, wilt-resistant; 'Super Princess', similar to 'Bouquet Powderpuff'.

Celosia (se-lo-se-a)
From the Greek *kelos*, burnt, referring to the burnt appearance of the flowers of

The Celosias are a group of half-hardy annuals resembling fluffy grasses.
1 The flowers of Celosia plumosa, the Cockscomb, reach 18 inches and are produced in pyramidal, often drooping, panicles.
2 This red Cockscomb with contrasting bronze foliage is sometimes used on its own in the open garden.

1 Chrysanthemum segetum is a hardy annual that grows to about 18 inches in height.
2 Cheiranthus are treated as biennials by sowing in May.

some species (*Amaranthaceae*). A genus of half-hardy annuals with brilliant flowers of golden-yellow, and glowing shades of red, which look more like bright grasses.

Species cultivated *C. argentea*, 2 feet, tapering spikes of creamy-white flowers all summer; var. *linearis*, leaves narrower, bronze-red in autumn. *C. cristata*, the cockscomb, has tightly packed flowers in rather congested form. There are many cultivars of this, including *nana* 'Empress', 1 foot, dark foliage, crimson 'comb'; 'Golden Beauty', 1 foot, flowers dark golden yellow; *nana* 'Jewel Box', very dwarf and compact, wide colour range, orange, cream, pink, red, and bronze, new; 'Kurume Scarlet', 3 feet, foliage bright red; 'Toreador', 1½ feet, bright red, good form, can be dried and retains colour if kept away from light. *C. plumosa*, 2½ feet, Prince of Wales's Feather, the leathery species with graceful spikes of flowers; vars. 'Golden Plume'; 'Scarlet Plume'; 'Lilliput Firebrand', 1 foot. Both *C. cristata* and *C. plumosa* are sometimes looked upon as varieties of *C. argentea* and may sometimes be so listed in catalogues.

Cultivation Celosias are very good greenhouse plants. Sow seed in seed compost in a temperature of 65°F (18°C) in February. Pot up the seedlings singly, never allowing them to become pot-bound. Keep the atmosphere moist and plants gently growing without any

check. Pot finally into 6 inch pots. Plants should be shaded throughout the summer. Bedding plants should be hardened off and planted out in the second week in June.

Centaurea (sen-taw-re-a)

From the classical myths of Greece; the plant is said to have healed a wound in the foot of Chiron, one of the Centaurs (*Compositae*). A genus of annual and perennial plants with flowers not unlike those of a thistle in structure. The annuals (cornflowers and sweet sultan) are good for cutting; some species of perennials are used as foliage plants for the silvery-white leaves.

Annual species cultivated *C. cyanus*, the cornflower, 2½ feet, a native plant, blue flower, summer. There are garden varieties in many colours, including *caerulea fl. pl.*, double blue; 'Julep', good reds. pinks and a white; 'Mauve Queen'; *nana* 'Polka Dot', 1 foot, mixed colours, good for bedding or edging, excellent range of colours including maroon; *nana* 'Rose Gem'; *rosea fl. pl.*, double pink; 'White Lady'. *C. moschata*, sweet sultan, 1½ feet, pale lilac purple, fringed petals, sweetly scented. The strain *imperialis* (Imperial Sweet Sultan), 3 feet, branching stems, mixed colours, is one of the best. Other cultivars are *alba*, white; *flava*, yellow; *rosea*, pink; 'The Bride', pure white.

Cultivation Annuals need a light friable soil with good lime content. Seed is sown in March or April where the plants are to flower and the seedlings thinned 9–12 inches apart. Tall kinds need staking. For early cut flowers, sow in August or September, keep the soil cultivated between the rows, but leave thinning until the spring.

Cheiranthus (ki-ran-thus)

Origin of name doubtful, possibly from the Arabic *kheyri*, a name for a fragrant

red flower, combined with the Greek *anthos*, flower (*Cruciferae*). These are the wallflowers; there are minor botanic differences only between this genus and the genus *Erysimum*.

Species cultivated *C. allionii*, Siberian wallflower, 1 foot, bright orange, spring, hybrid, thought by some botanists to be an erysimum. *C. alpinus*, 6 inches, yellow flowers, May, Scandinavia. *C. cheiri*, the wallflower or gillyflower (note: in the eighteenth century the gillyflower was the carnation), 1–2 feet, various colours, spring, Europe, including Britain. *C. × kewensis*, 1 foot, sulphur yellow, orange and purple flowers, November to May, a hybrid. *C. semperflorens* (syn. *C. mutabilis*), 1 foot, purple flowers, spring, Morocco.

Cultivars Dwarf: 'Golden Bedder', 'Blood Red'; 'Orange Bedder'; 'Golden Monarch'; 'Ruby Gem'; 'Vulcan', crimson; all about 1 foot. 'Tom Thumb', mixed colours, blood red and golden-yellow; 'Harpur Crewe', golden yellow, all about 9 inches.

Early flowering: 'Yellow Phoenix'; 'Early flowering Fire King'; 'Early Flowering Vulcan'; 'Feltham Early', red and brown.

Tall and sweet-scented: 'Blood Red'; 'Scarlet Emperor'; 'Cranford Beauty', yellow; 'Eastern Queen', salmon and apricot; 'Fire King', intense flame colour; 'Primrose'; 'Cloth of Gold'; 'Ellen Willmott', ruby; 'Rose Queen'; 'Carter's White'; 'Bacchus', wine red; 'Carmine King', all 1½–2 feet.

Cultivation Wallflowers grow well in an ordinary, not too heavy, well-drained soil. The plants like chalk, so lime or old mortar may be added with advantage. Put them in sunny borders or beds or into old walls, where plants may remain perennial. Sow seed broadcast or in drills, ½ inch deep, 6 inches apart, in May. When the third leaf has formed transplant the seedlings 6 inches apart both ways in a previously limed bed of firm soil. Seedlings may be attacked by the turnip flea beetle, and it is wise to take precautionary measures by dusting the soil and the seedlings with derris or a proprietary flea beetle dust, repeating the operation at weekly intervals for several weeks. Transplant them to their final quarters in September or October at least 1 foot apart either way and make the soil firm around the roots. It is usual, though not essential, to discard plants after flowering. To grow them in walls add a little soil and well-rotted manure to holes and sow a pinch of seeds in each hole in May, or transplant young seedlings to the sites.

Wallflowers make useful early-flowering pot plants for the greenhouse. Sow seed in ordinary good soil in 6 inch pots in September, put them in a cold frame until the flower buds form and then transfer them to a greenhouse, water them moderately only and supply weak liquid manure when in flower.

Discard the plants after flowering.

Wallflowers may also be propagated by cuttings made from side shoots rooted in sandy soil. *C. alpinus*, *C. × kewensis* and *C. semperflorens* are best grown in sunny rock gardens in a mixture of loam soil and old mortar. They may be top-dressed every year with well-rotted manure.

Chrysanthemum (kris-an-the-mum)

From the Greek *chrysos*, gold, *anthemon*, flower (*Compositae*). A genus of over 100 species of annuals, herbaceous perennials and sub-shrubs, distributed over Africa, America, Asia and Europe, including Britain. The well-known greenhouse and early-flowering (outdoor) chrysanthemums are descended from *C. indicum*, found in China and Japan, and *C. morifolium* (syn. *C. sinense*), from China, two closely related, variable plants. For full details of the cultivation of these chrysanthemums see Chrysanthemum cultivation.

Annual species cultivated *C. carinatum*, 2 feet, white and yellow flowers, summer, Morocco; cultivars include *burridgeanum*, white with a crimson ring; *flore pleno hybridum*, fringed double flowers, mixed colours; 'John Bright', pure yellow; 'Lord Beaconsfield', bronze-red and bronze rings on various ground colours; 'Northern Star' white, sulphur yellow ring; 'The Sultan' coppery-scarlet; 'W. E. Gladstone', coppery-scarlet; 'White Queen'. *C. coronarium*, 1–4 feet, yellow and white, double, southern Europe; vars. 'Golden Crown', 3–4 feet, butter-yellow; 'Cream Gen', 'Golden Gem', 1 foot; 'Golden Glory', 2 feet, single. *C. frutescens*, Paris daisy, marguerite, shrubby half-hardy plant, strictly a perennial but usually treated as an annual, $2\frac{1}{2}$–3 feet, white, blooming continuously, valuable greenhouse pot plant for winter, or out of doors in summer, Canary Islands; var. 'Etoile d'Or', lemon-yellow. *C. inodorum*, 9 inches, white, summer, good for cutting. *C. multicaule*, 9 inches, single golden yellow flowers, summer, Algeria. *C. nivellii*, 1 foot, white, summer, Morocco. *C. segetum*, corn marigold, yellow boy, $1\frac{1}{2}$ feet, golden-yellow, summer, Europe (including Britain), Africa, Asia; vars. 'Eastern Star', yellow; 'Evening Star', golden-yellow; 'Golden Glow', double; 'Morning Star', pale yellow.

Cultivation The annuals, with the exception of *C. frutescens*, are hardy and seed is sown out of doors in April or May where the plants are to flower, in open, sunny positions and ordinary soil. An earlier start may be made by sowing under glass in spring, hardening off the seedlings and planting out in May, 6 inches apart. They may also be grown as pot plants, planting four seedlings to a 5 inch pot, seven to a 6 inch pot, growing them on in a cold frame for indoor decoration, or in the greenhouse for display purposes.

C. frutescens is propagated from cuttings taken in summer and rooted in heat in the greenhouse. The rooted cuttings are potted on, kept in a sunny place out of doors until September then moved into a cold frame until November when they are brought into the greenhouse to flower in a temperature of 50–55°F (10–13°C). Moderate watering only is required, but plants should be fed with weak liquid manure when their pots are full of roots. For outdoor cultivation in the summer cuttings are taken early in the year, grown on, hardened off and planted out in May.

1 Chrysanthemum 'Fair Lady' comes into flower in late December, a time when cultivars of this colour are not appearing freely. These plants are of moderate height with strong constitutions.
2 The 'Keystone' Chrysanthemum is a large-flowered intermediate decorative which grows to about 4 feet in height. It is especially desirable for its high resistance to weather damage.

Chrysanthemum 'Florence Shoesmith' produces a huge reflexed bloom in late autumn or early winter. It is a strong-growing cultivar of medium height.

Chrysanthemum cultivation

There are very many different kinds of chrysanthemum; however, this article is concerned only with those garden and greenhouse plants which are descended from two original species, *Chrysanthe-mum indicum* and *Chrysanthemum morifolium* (syn. *C. sinense*).

These hybrids may be divided into three classes according to their season of blooming. The Early-flowering type blooms in the open garden before October 1st. Mid-season varieties flower in October and November under glass and are followed in December and January by the true Late-flowering section. The glasshouse types are nor-mally grown in pots but may be planted in the open garden for the summer and lifted into the greenhouse for blooming. Flowers may, therefore, be had from August to January and there is a great variety of form and colour.

Propagation of all types is by division or cuttings, the latter giving the best results particularly for exhibition. The stools are taken up a few weeks after flowering and when the soil has been removed by washing they are boxed up in fresh compost. Since a period of dormancy is essential the boxes are kept in a cool airy place such as a cold frame and the stools kept only just moist for about a month. Slight frost will do no harm but some protection should be given when conditions are severe. Cold wet soil will cause more loss than frost.

The stronger light and higher temper-atures of the spring season will cause the stools to start into growth but when cuttings have to be rooted early in the year, this process must be accelerated. A heated greenhouse is best but soil warming in the frame itself will certainly help. A temperature range of 45–55°F (7–13°C) is ideal and this must be asso-ciated with good light conditions. Once the new growth appears, watering can be increased, and the amount should be regulated according to the speed of growth. Cuttings are taken in the usual way when they are about 3 inches long. They root easily on an open bench if some muslin is stretched a few inches above them. The temperature range is as mentioned above. The time for inserting the cuttings will vary according to the facilities available and the varieties in-volved. Generally speaking, the early flowering-types are struck in February and March, together with those flower-ing in December. The mid-season varieties can be rooted from January to March.

The treatment of the young plants will vary according to the method by which they are to be grown. Plants intended for the open garden are best planted up in boxes 4 inches deep filled with potting compost or the equivalent soilless com-post. Another plan is to make up a bed of compost on the floor of the cold frame. In either case, space out well at not less than 4 inches to avoid thin spindly growth. If the plants are to be flowered in large pots they should be transplanted from the cutting bed into 3 inch pots using the same compost as for boxes.

At this stage it is important to keep the plants cool and a cold frame is quite suitable in most areas from the middle of March. Plenty of light and air will keep the growth sturdy. Water the plants moderately and allow the pots and boxes to dry out between waterings. Soil kept wet all the time will encourage soft growth but overdryness produces a hard plant which can never give satis-faction. The hardening off process will aim at fully exposing the plants to

unsheltered conditions by the end of April or early May.

Plants in pots will require repotting before this time and as soon as the small pot is full of roots the plant should be moved to a 5 inch or 6 inch size, using a rich potting compost or the equivalent soilless compost. Again the emphasis should be on good spacing for maximum light while the plants should only be watered sparingly, particularly for the first few weeks. A short stake is usually needed at this time, with the stem lightly looped to it.

Plants in boxes will normally grow well until planting-out time, but if there are any signs of starvation, give a few diluted liquid feeds at weekly intervals.

During these early stages of growth the three main pests are likely to be slugs, greenfly and leafminer. The first may be controlled with metaldehyde bait, while the others succumb to sprays of BHC which should be at half the normal strength to avoid scorching tender foliage.

From early May the treatment of plants varies according to type and it is necessary to follow each method separately.

Early-flowering chrysanthemums These are flowered in the open garden and the ground must be well prepared during the winter. The main aims are to provide

After lifting, the chrysanthemum stools are 1) washed free of soil and 2) the basal shoots cut away. Plant the stools in clean boxes as close together as is convenient. 3) Special attention needs to be paid to labelling. 4) To avoid confusion, keep one variety in each box, but if this is not possible, label each stool separately. 5) Use soil which has not previously been used as the rooting medium for chrysanthemums. 6) Water the stools in and stand in a light cool place. A cold frame is ideal. Growth will start when the temperature is raised to 45–50°F (7–13°C).

plenty of humus for moisture retention and sufficient nourishment to sustain the plants in full growth for a period of several months. The basic method is to dig the land one spit deep incorporating farmyard manure or compost at the rate of one bucket per square yard. At the same time, dust the trenches with bonemeal, using ½–¾ lb per square yard. The ground is left rough for weathering until the middle of April when a light forking over is given. This should never go deeper than 3–4 inches but this surface layer must be enriched by working in a base fertilizer or a similar general fertilizer at ¼ lb per square yard. This programme provides nourishment immediately available at the surface for the young roots and slow acting organic

material at lower levels to serve the mature plant. Lime is required only if the soil is rather acid (pH less than 6·5). Where plants are to be grown in rows on a separate plot, this cultivation should be given to the whole area but if plants are to form groups in a border the same kind of preparation may be given to the actual planting sites.

A careful raking will level the soil and prepare a good planting tilth in early May and the actual moving of the plants may be done from about May 10th in the south if the weather is suitable. The first step is to place the canes either in rows or groups according to the site. Plants should never be closer than 18 inches and rows can be double, leaving paths 2½ feet wide between each pair. Planting may be done when the soil is nicely moist without being sticky. A hole is taken out close to the cane and large enough to contain the root ball without cramping. If soil preparation was not well done or the soil tends to be poor, it is a good idea to incorporate a handful of peat and a sprinkling of base fertilizer in the bottom of the hole. Water the boxes some hours beforehand so that the plants may be removed from them with little damage to the roots. Plant firmly at the same level and immediately give one loose tie around the cane to avoid breakages. It is better not to water in

but if the weather is dry try to keep the plants going with overhead sprays of water until a shower comes. When watering is essential give a substantial amount so as to wet the soil quite deeply.

Slugs may still be troublesome and appropriate action must be taken. In built-up areas birds may become a problem, as they peck at leaves and growing points with unfortunate results. Black cotton string stretched in criss-cross fashion a few inches above the tips still seems to be the best answer. The birds stop attacking the plants after a few weeks and the string can be removed to make hoeing easier.

It is important to keep the plants growing steadily without any check and in dry weather a thorough watering may be necessary every week though a mulch of compost, peat or lawn mowings may help on light soils. Feeding will also help, but it should not be overdone. One application of fertilizer at the end of May and another at the end of June should be quite enough if the winter cultivation was well done. Each time use a fertilizer containing about twice the amount of nitrogen as potash. Throughout the growing season keep the ground free of weeds but resort to hand weeding after mid-June to avoid damaging the surface roots. Pests will cause trouble, and particular attention should be given in July and August when

capsid bugs are active. A fungicidal spray every ten days should prevent significant damage. Tying-in of the stems is also very important. They may either be looped to a strong central cane or enclosed in a framework of three canes. In either case allow some movement of the stems, for in this way they will bend before the wind. Too rigid a support often results in breakage.

The pinching and disbudding process for large blooms follows the same pattern for early-flowering and late-flowering and will be described fully in a later paragraph.

Late-flowering chrysanthemums These plants are grown on in the 5–6 inch pots for several weeks but before they become pot bound they must be potted on to their final sizes. The 9 inch size is the most useful pot but both 8 inch and 10 inch may be used. For the very best results the following crop may be taken:
Large exhibition blooms Two blooms in a 10 inch pot or one only to an 8 inch.
Incurveds and decoratives Three blooms in an 8 inch pot or four to a 9 inch. The 10 inch size is only used for the very vigorous plants when up to six blooms may be taken.
Singles Best quality is obtained when four blooms are taken from an 8 inch and two more for every inch increase in the size of pot.

These figures are for blooms of

exhibition quality but for good cut-flowers one may safely increase the crop by 50 per cent in each instance.

The final potting which is usually necessary in early June, must be done carefully. Potting compost is advised, or the equivalent soilless compost. The first step is to provide adequate drainage in the bottom of the pot, covering the bottom layer of large crocks with smaller ones and placing on top of this a thin layer of peat or the coarser material of the compost. Place the root ball on the coarse material and add compost until the final level is some 3 inches below the rim. New compost is added and some gentle firming must be done as each handful is placed. Modern practice does not favour the heavy ramming which was once the custom. When peat/sand composts are used, no firming of any kind is necessary.

If the plants were watered several hours before potting, there will be no need to water them in, indeed it is best to place the newly-potted stock in a cool, shady place and provide them with overhead sprays of water as long as possible. Under good conditions it may not be necessary to water for between four to seven days. When water is obviously needed give sufficient to fill the whole 3 inches of free space which has been left at the top of the pot. Thereafter, each plant should be watered according to its needs, allowing the soil to dry out almost to the point of causing the plant to flag a little before watering again. It is difficult to describe the precise state the soil should have reached, but the grower will soon become expert at judging the correct time to water.

Once the plants are established in their new pots they may be stood out in rows for the summer. The standing ground should be in full sun and the rows of plants set out with wide paths for easy access. The maximum room available should be given to each plant and it is best to stand the pots on slates, planks or gravel to discourage the entry of worms and to ensure free drainage of surplus water. The canes inserted at final potting must be securely tied to a straining wire stretched about 3½ feet above the pots. If these wires are supported by firm end posts, there will be no fear of damage by winds which always

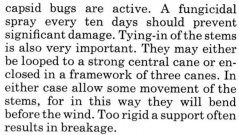

1 Cuttings of chrysanthemums are made from strong sturdy shoots taken from the base of the plant, 2 to 3 inches in length.
2 The lower leaves are removed and the cutting inserted firmly, about an inch deep, with a wooden dibber into a special compost covered with sand.
3 Each container should be clearly labelled with the variety name and the cuttings then watered in.
4 Stand the pots close together in a cool, shaded greenhouse or frame until rooting occurs.

seem to come in September when the plants are large.

Pest control, tying and watering will all need attention through the growing season but a major concern will be feeding, since the roots, being confined to a limited volume of soil, will need extra help to produce fine plants. Much could be written on this subject but a basic programme involves the application of dry fertilizer once weekly at the rate of one teaspoonful per pot or at such rates as the manufacturer may specify. This begins about the first week in July and the fertilizer should be of a fairly high nitrogen content to encourage the growth of leaf and stem. Later on when the bud arrives, the fertilizer is changed to one which has about equal quantities of nitrogen and potash. Liquid fertilizers are probably better and here one may give a feed every two days using a quarter-strength dilution. All feeding should stop when the plants are taken inside to flower.

This process of housing takes place

Individual blooms can be protected from damage and pollution with paper bags secured with waterproof glue. Two, one inside the other, are used. Inflate by blowing into them and place over buds which are opening.

about the end of September and is preceded by a thorough cleaning of the house followed by a fumigation with BHC or a sulphur candle to rid it of all pests. The plants themselves require preparation, and this involves the removal of the old leaves at the base and a spraying of all foliage with a combination of insecticide and fungicide. A good combination would be dinocap and BHC. It is important to wet the undersides of the foliage where many mildew troubles begin.

Once the plants are dry, they may be taken inside and arranged in convenient rows, giving them as much space as possible to allow light and air to flow around the lower leaves. For the first fortnight, every ventilator and door can

be left open by day and night but as the buds begin to open it will be necessary to regulate ventilation in conjunction with gentle heat to keep the air dry and moving and at a temperature of 50–55°F (10–13°C). Shading on the roof is an added refinement to prevent scorching from very bright morning sunshine. Indoors the plants may not require so much watering but it should be done carefully and early in the day, so that the air is dry before closing some of the ventilators at night. There must always be some ventilators left open except in very foggy conditions and even then it is better to have a little ventilation with enough heat to exclude the moisture. Pests may be controlled by the use of an aerosol or by routine fumigations.

Stopping If left to grow naturally the chrysanthemum plant will extend its single stem until a bud forms at the tip. This is the break bud which causes the plant to break into branching growth. Usually the grower will pinch out the tip of his plant before this bud forms

1

3

5

2

4

6

and this process is sometimes called 'stopping'. It has the same result in the formation of lateral branches and is a useful device to help in timing flowers for a particular date. Each of the side branches ultimately forms a bud at its tip. This is the first crown bud and is usually the one which is 'taken' or allowed to flower. In the few instances— such as the singles—where the second crown is the desired bud, the plant may be pinched or stopped a second time, thus producing further laterals and increasing the potential flower crop. Most chrysanthemum catalogues give the best dates on which to pinch each variety to obtain blooms at the normal show season, but the gardener who is growing for cut-flowers may ignore these dates and follow the following alternative plan.

Early flowering: Pinch the plants when they are about 6–9 inches high and take on four to six stems. For decorative plants in the border, double this number of stems may be kept. For exhibition

Early-flowering chrysanthemums are brought into flower in the open garden, in soil deeply dug in winter. In April prepare a tilth by forking 3 to 4 inches deep and applying a general fertilizer at 4 oz per square yard. In mid-May the plants are stood out in rows at least 18 inches apart. 1) At the time of planting, a hole is dug large enough to take the root ball without overcrowding. 2) The plant is knocked out of its pot. Water first to prevent damage to the roots. 3) Remove crocks and pebbles and 4) plant. 5) and 6) Firm the soil. If the ground is dry, water in the plants. They will also require staking at a later date.

quality three only are retained.

Mid season: Pinch when plants are about 9 inches high and allow the required number of stems to grow on. If the number produced is not sufficient, pinch again and allow the requisite number to extend to bud.

Late flowering: Pinch for the first time at 9 inches high and give a further

pinch at the end of July.

Disbudding If left to develop naturally, the chrysanthemum will flower in sprays but if it is desired to produce large specimen blooms the buds must be restricted to one per stem. Unless it has been damaged, the central or crown bud is retained and all the buds or sideshoots clustered around it removed. The removal should begin when the sideshoots are about $\frac{1}{2}$ inch long and it is advisable to take out one each day over a period. The sideshoots which are produced lower down the plant, together with the suckers appearing from the soil, may be removed as soon as they are seen so that all the energies of the plant are directed to the flowering stems.

Timing Production of blooms for a specific date is not the easiest task, since it is controlled by many factors. The dates on which the plants are rooted and pinched will have some bearing and the optimum dates for each variety can usually be ascertained from catalogues and other publications.

The buds of early-flowering types to give bloom in the first half of September should arrive from mid-July to the first week of August. The mid-seasons normally bloom in the first two weeks of November and buds should appear at the following times according to type:

Large Exhibition Incurveds and Decoratives — August 10-20th

end of August

Singles — around September 7-14th

There is little one can do to hurry a bud which is late but early buds can be dealt with in one of three ways. If the bud is more than three weeks earlier than desired, it is best to pinch each stem and allow the next crown bud to form. Buds only two or three weeks early may be 'run on.' This means that the bud is removed together with all the side shoots around it except for the topmost one. This is allowed to grow on as an extension of the main stem to form another bud in a few weeks. Buds which are only a few days early may be delayed somewhat by leaving the sideshoots around the bud to grow to an inch or so before disbudding begins.

Protecting blooms In exposed gardens or in areas of polluted air it may be necessary to protect the choicer outdoor blooms from damage. Light wooden frames covered with polythene may be firmly fixed over the beds. Another method widely used by exhibitors consists of enclosing individual blooms within paper bags specially made with waterproof glue. Two bags, one within the other are used, and after being inflated with the breath they are placed over the opening bud which has previously been sprayed and allowed to dry. The mouth of the bag is gathered up to the stem and secured firmly with two green twist ties about 2 inches apart. No protection of any kind should be placed on the buds until the stem immediately below is firm and strong and the first colour is seen in the florets. White and yellow blooms bag well but other colours tend to fade badly.

Soilless composts It is not always possible to rely on the quality of composts bought from the shops and the supply of good quality loam for home mixing is very limited. For these reasons it may be profitable to use soilless composts for all pot work. Experience suggests that these composts will satisfy most requirements, but the grower must be ready to follow the instructions quite closely. These composts are not recommended for boxing up the early-flowering plants, for the root action is so vigorous that it is almost impossible to separate the plants at planting-out time without causing very serious damage to the roots.

Recommended cultivars Because of the large number of cultivars available and the steady stream of novelties each year, the following list can only indicate some of the best varieties at the present time. They are set out according to the National Chrysanthemum Society of Great Britain's classification.

Indoor varieties: Section 1 Large Exhibition 'Duke of Kent' white, 3½ feet, reflexed, stop May 15th for first crown; 'Yellow Duke' is also very fine and treatment is the same. 'Gigantic', salmon, 4½ feet, reflexed, stop May 7th for first crown. 'Majestic', light bronze, 3 feet, reflexed, stop May 7th for first crown; 'Yellow Majestic' and 'Red Majestic' are equally as good and should be treated in the same way, 'Shirley Primrose', yellow, 5–6 feet, interlacing florets. Root in January and allow the plants to break twice to give second crown buds.

Section 2 Medium Exhibition 'Cosack', red, 4 feet, very reliable. Root in January and February and stop at mid-June for first crown. 'Connie Mayhew', yellow, 5 feet, deep primrose incurved bloom. Let

1 *Chrysanthemums with quilled petals are popular in flower arrangements.*
2 *Anemone-flowered chrysanthemums flower on second crown buds.*

plants form their break naturally and take the first crown.

Section 3 Exhibition Incurveds: *Large-flowered* 'Audrey Shoesmith', pink, 5 feet, strong healthy grower, blooms are very tight. Stop on June 1st for first crown. There is a 'White Audrey Shoesmith' which responds to the same treatment. 'Lilian Shoesmith' is a bronze. The plants are dwarfer at 4 feet and should be pinched at mid-June. 'Shirley Model' is of recent introduction. The rich pink blooms are borne on upright plants of about 4 feet. Stop third week of May.

Medium-flowered 'Maylen', white, 4 feet, is the parent of a large family including yellow, golden and buff coloured sports. All give good blooms if stopped twice, June 1st and July 7th for second crowns. 'Vera Woolman', yellow, is similar in height and stopping requirements. 'Minstrel Boy', light bronze, is possibly the best in this section. Reaching 4½ feet, this one also needs two stops, June 1st and June 30th.

Section 4 Reflexed Decoratives: *Large-flowered* There is a shortage of good cultivars in this section. 'Stuart Shoesmith' light bronze, 4½ feet, is a very easy grower. Stop June 15th for first crown. 'Elizabeth Woolman' pink, and the salmon sport reach only 3 feet, and should be allowed to make a natural break or be stopped in late June.

Medium-flowered 'Joy Hughes', pink, 4½ feet, deeply reflexing spiky florets. Root in February and allow to make a natural break for first crown. Often needs frequent watering. 'Princess Anne', pink, 3½ feet. Its only fault is a spreading habit which calls for careful

tying-up. There are several sports including 'Yellow Princess Anne' which is probably the best of the family. The whole family produces its best flowers on second crown buds after the plants have been stopped on June 1st and July 7th. 'Woking Scarlet', red, 3½ feet, an excellent cut flower when stopped about mid-June allowing the first crown bud to form and then rubbing it out to run-on for second crown.

Section 5 Intermediate Decoratives These are neither incurved nor fully reflexing. *Large-flowered* 'Balcombe Perfection', bronze, 3½ feet, parent of a family including red, and golden sports. For November flowering stop once only on June 1st. For December a second stop may be given at the end of July. 'Fair Lady', pink, 3½ feet, a most beautiful incurving form in carnation pink, with very neat habit. Stop June 15th for first crown. The bronze and orange sports are also highly desirable. 'Goldfoil', yellow, 3½ feet, clear yellow and very resistant to damping. Stop end of June. 'Daily Mirror', purple, 4½ feet, a recent introduction of great worth though not everyone's choice of colour. Stop twice, June 1st and 30th.

Medium-flowered 'Leslie Tandy', purple, 4 feet, very full blooms with a touch of silver. There is also a red sport. Stop June 7th for first crown. 'Woking Perfection', red, 4½ feet, hard, long-lasting blooms. Best rooted in February and stopped once only in mid-June.

Section 7 Singles: *Large-flowered* 'Albert Cooper', yellow, 4½ feet: 'Broadacre', white, 3½ feet; 'Preference', pink, 4½ feet; 'Woolman's Glory', bronze, 4½ feet; 'Red Woolman's Glory', red, 4½ feet. All should be stopped twice, mid-May and late-June.

Medium-flowered 'Golden Seal', yellow, 3 feet; 'Mason's Bronze', bronze, 5 feet, and several colours sports including 'Chesswood Beauty', red 'Jinx', white, 4 feet. Stopping times are as for the large-flowered.

Decoratives for December and Christmas 'Christmas Wine', pink; 'Bellona', pink; the Favourite family including white, golden, pink and red; 'Fred Shoesmith', and its sports; 'Loula', red. These should all be stopped twice, the first time when they are about 9 inches high and again at the end of July. 'Mayford Perfection', and its many sports are also very good but these must be grown on natural first crowns.

The so-called American Sprays are useful for the November–December period and there is a variety of form ranging from singles to pompons. It is

1 Chrysanthemum 'Pretty Polly' is a medium-flowered reflexed decorative.
2 Cascade chrysanthemums, widely used in Victorian conservatories, are still popular for decoration. Flowering occurs over a period of six months.

best to obtain young plants in June, for early rooting leads to excessive height. Stop once only when they are about 9 inches high and then leave them to branch naturally. No disbudding is practised and the flowers come in dainty sprays. 'American Snow', white; 'Christmas Greeting', red; 'Corsair', yellow; 'Galaxy', bronze; 'Minstrel', pink, can all be recommended.

Outdoor cultivars All are flowered on first crown buds.

Section 23 Incurved Decoratives: *Large-flowered* 'Ermine', white, 4½ feet, stands alone in this section. Thin stems but strong and healthy. There is a yellow sport of less quality. Stop June 7th. Bags well.

Medium-flowered 'Martin Riley', yellow, 4 feet, long-lasting blooms tending to come in August. Stop at mid-June. 'Yellow Nugget', yellow, 3½ feet, excellent flowers on a sturdy plant, bags well.

Section 24 Reflexed Decoratives: *Large-flowered* 'Ken Cooper', yellow, 3½ feet, of immaculate form and clear colour. Stop June 15th. 'Polaris', white, 3 feet, a quality flower with long, plunging florets, stop June 1st. 'Standard', bronze, 4 feet. Bright orange-bronze and top of its class, stop May 20th. 'Tracy Waller', pink with salmon, bronze and cherry sports, all at 5 feet. The height makes these a little difficult but the flowers are superb. Stop on June 1st.

Medium-flowered 'Early Red Cloak', red, 3½ feet, strong prolific grower. Flowers of fine form and the colour fades but little. Stop June 7th. 'Morley Jones', 3 feet, colour is rich amber with peach suffusion. Perfectly weather-proof and suitable for exhibition or bedding. Stop June 15th. 'Pretty Polly', purple, 2½ feet. Good for all purposes, the flowers being weatherproof. Stop June 1st. 'Sonny Riley', yellow, 4 feet, possibly the best in this section with high quality flowers. Bags well and always blooms well. Stop June 1st.

Section 25 Intermediate Decoratives: *Large-flowered* 'Evelyn Bush', white, 4½ feet, mainly an exhibitor's flower as it comes best out of bags. Stop June 1st. 'Gladys Sharpe', yellow, 3 feet, very strong grower with large foliage and full blooms. Stop mid-May. 'Harry James', bronze, 4 feet, reddish bronze florets which are broad and closely incurving. Blooms late in September, so stop mid-May. 'Keystone', purple, and its sport 'Red Keystone' reach about 4 feet. Highly resistant to weather damage Stop in early June.

Medium-flowered 'Cricket', white, with yellow and primrose sports, 4 feet, blooms last well after cutting. Stop June 7th. 'Jane Rowe', pale pink, 3½ feet, new but very promising though the delicate colour fades in bright sunshine. Stop June 15th. 'People', purple, 4½ feet, of exquisite form showing the reverse of the florets. Tends to bloom in the second half of September so stop mid-May.

Cineraria hybrida grandiflora is typical of modern strains.

'Topper', light bronze, 3½ feet, a lovely flower which bags well with little loss of colour. Stop June 1st.

Outdoor Singles are not very distinguished but 'Kitty' may be tried, while 'Premiere', an anemone-centred type, is also worth a place.

Any of the Pompons are good and they are available in varying heights and colour. Give one pinch when the plants are established outside, and then leave them to develop naturally.

A selection for bedding In addition to the shorter cultivars among those already listed, the following are recommended: August-flowering. 'Sweetheart', pink, and its many sports, 3 feet; 'Capstan', bronze, 2½ feet; 'Sunavon', yellow, 3 feet; 'Red flare', red, 3 feet.
September-flowering. 'Whiteball', white,

2½ feet; 'Catherine Porter', pink, 3 feet; 'Packwell', bronze, 3½ feet: 'J. R. Johnson', yellow, 3½ feet.

All these should be stopped about June 7th. They may be allowed to flower in sprays or be disbudded for larger blooms.

Cineraria (sin-er-air-e-a)
From the Latin *cinereus*, ash-coloured, referring to the colour of the undersides of the leaves. All but a very few species (none of which are likely to be found in cultivation) have been transferred to the genus *Senecio* and for information on cinerarias other than the florist's cinerarias, see Senecio.

Florist's cinerarias The florist's cinerarias, obtainable in a very wide range of beautiful colours, have been derived from *Senecio cruentus* (once known as *Cineraria cruenta*), a herbaceous perennial from the Canary Islands. Although

the plants are strictly perennials they are almost invariably grown as half-hardy annuals or biennials, for green-house display or for spring window boxes. Seed is obtainable of various strains in mixed colours, under such names as *hybrida grandiflora*, producing plants about 18–24 inches tall; 'Berlin Market', not quite so tall, in various rich shades; 'Hansa Strain', 18 inches, bright colours, compact plants; 'Rainbow', 18 inches, pinks and pale blues; 'Cremer's Prize', 18 inches, medium-sized flowers, freely produced; *stellata*, 2½ feet, large heads of small, star-shaped flowers in very varied colours; *multiflora nana*, 1 foot, dwarf plants, self-coloured flowers. In addition there are certain named colour cultivars growing to about 21 inches tall, including *atroviolacea*, large dark violet flowers; 'Matador', coppery scarlet; *sanguinea*, blood-red.

Cultivation To produce winter-flowering plants seed should be sown in April or early May in the heated greenhouse, in a temperature of 55–60°F (13–16°C). Seed for spring-flowering plants should be sown in an unheated frame in June or early July. Sow thinly in seed compost, covering the seed only lightly. When the seedlings have developed three leaves pot them up into deep seed boxes. Give

Cinerarias are colourful and deservedly popular as house plants, but they are suitable as well for window boxes and summer bedding. They need a cool airy position with full light.

them plenty of light and air; pot them on again singly into 3 inch pots before they become crowded, then into 6 inch pots when the 3 inch pots are filled with roots. Large, vigorous plants may need a further potting into 7 or 8 inch pots; this should be done by the end of October. Potting composts are perfectly suitable. Once they have been potted singly the plants should be moved out into the cold frame and kept shaded. They may remain there until about mid-October, given plenty of ventilation, both by day and by night. They will still need ample ventilation after they have been brought into the greenhouse where they should be placed on the staging as near to the glass as possible. Feed the plants with weak liquid manure or fertilizer, twice weekly from September onwards and spray them against attacks by aphids and leaf miners. From late October until the plants have finished flowering and are either discarded or used to provide cuttings, the temperature in the green-house should be 45–50°F (7–10°C). How

ever, cuttings are hardly ever used to propagate these plants, unless it is to increase a specially desirable variety.

Cladanthus (klad-an-thus)
From the Greek *klados*, branch, *anthos*, flower, referring to the flowers borne at the ends of the branched shoots (*Compositae*). A genus of a single species, a half-hardy annual with yellow-rayed flowers carried at the ends of the branches. The species is *C. arabicus* (syns. *C. proliferus, Anthemis arabica*), 2½–3 feet, a strong smelling plant, a native of Spain and Morocco.
Cultivation Seed should be sown in the greenhouse in spring and the plants set out in their flowering quarters in late May. The plants will grow in any ordinary garden soil.

Clarkia (klar-ke-a)
Commerating Captain William Clark, who with Captain Meriwether Lewis made a famous journey through America and across the Rocky Mountains early in the nineteenth century (*Onagraceae*). A small genus of hardy annuals from North America, of which one species only, the popular *C. elegans*, is likely to be encountered in general cultivation. Of this, however, there are

many fine cultivars in a good colour range.

They include 'Brilliant', double carmine; 'Enchantress', double salmon-pink; 'Fire-brand', scarlet; 'Glorious', bright crimson, dark leaves; 'Illumination', orange and rose-pink; 'Lady Satin Rose', double; 'May Blossom', double pink; 'Orange King'; 'Purple King', double; 'Salmon Bouquet'. All these grow to about 2 feet tall. There are also mixed strains available as well as the 'Royal Bouquet' mixed strain, slightly dwarfer.

Cultivation Clarkias do best in a light rich soil in a sunny border or bed. Space the plants well apart to obtain the best results. Propagate from seed sown ⅛ inch deep in April, May or June in rows or clumps where the plants are required to flower, as they do not transplant well. Thin the seedlings to 8 inches apart when they are 3 inches high. Clarkias may also be grown as greenhouse plants. Sow seeds in small pots of loamy soil in September and grow the plants on in cool, airy conditions until spring, when they should be re-potted into loamy soil for flowering. The stems, whether grown in pots or out of doors, may need a few twigs among them for support.

Cleome (kle-o-me)

The old Greek name (*Capparadiceae*). A genus, mainly of half-hardy or greenhouse annuals of which the best known is *C. spinosa*, the spider flower, a striking half-hardy annual with spidery flowers which can be grown outside in summer.

Species cultivated *C. hirta*, 4 feet, bluish-green foliage, pinkish-mauve flowers, summer. *C. lutea*, 1 foot, yellow-orange flowers, July and August. *C. spinosa*, spider flower, 3–4 feet, white, pale pink or rose-pink flowers, June to September; cultivars include: 'Helen Campbell', white; 'Mauve Queen'; 'Pink Queen'; 'Rose Queen'; all colours as indicated by their names.

Cultivation Sow seed 1/16 inch deep in a temperature of 65–70°F (18–21°C) in March, potting the seedlings into individual pots when they are 1 inch tall. If they are to be grown out of doors, grow them on steadily, potting on as required, harden off in May for planting out in a light, rich soil in a sunny dry spot in early June. They make fine greenhouse pot plants, grown in potting compost. Water only moderately at all times.

Cobaea (ko-be-a)

Commerating Father Barnadez Cobo, a Spanish Jesuit and naturalist, who

1 Cladanthus arabicus is a half-hardy annual with a strong pungent odour.
2 Clarkia, a genus of four or five species from North America, has many colour forms.

lived in Mexico, the home of these plants (*Polemoniaceae*). A small genus of tender perennial plants, climbing by means of tendrils, usually grown as annuals. One species only is likely to be found in cultivation. This is *C. scandens*, the cup-and-saucer vine, so named because of the shape of the beautiful long-stemmed flowers, which resemble those of a Canterbury bell. They open cream and gradually turn deep purple. They appear continuously from May to October, or even throughout the winter. A quick-growing evergreen climber to 20 feet, this is particularly useful for large conservatories where two or three plants can soon cover a wall. There is a white-flowered form, *flore albo*, and a variegated form, *variegata*.

Cultivation Seed should be sown (edgeways in the pots) in a temperature of 50–55°F (10–13°C) in late February, or in a frame in April and young plants potted up singly when they have made two or three leaves. They can then either be planted out-of-doors in June in sheltered gardens or planted in a cold greenhouse or conservatory border. Alternatively, they can be potted in large pots or tubs in a compost of equal parts of leafmould and loam with a scattering of sand, and the laterals pinched back to two or three buds to prevent straggly growth. Water regularly and feed weekly with a liquid feed during the early summer.

Plants occasionally survive the winter out of doors in the south but are usually so slow to make new growth that much quicker results are obtained by raising new plants from seed. They may be grown in a light, warm living room, but need ample space and adequate support for their tendrils. A sticky nectar is liable to drop from the open flowers, so the position indoors should be chosen with some care.

Collinsia (kol-in-ze-a)
Commerating Zaccheus Collins, American naturalist (*Scrophulariaceae*). Hardy annuals from North America and Mexico, related to *Penstemon*, easy to grow and bearing spikes of attractive blossom during summer. The only species likely to be found in cultivation is *C. bicolor*, 12–15 inches, with lilac and white flowers. It has several varieties including *alba*, white; *multicolor*, rose, lilac and white; 'Salmon Beauty', salmon rose. Seed of mixed varieties is also available.

Cultivation Collinsias like sunny borders,

1 Cleome spinosa, the Spider Flower, is an annual discovered in the West Indies. It thrives outside in summer or as a greenhouse pot plant in cold weather. 2 Cobaea scandens, a half-hardy climber from South America, is best grown in a pot or tub that can be moved indoors for the winter months.

and look especially effective among mixed annuals. They do well in ordinary soil. Propagation is by seed sown out of doors during the spring, where plants are intended to flower. It pays to sow thinly. Final thinning should take place when young plants are 2 inches high; allow 6 inches between each. Collinsias may also be sown out of doors in a sheltered spot during September and allowed to stand throughout the winter for flowering during June.

Convolvulus (kon-vol-vu-lus)
From the Latin *convolvo*, to entwine, as some of the species do (*Convolvulaceae*). A valuable race of plants both annual and perennial, herbaceous or sub-shrubby. Flowers are bell-shaped throughout and highly attractive.

Hardy annual species cultivated *C. tricolor* (syn. *C. minor*), 1 foot, blue, pink and white flowers, late summer; cultivars include 'Cambridge Blue'; 'Crimson Monarch', cherry red with white and gold centre; 'Lavender Rosette'; 'Royal Ensign', Wedgwood blue with gold centre; 'Royal Marine', rich blue. For *C. major* see *Ipomoea purpurea*.

Cultivation These convolvulus can be grown in beds and borders and appreciate good soil and sun. Trailing species may be provided with support if preferred. A sunny, sheltered rock garden is especially suitable for *C. cneorum*, *C. mauritanicus* and other dwarf and trailing species. Propagation of hardier kinds is by seed sown out of doors in spring. Strike cuttings of *C. cneorum* and *C. mauritanicus* in sandy soil in a frame in July and August. Bottom heat is an advantage.

Coreopsis (kor-e-op-sis)
From the Greek *koris*, a bug or tick, *opsis*, like, a reference to the appearance of the seeds (*Compositae*). Tickseed. The annual species are often catalogued under *Calliopsis*. Hardy perennials and annuals with showy flowers, excellent for borders.

Annual species cultivated *C. atkinsoniana*, 2–4 feet, yellow and purple flowers, summer. *C. basalis* (syn. *C. cardaminifolia*), 6 inches–2 feet, yellow and purplish flowers, summer. *C. coronata*, 2 feet, orange and crimson flowers, summer. *C. drummondii*, 2 feet, yellow and crimson flowers, summer: a cultivar is 'Golden Crown'. *C. tinctoria* (syn. *C. bicolor*), 2 feet, yellow and crimson

1

2

1 Collinsia bicolor, a hardy annual growing to 2 feet, flowers in late summer. First discovered in California, Collinsias resemble, and are closely-related to, Penstemons, but there are minor botanical differences. Seed can be sown either in spring or in autumn.
2 Convolvulus cneorum is a half-hardy sub-shrub from southern Europe which requires a cold greenhouse in cooler areas.

flowers, summer; cultivars include 'Crimson King', 9 inches; 'Fire King' 9 inches, scarlet; 'Golden Sovereign', 9 inches; 'Dazzler', 9 inches, crimson and yellow; 'Star of Fire', 9–12 inches, red; 'Evening Star', 9 inches, yellow and scarlet; 'The Garnet', 1½ feet crimson-scarlet; 'Tiger Star', 12 inches, bronze and yellow; 'Golden Blaze', 2–3 feet, gold and maroon, yellow and maroon; 'Sovereign', 9 inches, golden-yellow.

Cultivation Coreopsis do well in ordinary well-drained garden soil and in sunny positions. Plant perennials during autumn and spring. Propagate single perennial species from cuttings in April, or seed sown a month later; double forms by cuttings in April. Split large clumps in autumn. The annuals are raised from seed sown out of doors during spring and early summer, where they are intended to flower, thinning the seedlings to 9 inches. Alternatively, seed may be sown under glass in a temperature of 65°F (18°C) in March.

Cosmos (koz-mos)

From the Greek *kosmos*, beautiful (*Compositae*). Half-hardy annuals and perennials, mainly from tropical America, with ferny foliage and broad-petalled, daisy flowers, single and sometimes double. They are sometimes found in catalogues under the name *Cosmea*.

Species cultivated *C. atrosanguineus*, 1–3 feet, dark brownish-red flowers, late summer to early autumn, perennial, treated as an annual. *C. bipinnatus*, 3 feet, rose or purple, late summer. *C. diversifolius* (syn. *Bidens dahlioides*), 3 feet, lilac flowers, late summer to early autumn. *C. sulphureus*, 3–4 feet, pale yellow flowers, mid to late summer. Cultivars and strains in many hues are numerous. Those of *C. bipinnatus* include 'Early Flowering Crimson-Scarlet',

'Fairy Queen', bright rose; 'Sensation' pink and white; 'Sensation Purity' white; 'Sensation Radiance', rose and crimson bicolor; 'Crested Mixed', double in varied colours. Cultivars of *C. sulphureus* are 'Klondyke Orange Flare' and 'Klondyke Yellow Flare'.

Cultivation Cosmos will grow in almost any good garden soil, especially the lighter kinds and should be given a sunny position. Propagation is by seed sown in a temperature of 55–60°F (13–16°C) from February to March. Prick out the seedlings into boxes in which they are grown on and finally hardened off. Plant out at the end of May, 1 foot apart. Plants will become large and in high summer are loaded with flowers which are ideal for cutting.

Delphinium (del-fin-e-um)

From the Greek *delphin*, a dolphin, the flowerbuds having some resemblance to that sea creature (*Ranunculaceae*). Larkspur. The genus consists of annual, biennial and herbaceous perennial plants, mostly hardy and showy plants for border cultivation, with some dwarf species suitable for the rock garden.

Species cultivated: Annual *D. ajacis*, 1–2 feet, blue, violet, rose-pink or white, summer, Europe, *D. consolida*, branching larkspur, 2 feet, purple or deep violet, summer, Europe. *D. paniculatum*, Siberian larkspur, up to 3 feet, single, violet, July to September, also grown as a biennial. Seedsmen list many beautiful varieties of these annual larkspurs, mainly 2½–3 feet tall, derived mainly from *D. ajacis* and *D. consolida*. They

1 Cultivars of Coreopsis, the Tickseed, are easy to raise from seed.
2 and 3 Cosmos bipinnatus, a Mexican annual, reaches 3 feet in height and flowers in late summer.

include such strains as 'Giant Hyacinth flowered'; 'Giant Imperial'; 'Regal', 4 feet; 'Supreme', 4 feet, and named cultivars such as 'Blue Spire', dark blue; 'Carmine King'; 'Dazzler', bright scarlet; 'Exquisite Pink'; 'Lilac Spire'; 'Los Angeles', rose and salmon; 'Miss California', salmon rose; 'Rosamond', bright rose and 'White Spire'.

Cultivation Sow annual varieties in a sunny, open border in April where they are to flower, or in boxes of light soil under glass in March in a temperature of 55°F (13°C). Prick out seedlings when large enough to handle and transplant in the open in May.

Cultivation of modern hybrid delphiniums Fast growing plants, delphiniums require a deeply-dug, rich soil with adequate drainage. A medium loam is preferable to a light sandy soil. Where the soil is light, dig in deeply plenty of compost or old farmyard manure before planting and during the summer a mulch of garden compost is excellent. Nitrogenous fertilizers should be used with care as they may only result in producing weak stems. If the stems are cut back immediately after flowering a second crop of spikes may be produced,

3

1

2

1 This border of Delphiniums in various shades of purple is in Regent's Park, London.
2, 3 and 4 Delphiniums are available in a wide range of colour and bloom type.

but these should only be encouraged with strong-growing varieties. Adequate moisture will be required to produce this second crop during what may be hot, summer weather. Slugs can be a menace with the tender young delphinium shoots, especially in the early spring, so precautions should be taken with slug pellets or other repellents. Varieties that grow to about 4–5 feet in height are more suitable for small gardens than those that tower to 7 feet or more, and they are less liable to damage by summer gales. Pea sticks, brushwood or twigs can be used to support the young growths but these should be put in position around the plants in good time so that the stems grow up through them. This is often left too late, with the result that the tender stems get broken when the sticks are being pushed into the soil. Staking for exhibition spikes must be carefully done, using one stout cane to each spike. When growing the large flowering varieties it is usual to restrict one-year-old plants to one spike and two-year-old plants to two or three spikes. Pea sticks, however, provide adequate support for the lighter, less tall graceful belladonna types of delphinium, with their branching stems, which are also so attractive for floral arrangement. Exhibition spikes should be straight, tapering and well-filled with large circular florets (but not overcrowded) and bearing few laterals. The foliage should be clean, healthy and undamaged. As soon as spikes are cut they should be placed in deep containers filled with water and stood in a cool, but not draughty, place. There they should remain for some hours or overnight. Each stem should be wrapped in a large sheet of tissue paper (30×40 inches) before being taken to the show. A further step to ensure that the spike does not flag is to turn it upside down, immediately before final staging, fill the hollow stem with cold water and plug with cotton wool.

As it is easily raised from seed, the delphinium has been of much interest to the plant breeder who has produced many stately varieties. The era of immense spikes has passed its zenith and the trend is to develop a range of hybrids not exceeding about 4½ feet in height. These are of much more general use in gardens which are ever becoming smaller, but more numerous. From the glorious shades of blue the colour range has been extended from white and cream through pink, carmine, mauve, lavender, purple and violet. Now, thanks to the work done by Dr Legro, the celebrated Dutch hybridist, the range includes shades of cerise, orange,

1 The flowers of Dimorphotheca ecklonis, a half-hardy South African plant, open only in bright sunlight.
2 Dimorphotheca 'Giant Goliath' produces extra-large blooms.

peach and tomato-red. Our garden hybrids have been mainly derived from *Delphinium elatum*, a natural tetraploid species, but Dr Legro succeeded in overcoming the sterility barrier when he made a number of species crosses at diploid level, tetraploided the resulting plants and then successfully married them to hybrid elatums. The rediscovery of the white African species, *D. leroyi*, which has a freesia-like fragrance, also opens up pleasing possibilities. First crosses at diploid level have shown that this quality is not recessive, so hopes are high, but all this work takes time. In England Dr B. J. Langdon has also been working on these problems and during the next few years we should see a truly remarkable range of hybrid delphiniums.

Dimorphotheca (di-mor-foth-e-ka)

From the Greek *di*, two, *morphe*, shape, *theca*, seed, because the flower produces two different shapes of seed, one from the disk florets and another from the ray florets (*Compositae*). Cape marigold, star of the veldt, Namaqualand daisy. A genus of half-hardy annual, herbaceous perennial and sub-shrubby plants from South Africa, grown for their long-lasting daisy-like flowers in bright colours. Considerable confusion in naming exists in many books and catalogues and according to some authorities those plants known as dimorphothecas should be split up between the genera *Castalis*, *Chrysanthemoides*, *Dimorphotheca* and *Osteospermum*. Here, for the sake of convenience, they are all treated as belonging to the genus *Dimorphotheca*.
Species cultivated *D. aurantiaca* (syn. *Castalis tragus*, *D. flaccida* and apparently the true name for many of the plants grown in gardens under the names of *D. calendulacea* and *D. sinuata*), 1–1½ feet, bright orange flowers with a dark brown disk, edged with metallic blue, June to September, a perennial usually treated as a half-hardy annual. This species has given rise to several garden hybrids (listed in catalogues) such as 'Buff Beauty'; 'Goliath', extra large, mainly orange flowers; 'Lemon Queen'; 'Orange Glory'; 'Glistening White' and 'White Beauty'. *D. barberiae* (syn. *Osteospermum barberiae*), 1½ feet, aromatic foliage, long stemmed rosy-lilac flowers, summer to autumn, with occasional flowers appearing at almost any time, sub-shrubby. This plant is hardier than is generally supposed and will usually survive out of doors in the south of England, making large spreading clumps. There is a dwarf form, *compacta*, which is said to be hardier still. *D. calendulacea* see *D. aurantiaca*. *D. ecklonis*, 2–3 feet, flowers white with reverse of petals purple and a deep purple zone on the petals, perennial treated as annual. *D. pluvialis* (syn. *D. annua*), 1 foot, almost hardy, white above, purple below; var. *ringens*; violet ring round disk, June onwards.

D. sinuata see *D. aurantiaca*.
Cultivation Sun is essential for all species and in a poor cloudy summer, nothing can be done to improve the results since the flowers of most kinds open only in sunny weather, closing or failing to open when the sky is overcast, or in late afternoon. Out of doors they do best in the lighter soils, although *D. barberiae* will thrive on any kind of soil, even heavy clay. In the sunny greenhouse dimorphothecas are grown in pots containing a compost of 3 parts of sandy loam, 1 part of leafmould, plus silver sand. The minimum temperature in winter, when they need moderate watering only, should be 40°F (4°C). Propagation is by seed sown in March in pans or boxes in heat and, after hardening off, the seedlings may be put out in the border in late May or early June. The plants grow quickly and will start flowering in June. Perennial species may be propogated by cuttings taken in late summer and rooted in a greenhouse or frame. *D. pluvialis* is probably the hardiest of those grown as annuals and seed of this species may be sown out of doors in early April in fine soil, the seedlings later thinned, to start flowering at the end of June.

Dorotheanthus (dor-o-the-an-thus)

Named in honour of Frau Dorothea Schwantes, wife of a German botanist (*Aizoaceae*). Greenhouse succulents from South Africa, often found under *Mesembryanthemum*. They may be used for bedding out or as pot plants.
Species cultivated *D. bellidiformis*, dwarf spreading plant, leaves fleshy, flowers open in sunshine, colours, white, pink, red and orange. *D. gramineus*, short-stemmed and spreading, flowers bright carmine. *D. tricolor*, spreading habit, leaves long and curved, flowers white below and purple above. All these are natives of Cape Province.
Cultivation An open compost is needed; out of doors see that the soil is well-drained and plant in sunny positions. These plants are annuals and three plants in a pot make a good display; they do not require high temperatures. Propagation is by seeds sown on seed compost. Do not cover the seed. The temperature should be 70°F (21°C). Keep the seed pans moist and shaded while germination is taking place, prick out the seedlings and grow them on in a frame. The plants should be potted up or planted out in June.

Dorotheanthus (sometimes called Mesembryanthemum) flowers freely at the Karoo Garden, Worcester, South Africa. They need a position in full sun, as they only open in bright sunlight.

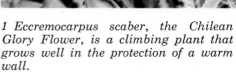

1 Eccremocarpus scaber, the Chilean Glory Flower, is a climbing plant that grows well in the protection of a warm wall.
2 Echium vulgare is a biennial that grows to 3 feet in ordinary soil.

Eccremocarpus (ek-re-mo-kar-pus)

From the Greek *ekkremes*, pendant, and *karpos*, fruit, describing the pendulous seed vessels (*Bignoniaceae*). An attractive evergreen half-hardy annual climbing plant. There are very few species and of these one only is in cultivation. This is *E. scaber*, the Chilean glory flower. It grows up to 15–20 feet, clinging to suitable supports by means of tendrils at the ends of the leaves. The flowers, borne in clusters from late spring to autumn, are tubular in shape, scarlet or orange-red and yellow in colour. There is a golden-flowered variety, *aureus*, and an orange-red variety, *ruber*.

Cultivation *E. scaber* is very easily raised from seed sown in pots of sandy soil in March or April and germinated in a temperature of about 60°F (16°C). Seed will even germinate out of doors in milder gardens if sown in April or May. Plant out in June in a light, rich soil against south or southwest facing walls, with trellis, wires, etc., for support. The growths are weak, so that they will do no harm if the plant is allowed to scramble over shrubs. In mild winters the roots are hardy, but in exposed gardens should be covered with old ashes or matting in severe weather. In favoured gardens, the plant appears to be quite hardy except, perhaps, in very severe winters, when it may be cut to the ground only to spring

again from the base. Seed is set very freely in long capsules which turn dark brown as they ripen. Self-sown seedlings occasionally appear in the spring, particularly where they have germinated between paving stones and thus the seed has had some protection during the winter.

Echium (ek-e-um)

From the Greek *echis*, a viper, referring either to the supposed resemblance of the seed to a viper's head or the belief that the plant was efficacious against the adder's bite (*Boraginaceae*). Viper's bugloss. Hardy and half-hardy annual, biennial and perennial plants mainly from the Mediterranean region and the Canary Islands.

Species cultivated: Annual and biennial *E. creticum*, 1–1½ feet, violet, July, annual. *E. plantagineum*, 2–3 feet, rich bluish-purple, summer, annual or biennial. *E. vulgare*, 3–4 feet, purple or blue, summer, biennial, native. *E. wildpretii*, 2–3 feet, rose-pink, summer, biennial.

Cultivation Plant out the perennial kinds in ordinary well-drained soil and in a sunny position in May. Seed of the annual kinds is sown in a sunny position in the open in April or August. The perennials are propagated by seed sown out of doors in spring.

Eschscholzia (esh-olt-se-a)

Commemorating Johann Friedrich von

Eschsholz, physician and naturalist, member of a Russian expedition to northwest America in the early nineteenth century (*Papaveraceae*). A small genus of hardy annuals from northwest America, bearing saucer-shaped flowers which open to the sun and close up during damp and cloudy weather.

Species cultivated *E. caespitosa*, 6 inches, flowers yellow, 1 inch across, summer; 'Sundew' with lemon-yellow flowers is a cultivar. *E. californica*, the Californian poppy. This grows 1–1½ feet tall and has 2 inch wide bright yellow or orange flowers in summer; var. *alba flore pleno* has double white flowers. There are numerous named varieties and strains to be found seedsmen's lists, in which the flowers vary from the palest lemon and apricot to a clear orange-red. Both single and double varieties are available, in heights from 9 inches–1 foot or so. The foliage is a consistent pale silvery-green, light, feathery and an exquisite foil for the flowers. They will be found under such names as 'Monarch Art Shades'; 'Carmine King'; 'Golden Glory'; 'Mandarin' and 'Toreador'. New strains are constantly being developed.

Cultivation A light, well-drained soil is most suitable, although these annuals will grow in any ordinary garden soil.

Where they flourish they will seed themselves freely. Sow seed out of doors in open, sunny positions in September or March to April where the plants are to flower and thin the seedlings to 6 inches apart, as soon as they are large enough to handle, to prevent them from becoming spindly. Once the flowers begin to fade cut them off to prevent the formation of seed and thus prolong the flowering season unless, of course, self-sown seedlings are required.

Exacum (eks-ak-um)
From the Latin *ex*, out of, *ago*, to drive; the plant was thought to expel poison (*Gentianaceae*). Hot-house annuals, biennials and perennials first grown here in the middle of the nineteenth century for their freely-produced flowers.

Species cultivated *E. affine*, 6 inches, fragrant, bluish-lilac flowers, June to October, Socotra; var. *atrocaeruleum* gentian-blue. *E. macranthum*, 1½ feet, purple, summer, Ceylon. *E. zeylanicum*, 2 feet, violet-purple, summer, Ceylon.

Cultivation Exacums like a compost of equal parts of loam, peat, sand and leafmould and need a minimum winter temperature of 50°F (10°C). Sharp drainage is essential as the plants are particularly liable to damp off. The atmosphere should be moist and shade is needed from hot sun. Propagation is from seed, sown in August and September, the seedlings over-wintered in small pots and potted on into 5-inch pots in March for summer flowering.

Felicia (fel-is-e-a)
From the Latin *felix*, cheerful, a reference to the bright flowers(*Compositae*). Half-hardy annual or greenhouse evergreen plants, some of them sub-shrubs, from South Africa and Abyssinia.

Species cultivated *F. amelloides* (syn. *Agathaea coelestis*), blue daisy, blue marguerite, 1–1½ feet, half-hardy perennial, blue daisies, June to August, an attractive pot plant for the cold greenhouse or conservatory. *F. bergeriana*, kingfisher daisy, 6 inches, half-hardy annual, blue flowers, June onwards. *F. petiolata*, prostrate evergreen sub-shrub, pink to blue flowers, summer. *F. tenella* (syn. *F. fragilis*), 1 foot, half-hardy annual, small violet-blue flowers with yellow centres, July and August.

Cultivation Seeds of the half-hardy annual kinds should be sown in the greenhouse in March in light soil, and the seedlings gradually hardened off and planted out in late May where they are

1 Eschscholzia californica 'Monarch Art Shades', the Californian Poppy, produces semi-double blooms of various shades and flowers over a long period.
2 Exacum affine has fragrant bluish-lilac flowers with prominent golden stamens. It is especially attractive as a pot plant.

to flower. The greenhouse kinds can be raised from seed sown at the same time, pricked off into small pots and then into 5 inch pots in which they will flower. Cuttings of young shoots can be made in spring or August and inserted round the edge of a pot in sandy compost in a propagating case or where a temperature of 55–65°F (13–18°C) can be maintained.

Gilia (gil-e-a)

Commemorating Felipe Luis Gil, eighteenth-century Spanish botanist (*Polemoniaceae*), A genus of annuals, biennials, perennials and a few subshrubs from both North and South America. Although they are attractive plants, few species are in general cultivation.

Annual species cultivated *G. achilleifolia*, 1 foot, purplish-blue flowers; var. *major*, larger flowers, August. *G. androsacea* (syn. *Leptosiphon androsaceus*), 1 foot, white, pink or lilac flowers with yellow throats, August. *G. capitata*, Queen Anne's thimbles, 12–15 inches, lavender-blue flowers, summer; var. *alba*, white. *G. densiflora* (syn. *Leptosiphon densiflorus*), 1–2 feet, lilac or white flowers, June. *G. hybrida* (syn. *Leptosiphon hybridus*), 3–6 inches, various colours, summer. *G. micrantha*, 9 inches, rose-pink flowers, summer, useful for the rock garden and paved paths. *G. tricolor*, 1–2 feet, lavender and white, with dark throats, summer.

Biennial *G. rubra* (syn. *G. coronopifolia*), 3 feet or more, plumed spikes of brilliant red flowers, July to October; colour variations occur in pinks and yellows.

Shrubby *G. californica*, prickly phlox, 3 feet, pink flowers, July. *G. montana* (syn. *Linanthus montanus*), 10 inches, white flowers, summer.

Cultivation Sunny borders out of doors are ideal for the annuals which can be propagated by seed sown shallowly in April. The biennial *G. rubra* can be treated as a half-hardy annual and potted up to flower under glass the same year, but far better flowers result from a sowing the previous autumn under glass.

Godetia (god-ee-she-a)

Commemorating Charles H. Godet, nineteenth-century Swiss botanist (*Oenotheraceae*). A genus of hardy annuals, popular and showy, greatly improved in recent years, related to the evening primrose (*Oenothera*) in which genus they were formerly included.

Species cultivated Few original species are grown, with the possible exception of *G. dasycarpa*, 9 inches, from the Andes, with mauve flowers and steely blue-green foliage, the parent of many lavender-flowered varieties. The original species have been superseded by the garden varieties now available, mainly the results of crosses between *G. grandiflora*, 6–12 inches, a showy plant of compact habit and the tall-growing

G. amoena, 1–2 feet, with loose habit, both variable in colour.

Cultivars include 'Firelight', crimson; 'Kelvedon Glory', salmon; 'Orange Glory', a deeper salmon and 'Sybil Sherwood', salmon pink, orange and white, all 1–1½ feet tall. Double-flowered cultivars include 'Cherry Red'; 'Rich Pink'; 'Rosy Queen'; 'Schaminii', salmon-pink, all 2–2½ feet tall; 'Whitneyi azalaeiflora pleṅa', pink with a crimson blotch, and 'Carmine Glow' about 1 foot tall.

Another kind, tall but with single flowers, is represented by such cultivars as 'Lavender Gem' and 'Lavender', with dark prominent stamens. These probably come from the 2 foot tall species *G. viminea*, from California.

Cultivation Sow in beds and borders in full sun in April; thin according to ultimate height. The tall double-flowered kinds are the hardiest and may be sown in autumn in a well-drained position and will produce spikes of flower up to 3 feet in height the following summer.

Gomphrena (gom-free-na)

Probably from the Greek *gomphos*, a club or wedge, a reference to the shape of the flower-heads (*Amaranthaceae*). A genus of half-hardy annuals of which only one species is cultivated. Its

1 *Gilia rubra is a biennial usually treated as a half-hardy annual.*
2 *Godetia 'Sybil Sherwood' is a summer-flowering cultivar.*
3 *The showy flowers of Godetia bloom in summer.*

Helianthus (hel-ee-an-tuhs)

From the Greek *helios*, the sun, *anthos*, a flower. (*Compositae*). Sunflower. A genus of tall, coarse-growing plants, annuals and perennials, gross feeders, dominating the border in which they are planted. *H. annuus*, the common sunflower, is a plant of some economic importance as the seeds are fed to fowl and produce an edible oil, and the flowers yield a yellow dye.

Annual species cultivated *H. annuus*, 6–10 feet, common or giant sunflower, large yellow flowerheads, late summer, coarse growing; var. *floreplenus*, double flowers. Cultivars and strains include 'Dwarf Chrysanthemum-flowered', 3 feet, golden-yellow, fringed petals; 'Gaillardia flora', 5 feet, brown and yellow gaillardia-like flowers; 'Primrose', 5 feet, sulphur-yellow, darker disk; 'Red', 5 feet, a strain with chestnut-brown flowers; 'Russian Giant', 8 feet, large, yellow; 'Sungold', 6 feet, golden-yellow, double; 'Tall Chrysanthemum-flowered', 5 feet, golden-yellow, fringed petals; 'Yellow Pygmy', 2 feet, double yellow, dwarf. *H. debilis* (syn. *H. cucumerifolius*) 3–4 feet, branched plants with somewhat glossy leaves, yellow flowers, summer. Cultivars include 'Autumn Beauty', 2 feet, yellow, coppery zone; 'Dazzler', 3 feet, chestnut, orange-tipped rays; 'Excelsior', 3 feet, yellow, red zones; 'Starlight', 4 feet, yellow, twisted petals; 'Stella', 3 feet, golden-yellow, starry flowers.

Cultivation The best plants are grown in a stiff loam in full sun. Seeds of annual kinds can be sown *in situ* in April, and to get the largest flowerheads water, and give liquid feeds occasionally up to flowering time. The perennials can be divided in autumn or spring. *H. laetiflorus* needs constant checking to prevent it from dominating the surrounding area, and is best planted in rough corners where it will provide useful flowers for cutting.

Helichrysum (hel-ee-kry-sum)

From the Greek *helios*, the sun, *chrysos*, gold, referring to the yellow flowers of some species. (*Compositae*). Everlasting-flower, immortelle-flower. A large genus of plants ranging from alpines to shrubs, bearing daisy-like flowers. Some are commonly dried as everlasting flowers. Not all are hardy.

Annual species cultivated *H. bractetuam*, 2–4 feet, bracts yellow or pink, summer, Australia; *album*, white, *monstrosum*, flower-heads double. Cultivars and strains of *H. b. monstrosum* include 'Fireball', scarlet, 'Golden', 'Rose,' and 'Salmon Rose'.

Cultivation Treat the annuals as half-hardy, sowing in gentle heat in March, gradually hardening off and planting out in May. Late sowings can be made out of doors in early May. The rock garden kinds all like dry sunny spots with sharp drainage, and make good

---

varieties are usually grown in a cool greenhouse either for pot work or to be cut and dried for winter use. The conspicuous papery bracts of the flowers are their chief attraction.

Species cultivated *G. globosa*, the globe amaranth, from India, a plant 1–1½ feet tall, seed of which is available either in mixed colours or, in selected colours including orange-yellow, purple, rose and white. There is also a dwarf form *nana*, 6 inches high, of which 'Buddy' is a purple-flowered cultivar, and seed of a form with variegated leaves is also offered.

Cultivation Sow seed in warmth, either in spring or autumn, and transplant the seedlings to small pots when they are about 1 inch high. Pot on as required in a compost of loam, leafmould and well-decayed manure in equal proportions, with a good sprinkling of sand added. Water regularly and give a liquid feed weekly until the plants flower, always keeping them as near the light as possible. Plants will flower between April and September according to the time of sowing. For winter use in dried arrangements and the like, cut the flowers as soon as they have developed fully and hang them up to dry.

Gypsophila (jip-sof-ill-a)

From the Greek *gypsos*, chalk, *phileo*, to love; the plants prefer chalky soils (*Caryophyllaceae*). Hardy annuals and perennials of great value in both the

---

The purple Gomphrena globosa, the Globe Amaranth, is an everlasting annual from India. Its papery bracts can be cut for drying or used to brighten up a group of pot plants.

border and rock garden; the dwarf kinds also look well in pans in the alpine house. They are mainly natives of the eastern Mediterranean region.

Annual species cultivated *G. elegans*, 1–1½ feet, clusters of small white flowers; vars. *alba grandiflora*, larger flowered, *rosea*, bright rose. 'London Market Strain' and a crimson strain are sometimes offered. *G. muralis*, 6 inches, rose-pink flowers.

Cultivation Plant both rock garden and border kinds in autumn or spring, the rock garden sorts in pockets containing a large amount of mortar rubble or limestone chippings. Although the border kinds like limy soil, they are tolerant of other soils but need a sunny spot with good drainage. They provide useful cut flower material when well grown. Propagation of the annual species and *G. repens* and *G. pacifica* is from seed. *G. paniculata* itself comes true from seed but cuttings of the varieties should be taken in June. These should be of young growth with a heel, 2 inches long, inserted in silver sand with gentle bottom heat. Commercially named forms are propagated by root grafting. Trailing species can be increased by cuttings or by division in spring.

scree plants. The shrubby kinds are rather tender and need wall protection in all except mild localities. Plant in April and fasten the main branches to a trellis or wire support. Prune away unwanted branches early in April. They may be grown as attractive greenhouse shrubs in a gritty compost of sand, peat and loam. Propagation of the perennial species is by division in April or by cuttings in a cold frame in spring, and of the shrubby kinds from cuttings of half-ripened wood in August, inserted round the edges of a pot of sandy soil and put in a cold frame.

Heliophila (he-le-off-ill-a)
From the Greek *helios*, the sun, and *philein*, to love (*Cruciferae*). A genus of attractive plants, from South Africa, mostly annuals, particularly effective when grown in masses.
Species cultivated *H. linearifolia*, 1½ feet, blue flowers, summer, a sub-shrubby plant usually treated as an annual. *H. longifolia*, 1½ feet, blue flowers with a white eye, freely produced on long racemes in summer, annual.
Cultivation A light, well-drained soil in a sunny spot suits the heliophilas and they also make attractive pot plants for the cold greenhouse. The seedlings are raised under glass from a March sowing. Those to be grown on under glass are potted up singly into 5-inch pots in potting compost and those to be

1 The annual Sunflower, Helianthus annuus, is a favourite plant which dominates any border in which it is grown.
2 Helichrysum vestitum, the Felted Everlasting, grows wild in South Africa.
3 Heliophila longifolia is a sun-loving mid-summer annual which produces small blue flowers freely in summer. It is equally effective massed in a sunny border or as a pot plant.

planted out of doors need hardening off and planting out 6 inches apart in May. Alternatively seed can be sown out of doors in May on a well-prepared seed bed.

Heliotropium (he-le-o-tro-pe-um)
From the Greek *helios*, the sun, *trope* to turn; the flowers were thought to turn towards the sun (*Boraginaceae*). Heliotrope, cherry pie. Half-hardy shrubs with fragrant flowers, one of which is treated as a half-hardy annual raised afresh each year for summer bedding.
Species cultivated *H. amplexicaulis* (syn. *H. anchusifolium*) 1 foot, lavender flowers, summer, Peru. *H. peruvianum* (syn. *H. arborescens*) 1–6 feet, heliotrope and white flowers from spring to winter according to cultivation, Peru. Cultivars

include 'Lemoine's Giant', heliotrope; 'Lord Roberts', dark blue, large flowers; 'Marguerite', dark blue; 'President Garfield', mauve-blue; 'Vilmorin's Variety' deep purple; 'White Lady', white.
Cultivation A minimum winter temperature of 45°F (7°C) is required and the compost should consist of 2 parts of loam, 1 part each of leafmould and silver sand. Repot in spring or plant in greenhouse borders where plants may be used to clothe a wall. Prune in February, cutting back the previous year's growth to within 2 or 3 inches of its base. By taking cuttings in autumn or spring a supply of small plants for pot work or for bedding out of doors can be maintained, autumn rooted cuttings usually making the better plants. Pinch out the tops when about 5 inches of growth has been made to produce bush plants. Water frequently and feed before flowering. Standard heliotropes are obtained by stopping at the desired height and side shoots stopped subsequently to form a head.

Helipterum (hel-ip-ter-um)
From the Greek *helios*, the sun, *pteron*, a wing or feather; the seed pappus is plumed (*Compositae*). Australian everlasting, immortelle-flower. A genus of sun-loving annuals and perennials, some of them shrubby, the annuals bearing everlasting flowers excellent for winter decoration.
Species cultivated *H. humboldtianum*, 1 foot, yellow, summer. *H. manglesii* (syn. *Rhodanthe manglesii*), 12–18 inches, pink and white, June to September, out of doors; April to June under glass, Australia. *H. roseum* (syn. *Acroclinium roseum*), 15–18 inches, shades of pink and white with yellow or bronze-copper centres, from July onwards out of doors, earlier under glass; vars. *flore plenum album*, double white, *grandiflorum*, larger flowers, various colours, Australia. 'Red Bonnie' is a bright red cultivar.
Cultivation Seeds are sown under glass in March and the seedlings are pricked out and hardened off, ready for planting out of doors in May. Seed may also be sown under glass in September and the seedlings pricked out, and potted on through the winter to provide spring blooms under glass. Water freely and give a liquid feed weekly after the plants are 6 inches high. Light staking will be required, and a minimum temperature of 45–50°F (7–10°C).

Iberis (eye-ber-is)
From the ancient name for Spain, Iberia (*Cruciferae*). Candytuft. A genus of about 40 species of hardy annual, biennial, evergreen and perennial herbs, from Spain and the Mediterranean region. All the species are easily grown, provided they have plenty of sun in a well-drained ordinary soil. The annuals make a useful addition to the annual border,

while the perennials are invaluable as a margin plant, or for rock gardens and pillars where there is no fear of damp conditions.

Species cultivated Annual *I. amara*, 1 foot, white, summer. *I. umbellata*, 1 foot, purple, summer; vars. *albida*, white, 'Dunnett's Crimson,' bright crimson; 'Giant Pink', rose-pink, 15 inches; *purpurea*, dark purple. Shrubby *I. saxatilis*, 4–6 inches, white, tinged purple, May. *I. sempervirens*, 9 inches, white, May; vars. 'Little Gem', 9 inches; 'Snowflake', 1 foot.

Cultivation For summer-flowering species sow the annual and biennials ⅛ inch deep, in March or April in light workable soil or in August for flowering in spring. Thin seedlings to 2 inches apart. Prevent the ground from drying out or the plants will run to seed. Remove seed pods. Propagate the sub-shrubs by seed sown in boxes in April by cuttings 1–2 inches long in July–October, or by division of roots October–March.

Impatiens (im-pa-she-ens, or im-pat-e-ens)

From the Latin *impatiens* in reference to the way in which the seed pods of some species burst and scatter their seed when touched (*Balsaminaceae*). Balsam, or Busy Lizzie. A genus of about 500 species of annuals, biennials and sub-shrubs mostly from the mountains of Asia and Africa. The succulent hollow stems are brittle and much branched. Few species are now cultivated and those that are may be grown in flower borders or under glass, or in the home as house plants.

Species cultivated *I. balsamina*, 1½ feet, rose, scarlet and white, summer, annual, greenhouse. *I. holstii*, 2–3 feet, scarlet, almost continuous flowering, half-hardy, greenhouse perennial; var. Imp Series F_1, low growing, brilliant mixed colours, in shade and sun. *I. petersiana*, 1 foot, reddish-bronze leaves and stems, red, almost continuous flowering, half-hardy, greenhouse perennial. *I. sultanii*, 1–2 feet, rose and carmine, almost continuous flowering, greenhouse perennial. *I. amphorata*, 5 feet, purple, August, annual. *I. roylei* (syn. *I. glandulifera*), 5 feet, purple or rose-crimson, spotted flowers in profusion, summer, annual.

Cultivation Greenhouse plants are potted in a mixture of equal parts loam, leaf-mould and sharp sand in well-drained pots, during February or March. They do best in well-lit conditions, and require moderate watering March–September, but only occasionally otherwise. They require a temperature of 55–65°F (13–18°C) from October to March, 65–75°F (18–24°C) March to June, and about 65°F (18°C) for the rest of the time. Pinch back

1 Heliotrope, or Cherry Pie, is a summer-flowering plant grown for its perfume.
2 The common Candytuft, Iberis umbellata, is available in various colours.

1 *Impatiens roylei has attractive red buds and blooms in early summer.*
2 *Ipomoea is a twining climber.*
3 *Ipomoea hederacea is the popular Morning Glory.*

the tips to make them bushy during February. Hardy species do well in ordinary soil in a sunny position, about 6 inches apart. *I. holstii* can be grown as a bedding plant and prefers light shade out of doors; it will tolerate varied temperatures. Propagate by seed in spring, sown in heat for the greenhouse species, and out of doors where the plants are to grow, for the hardy species, or by cuttings taken March to August, and placed in sandy soil in a temperature of 75°F (24°C).

Ipomoea (i-po-mee-ya)
From the Greek *ips*, bindweed, and *homoios*, like, in reference to the twining habit of growth (*Convolvulaceae*). A genus of 300 species of evergreen and deciduous climbing and twining herbs, including the sweet potato, and a few trees and shrubs, mostly from the tropics, Asia, Africa and Australia. First introduced in the late sixteenth century. Some of the greenhouse species, which like plenty of root room, are amongst the prettiest of climbing plants. They do best if planted in borders.
Species cultivated *I. batatas*, sweet potato, 2–4 feet, tubers, edible, greenhouse. *I. tricolor* (syn. *I. rubro-caerulea*), red, summer, greenhouse. *I. hederacea*, Morning Glory, blue, summer, half-hardy. *I. purpurea*, purple, summer, half-hardy. *I. pandurata*, white and purple, perennial, summer.
Cultivation The seeds of annual species, whether greenhouse or half-hardy, should be sown (notch seed slightly with

file) 2–3 in a 3-inch pot in a warm house in early spring using a compost of fibrous loam, decayed manure and lumpy leafmould. Otherwise the plants are prone to a chlorotic condition. Transfer the plants to a larger pot as required, without disturbing the roots. Train up a tripod of canes until ready for planting. The half-hardy species may be planted out at the beginning of June in a sheltered border on a south wall. Evergreen ipomoeas may be propagated by cuttings or layers.

Kochia (kok-e-a)
Named after W. D. J. Koch, 1771–1849, a German botanist (*Chenopodiaceae*). A half-hardy annual that is prized as a foliage plant; the small bushes, growing to as much as 3 feet, are green in the early stages, changing to crimson later in the season. They make ideal specimen plants dotted in sunny annual or other border, and they also look well as a low background for smaller plants. Only one species is cultivated, *K. scoparia*, belvedere, seldom grown, and its variety *trichophila*, the summer cypress.
Cultivation Seeds are sown in March in slight heat, and the seedlings pricked out and transplanted into their permanent quarters in June after being hardened off. They also make good plants for the unheated greenhouse.

Lathyrus (lath-eye-rus)
Lathyrus is the ancient Greek name for the pea (*Leguminaceae*). A genus of hardy annual and herbaceous perennial

climbers, from temperate zones and tropical mountains. The sweet pea, *L. odoratus*, is dealt with in detail under Sweet peas.

Species cultivated Annual: *L. sativus azureus*, 2 feet, blue, June–July, southern Europe. *L. tingitanus*, 6 feet, purple and red, summer, North Africa.

Cultivation Any good rich soil is suitable. The perennial species are propagated by seeds or by division of the roots in the spring. The annual species are propagated by sowing seeds in spring, either under glass and then planting the seedlings out of doors after they have been hardened off, or out of doors where they are to flower.

Lavatera (la-vat-ear-a)

Commemorating a seventeenth-century Swiss naturalist J. K. Lavater (*Malvaceae*). A genus of some 20 species of annuals, biennials, herbaceous perennials and sub-shrubs, mostly from southern Europe and the Mediterranean region. All bear mallow-like flowers.

Species cultivated *L. trimestris* (syn. *L. rosea*), 3–5 feet, pink, summer, annual; var. *alba splendens*, white. Named cultivars include 'Loveliness', 2 feet, deep rose, and 'Sunset', 2 feet, deeper in colour. *L. arborea*, tree mallow, 6–10 feet, flowers pale purple, summer to autumn, biennial; var. *variegata*, white variegated leaves. *L. cashmiriana*, 5–6 feet, pale rose, summer, perennial, India. *L. assurgentiflora*, 10 feet, purple, July,

1 Kochia scoparia trichophilia, the Summer Cypress, is a small annual foliage plant.
2 The Kochias are also called Fire Bushes, because in autumn the foliage turns fiery crimson.
3 Lathyrus tingitanus is a climbing annual Pea, closely related to the Sweet Pea.
4 Lavatera 'Loveliness' is one of the best of the annual Mallows.
5 Lavatera olbia rosea, the Tree Mallow, is not entirely hardy.

shrub, California. *L. olbia*, 6 feet, reddish purple, June–October; var. *rosea*, rose-pink.

Cultivation All these lavateras like hot, dry positions and make good plants for the back of a border. The tree mallow is not entirely hardy and may be cut down by frosts, but it usually shoots up again from the base in the spring. The perennial species are planted out in June from sowings made under glass in February or March in a temperature of 60°F (16°C) or from sowings made out of doors in late spring. The variegated tree mallow is propagated by cuttings taken in mid-summer and kept in a closed propagating case until rooted. The annual species are sown in September or April in the beds or borders where they are to flower.

Leptosyne (lep-to-sy-knee-)
From the Greek *leptos*, slender, describing the growth of these plants (*Compositae*). A small genus of hardy annuals and perennials that deserve to be better known, as they are showy in the garden and good as cut flowers. They are very similar in appearance to *Coreopsis*, to which they are closely related, and are natives of America.

Species cultivated Annual: *L. calliopsidea*, 1½ feet, yellow, late summer. *L.*

There are few low-growing annual plants that can surpass Limnanthes douglasii for summer colour.

douglasii, 1 foot, *L. stillmanii*, 1½ feet, bright yellow, autumn.

Cultivation Any ordinary soil will suit these plants but they like an open, sunny position. Sow seeds of the annual species in the spring in the open ground where the plants are to flower, or sow them under glass and transplant the seedlings to their flowering positions in late May or early June.

Limnanthes (lim-nan-thes)
From the Greek *limne*, a marsh, and *anthos*, a flower, referring to the liking some of these plants have for damp ground (*Limnanthaceae*). A small genus of hardy annuals from California, which deserve to be grown more. They will always have a cloud of bees hovering over them, to which they seem to be very attractive, and a common name for them is the bee-flower. In the right soil they are prolific in their production of flowers and if left to seed, will bloom again in the same year, in September and October. One species only is cultivated, *L. douglasii*, which grows 6 inches tall and has delicate fern-like leaves and shining, lemon-yellow and

white flowers, in May–June. The flower colours have also led to the plant being given the popular name, butter and eggs.

Cultivation Ordinary soil will do, but limnanthes grow best in moist soils. Plants should be given a sunny position and they give good displays if grown in clumps. Propagate by seed sown in autumn and spring where the plants are to flower, thinning the seedlings to 3–4 inches apart.

Limonium (li-mo-nee-um)
From the Greek *leimon*, a meadow, because certain species are found growing in salt marshes (*Plumbaginaceae*). Sea lavender. A genus of annuals, perennial herbaceous plants and sub-shrubs, hardy, half hardy and tender. Once known as *Statice*, these plants are natives of all parts of the world, particularly coasts and salt marshes. The numerous small flowers, usually borne in branched spikes, are easily dried and are much used for long-lasting flower arrangements. All flower in summer.

Annual species cultivated *L. bonduellii*, 1 foot, yellow, North Africa, strictly a perennial but treated as a half-hardy annual. *L. sinuatum*, 1–2 feet, blue and cream, Mediterranean region; there are several cultivars including 'New Art Shades', a strain containing a mixture of

colours; 'Chamois Rose', shades of apricot-pink; 'Lavender Queen', 'Market Grower's Blue'; 'Pacific Giants Mixed', large-flowered strain in mixed colours; 'Purple Monarch', rich purple. *L. spicatum*, 6 inches, rose and white, Caucasus, Persia. *L. suworowii*, 1½ feet, lilac pink, Turkestan.

Greenhouse: *L. imbricatum*, 1½–2 feet, blue, Canary Isles. *L. macrophyllum*, 1–2 feet, blue, Canary Isles. *L. ×profusum*, 2–3 feet, blue, late summer to autumn, hybrid.

Cultivation All the limoniums prefer well-drained, sandy loam and a sunny position. The outdoor species are suitable for borders, the dwarf kinds for rock gardens. Plant the hardy perennials in spring and the annuals in late May. Greenhouse species are potted in the spring and fed occasionally with a weak liquid fertiliser. They require a summer temperature of 55–65°F (13–18°C) and 40–50°F (4–10°C) in the winter. Propagation is by seeds sown in sandy soil in early spring, when the temperature should be 55–60°F (13–16°C). Root cuttings of the perennials can be taken in late winter or early spring and rooted in a cold frame.

Linaria (lin-ar-ee-a)

From the Latin *linum*, flax, referring to the flax-like leaves (*Scrophulariaceae*). Toadflax. Linarias are in the main hardy annual or perennial plants from the Northern Hemisphere; the European plant, once known as *L. cymbalaria*, the Kenilworth ivy or mother of thousands, widely naturalised in Britain, is correctly known as *Cymbalaria muralis*. The yellow flowers of the native species *L. vulgaris*) can be seen on roadside verges, banks and in fields throughout the summer.

Annual species cultivated *L. heterophylla*, 1–3 feet, yellow, July, Morocco. *L. maroccuna*, 9–12 inches, violet-purple, June, Morocco; cultivars include 'Fairy Bouquet', mixed colours; 'Northern Lights', mixed colours, 'White Pearl' and 'Yellow Prince'. *L. reticulata*, 2–4 feet, purple and yellow, summer, Portugal. *L. tristis*, 1 foot, yellow and brown, summer, Portugal and Spain.

Cultivation The soil should be well-drained and rather moist. Sunny borders or rock gardens are suitable positions. Plants can be moved and replanted in autumn or spring. Propagation is by seeds sown where the plants are required to flower, in September for flowering in spring, and in April for summer flowering.

Linum (li-num)

From the old Greek name, *linon*, used by Theophrastus (*Linaceae*). Flax. This important genus contains, besides the economically valuable annual which supplies flax and linseed oil, a number of very decorative garden plants. The

flower colour which seems characteristic of the genus is a fine pale blue but there are a number of shrubs with yellow blossoms, and a lovely scarlet annual. The genus is widely distributed in the temperate regions of the world.

Annual species cultivated *L. grandiflorum*, 6–12 inches, rose, summer, North Africa; vars *coccineum*, rose-crimson; *rubrum* brighter than type; 'Venice Red' is a large-flowered cultivar with carmine-scarlet flowers. *L. usitatissimum*, common flax, 1½ feet, blue, June–July, Europe. Historically this is the world's most famous fibre plant; it was known to the Egyptians. Shrubby: *L. arboreum*, 1 foot, yellow, May–June, Crete.

Cultivation The flaxes are not fussy about soil provided it is well-drained and will do very well on an alkaline medium. The annuals need the standard treatment for this group. Sometimes *L. grandiflorum* is sown in pots in July to decorate the greenhouse in the autumn, but whether grown outside or in, it is one of the best annuals for display.

Lobularia (lob-u-lar-i-a)

From the Greek *lobulus*, a little lobe, a diminutive of *lobos*, the lower part of the ear, possibly referring to the forked hairs on the leaves (*Cruciferae*). A small genus of plants closely related to *Alyssum*. There are four species, natives of the Mediterranean region, but only one of any garden value. This is *L. maritima* (syn. *Alyssum maritimum*), 9–10 inches tall, the well-known sweet alyssum or sweet Alison. Though it is really a

1 The Limonium suworowii from Turkistan has lilac-pink, papery flower spikes which are long-lasting and useful for winter flower arrangements.
2 Linaria reticulata, an annual Toadflax, can grow to 4 feet or more in height.

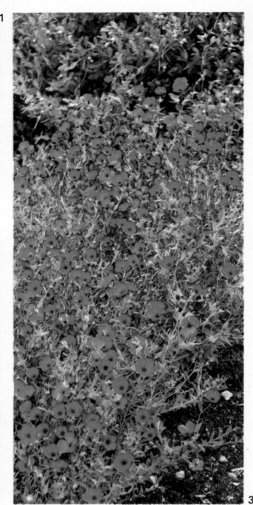

1 Cultivars of the annual Toadflax, Linaria maroccana, appear in a variety of colours.
2 Lobularia maritima, Sweet Alyssum, has white flowers and is usually grown as an annual.
3 Linum rubrum grandiflorum, the annual Flax, has deep rose-red blooms.

perennial it is treated as a hardy annual and flowers in early summer. It is a popular edging plant grown for the sake of its sweetly-scented white flower.

Some varieties and cultivars are: *minimum*, very small-growing, white; *nanum* ('Little Dorrit'), compact, short-growing, white; 'Lilac Queen', pale lilac; 'Pink Heather', compact; 'Rosie O'Day', deep rose; 'Violet Queen', bright violet, very floriferous; *procumbens* 'Snow Cloth', compact mass of pure white flowers; 'Royal Carpet', very dwarf, dark purple.

Cultivation There is no difficulty in growing this fragrant plant, which can be put in open borders or rock gardens. Seeds are sown in spring or autumn where the plants are to grow, and plants will survive through a mild winter. Cuttings can be made, but lobularia will reproduce itself quite readily from self-sown seeds. It thrives in any soil, although it does not like a heavy wet medium one, and prefers a position in full sun to all others.

1 The annual Lupins are useful and long-lasting cut flowers.
2 Lupin 'Lilac Time' has mauve and white flower spikes.
3 Lupin 'Tom Reeves' comes into flower in mid-June.
4 Lupin 'Fireglow' is a sturdy cultivar with orange and gold flowers.
5 Lupin 'Whitesheaf' is a cultivar with flat-topped flower spikes which mature from yellow to a deep golden orange.
6 The apricot-pink flower spikes of Lupin 'Harvester' are extra-long.

Lonas (lo-nas)

Derivation uncertain (*Compositae*). There is but one species in the genus, *L. annua*, African daisy, an uncommon and hardy annual, a branching plant, 1 foot tall. The clustered flowers, produced from July to October, resemble those of an ageratum but they are golden-yellow. An added attraction of this Mediterranean plant is that the flowers may be treated as everlasting to combine with other dried material to use as winter decoration.

Cultivation The plant will grow in any kind of soil, but needs a sunny aspect. Propagate by seed sown out of doors in April, where the plants are to flower.

Lupinus (lu-py-nus)

From the Latin *lupus*, a wolf (destroyer), because it was thought that the plants depleted the fertility of the soil by sheer numbers (*Leguminosae*). Lupin. A genus of over 300 species of annuals, perennials and sub-shrubs, mainly from North America, though there are a few Mediterranean species which, since Roman times, have been used for green manuring. This is surprising since the Roman farmers did not know that within the root nodules were colonies of bacteria capable of utilising nitrogen to produce valuable nitrates. The fine Russell hybrid lupins are among the most showy of herbaceous perennials and have a wide colour range embracing the three primary colours: red, yellow and blue. They do not, however, thrive on

1 *Malcolmia maritima, Virginia Stock, is among the simplest of all annuals to grow. It comes in many shades of pink, mauve and white.*

2 *Malope trifida with its shiny purple flowers is sometimes included in the herb garden because of its medicinal properties.*

alkaline (chalky or limy) soils.

Species cultivated Annual: *L. densiflorus*, 1½–2 feet, yellow, fragrant, July–August, California. *L. hartwegii*, 2–3 feet, blue, white and red, July–October, Mexico. *L. hirsutissimus*, 1 foot, with stinging hairs, purple flowers, July, California. *L. hirsutus*, 2–3 feet, blue and white, July–August, Mediterranean region. *L. luteus*, 2 feet, yellow, June–August, south Europe. *L. mutabilis*, 5 feet, white, blue and yellow, summer, Colombia. *L. pubescens*, 3 feet, violet, blue and white, summer, Mexico. *L. subcarnosus*, 1 foot, blue and white, July, Texas.

The annuals are treated as hardy and seeds are sown in drills in April. In May the seedlings must be thinned out to 9 inches apart. It is important with both annual and perennial lupins to remove the forming seed pods before they can grow large enough to retard the flowering capacity of the plants.

The tree lupin, *L. arboreus*, may be raised from seed with extreme ease. These shrubs make rapid growth and will flower in their second season. They are, however, not long-lived, but generally manage to renew themselves by self-sown seedlings. The shrubby lupin, *L. excubicus*, makes a fine large plant,

but needs some frost protection. Like most lupins this has very fragrant flowers.

Malcolmia (often spelt Malcomia) (mal-ko-me-a)

Commemorating William Malcolm, nurseryman, botanist, and associate of the naturalist Ray (*Cruciferae*). Though there are 35 species in this genus of hardy annual and perennial plants, and many quite decorative plants among them, there is one only which is commonly grown, the Virginian stock, *M. maritima*. The vernacular name is a misnomer as this plant is a native of Southern Europe and has been grown in British gardens since its introduction in 1713. *M. maritima*, which is perhaps the simplest of all hardy annuals to grow, is a 1-foot tall plant with a colour range including white, pink, red, yellow and lilac. There is a 6-inch tall variety in various colours, known as *nana compacta*. It is sometimes used to edge beds of annual plants and may be sown quite thickly where it is intended to grow, thinning the seedlings to ½–1 inch apart when they are 1 inch tall. The seeds may be sown in spring for summer blooming, in early summer to flower in late summer and autumn, or in September to bloom in the following spring. Plants may also be grown in 5-inch pots to decorate a sunny windowsill or cold greenhouse.

Malope (mal-o-pe)

The old Greek name for a kind of mallow, meaning soft or soothing, from the leaf texture, or the plant's medicinal properties (*Malvaceae*). This is a small genus of hardy annuals from the Mediterranean

region, with showy rose or purple flowers.

Species cultivated *M. malacoides*, 1 foot, rose-pink and purple, June, Mediterranean region. *M. trifida*, 2–3 feet, purple, summer, Spain; vars. *alba*, white; *grandiflora*, large rosy-purple flowers; *rosea*, rose.

Cultivation Good soil and full sunshine are appreciated and water should be given in dry periods. Soluble stimulants should be given occasionally when the plants are in full growth. Propagation is by seed sown in boxes or pots under glass in March in a temperature of 50°F (10°C), potting the seedlings on as necessary and planting them out 6 inches apart in their flowering positions in May or June. Or seed may be sown ½ inch deep out of doors in April or May where the plants are to flower.

Matthiola (mat-te-o-la)

Commemorating Pierandrea Mattioli 1500–77, Italian physician and botanist (*Cruciferae*). This genus of 50 species is important for the gardener's benefit because it contains those annual and biennial species known as stocks. They are showy plants and most have the additional quality of sweet scent. In the wild state stocks are found in the Mediterranean, Egypt, South Europe and in South Africa, and two species, *M. incana* and *M. sinuata*, are among the rarer British natives. *M. incana* is, in fact, the parent plant from which the annual ten-week stocks have arisen; it is also the parent of the biennials: the East Lothian, Brompton, queen and wallflower-leaved stocks.

The sweetly fragrant night-scented stock, *M. bicornic*, looks a dowdy thing during the daytime but as evening comes the air is filled with its scent. For the sake of its fragrance it may well be grown beneath a window, but not in too prominent a place as it has no beauty of appearance. It is sometimes listed as *Hesperis tristis*.

Species cultivated *M. bicornis*, the night-scented stock, 1 foot, purplish, fragrant, annual, Greece. *M. fenestralis*, 1 foot, scarlet or purple, biennial, Crete. *M. incana*, 1½ feet, purple, summer, biennial. It is from this last species that most of the showy garden stocks have arisen, and any seedsman's catalogue will offer a great choice of colours in various strains. Named cultivars and strains include:

Beauty or Mammoth stocks, all 1½ feet tall 'Abundance', crimson-rose: 'American Beauty', carmine rose; 'Beauty of Naples', old rose; 'Beauty of Nice'; flesh-pink; 'Cote d'Azur', light blue; 'Crimson King', scarlet, double; 'Monte Carlo', yellow; 'Queen Alexandra', rosy-lilac; 'Salmon King'; 'Snowdrift', pure white; 'Summer Night', purple; 'Violette de Parme', violet.

Brompton stocks, mainly 15–18 inches tall 'Crimson King'; 'Giant Empress

Elizabeth', rosy carmine: 'Ipswich Carmine King', 2 feet; 'Ipswich Pink King', 'Lavander Lady', 'White Lady'; *Hybrida* 'Harbinger', early flowering.

East Lothian stocks, 15 inches to 2 feet tall, available in lavender, rose, crimson, scarlet and white and in strains such as 'Giant Imperial', 1½ feet, double flowers in various colours; 'Giant Perfection', 2 feet, mainly double, various colours; 'Improved Mammoth Excelsior', non-branching strain, mainly double flowers, various colours.

Ten-weeks stocks, 15 inches tall, various colours.

Of both Brompton and ten-week stocks, there are available strains known as 'Hanson's Double'. With these it is possible at the seedling stage to select the double varieties as these have light green leaves, whereas those with darker leaves will produce single flowers if grown on. This colour distinction can be emphasised by sowing seeds in a temperature of 54–60°F (12–16°C), lowering it to below 50°F (10°C) when the seedlings have formed their first pair of leaves.

In addition to the above there is a newer strain called 'Trysomic Seven Week Stocks', earlier to flower than all others, which produces plants above 1 foot tall with mainly double flowers in carmine, pink, light blue and white.

Cultivation Ten-week stocks are grown from seed sown under glass in March. Plant out the seedlings in May or June, leaving 9 inches between plants. The soil should be deep and well manured. The night-scented stocks are sown out of doors in April where the plants are intended to remain. The biennials of the Brompton group should be sown in frames in June and July. Transplant when 1 inch high to the places where the plants are to flower in the following year, spacing them 1 foot apart. Or, over-winter them in pots in a frame to plant out in the following March. The intermediate and the East Lothian stocks may be given much the same treatment as the Bromptons but will flower much earlier in the year. Though some seedsmen apply the term 'hardy annual' to many of the stocks, it is in fact not advisable to give hardy annual treatment to any but the night-flowering *M. bicornis*.

Maurandia (maw-ran-de-a)
Commemorating Mme Catharina Maurandy, student of botany, Carthagena, c.1797 (*Scrophulariaceae*). This small genus, mainly of half-hardy climbing

1 *Matthiola incana is the parent plant for all the various types of Stocks, which are available in various shades of pink and purple or in white.*
2 *The Stocks are useful summer-flowering plants. They lend themselves especially well to informal borders and bedding schemes.*

Mentzelia (ment-ze-le-a)

Commemorates Chritian Mentzel, 1622–1701, a German botanist (*Loasaceae*). Annual, biennial and perennial plants from North and South America, numbering about 50 species, few of which are in cultivation.

Species cultivated *M. hispida*, 1½–2 feet, yellow flowers in June and July. Perennial which should be over-wintered in a greenhouse or frame with little water at that period, Mexico. *M. lindleyi* (syn. *Bartonia aurea*), blazing star. 1½–2 feet, with golden-yellow flowers and a mass of feathery stamens resembling a St John's wort. The slightly fragrant flowers open only during sunny weather. A delightful hardy annual to be sown in the open in April and May where it is to flower, California. *M. nuda*, 2–3 feet, with creamy-white flowers about 2 inches across borne on slender stems in August and opening in the evening; biennial, for a cool greenhouse, Missouri.

Cultivation The hardy annual *M. lindleyi* does well in ordinary garden soil and a sunny position. The tender species should be grown in pots containing a well-drained potting compost and given little water during the winter. Propogate by seed sown in the spring in a heated greenhouse. Cuttings of *M. nuda* will root if inserted in sand in a propagating frame with bottom heat.

Mesembryanthemum

(mes-em-bre-an-the-mum)

From the Greek *mesos*, middle, *embryon*, fruit, and *anthemon*, flower; not from *mesembria*, mid-day and *anthemon*, as is usually suggested. The earliest species known flowered at mid-day, but when night-flowering species were discovered the name was changed to give a change of sense without a change of sound (*Aizoaceae*). These are greenhouse succulent plants, many suitable for bedding out for the summer with a creeping habit of growth, fleshy leaves and brilliant coloured flowers.

Species cultivated *M. albatum*, branching, green and pinkish-red flowers, Cape Province. *M. crystallinum*, ice plant, spreading branches, white flowers, south-west Africa. *M. fulleri*, annual, white flowers, Cape Province. *M. intransparens*, erect stem, white and pink flowers, Cape Province. *M. macrophyllum*, prostrate, violet-pink flowers, Namaqualand. *M. nodiflorum*, cylindrical leaves, white flowers, Africa, the Middle East and California. *M. setosum*, pink and greenish flowers, Cape Province. *M. striatum*, prostrate, white flowers, Cape Province. The plant popularly known as *M. criniflorum* is now called *Dorotheanthus criniflorum*.

Cultivation They should be grown in a very porous compost with ⅕ part added of coarse sand, grit, broken brick and granulated charcoal. The greenhouse kinds require a sunny position with plenty of ventilation in hot weather.

perennials has a few Mexican species worthy of cultivation in the greenhouse. The climbing kinds climb by the aid of their sensitive leaf-stalks, in the manner of a clematis, and are quite suitable for cultivation in a suspended wire basket. The funnel-shaped flowers are large and showy, and their effect is enhanced by the delicate growth.

Species cultivated *M. barcaliana*, to 6 feet, violet-purple, rose or white summer. *M. erubescens*, to 6 feet, rose and white, summer. *M. lophospermum*, to 6 feet, rosy-purple, summer. *M. scandens*, to purple and violet, summer.

Cultivation A mixture of equal parts of loam and leafmould or peat and a little sand suits them. Pots or wire baskets are suitable and these climbers need some sort of support upon which to fix their leaf-stalks, such as trellis work or twiggy sticks. In the growing season

Maurandia scandens is an annual climbing plant which uses its sensitive leaf-stalks to cling to its support.

when plants are flowering, water with a weak liquid fertilizer, but in winter keep the plants nearly dry, but with a minimum temperature of 45–55°F (7–13°C). Though perennial, the mauradnias are sometimes treated as hald-hardy annuals. Plants may also be grown out of doors from June onwards in sunny, protected places, such as against south-facing walls. They should be lifted and taken into the protection of the greenhouse in September. Propagation is by seed sown in seed compost in March in a temperature of 60–70°F (16–21°C), potting the seedlings into individual small pots when they are 1 inch high. Cuttings will root in spring or summer in a closed propagating frame with bottom heat.

Give them a minimum winter temperature of 45°F (7°C), and normal greenhouse temperature during summer. Water only when the soil has dried out and keep dry during the winter. Propagate from seed sown in seed compost in March in a temperature of 65–70°F (18–21°C). Do not cover the seeds but keep moist and shaded until the seedlings are pricked out. Also by cuttings taken during the summer and rooted in equal parts of sharp sand and peat. These can then be put out in a sunny position in well-drained soil as bedding plants, or on a rock garden.

Mimulus (mim-u-lus)

From the Greek *mimo*, ape; the flowers were thought to look like a mask on a monkey's face (*Schrophulariaceae*). Monkey flower, monkey musk, musk. A genus of hardy annual, half-hardy perennial and hardy perennial plants grown for their showy flowers. They are found in many temperate parts of the world, particularly in North America.

Species cultivated Annual *M. brevipes* 1½–2 feet, yellow flowers, summer. *M. fremonti*, 6–8 inches, crimson flowers summer.

Cultivation Annual species do best in moist, shady positions, though they will grow in sunny places provided the soil is sufficiently moist. Propagation is by seed sown under glass in a temperature of 55–65°F (13–18°C) in spring. The seedlings are pricked out, and gradually hardened off, finally in a cold frame, before being planted out at the end of May or the beginning of June.

Mirabilis (mir-ab-il-is)

From the Latin *mirabilis*, wonderful, to be admired (*Nyctaginaceae*). A small genus of annuals and perennials, some with tuberous roots, from the warmer regions of America: all those in cultivation are half-hardy plants. *M. jalapa* is unusual in that flowers of different colours often appear on different stems of the same plant.

Species cultivated *M.* × *hybrida*, 2 feet, flowers white, summer, opening in afternoon. *M. jalapa*, marvel of Peru, four o'clock plant, 2–3 feet, fragrant flowers, various colours, summer, opening in late afternoon, hence one of the common names; 'Pygmee', 1 foot, is a dwarf strain. *M. longiflora*, 3 feet, mixed colours, fragrant, summer, opening in afternoon. *M. multiflora*, 2–3 feet, rosy-purple flowers, summer, remaining open in sun, unlike other species.

Cultivation Sunny positions and quite

1 The Mentzelia lindleyi, Blazing Star, with its glossy yellow flowers, will flourish in any ordinary garden soil and provides bright colour in early summer borders.
2 Mesembryanthemums are multi-coloured creeping plants that are useful in summer bedding schemes.

1 Mirabilis jalapa, the Four O'Clock Plant or the Marvel of Peru, has flowers in shades of deep pink which open in the late afternoon.
2 The wide open blooms of Mirabilis jalapa are especially fragrant in the early evening.
3 The dried calyces of Moluccella laevis are useful for bright floral decoration in the winter.

ordinary garden soil suit these plants, which should be planted out in May or early June, after the danger of frost is over. The tubers may be lifted during October, to be stored, like those of dahlias, in frost-free places in peat, sand, or other material, until they are required for planting again. In the milder localities the black tubers of *M. jalapa* may be left in the ground during the winter and most of them will survive. Quicker results are obtained, however, by growing plants from seed each year. Propagation is by seed sown $\frac{1}{8}$ inch deep during February or March, in seed compost in a temperature of 65–75°F (18–24°C). Young plants should be gradually hardened off, completing this process in a cold frame in late spring to early summer, and finally planted out in June. Overwintered tubers may also be divided at planting time.

Moluccella (mol-u-sel-a)

The name is taken from the Moluccas, islands in the Malay Archipelago, from whence one of the two species is thought to have come (*Labiatae*). Their flowers are curious, the white-veined and enlarged calyces are pale green in colour and look like petals. One of the species, *M. laevis*, is treated as a half-hardy annual and is much sought after by flower arrangers, who grow it specially for this purpose. These flowers are also very useful for winter decoration as they dry well. The 'flowers' have a papery appearance and are green and look like shells, hence the name shell flower or bells of Ireland. The flowers are arranged in whorls along the flowering stem.

Species cultivated *M. laevis*, 1½ feet, white flowers cupped in white-veined pale green calyces, August, Syria, treated as a half-hardy annual. *M. spinosa*, to 8 feet, white flowers, spined calyces, summer, eastern Mediterranean, usually treated as an annual.

Cultivation Moluccellas do best in a sandy loam soil and a sunny position. They should be treated as half-hardy annuals, sowing the seed in heat in February or March. The seedlings are then pricked off and hardened off, ready for planting out in May.

Myosotis (my-o-so-tis)

From the Greek *mus*, a mouse, and *otes*, an ear, in reference to the leaves (*Boraginaceae*). Forget-me-not, scorpion grass. The common forget-me-not is a popular plant for use in spring bedding schemes in combination with other plants such as tulips and wallflowers. There are some 40 species of annuals, biennials or perennials in the genus, natives of temperate regions, particularly Europe and Australia. Those used for bedding purposes are hardy perennials but are usually treated as biennials.

Species cultivated *M. alpestris*, 3–8 inches, azure-blue with yellow eyes, June–July, European mountains; vars. *alba*, white flowers, *aurea*, golden yellow leaves. *M. australis*, 1–1½ feet, yellow,

1 Myosotis, the popular Forget-Me-Not, is a useful plant for spring bedding schemes. Here is it used as a border for a bed of tulips.
2 Myosotis azorica produces mauve-purple flowers in the summer.
3 The dwarfish Myosotis alpestris, with its pale blue flowers with yellow eyes, is a native of the mountains of Europe.

sometimes white, summer, New Zealand. *M. azorica*, 6–10 inches, violet-purple, summer, Azores; var. *alba*, white flowers. *M. caespitosa*, 6 inches, sky-blue, yellow centre, summer, European mountains; var. *rehsteineri*, 2 inches, tufted, April–May. *M. dissitiflora*, 8–10 inches, sky blue, May to July, European Alps; var. *alba*, white. *M. scorpioides* (syn. *M. palustris*), forget-me-not, 6-12 inches, blue flowers with yellow eye, May and June; vars. *alba*, white flowers, *semperflorens*, dwarf. *M. sylvatica*, 1–2 feet, blue with yellow eye, spring, Europe, including Britain, North Asia. Cultivars: 'Anne Marie Fischer', deep blue flowers, compact plant; 'Blue Ball', deep blue; 'Blue Bird', deep blue, winter flowering; 'Carmine King'; 'Compindi', deep indigo-blue, compact; 'Marga Sacher', deep sky blue; 'Royal Blue'; 'Rosea', pale rose; 'Ruth Fisher', very large blue flowers; 'Star of Love', blue, dwarf; 'Victoria', blue.

Cultivation *M. alpestris* requires a lightly shaded place in the rock garden, and should be planted in March or April. Other kinds are best grown as biennials by sowing seed in shallow drills outdoors from April to June. Transplant the seedlings to spring-flowering beds, in October, planting them 4-6 inches apart in ordinary soil. Perennial plants may be increased by division in March or October. *M. azorica* may not prove reliably hardy as a perennial in some years.

Nemesia (nem-e-ze-a)

An ancient Greek name used for a similar plant (*Schrophulariaceae*). Although there are some 50 species in the genus of annuals, perennials and subshrubs, mainly natives of South Africa, the majority of plants grown by gardeneres are hybrid races and cultivars originating mostly from the South African species *N. strumosa*. These are mainly grown as half-hardy annuals, chiefly to provide bright mixtures of colour in summer-flowering bedding schemes. Cultivars include *N. strumosa* 'Aurora', 9 inches, carmine and white flowers: 'Blue Gem', 9 inches, pale blue flowers; 'Fire King', 9 inches, flowers crimson scarlet; 'Orange Prince', 9 inches, rich orange flowers, *superbissima grandiflora*, 9 inches, a strain with large flowers in a wide range of

1 Nemesia strumosia suttonii is a selected race with large flowers found in the wide range of colours that characterize this genus. They are effective in a mixed border.

2 Nemesia strumosa with its pale blue flowers is usually grown as a half-hardy annual, producing numerous flowers throughout the summer.

colours. *N. strumosa suttonii* is a selected race with large flowers and a range of all colours found in nemesias. Other hybrid selections include 'Dwarf Compact Hybrids', 9 inches; 'Dwarf Gem Mixture', 9 inches; 'Dwarf Triumph Strain', 9 inches; 'Carnival Mixture', 9-12 inches; 'Red Carnival', 9–12 inches, a tetraploid cultivar.

Cultivation Sow seed in well-drained pans, pots or boxes in the greenhouse in April in a temperature of 55°F (13°C), and transplant the seedlings 1 inch apart in seed boxes until the plants are ready for setting out in the open garden in June, at 4 inches apart. Keep the plants cool at all stages, at a temperature not above 55°F (13°C), and ensure that seedlings are never allowed to dry at the roots nor become overcrowded in their boxes. Seed may also be sown directly into flowering beds, in May and June, thinning the seedlings to 4 inches apart when they are large enough to handle. A sowing under glass in July or August will provide winter-flowering pot plants for the greenhouse. For flowering under glass in early spring sow seed between mid-September and mid-October. Prick off the seedlings first into seed boxes and later pot them on individually into

3-inch pots, finally moving them to 5-inch pots. Forcing in extra heat should not be attempted.

Nemophila (nem-of-il-a)
From the Latin *nemos*, a glade, and the Greek *phileo*, to love, because the plant was found growing in glades or groves (*Hydrophyllaceae*). Baby blue eyes. A genus of nearly 20 species of annual plants from North America of which a few are grown in temperate gardens as hardy annuals.

Species cultivated *N. maculata*. 6–12 inches, flowers white, prominently veined flowers blotched violet, summer. *N. menziesii* (syn. *N. insignis*), 6 inches, spreading in habit, flowers light blue with white centres, summer; var. *alba*, flowers white with black centres.

Cultivation These little annuals are easily grown in any ordinary garden soil. Seeds are sown in March or April, where the plants are to flower in summer, choosing sunny places. Spring-flowering plants are raised from seed sown in August or September, but they may need cloche protection during severe spells. The seedlings should be thinned when young to 3 inches apart. Nemophilas make attractive pot plants for unheated greenhouses or sunny window-sills, if seed is sown in pans or pots and the seedlings into potted-on 3½-inch pots and later into final 5–6-inch pots. Keep them in a cool, shady place until the plants are about to flower.

Nicotania (nik-o-shee-ana)
In honour of Jean Nicot (1530–1600), a French Consul in Portugal, who introduced the tobacco plant into France and Portugal (*Solanaceae*). A genus of some 66 species, mainly annual and perennial herbaceous plants, treated as half-hardy plants, 45 species from the warmer regions of north and south America, 21 from Australia. The most important economic species is *N. tabacum* and its many varieties, grown commercially for the sake of its leaves which when dried provide the tobacco of commerce, although *N. rustica*, still used for this purpose, was the first species used to provide tobacco for smoking in Europe. They all have sticky stems and very hairy leaves, exceptionally large in *N. tabacum*. The long-tubed flowers of the ornamental species are carried in racemes or panicles. The colours vary considerably, due mostly to hybridisation between the white of *N. alata* and carmine of *N. × sanderae*. The flowers

1 The delicate and popular Nemesia is native to South Africa and requires cool, dry conditions before being planted out.
2 The dwarf Nemophila menziesii reaches only 6 inches in height, but because of its spreading growth and profuse flowering habit, it is an ideal summer bedding plant. The light blue flowers have a white centre.

of most of the ornamental species are very fragrant, some of them particularly so at night.

Species cultivated N. alata, 2 feet, flowers white with greenish-yellow reverse, very fragrant, summer; var. grandiflora (syn. N. affinis) has large flowers which are yellowish on the reverse; cultivars include 'Daylight', 2½ feet, flowers pure white, remaining open all day; 'Dwarf White Bedder', 15 inches, flowers remaining open all day; 'Lime Green' 2½ feet, greenish-yellow, popular with flower arrangers; 'Sensation', 2½ feet, a strain with flowers in various colours. N. glauca, half-hardy shrubby plant, normally about 8 feet tall, sometimes considerably more, leaves glaucous, flowers yellow, August to October, naturalized in southern Europe. N. × sanderae, 2–3 feet, flowers in shades of pinks and carmines, summer hybrid; cultivars are 'Crimson Bedder', 15 inches, deep crimson; 'Crimson King', 2½ feet, crimson-red; 'Knapton Scarlet', 3 feet. Mixed colours are also available. N. suaveolens, 1½–2 feet, white flowers, greenish-purple outside, summer. N. sylvestris, 5 feet, leaves to 1 foot long, flowers white, long-tubed, fragrant. N. tabacum, the common tobacco, to 6 feet, very large hairy leaves, insignificant pink flowers, summer; cultivars include 'Burley', a popular kind for making home-grown tobacco; 'Havana', leaves used for cigar making; 'New Zealand Gay Yellow'; 'Virginica No. 25'. All the above species and hybrids are annuals, except where stated, and all are from north or south America.

Cultivation The ornamental species, grown as half-hardy annuals, will thrive in full sun or partial shade in any good garden soil. The seeds are sown in the greenhouse in a temperature of 55–60°F (13–16°C), in March or April in any good seed compost. The seedlings are hardened off and planted out 1 foot or so apart in June. Seeds may also be sown out of doors in May, where the plants are to flower. In the southern part of the country, at least, self-sown seedlings often appear in late spring. Although N. alata is treated as an annual, it is, in fact, a perennial and in sheltered gardens plants may survive through a mild winter, especially if the roots are protected in some way, to flower again the following summer. The roots are thick and tuberous, not unlike those of the dahlia. The common tobacco is also treated as a half-hardy annual, the leaves being gathered in September for curing. For greenhouse decoration N. suaveolens is suitable and also the 'Daylight' and 'Sensation' hybrids. The

1 and 2 Cultivars of Nicotiana alata grandiflora have large, fragrant flowers and come in a variety of colours. Because its fragrance is especially strong in the evening, it is very effective when grown under a window.

taller species and varieties need a good deal of space but otherwise make good greenhouse plants. Seeds can be sown in September in a temperature of about 50°F (10°C), the plants being potted on eventually into 6-inch pots. For early summer flowers sow seeds again in February. A fairly rich compost should be used or the plants will be of poor quality. Water plants freely when they are in full growth.

Nigella (ni-jel-la)

From the Latin *nigellus*, a diminutive of *Niger*, black, referring to the black seeds (*Ranunculaceae*). Fennel-flower. A genus of 20 species, natives of the region stretching from Europe to eastern Asia. Those in cultivation are popular, easily-grown hardy annuals with feathery foliage and, in the main, blue flowers though other colours have been introduced in recent years. *N. damascena* has given us the majority of cultivated forms. The dried seed heads may be used for ornamental purposes.

Species cultivated *N. damascena*, love-in-a-mist, devil-in-a-bush, 1–2 feet, flowers blue, summer; vars. *alba*, white flowers; *flore-pleno*, double flowers. Cultivars include 'Miss Jekyll', bright blue flowers; 'Oxford Blue', flowers open light blue and become darker; 'Persian Jewels', mixture including shades of rose, pink, carmine, mauve, lavender, purple and white; 'Persian Rose', flowers open pale pink and become darker seeds of mixed colours are also available. *N. hispanica*, 1–2 feet, deep blue flowers with red stamens, summer.

Cultivation Sow seed in ordinary garden soil, in March or April, where the plants are intended to flower, later thinning the seedlings to 6 inches apart. Seed may also be sown in early September in sheltered borders with a minimum of winter protection, to provide the best plants. If they are raised in a nursery bed, seedlings may be transplanted in spring.

Papaver (pap-a-ver)

An ancient Latin plant-name of doubtful origin, but possibly derived from the sound made in chewing the seed (*Papaveraceae*). Poppy. A widespread genus of 100 species of colourful hardy annual and perennial plants. Poppies like full sun, although some will flower reasonably well in partial shade. The newly unfolded petals have the appearance of crumpled satin and many varieties have a glistening sheen on the blooms. They produce seed freely and many hybrids have been raised which are most

1 Nigella hispanica has deep blue flowers with purple-red stamens that appear as a dark centre to the flower. They bloom in summer.
2 Nigella damascena, Love-in-a-Mist, gets its name from the way the fern-like leaves surround the flowers.

decorative and easily grown. When used as cut flowers they will last longer if the stems are burned when they are cut and before putting them in water. This seals the milky sap in the stems.

Annual species cultivated *P. commutatum* (syn. *P. umbrosum*), 18 inches, bright crimson flowers with a conspicuous black blotch on each of the four petals, summer, Caucasus, Asia Minor. *P. glaucum*, tulip poppy, 18 inches, deep scarlet, summer, Syria. *P. rhoeas*, corn poppy, 1–2 feet, scarlet flowers with a black basal blotch, summer, Europe, including Britain. *P. somniferum*, opium poppy, 2–3 feet, pale lilac, purple, variegated or white flowers in summer, widely distributed in Europe and Asia.

Cultivation Sow annual varieties in April in patches where they are to flower. They prefer a sunny position and reasonably good soil. Thin the seedlings to 2 or 3 inches apart when quite small. Plant the perennial varieties in October or early spring in deeply dug, loamy soil in full sun, and top-dress with old manure or compost in March or April.

Perilla (per-il-la)

Possibly from the native Indian name (*Labiatae*). This is a small genus, containing 4 to 6 species only, of which there is one plant which is of value in the garden. This is *P. frutescens nankinensis*, a half-hardy annual from China, which has been grown by gardeners for the sake of its striking purple-bronze foliage, the margins of which are crisped and fringed. It was much in favour

1 Perilla frutescens nankinensis is a half-hardy annual grown for its striking bronze foliage. It is very effective as a summer bedding plant.
2 Papaver rhoeas, the Corn Poppy, is a weed commonly found on arable land. The Shirley Poppies were derived from P. rhoeas.
3 Papaver commutatum is an annual Poppy from the Caucasus and Asia Minor.
4 The summer-flowering Shirley Poppy is an annual with a wide range of colours.
5 A paeony-flowered form of Papaver somniferum, the Opium Poppy, has flowers that are fully double.

during the late Victorian vogue for carpet bedding and is still seen today, particularly in public parks. There is a form *laciniata* (syn. *N. frutescens foliis atropurpurea laciniata*), in which the leaves are cut nearly to the middle, and *rosea*, the leaves of which are red, pink, light green and whitish.

Cultivation Seed should be sown under glass in sandy compost during mid-March, in a temperature of 65–70°F (18–21°C). Transplant the seedlings when they are large enough to handle to individual pots and keep the temperature at 55–65°F (13–18°C) until May. Then transfer the pots to a cold frame and gradually harden off the plants until they are planted out 6 inches apart in June, in ordinary good garden soil and sunny positions. The leaf colour of seedlings varies to some extent. To form bushy plants the growing points should be pinched out from time to time. The full effect is gained when plants are massed together.

Petunia (pe-tu-ni-a)
From *petun*, the Brazilian name for tobacco to which petunias are nearly related (*Solanaceae*). A genus of 40 species of annual or perennial herbaceous plants from South America, two of which have been crossed to produce the many named varieties given in catalogues.

Species cultivated The two species concerned are *P. nyctaginiflora* and *P. integrifolia*, from the Argentine, and the resultant plants, though in fact

The brightly-coloured Petunias are among the gayest of summer bedding plants, and although they are really perennials, they are treated as half-hardy annuals in the open garden.
1 The flowers of Petunia 'Moonglow' are yellow, an uncommon colour.
2 Petunia 'Sugar Plum'.
3 A group of mixed Petunias are among the gayest of summer bedding plants.

67

perennial, are best treated as half-hardy annuals for the open garden. They are handsome plants, very varied in colouring, marking and form, and make extremely effective and colourful displays when used as bedding plants, in sunny situations, during late summer and autumn. Cultivars include 'Bedding Alderman', dark violet; 'Blue Bee', violet-blue; 'Blue Lace', light-blue fringed flowers with violet throat; 'Blue Danube' (F_1), lavender-blue, double; Blue Magic' (F_2), velvety blue; 'Canadian Wonder' (F_1), double flowers, fine colour range' 'Cascade' (F_1), large-flowered, wide range of colours; 'Cheerful', bright rose; 'Cherry Tart' (F_1), rose-pink and white; 'Confetti' (F_2), wide colour range; 'Commanche Improved' (F_1), scarlet-crimson; 'Fire Chief', fiery scarlet; 'Great Victorious' (F_1), double flowers, up to 4 inches across, wide colour range; 'Gypsy Red', brilliant salmon-scarlet; 'Lavender Queen'; 'Moonglow', yellow; 'Mound Mixed', various colours, useful for bedding; 'Pink Beauty'; 'Plum Dandy' (F_1), reddish-purple; 'Red Satin' (F_1), bright red, dwarf; 'Rose Queen'; 'Salmon Supreme'; 'Snowball Improved'; 'Sunburst' (F_1), light yellow, ruffled petals; 'Tivoli', scarlet and white bicolor; 'Valentine' (F_1), red, double, large flowered; 'White Magic' (F_1). There are also strains with fimbriated (fringed) petals in various colours. It is wise to consult current seedsmen's catalogues as very many other kinds are available and new ones appear annually.

Cultivation For growing out of doors, petunias should be treated as half-hardy annuals, sowing the very fine seed carefully in boxes in February or

1 Petunia 'Cherry Tart'.
2 Petunia 'Pink Bountiful' is an F_1 hybrid with rose-pink flowers.
3 This Petunia cultivar has large flowers and fimbriate petals.
4 Petunia 'Cascade' is a popular F_1 hybrid with a wide range of colours.

March in the greenhouse. Use a compost of equal parts of loam, leafmould and sand or seed compost. Make the surface firm, with a layer of finely-sifted compost on top and do not cover the seed with any further compost once it has been sown. Keep the seed boxes in a temperature of 65–75°F (18–24°C) and do not allow the soil to dry out. Transplant the seedlings when they are large enough to handle; begin to harden them off and continue this operation until the plants are set out at the beginning of June. If seed-raised plants are required for increase, overwinter the mature plants in the greenhouse, and take cuttings in the spring, placing them in a sandy compost in a frame in a temperature of 55–65°F (13–18°C). Greenhouse cultivation is similar, but cut the plants back in February or March. Water them freely during the growing season, but moderately at other times. Feed them with a liquid fertiliser twice a week while growing, and keep them in a temperature of 55–65°F (13–18°C) during the summer. In winter do not allow the temperature to fall below 40°F (4°C), and it should preferably be higher. It may be necessary to train the growths, which can be lax and rather sappy, to stakes. For cultivation in hanging baskets or window-boxes or ornamental plant containers it is best to choose such strains as 'Cascade', or 'Pendula Balcony Blended'.

Phacelia (fa-se-lee-a)

From the Greek *phakelos*, a bundle, in reference to the arrangement of the flowers (*Hydrophyllaceae*). A genus of 200 species, natives of North America and the Andes, of hardy annual and perennial plants, of which a number of blue, purple, mauve or white flowering annuals are of great value in the garden. One species in particular, *P. campanularia* has flowers of great depth and intensity of blue colouring, comparable with those of certain gentians.

Species cultivated *P. campanularia*, 9 inches, flowers bell-shaped, intense blue, June to September, southern California. *P. ciliata*, 1 foot, flowers fragrant, lavender, June to September, California. *P. congesta*, 1½ feet, lavender-blue, July to September, Texas, northern Mexico. *P. divaricata* (syn. *Eutoca divaricata*), 1 foot, flowers large, bright blue, July to September, California. *P. grandiflora*, 2 feet, large flowers lavender veined violet, July to September, southern California. *P. minor* (syn. *Whitlavia minor*), Californian bluebell, 1½ feet, flowers bell-shaped, deep

1 *Pharbitis tricolor is a climbing plant with a profusion of funnel-shaped flowers. It is closely related to the genus Ipomoea.*
2 *Phacelia campanularia, from southern California, bears blooms of deep, intense blue from June to September. It should be sown as a hardy annual in the sunny spot where it is to flower.*

violet, July to September, California. *P. parryi*, 1½ feet, flowers cup-shaped, deep violet, July to September, California. *P. tanacetifolia*, to 3 feet, soft lavender heliotrope-like flowers, July to September, California. *P. viscida* (syn. *Eutoca viscida*), 2 feet, flowers deep rich blue with white centre, July to September, California; 'Musgrave Strain' is an improved strain.

Cultivation All the species listed should have hardy annual treatment. Sow seeds thinly in April, where the plants are to flower and thin the seedlings to 6–8 inches apart in June. Any garden soil suits them, and they should be grown in the sunniest position possible. Seedlings transplant badly. As these are hardy annuals, seeds may be sown in September and will generally survive to make excellent plants for early flowering the following summer. Seed is available of most of the species described above.

Pharbitis (far-by-tis)

From the Greek *pharbe*, colour, in reference to the brilliantly coloured flowers (*Convolvulaceae*). This widespread genus of 60 tropical and subtropical, tall, twining, annual and evergreen plants differ only in botanical details from *Ipomoea* and *Convolvulus*, and the species are often placed in the former genus. Those grown are cultivated for the sake of their colourful funnel-shaped or bell-shaped flowers, usually borne in great profusion. It is a remarkable experience to see, in a large greenhouse, the vigorous growths of *P. learii* mounting to the roof and bearing huge clusters of its large, funnel-shaped bright blue flowers, which later turn to pinkish-mauve.

Stovehouse species cultivated *P. cathartica* (E), to 16 feet, purple, August to September, West Indies. *P. hirsutula*, annual, violet to white, Mexico. *P. learii* (E), blue dawn flower, 20 feet, blue to pinkish-mauve, tropical America. *P. mutabilis* (E), blue to purple with a white throat in clusters, South America.

Coolhouse species cultivated *P. lindheimeri*, perennial, light blue, Texas. *P. triloba*, annual, pink or purple, tropical America. *P. tyrianthina* (D), shrubby twiner to 10 feet, dark purple, August to November, Mexico.

Cultivation Stovehouse species grow well in potting compost and should be potted between February and April. A temperature of 65–75°F (18–24°C) is required in summer, and between 55–65°F (13–18°C) in winter. Water generously in the growing season, but moderately at other times and prune into shape if necessary in February.

Phlox (flocks)

From the Greek *phlego*, to burn, or *phlox*, a flame, referring to the bright colours of the flowers (*Polemoniaceae*). A genus of nearly 70 species of hardy,

half-hardy, annual and perennial herbaceous plants all, with one exception, natives of North America and Mexico. Almost all the most important species are from the eastern United States, though the popular annual, *P. drummondii*, is from Texas and New Mexico. The fine herbaceous plants derived originally from *P. paniculata*, the garden forms of which may sometimes be listed as *P.* × *decussata*, have a most important part to play in the garden as they give colour at a time—July and August—

1 The leaves of Portulaca oleracea, Purslane, are sometimes used for flavouring in salads.

2 Mixed cultivars of the annual Portulaca grandiflora, with its spreading habit and bright flowers, are available in a wide range of colours.

3 Primula vulgaris, the Common Primrose, is a native plant that flowers in the spring. Its creamy yellow blooms are found throughout southern and western Europe, and its cultivars appear in a huge range of bright colours.

when it very much needs their bright colours. They are extremely easy to grow and all have fragrant flowers. Our rock gardens would be much poorer if they lacked the various forms of either *P. douglasii* or *P. subulata* or their hybrids.

Annual species cultivated There is one annual. *P. drummondii*, to 1 foot, flowers in a wide colour range, July onwards, from Texas and New Mexico. This is among our most floriferous of annuals.

Annual cultivars *P. drummondii cuspidata* (stellaris), star phlox, 6 inches, flowers starry, mixed colours; 'Brilliant', deep rose with darker eye; 'Isabellina', light yellow; *kermesina splendens*, crimson with white eye; *rosea*, bright rose; *rosea-albo ochlata*, rose with white eye; *nanum compactum*, dwarf strain available in various named colours including blue, pink, red, violet, white. Others are listed by seedsmen.

Cultivation The annual species, *P. drummondii*, needs the standard half-hardy annual treatment. Sow in pans or boxes in March, under glass, and harden off the seedlings and plant them out in June, 6 inches apart. Nip out the points of the shoots to induce bushy growth, and water generously. They make excellent edging plants, and, if allowed to develop naturally, make good plants for tubs, ornamental containers, hanging baskets or window boxes.

Portulaca (por-tu-lak-a)
An old Latin name, possibly from the Latin *porto*, to carry, and *lac*, milk, in allusion to the milky juice (*Portulacaceae*). These are succulent annual and perennial herbaceous plants, with fibrous or thickened roots and small fleshy leaves. Of the 200 or more species in this genus, widespread in tropical and sub-tropical regions, many are considered to be weeds and the group is not very important for garden cultivation. The leaves of *P. oleracea* can be used in salads.

Species cultivated *P. grandiflora*, annual, stems procumbent and spreading, flowers white, yellow, pink, red or orange, June–July, Brazil. *P. lutea*, coarse-stemmed perennial, yellow flowers, summer, Pacific Islands. *P. oleracea*, purslane, annual, a fleshy-leaved plant, flowers yellow, summer, southern Europe.

Cultivation The half-hardy annual species are grown from seeds sown in seed compost at a temperature of 60°F (16°C), and the seedlings pricked off when they are large enough to handle into small pots. Finally they are planted out on rock gardens or in sunny borders in well-drained soil. When grown in the greenhouse in pots, they are placed in very sandy soil and kept in a sunny position, being watered freely in late spring and summer. The temperature in summer should be between 65–70°F (18–21°C), and in winter about 50°F (10°C).

Propagation is by seed, as for most succulents, covered very lightly or not at all, or from cuttings, rooted in sandy soil at any time.

Primula (prim-u-la)
The name is derived from the Latin *primus*, first, referring to the early flowering of some of the species, such as the primrose (*Primulaceae*). A diverse and widely distributed genus of over 500 species including those from the high Alps, moisture-loving perennials and tender greenhouse varieties. All are natives of the northern hemisphere. The one thing most primulas demand is a cool, moist soil containing plenty of peat or leaf soil. Most of the Asiatic primulas —and this is a considerable number of species—are lime haters, but they can be grown in neutral or acid soil, together with the European species. The genus has been divided by botanists into 30 or so different sections, some of which are large and have been further sub-divided, but of these sections, about a dozen or so only are of importance to the gardener. The section to which the species belongs is indicated in brackets after the name of the species.

Hardy species cultivated *P. allionii* (Auricula), 2 inches, grey-green leaves, rose-pink to deep red flowers, March and April, Maritime Alps; var. *alba*, a pure white form; easy plants to grow in pans in an alpine house or cold frame. *P. alpicola* (Sikkimensis), 1–1½ feet, with variable, cowslip-like, fragrant flowers in shades of yellow, violet or white. May and June, Tibet. *P. anisodora* (Candelabra), 2 feet, purple flowers with a green eye in June, Yunnan. The whole plant is aromatic. *P. altaica* (Vernales), of gardens, is now *P. vulgaris rubra*, a pale pink primrose of European origin. *P. aurantiaca* (Candelabra), 1 foot, flowers reddish-orange, bell-shaped, in whorls, July, Yunnan; moist soil. *P. auricula* (Auricula), 3–6 inches, yellow, fragrant flowers in spring and more or less farinose leaves about 3 inches long, European Alps. *P. beesiana* (Candelabra), 1½–2 feet, bright rosy-purple flowers with a yellow eye, borne on erect stems in tiers, June and July, Yunnan. It will soon naturalize itself in moist soil and partial shade. *P. bulleyana* (Candelabra), 1½–2 feet, orange, shaded apricot, June and July, for similar conditions, Yunnan. *P. capitata* (Capitatae), 6–9 inches, with heads of fragrant, violet flowers from June to August, Tibet, Sikkim. Suitable for a moist place on the rock garden. *P. carniolica* (Auricula), 4–6 inches, soft rose-purple, bell-shaped, fragrant flowers

1 The native Primula veris, the Cowslip, is an early-flowering summer plant found in Europe and western Asia.
2 Primula vialii bears lavender-pink flowers on long spikes, made more colourful by the red buds at the tips.

1 The summer-flowering Primula florindae grows best in boggy conditions.
2 The dwarf Primula allionii is only 2 inches high and flowers in spring.
3 The magenta flowers of Primula werringtonensis appear in early summer.
4 The large, pale blue flowers of Primula bhutanica bloom in spring.

in May, Maritime and Julian Alpa. *P. chungensis* (Candelabra), 2 feet, flowers light-orange, bell-shaped, tube red, borne in whorls, June, Burma, China, Assam; moist soil. *P. clarkei* (Farinosae), 2–3 inches, foliage coppery-red, flowers rose-pink, April, Kashmir, rock garden or alpine house. *P. cockburniana* (Candelabra), 1 foot, with dark orange-red, bell-shaped flowers, June, China. Best treated as a biennial in fairly most soil and partial shade. *P. denticulata* (Denticulata), the drum-stick primula, 1 foot, with large, globular heads of lilac flowers from March to May, Himalaya; var. *alba*, is a good white form and 'Prichard's Ruby' is a rich ruby-red; easily grown in moist soil in the border or rock garden in light shade. *P. florindae* (Sikkimensis) 2–4 feet, with large heads of sulphur-yellow, drooping flowers June and July, Tibet. Requires a really moist soil and is admirable beside a pool. *P. frondosa* (Farinosae), 3–6 inches, with rosy-lilac flowers with a yellow eye, April, Balkans. *P. gracilipes* (Petiolares), almost stemless blue or mauve flowers with a yellow eye produced in spring

from a rosette of leaves up to 6 inches long, Nepal, Sikkim, Tibet. A charming little plant for the alpine house. *P. helodoxa* (Candelabra), 2–8 feet, with golden-yellow, bell-shaped flowers in June and July, Yunnan. The common name, glory of the marsh, indicates that it likes a boggy place. *P. involucrata* (Farinosae), 6–9 inches, flowers white with a yellow eye in May and June, Himalaya. *P. ioessa* (Sikkimensis), 9 inches, flowers bell-shaped, pinkish mauve to violet, summer, Tibet, moist soil. *P. japonica* (Candelabra), 1½ feet, with purplish-red flowers in whorls in May and June, Japan; var. 'Miller's Crimson' is a striking plant, and 'Postford White' is a clear white with a pink eye. These will seed themselves readily in moist conditions. *P. juliae* (Vernales), 2 inches, forms mats of foliage, flowers, lilac-purple, winter and early spring, Transcaucasia, parent of a number of hybrids, requires moist soil. *P. marginata* (Auricula), 6 inches, with umbels of fragrant, deeply farinose lavender flowers in May, Maritime and Cottian Alps; var. 'Linda Pope', rich lavender-blue with a white eye. *P. minima* (Auricula), almost stemless rose-pink flowers in April, and short, shiny green leaves, southern European Alps. *P. nutans* (Soldanelloideae), 9–12 inches, with compact heads of lavender-blue, fragrant flowers in June, Yunnan. Charming, but short-lived and requires to be kept on the dry side during the winter, so should be grown in an alpine house. *P. × pubescens* (Auricula), 3–6 inches, flowers rosy-purple, April–May, hybrid group; 'Faldonside', 3 inches, flowers rich crimson; 'Mrs J. H. Wilson', 3–4 inches, flowers rich purple with paler centre. *P. polyneura* (Cortusoides), 9–12 inches, pale pink to wine-red flowers in whorls in May and leaves up to 4 inches in length, sometimes hairy, Yunnan, Tibet. *P. pulverulenta* (Candelabra), 2–3 feet, with whorls of claret-red flowers with a darker eye in June and July, China. The 'Bartley Strain' has delightful soft pink flowers. *P. rosea* (Farinosae), 3–6 inches, brilliant carmine flowers in April before the leaves develop, Himalaya; var. 'Delight' is a brilliant carmine-red. For a moist, reasonably sunny place in the rock or bog garden. Once established self-sown seedlings will appear. *P. rubra* (syn. *P. hirsuta*) (Auricula), 3 inches, with rose or lilac trusses of flowers in March and narrow leaves, central European Alps and Pyrenees. *P. rusbyi* (Parryi), 6 inches, red-purple, nodding heads in loose clusters in late summer. The tufts of leathery leaves are lance-shaped and toothed, Rocky Mountains. *P. sieboldii* (Cortusoides), 6 inches, variable rose to purple, with tufts of soft, heart-shaped leaves, Japan, suitable for the alpine

The colour range of Primula vulgaris, the Common Primrose, is quite extensive.

house. *P. sikkimensis* (Sikkimensis), 2 feet, with pendent, funnel-shaped, fragrant flowers in May and June, Sikkim, Tibet, Yunnan. Admirable beside a pool. *P. veris* (Vernales), cowslip, 2–6 inches, deep yellow, fragrant flowers in April and May, Europe, including Britain (rare in parts of Scotland and Ireland), western Asia. *P. vialli* (syn. *P. littoniana*) (Muscarioides), 1½ feet, a slender spike of lavender flowers with bright red buds at the tip in June and July, Yunnan. *P. viscosa* (Auricula) 4, inches, deep violet flowers in one-sided umbels in May, Swiss Alps and Pyrenees. Often confused with *P. rubra*. *P. vulgaris* (syn. *P. acaulis*) (Vernales), primrose, 1–4 inches, creamy-yellow, March and April, western and southern Europe, including Britain. Coloured primroses include: 'Garryarde Guinivere', 6 inches, leaves reddish-bronze, large pink flowers in big heads; 'Garryarde Victory', 4 inches, leaves tinted crimson, flowers wine-red; 'Lingwood Beauty', cherry-red, leaves bright green; 'Wanda', deep

claret-crimson and unnamed blue and pink shades. *P. whitei* (Petiolares), rosettes of ovate leaves, almost stemless pale blue flowers in April covered with farina, Bhutan.

Greenhouse species cultivated *P. × kewensis* (*P. floribunda × P. verticillata*) (Floribundae), 9–12 inches, yellow, fragrant flowers in winter and early spring in a cool greenhouse; a hybrid which originated at the Royal Botanic Gardens, Kew. *P. malacoides* (Malacoides), 12–18 inches, whorls of lavender flowers in winter and early spring, China; cars. 'Pink Pride', 8 inches, carmine-pink; 'Rose Bouquet', 15 inches, carmine-rose; 'Snow Queen', 15 inches, white. *P. obconica* (Obconica), 6 inches, pale lilac with a yellow eye in winter, continues to flower for months, China. The hairs on the stems and underside of the leaves are liable to cause a skin rash on some people; var. *alba* is a white form; 'Red Chief', scarlet-crimson; 'Salmon King', salmon-pink. *P. sinensis* (Sinensis), Chinese primrose, 9 inches,

purplish-rose with a yellow eye in spring, China; vars. *alba*, white; 'Dazzler', vivid orange-scarlet; 'Pink Beauty', rose suffused salmon.

Cultivation of hardy species These are best planted in September and October, or March and April, those suitable for the alpine house in pans containing an open, gritty sandy loam with peat or leaf soil in it, are: *P. allionii, P. carniolica, P. frondosa, P. marginata* and *P. nutans.* For waterside planting or in moist soil in partial shade suitable species are: *P. alpicola, P. beesiana, P. bulleyana, P. lentculata, P. florindae, P. japonica, P. pulverulenta, P. rosea* and *P. sikkimensis.* Mulch plants growing in the open with old manure or compost in February. Propagation is by seed sown as soon as it is ripe in a cold frame or by division of the roots soon after they have finished flowering.

Cultivation of greenhouse species Sow seed of *P. malacoides* in June and July on the surface of a compost consisting of leaf soil, loam and sharp sand. Cover the pan with a piece of glass, shade from the sun and germinate in a temperature of 55–60°F (13–16°C). Prick out the seedlings when they are large enough to handle, and when they have grown larger pot them into individual 3-inch pots, harden them off and place the pots in a cold frame. Finally, pot them into 5-inch pots in potting compost and bring them into the greenhouse in September. Keep them in a temperature of about 50–55°F (10–13°C) and feed them with a liquid fertilizer when they are flowering. When potting, allow the base of the leaves just to touch the compost, and pot fairly firmly. *P. × kewensis, P. obconica* and *P. sinensis,* may be sown from April to August and treated in a similar way.

Quamoclit (qua-mo-klit)

A genus of 12 species of annual and perennial climbers, natives of America (*Convolvulaceae*). They are treated as half-hardy annuals, though *Q. lobata,* at least, is a perennial in its native Mexico. By some botanists they are included in the closely related genus *Ipomoea.* They are grown for the sake of their colourful tubular flowers.

Species cultivated *Q. coccinea,* to 10 feet, flowers scarlet with yellow throat, August to October, tropical America. *Q. lobata,* to 15 feet, flowers crimson quickly fading to white, July to September, tropical America. *Q. pennata,* cypress-vine, to 15 feet, flowers scarlet, July to October, tropical America. *Q. × sloteri,* flowers crimson with white eye, hybrid.

Cultivation These are tender plants and if they are planted out they must have an exceptionally warm protected spot. They are best grown in the cool greenhouse. Seeds are sown in pots in heat in March or April. Young plants must be potted on and given twiggy sticks as supports. If they are to be planted out of

The unusual flowers of Quamoclit coccinea are scarlet with a yellow throat.

doors, this should be done in June.

Reseda (re-se-da)

Derived from *resedo,* to heal, a name given by Pliny for a species of mignonette which was credited with certain medicinal qualities in healing external bruises (*Resedaceae*). A genus of some 60 species of annual and biennial hardy plants, two of which are decorative in gardens. Sprays of flower cut from the garden in late autumn will keep indoors in a cool room in water throughout the winter and retain their refreshing fragrance. They are natives of southern Europe and North Africa to central Asia.

Species cultivated *R. alba,* 1½–2 feet, a biennial producing spikes of white flowers with brownish anthers from May to September, southern Europe; it is sometimes grown as a decorative pot plant in a cool greenhouse. *R. odorata,* mignonette, hardy annual, 9 inches, with heads of fragrant, yellowish-white flowers from June to October, North Africa, Egypt; vars. 'Goliath', 10 inches, large, very fragrant, reddish spikes; 'Red Monarch', 10 inches, large, deep red heads.

1 Reseda odorata, the Mignonette, bears fragrant flower spikes from late spring through early autumn.
2 Rhodochiton atrosanguineum (syn, R. volubile) is the Purple Bellerine, a climber with bell-shaped flowers.*

Cultivation Seed of mignonette should be sown in April or May where it is to flower, in a sunny position; it is not particular about soil. The seed should be covered with a thin layer of fine soil only and will germinate better when the soil is made firm after sowing. Plants do not transplant readily, but a few seeds sown in a pot will make most attractive cool greenhouse plants.

Rhodochiton (ro-do-ky-ton)
From the Greek *rhodo*, red, and *chiton*, a cloak, with reference to the swollen shape of the calyx (*Scrophulariaceae*). A genus of a single species, a deciduous flowering climber from Mexico, related to *Maurandia*, requiring greenhouse treatment in cooler climates. The species is *R. atrosanguineum* (syn. *R. volubile*), the purple bellerine, which climbs to 10 feet, and has large, showy blood-red, bell-shaped flowers with dark purple calyces, from June onwards, and slender-pointed leaves. The leaf stalks and flower stalks twist round supports, thus enabling the plant to climb.
Cultivation A sandy loam and cool greenhouse conditions are required, or the plant may be grown in the open in

warm, sheltered gardens as an annual climber. Wherever it is grown it should be provided with some support such as trellis-work or wire-netting for its twining leaf and flower stalks. Under glass the plant is grown as a perennial, provided a minimum temperature of 45°F (7°C) can be maintained in winter. So treated the plant should be lightly pruned in February, thinning and shortening the shoots and cutting out any dead or dying growth. Propagation is by seed sown in the spring in well-drained soil under glass in gentle heat, or by cuttings taken in August and rooted in a warm propagating frame.

Ricinus (riss-i-nus)
The Latin for a tick, which the seeds are thought to resemble (*Euphorbiaceae*). Castor bean, castor oil plant, Palma Christi. A genus of a single species, which is treated as a half-hardy annual in this country, but is perennial in the tropics. It is much used in tropical bedding, particularly in its coloured leaf forms. Castor oil is extracted from the seeds, which also contain a poisonous alkaloid, ricinin. The species is *R. communis*. The stems rise from

3 to 5 feet high and bear large peltate, palmate leaves which are deeply lobed with 5–12 lobes. The inflorescences are borne at the end of the stems, but the stems branch below the inflorescence, so that the panicles appear to be lateral. The flowers are greenish and unisexual, the males being at the top of the panicle and the females below. The round seed capsules are generally prickly. A number of forms with coloured leaves have been given varietal names, such as *cambodgensis*, with purple leaves and blackish stems; *gibsonii* which is rather compact with dark red stems and leaves; *sanguineus* with reddish leaves; and *zanzibarensis*, with very large green leaves with conspicuous white midribs and which can reach up to 8 feet high. The plant is probably a native of tropical Africa.
Cultivation The seeds, which are large, should be sown separately in 3-inch pots in early March in a temperature of 55–60°F (13–16°C). If higher temperatures can be provided, germination and growth will be more rapid. The plants are kept growing under glass until early June and may require being potted on to 5-inch pots before this. They are then stood out of doors to harden off and are planted out in the open garden about the middle of the month. The plants resent damage to the roots, so if any potting on is necessary, it should be done before the plants

1 *Ricinus communis cambodgensis, the Castor Bean, is grown for its unusual black stems and purplish leaves, and for the seeds, which are the source of castor oil.*
2 *Salpiglossis sinuata, the species from which most cultivars are raised, is noted for the wide range of bright colours of its trumpet-shaped blooms.*

have become at all pot bound. Plants may also be grown in 5-inch or 6-inch pots for decorating the cool greenhouse, conservatory or living room, when they will require moderate watering during the summer.

Salpiglossis (sal-pi-glos-sis)

From the Greek *salpin*, a tube, and *glossa*, a tongue, referring to the tongue-like style in the corolla tube (*Solanceae*). A genus of 18 species of half-hardy annuals, biennials and herbaceous perennials, of which the only species cultivated is *S. sinuata*, sometimes called the scalloped tube tongue or painted tongue, a plant of Chilean origin, which is remarkable for the richness of colour of the large trumpet-shaped flowers and the elegant veining and flushing. It makes an admirable pot plant for a cool greenhouse, and is useful as a cut flower. *S. sinuata* grows 2–3 feet tall and has flowers in shades of rose-pink, crimson, purple, yellow and cream, many of which are beautifully veined. Various improved strains are offered from time to time under such names as *grandiflora*, and 'Splash' is a modern F_1 strain, compact in habit, free-flowering, in a good colour range.

Cultivation Sow the seed in late February or March under glass in a temperature of about 55°F (13°C) in seed compost, and when they are large enough to handle prick out the seedlings singly into small pots of potting compost and grow them on steadily until they are planted out in early June in a sunny border, to flower in late July and August. Seed may also be sown in the open in late April or May where they are to flower. Such plants will come into flower somewhat later than those sown under glass and will thus prolong the display. If they are required to flower in the greenhouse in the spring, sow the seed in July and August and transplant when three leaves have formed, into a 2½-inch pot containing potting compost. Keep them close to the light in a temperature of 55–65°F (13–18°C), and move to 5–6-inch pots when well-rooted. When 6 inches high, take out the tips of the shoots to encourage bushy growth. These fast-growing plants require ample water in dry weather and when grown in a cool greenhouse. An occasional application of liquid fertilizer is also of help.

Salvia (sal-vee-a)

From the Latin *salveo*, meaning save or heal, used by Pliny with reference to the medicinal qualities of some species (*Labiatae*). A large genus of over 700 species of hardy, half-hardy and tender annual, biennial, perennial plants and shrubs, some with aromatic leaves, widely distributed in the temperate and warmer zones. It includes the common sage, *S. officinalis*, a valuable culinary plant, as well as many colourful summer and autumn flowering border plants.

Species cultivated *S. ambigens*, about 5 feet, perennial or sub-shrub, flowers deep sky-blue, September–October, South America, slightly tender, *S. argentea*, 2 feet, most decorative, leaves large, silvery-grey, felted, flowers white, small, in spikes, June and July, Mediterranean region; for a dry soil and a sunny position. *S. aurea*, shrub, leaves rounded, covered with fine hairs, flowers yellowish-brown, South Africa, hardy in mild areas. *S. azurea*, 4 feet, sub-shrub, flowers deep blue, autumn, North America, hardy; var. *grandiflora*, flower spikes denser. *S. fulgens*, Mexican red sage, 2–3 feet, shrub, flowers scarlet, in whorls, July, Mexico, tender. *S. gesneraeflora* 2 feet, sub-shrub, flowers bright scarlet, summer, Colombia, tender. *S. grahamii*, shrub, to 4 feet, flowers deep crimson, July onwards, Mexico, somewhat tender. *S. greggii*, shrub, 3 feet, flowers scarlet, summer, Texas, Mexico, tender. *S. haematodes*, biennial, 3 feet,

The widely-cultivated Salvia has varieties which are used in cooking and medicine, or grown for their beauty alone.
1 Salvia carduacea, the Thistle Salvia, produces unusual bluish-purple flowers.
2 The grey-green leaves of Salvia officinalis tricolor, the common culinary Sage, mature marked with flecks of yellow and red.
3 Salvia farinacea, the Mealycup Salvia, has long-toothed violet-blue flower spikes.

leaves large, wrinkled, heart-shaped, light blue flowers on branching stems from June to August, Greece. *S. interrupta*, 2–3 feet, sub-shrub, leaves 3-lobed, aromatic, flowers violet purple with white throat, May to July, Morocco, nearly·hardy. *S. involucrata*, sub-shrub, 2–4 feet, flowers rose, summer and autumn, Mexico, not quite hardy; var. *bethelii*, flowers rosy crimson in longer spikes. *S. juriscii*, perennial, 1 foot, flowers violet, June, Serbia, hardy. *S. lavandulifolia*, perennial, 9–12 inches, leaves grey, flowers lavender, early summer, hardy. *S. mexicana minor*, sub-shrub, to 12 feet in nature, flowers violet-blue, February, Mexico, tender. *S. neurepia*, sub-shrub, 6–7 feet, flowers scarlet, late summer and autumn, Mexico, hardy in the milder counties. *S. officinalis*, common sage, sub-shrub, 2–3 feet, leaves wrinkled, aromatic, flowers variable purple, blue or white, June and July, southern Europe, hardy; vars. *purpurascens*, reddish-purple stems and leaves, strongly flavoured; *aurea*, leaves golden, flowers rarely produced. *S. pratense*, perennial, 2 feet, flowers bright blue, June to August, Europe, including Britain, hardy; var. *rosea*, flowers rosy-purple. *S. rutilans*, pineapple-scented sage, sub-shrub, 2–3 feet, flowers magenta-crimson, summer, tender. *S. sclarea*, clary, biennial or short-lived perennial, leaves and stems sticky, flowers pale mauve, bracts white and rose, conspicuous, June to September, Europe; various strains are offered; var. *turkestanica*, flowers white, bracts and stems pink. *S. splendens*, scarlet sage, sub-shrub, 3 feet, flowers scarlet, in spikes in summer, Brazil, usually grown as half-hardy annual; vars. for summer bedding: 'Blaze of Fire', 9–12 inches, scarlet; 'Fireball', 15 inches, rich scarlet; 'Harbinger', 15 inches, long scarlet spikes; 'Salmon Pygmy', 6 inches. *S. × superba* (syn. *S. nemorosa*), 3 feet, bracts reddish, persistent, flowers violet-purple in spikes, July to September, hybrid, hardy; var. *lubeca*, identical but 1½ feet tall only. *S. uliginosa*, bog sage, 4–5 feet, leaves shiny green, deeply toothed, flowers azure-blue in spikes, August to October, eastern North America, hardy.

Cultivation Salvias are easily grown in ordinary, well-drained garden soil and in a sunny position. *S. argentea* particularly likes dry soil, as well as sun, and *S. officinalis* should be cut back in spring to encourage new bushy growth. *S. × superba* makes a particularly good border plant when planted in a bold group. *S. uliginosa* prefers moister conditions than the others, and its creeping rootstock should be given a covering of bracken or dry peat in cold districts. Those described as tender will succeed in the milder counties, given the shelter of a warm wall, or they may be grown in the greenhouse in pots in a compost of loam and well-rotted manure or leafmould plus some sand to provide drainage. The pots may be placed out of doors in June and brought in again in September. Water freely from spring to autumn, moderately in winter. Maintain a temperature in winter of 45–55°F (7–10°C). Propagate the shrubs, sub-shrubs and hardy perennial kinds by division in the spring or by soft-wood cuttings, rooted in sandy soil in a propagating case in spring in a temperature of 65°F (18°C). *S. splendens* is increased by seed sown under glass in February or March in a temperature of 60°F (16°C) and planted out in late May or June.

Sanvitalia (san-vit-arr-lee-a)
Named in honour of the Sanvitali, a noble Italian family who lived in Parma (*Compositae*). A genus of seven species, natives of the south-western United States and Mexico, of which one only is in cultivation. This is *S. procumbens*, a native of Mexico, a half-hardy annual, a spreading plant, not more than 6 inches high, with ovate leaves and small daisy-like flowers from July onwards. The ray florets are yellow, while the disk florets are dark brown. A double form, var. *flore pleno* is also known.

Cultivation Seed may either be sown in gentle heat in March and the seedlings planted out after the risk of frost has one, or they can be sown out of doors at the end of May. A sandy loam seems to suit these plants best, but they are not fussy and will grow in most soils, although they will not do so well in very heavy ones. They should be grown in full sun.

Saponaria (sap-on-air-ee-a)
From the Latin *sapo*, soap, the crushed leaves of *S. officinalis* producing a lather when mixed with water, and at one time used as a soap substitute (*Caryophyllaceae*). Soapwort. A genus of some 30 species of hardy perennials and annuals, mainly from the Mediterranean area. They are easily grown, and some of them can become invasive.

Species culvitated *S. caespitosa*, perennial, 3 inches, flowers large, pink on a green turfy cushion of leaves, May and June, Pyrenees. *S. calabrica*, hardy annual, 9 inches, flowers deep rose, freely produced, summer, Italy, Greece. *S. ocymoides*, perennial, 6 inches, a vigorous trailer, flowers rose-pink, on slender, ruddy-brown 2-inch stems, June to August, southern Alps, Sardinia, Caucasus; it may seed itself too freely. *S. officinalis*, bouncing Bet, 1-3 feet, flowers rose-pink, in panicles, August and September, central and southern Europe to Japan, naturalized in Britain. Its spreading roots must be watched; vars. *alba plena*, double white, *rosea plena*,

1 Sanvitalia procumbens is a spreading half-hardy annual.
2 Saponaria calabrica compacta forms small tufts smothered with purple blooms.

semi-double pink, are better garden plants.

Cultivation Plant the perennial kinds from October to April in a sunny position and in deep, good soil. They are propagated by seed sown under glass in early spring, or out of doors in April, by cuttings rooted in a cold frame in autumn, or by divisions of the clumps from October to March. Sow seed of the annual species in a sunny border in ordinary garden soil in April for summer flowering, or sow in the open in September for spring flowering.

Scabiosa (skay-bee-o-sa)

From the Latin *scabies*, itch, for which some of these plants were used as remedies, or from the Latin *scabiosus*, rough or scurfy, referring to the grey felting on the leaves of some species (*Dipsacaceae*). Scabious. This genus of 100 species of hardy biennial and perennial herbaceous plants, mainly from the Mediterranean region, gives a number which are good decorative plants for the garden. The three species which are British native plants, *Scabiesa arvensis*, *S. columbaria* and *S. succisa*, are among our prettiest-flowering wild plants and are quite suited to garden cultivation. *S. succisa*, the devil's bit, is especially good as it has flowers of a bright blue colour. In the plants in the *Dipsacaceae* family the so-called flower is made up of a large number of small florets gathered into a head, or *capitulum*, somewhat as in *Compositae*.

Annual species cultivated *S. atropurpurea*, sweet scabious, mournful widow, pincushion flower, 2–3 feet, flowers deep crimson to purple, July to September, south-western Europe; cultivars include 'Azure Fairy', blue; 'Blue Moon', pale blue; 'Black Prince', very dark purple; 'Cherry Red'; 'Cockade Mixed', large almost conical flowers in various colours; 'Coral Moon', light to dark salmon; 'Fire King', scarlet; 'Loveliness', salmon-rose; 'Parma Violet'; 'Peach Blossom', pale rose; 'Rosette', deep rose and salmon; 'Snowball', white.

Cultivation These plants all do well in chalky or limy soil, which, however, should be enriched. *S. caucasica* is suitable for the herbaceous border, but may also be grown to supply cut flowers, for which purpose its long clean stems make it very suitable. These plants should be lifted and divided every three or four years, moving them in spring as disturbance in autumn can kill them. *S. graminifolia* and *S. ochroleuca webbiana* are suitable for the rock garden. *S. atropurpurea* can be raised from seed sown in February or March in a temperature of 60°F (16°C). Plant out the seedlings in May to flower as annuals, or later disturbance (July) will cause them to behave as biennials. In the latter case, over-winter them in a cold frame and plant out in April. They are good for cutting. Other species may be propagated by division of the clumps in March.

Schizanthus (skiz-an-thus; shy-zan-thus)

From the Greek *schizo*, to cut, and *anthos*, flower, in reference to the deeply cut corolla (*Solanaceae*). A genus of 15 species of showy and attractive annual plants from Chile, sometimes known as the butterfly flowers, or the poor man's orchids. They are suitable for cold greenhouse cultivation or can be sown in heat and bedded out in late spring or early summer.

Species culvitated *S. grahamii*, 2 feet, lilac, rose and yellow, June to October. *S. pinnatus*, 2 feet, violet and yellow, but may be other colours, June to October. *S. retuses*, 2½ feet, rose and orange, July to September. *S. × wisetonensis*, hybrid of first two species, combines their characteristics. Garden strains which have evolved from hybridising include: 'Danbury Park Strain', pansy-flowered, pink crimson, purple and white; 'Dr Badger's Hybrids Improved' large flowers, colours ranging from white and yellow through lilac and rose; 'Dwarf Bouquet', bright rose, crimson, salmon, amber, and pink; Wisetonensis 'Monarch Signal', feathery leaves, cherry red orchid-like flowers.

Culvitation Schizanthus are usually grown as cold greenhouse plants and provide a most attractive display in late winter and early spring. Sow the seeds in August in seed compost in a frame or cool greenhouse, and transplant the seedlings when large enough to handle, to 3-inch pots containing potting compost, giving them as much light as possible, and a temperature of 45–55°F (7–13°C) until January. Then put them in 6-inch pots and grow them in a light position, but do not allow them to become pot-bound. Stop the plants frequently to keep them bushy, and support them by tying them to stakes. In winter they should be moderately watered, but freely at other times, and they benefit from the application of liquid fertilizers occasionally while flowering.

When grown as half-hardy annuals for planting out of doors, seed is sown under glass in February–March in a temperature of 65–75°F (18–24°C). The seedlings are pricked off when they are about 1 inch high, and then planted out in May after being hardened off. They can also be sown where they are required to grow, in May, but require a warm shel-

1

2

The unusual blooms of Scabiosa are wild flowers that are easily adaptable to cultivation in the garden, where they frequently behave as biennials.
1 The globular flowerhead of Scabiosa stellata is creamy-white and extremely delicate-looking.
2 The range of colours and cultivars of the annual Scabiosa atropurpurea is quite extensive.

tered site if this is to be done; they will then flower in August.

Senecio (sen-e-see-o)

From the Latin *senex*, an old man, in allusion to the grey and hoary seed pappus (*Compositae*). The largest genus in the plant world; containing between 2,000 and 3,000 species, it covers a wide range of plant types including greenhouse and hardy annuals, evergreen herbaceous plants, climbers, shrubs, an aquatic species and a dozen or more species of tree-like dimensions. The genus is of world-wide distribution. The greenhouse cinerarias are hybrids of one species, *Senecio cruentis* (for their cultivation see Cineraria).

Annual species cultivated *S. arenarius*, 1 foot, flowers lilac, summer, South Africa, *S. elegans*, 1–2 feet, single and double flowers of various colours, summer, South Africa.

Greenhouse species cultivated *S. cineraria* (syn. *Cineraria maritima*), dusty miller, 2 feet, yellow flowers, summer, silver leaves, Mediterranean. *S. cruentus* (syn. *Cineraria cruentus*), parent of the greenhouse cineraria hybrids, 1–2 feet, purple, summer, Canary Isles; many cultivars are available in a wide range of colours from light pink to deep blue. *S. glastifolius*, shrub, 4 feet, flowers purple and yellow, June, South Africa. *S. grandiflorus*, to 5 feet, purple and yellow, August, South Africa. *S. heretieri*, 3–4 feet, white and purple, May to July, Tenerife. *S. leucostachys*, 2–3 feet, yellow, summer, silver foliage, Patagonia. *S. macroglossus*, Cape ivy, climbing, thick, ivy-shaped leaves, flowers yellow, winter, South Africa. *S. mikanioides*, German ivy, climbing, ivy-shaped leaves, flowers fragrant, yellow, winter, South Africa. *S. petasites* (E), velvet groundsol, shrub, 5 feet, yellow, winter, Mexico.

Cultivation of annuals Sow seeds ⅛ inch deep in patches or drills where they are to grow in ordinary soil which has been previously enriched. A sunny aspect in beds or borders is suitable. Thin the seedlings to 3–6 inches apart.

Cultivation of greenhouse species Use a compost of 2 parts of sandy loam, 2 parts of peat and 1 part of coarse sand and sow the seeds in well-firmed, well-drained compost, in 6-inch pots in April. Use the seed sparingly and cover with sifted compost very thinly. Place the

The showy hybrid Schizanthus, known as Butterfly Flower or Poor Man's Orchid, can be grown as a half-hardy annual out doors or makes a colourful display for the cool greenhouse.

pots in a cool greenhouse, frame or window, and when the seedlings are 1 inch high, thin to 2 inches apart. The climbing species should be given a permanent position where they can be trained up to the greenhouse roof or round a window frame, and the seedlings potted up separately rather than thinned. Water freely during the growing season and feed also, but give little water in winter. The minimum winter temperature should be 40°F (4°C).

Specularia (spek-ul-air-ee-a)

From the Latin *speculum*, a mirror; Venus's looking-glass was the common name of one of the species (*Campanulaceae*). Once known as *Legousia*, under which name they are still known by many botanists, these are hardy annuals from the northern hemisphere. They are much like campanulas. Of the 15 species there is one only commonly grown, *S. speculum* (syn. *Campanula speculum*), a native of Europe. This grows about 1 foot tall and bears purple, somewhat bell-shaped flowers in summer; var. *alba* has white flowers; var. *procumbens* is spreading in habit.

Cultivation Ordinary soil and a sunny position suit these plants. Seeds should be sown in April, thinly, about 1/16 inch deep. Thin when the seedlings are 1–2

inches high, to 3–6 inches apart. When the plants are over 3 inches tall they should be supported with twigs.

Sweet Pea

The annual sweet pea, *Lathyrus odoratus*, was introduced to England from Sicily in 1699. It was not until 1870, however, that the breeding of sweet peas started to interest Henry Eckford, a Scot, who was a gardener in Gloucestershire at that time. Later he moved to Wem in Shropshire where he made his name for raising sweet peas. The fragrant flowers of the species are in various colours: shades of purple and red, or white and red. In 1901 a new frilled rose-pink variety, 'Countess Spencer' was shown in London and caused a great sensation as it was the first with frilled petals. It was raised by Silas Cole, gardener to Earl Spencer, at Althorp Park, Northamptonshire. Many new varieties were raised and the popularity of the sweet pea became so great that in 1912 a national newspaper offered a prize of £1,000 for the best vase of 12 stems shown at the Crystal Palace. The competition brought in some 35,000 entries.

Of recent years breeding has been continued apace in the British Isles and the United States, and there are now many distinct types in a wide range of colours and heights. The 'Spencer' varieties have the most elegant flowers and are widely grown for exhibition and for decoration. They are available in many beautiful separate colours. The new, early-flowering 'Galaxy Hybrids' produce as many as seven large, fragrant flowers on a stem, many of them opening at the same time. These are also now obtainable in separate colours.

'Knee-Hi' varieties are less tall and grow to about 3 feet in English gardens, although they are reputed to be of shorter growth under Californian conditions where they were first raised. They are free-flowering, with five to seven flowers on quite a long, straight stem which makes them useful for cutting, and they have the advantage of requiring light support only. This is a useful sweet pea for the small, modern garden, or even for growing in a deep container on a reasonably sheltered balcony. The 'Bijou' type do not exceed 1½ feet in height, yet they carry a good crop of flowers and have long-lasting, short-stemmed flowers. With all these types fading flowers should be snipped off, for if they are left to produce seed the flowering season will be much reduced.

Those who grow for exhibition purposes or like to have an early display

1 *Senecio elegans, the Purple Senecio or Wild Cineraria, is a native plant of South Africa.*
2 *The delicate Specularia speculum makes a charming addition to the summer border.*

of sweet peas sow the seed in October, five seeds in a 3-inch pot and over-winter in a cold frame or cold green-house. Once the seed has germinated the seedlings should be ventilated freely except in the coldest weather. Mice can be a menace as they devour the seed and, during the winter, they are liable to eat off the young green shoots, particularly in hard weather when they may be covered in a frame. By making a further sowing in February or March, flowers will then be available over a long period, well into September. Seed may also be sown in the open, where it is to flower, in late March or April, and if the rows are covered with cloches, these will assist germination.

Some varieties have particularly hard-coated seed, and to assist germination such seeds should be chipped. With the aid of a sharp knife a small piece of the outer coat is removed—on the opposite side to the eye—care being taken not to injure the inner white tissue. For a large number of seeds an easier method is to soak them in water for about 24 hours before sowing. This will cause the seeds to swell and any that remain hard can be chipped so that all should germinate about the same time.

Another important point, particularly with spring-sown seedlings is the ques-tion of stopping. The growing tip is pinched out immediately when the first or second pair of leaves has opened which will ensure that a strong, bushy plant develops.

Sweet peas are deep-rooting, hungry plants making rapid growth when the days are warm. Therefore they require a deeply dug trench and a rich soil. Those who grow prize-winning stems go to a great deal of trouble in preparing trenches two or three spits deep and work in generous quantities of manure, but perfectly good flowers for cutting purposes can be produced when only the top spit is dug and hop manure, or processed animal manure, obtainable in polythene bags, is worked into the soil. During the growing season oc-casional doses of liquid manure should be given and the plants require ample watering in dry spells.

Plants that have been over-wintered under glass should be planted out in the prepared ground in March or early April, and in some districts it may be necessary to protect the young plants with short pea-sticks or netting against damage by pigeons and other birds. With tall-growing sweet peas the pea-sticks should be placed in the ground

1 Rose-pink Sweet Pea 'Zetra' (left); salmon-pink 'Percy Izzard' (centre) and pale 'Pink Pearl' (right).
2 Unwanted tendrils and side shoots are pinched out of Sweet Pea vines grown by the cordon method.

first and then plant one pea beside each stick, or 8–10 foot cane, if it is intended to grow them on the cordon system for exhibition. However they are grown, the supports should be in a double row 8 inches apart in the row and about 1 foot between the rows. Sweet peas may also be grown on netting, trellis or polythene covered mesh, securely fixed to stout metal or wooden stakes. Where sweet peas are grown in a mixed border the pea-sticks can be in the form of a wigwam with the top tied together so that it will withstand summer winds.

When planting out pot-grown seed-lings, care must be taken not to break the long, slender roots and these should be spread out as much as possible in a deep hole made by a trowel. Or cut the soil with a spade and then firm the soil around the roots leaving the bottom side-shoot joint at soil level.

It may not always be possible to raise one's own seedlings but seedlings may be purchased from reliable sweet pea growers. As stocks of strong seedlings are limited, it is usually necessary to order not later than January for delivery in March. Seedlings may also be purchased at market stalls, but beware of thin, weedy seedlings that may have a yellow, starved appearance through lack of water and poor soil, for it is a waste of time to plant out such miserable specimens.

Sweet pea seedlings are reasonably

The 'Bijou' form of the Sweet Pea is a low-growing type of this eternally popular flower which produces a good crop of blooms on short stems and flowers over quite a long period of time if fading flowers are cut back before they seed.

hardy and will withstand normal spring frosts but perishing east winds can be damaging to newly planted seedlings in exposed gardens and any form of temporary windbreak should be used.

Straw or bracken can be laid along the rows, or hessian or polythene stretched along the canes or pea-sticks. This may appear a little unsightly but it is likely to be required for a short period only, in the early days after planting, and it is one of those little attentions that will make all the difference between success and poor results.

Among the leading prize-winning varieties at National Sweet Pea Society's and other shows, are 'Leamington', deep lilac; 'White Ensign'; 'Royal Flush', salmon-pink on a cream ground;

'Herald', orange-cerise on a white ground; 'Gipsy Queen', crimson; 'Larkspur', pale blue; 'Margot', cream and ivory; 'Noel Sutton', rich blue, and 'Festival', salmon-pink on a cream ground. (See also Lathyrus.)

Tagetes (ta-ge-tez)

From the Latin *Tages*, an Etruscan divine (*Compositae*). A genus of 50 species of half-hardy annuals or herbaceous perennials commonly called marigold, but not to be confused with the English or pot marigold (*Calendula officinalis*). There are now many cultivars with single or double flowers of various forms. They have acquired the names African and French marigold, although the original species from which they have been bred were introduced from Mexico and the southern United States.

Species cultivated *T. erecta*, African marigold, annual, 2 feet, leaves much divided, flowers yellow to orange, 2–4 inches across, July, Mexico. There are numerous cultivars and strains, ranging

in height from 1 to 4 feet, free-flowering, branching plants. A selection includes: 'All Double Orange', $2\frac{1}{2}$ feet; 'All Double Lemon', $2\frac{1}{2}$ feet; 'Carnation-flowered Alaska', 2 feet, flowers pale primrose, to 4 inches across; 'Crackerjack', 3 feet, golden-yellow to orange; 'First Lady' (F_1), 1 foot, pale yellow, double; 'Golden Age', 2 feet; 'Guinea Gold', $2\frac{1}{2}$ feet; 'Hawaii', 2 feet, bright orange; 'Cream Puff', $1\frac{1}{2}$ feet, creamy-white ageing almost to white, double; 'Chrysanthemum-flowered Super Glitters,' $2\frac{1}{2}$ feet, lemon; 'Golden Fluffy', 'Orange Fluffy', 'Yellow Fluffy', all $2\frac{1}{2}$ feet; 'Collarette Crown of Gold', 2 feet, centre petals incurved, outer petals broad; 'Diamond Jubilee' (F_1), 2 feet, yellow; 'Golden Jubilee' (F_1), 'Orange Jubilee' (F_1), both 2 feet; 'Climax Toreador', 3 feet, flowers mid orange, ruffled; 'Sunset Giants', 4 feet, flowers yellow, broad-petalled. *T. lucida*, sweet-scented 'Mexican Marigold', annual, 1 foot, yellow, August, Mexico, South America. *T. minuta*, annual, 4–6 feet, pale yellow, October, South America, secretions from the roots are said to keep down weeds and research on this is proceeding at present. *T. patula*, French marigold, annual, $1\frac{1}{2}$ feet, leaves much divided, flowers brownish-yellow, July onwards, Mexico. Numerous strains and cultivars are available, in a wide colour range and in heights ranging from 6 inches to 2 feet. These include: 'Sovereign', 2 feet, early-flowering, golden-yellow and brown to brownish-red, double; 'Dainty Marietta', 6 inches, golden-yellow blotched maroon; 'Flame', 9 inches, deep scarlet, double, 'Golden Ball', 1 foot, large flowers, double; 'Gold-laced', 9 inches, dark red, petals edged orange; 'Harmony', 9 inches, centres orange, collar dark red; 'Golden Bedder', 9 inches, double; 'Legion of Honour', 9 inches, yellow, flecked brown at base, single; 'Lilliput Fireglow', 6 inches, dark scarlet, golden centres; 'Miniature Lemon Drop', 9 inches, golden-yellow, blotched maroon; 'Pygmy Mixed', 6 inches, various colours; 'Samba', 1 foot, various colours; 'Spanish Brocade', 9 inches, golden-yellow, tipped dark red. *T. tenuifolia* (syn. *T. signata*), striped Mexican marigold, annual, $1\frac{1}{2}$ feet, yellow, summer, Mexico; var. *pumila*, 6 inches. Cultivars and strains include: 'Gnome', 6 inches, deep orange; 'Golden Gem Selected', 6 inches; 'Lulu', 6 inches, canary-yellow. 'Irish Lace', 9 inches, is a foliage plant, recommended for edging, which makes mounds of slender, lacy-green foliage.

Cultivation Sow seed thinly in boxes of light soil in a heated greenhouse in March or cold greenhouse in April. Prick out seedlings into seed trays when they are large enough to handle and place in a cold frame and after hardening off, plant out, 12–15 inches apart (dwarf kinds, 6 inches apart) in a sunny bed in late May or June. Water freely

during dry weather, and give a liquid feed occasionally. Seed of *T. minute* is sown under glass in April and the young plants set out 8–9 inches apart in May, after weeds have been cleared.

Thelesperma (thel-es-per-ma)
From the Greek *thele*, nipple, and *sperma*, seed, referring to the papillose achenes (*Compositae*). A genus of 12 annual or perennial herbaceous plants, very similar in appearance to the genus *Cosmos*, and the generic synonym is in fact *Cosmidium*, but they differ botanically slightly in the inflorescence characters. They are natives of the warmer parts of North and Central America.

Species cultivated *T. burridgeanum*, 1–2 feet, half-hardy annual with a loosely branching habit, flowerheads to 1½ inches across with deep orange ray florets with a reddish-brown basal blotch, June to September, Texas. *T. trifidum*, very similar but the ray florets lack the basal blotch, June to September, south-western United States.

Cultivation Both these species should be treated as half-hardy annuals, sowing the seed in situ out of doors in late May, or earlier, under glass, planting out in June. They grow satisfactorily in ordinary soil, in a sunny position.

Thunbergia (thun-ber-gee-a)
Named after Dr Carl Pehr Thunberg (1743–1822), professor of botany at Uppsala (*Acanthaceae*). A genus of 200 species of twining and dwarf annuals and perennials, mainly from Africa. Most require warm greenhouse conditions.

Species cultivated *T. affinis*, hairy-stemmed shrub, flowers violet, 2 inches across, tube yellow, September. *T. alata*, black-eyed Susan, twining annual, flowers yellow and purple, 1½ inches long but varying greatly in colour, summer; vars. *alba*, white with dark centre; *aurantiaca*, deep yellow, dark centre; *bakeri*, white; *doddsii*, leaves white-bordered, flowers orange with a purple centre; *fryeri*, pale yellow, white centre; *lutea*, yellow; *sulphurea*, sulphur-yellow. *T. grandiflora*, large climber, leaves up to 6 inches long, flowers blue, 3 inches long and across, July to September, India; var. *alba*. white. *T. gregori* (syn. *T. gibsonii*), perennial climber, orange waxy flowers 1½ inches across with lobes half as long as the tube, summer.

Cultivation A well-drained, rich fibrous compost is most suitable. Keep the greenhouse at a minimum winter temperature of 60°F (16°C). Some kinds of *T. alata* will tolerate lower temperatures but it is necessary to maintain the humidity. Propagate from seed, for *T. alata* and *T. gregori* in March–April, or from soft cuttings, using mild bottom heat.

There are many kinds of Tagetes, the French or African Marigold, varying in height and bloom size. All flower over a long period of time.
1 Tagetes 'Cordoba'.
2 Tagetes patula 'Dainty Marietta'.
3 The fully-double Tagetes erecta.

Torenia (tor-e-nee-a)
Named after the Rev Olof Toren (1718–53), chaplain of the Swedish India Company (*Scrophulariaceae*). A genus of 50 species of attractive annual and perennial plants, mainly from tropical Asia, requiring warm greenhouse conditions in this country. The flowers, typified by the well-known *T. fournieri*, are borne in short racemes, with a winged tubular calyx, and corolla with a broad upper lip, the lower three-lobed and spreading.

Species cultivated *T. atropurpurea*, perennial, drooping branches up to 2 feet long, flowers usually single, 1–2 inches long, calyx not winged, corolla tube slender, red-purple, summer, Malaya. *T. baillonii*, low and branched, flowers terminal and axillary, calyx keeled, corolla 1 inch long, upper part red-purple, otherwise bright yellow, Indo-China. *T. fournieri*, erect branching annual, 1 foot, flowers in short terminal racemes, broad wings on calyx, upper part of corolla lilac, lower lip violet, centre lobe yellow-blotched at base, tube to 1 inch long, violet, yellow on back, summer, Indo-China; a number of

1

2

3

1 Thunbergia mysorensis, a greenhouse climber, produces unusual strands of flowers which hang downward from their support in chains of yellow and orange.
2 Thunbergia alata is a popular twining annual with brightly-coloured blooms of yellow and purple. Known as Black-Eyed Susans, presumably because of the large dot or 'eye' in the centre, they flower in summer.
3 Torenia fournieri is a summer-flowering greenhouse annual, a native of Indo-China, which produces dainty lilac and violet blooms on upright stems.

cultivars are available with colour and flower size variations. *T. hirsuta*, annual, spreading, flowers axillary, calyx hairy, not winged, corolla violet-blue with darker tube, India.

Cultivation Species other than *T. four-nieri* are suitable for hanging baskets in a stovehouse or warm greenhouse. *T. fournieri* makes an attractive pot plant if supported with slim canes. Sow seed in spring in heat. Potting compost with added organic matter is suitable. Soft cuttings root easily in a propagating frame.

Tropaeolum (trop-e-o-lum)

From the Latin *tropaeum* (or Greek *tropaion*), a trophy, possibly in allusion to the likeness of the flowers and leaves to helmets and shields displayed after Roman victories (*Tropacolaceae*). A diverse genus of 90 species of annuals perennial herbaceous climbers, some tender, others hardy, natives of Mexico and temperate South America.

Species cultivated *T. majus*, nasturtium, hardy or half-hardy annual climber, flowers orange, summer in the wild, Peru; cultivars include 'Golden Gleam', double; 'Indian Chief', flowers scarlet, double, dark leaves; 'Mahogany', mahogany-red, double; 'Orange Gleam', deep orange and mahogany, double; 'Primrose Gleam', double; 'Salmon

Gleam', golden salmon, double; 'Scarlet Gleam', orange and scarlet, double; var. *nanum* is a non-climbing form commonly called the Tom Thumb nasturtium. Cultivars of this are: 'Cherry Rose', cerise, rose, double; 'Empress of India', deep crimson, dark leaves; 'Feltham Beauty', bright scarlet, compact; 'Fire Globe', brilliant red, double; 'Golden Globe', compact, double, gold and crimson. 'Jewel Mixed', double, various colours, flowers held well above the leaves; 'King of Tom Thumbs', scarlet, dark leaves; 'Mahogany Gem', deep mahogany-red, double; 'Queen of Tom Thumbs', various, silver-variegated leaves; 'Rosy Morn', rose-scarlet; 'Vesuvius', salmon-rose, dark leaves. *T. pelto-phorum* (syn. *T. lobbianum*), hardy or half-hardy annual or perennial climber, flowers yellow or orange, summer, Chile, Argentine. *T. peregrinum*, Canary creeper, 3–10 feet, half-hardy annual or

1 Mixed Nasturtiums, Tropaeolum majus, are half-hardy annuals which include both climbing and dwarf varieties and cultivars. They flourish in a poor soil, provided the position is well-drained and sunny.
2 Tropaeolum peregrinum, the Canary Creeper, is grown as a half-hardy annual climber in cooler climates. It is a perennial in mild areas.
3 Ursinia speciosa is an annual with yellow daisy-like flowers.
4 Ursinia anethoides is a native of South Africa.

perennial climber in mild districts, flowers golden-yellow fringed, July onwards, entirely different from the common nasturtium, and requiring a richer soil, Peru. *T. speciosum*, flame nasturtium, hardy perennial, 6–9 feet when established and climbing through a shrub or hedge, flowers brilliant scarlet, June to September, Chile. *T. tuberosum*, tuberous-rooted perennial, 4–5 feet, flowers orange-scarlet, September, Peru.

Cultivation The annual nasturtiums should be sown in spring where they are to flower, in well-drained soil and a sunny position. The young seedlings are tender and are liable to frost damage, therefore nothing is gained by sowing before the end of April or later in cold districts, although following mild winters self-sown seedlings often appear. Sow *T. peregrinum* in light soil under glass in March with a temperature of 50°F (10°C), and harden off the seedlings before planting out against a fence or wall in mid-May. It does well on a north-facing wall. The perennial species like a well-drained loamy soil, *T. speciosum* thriving in a cool, north-facing aspect beside a wall on which there are plants

up which it can clamber. It does best in the north, where it is often seen scrambling into yew hedges. *T. tuberosum* does best in poorish, lime-free soil and a sunny position; the tubers should be planted in March or April and in colder districts lifted in autumn and stored in the same way as dahlia tubers. *T. speciosum* is raised from seed, although seed is difficult to germinate. The seedlings are best grown on in separate pots as they can prove tricky to transplant.

Ursinia (ur-sin-ee-a)

Commemorating Johann Ursinus of Regensburg (1608–66), author of *Arboretum Biblicum* (*Compositae*). A genus of 80 species of annuals, herbaceous perennials or sub-shrubs, natives of South Africa, with one species found in Abyssinia. Those grown in Britain are treated as half-hardy annuals. The daisy-like flowers, in shades of orange and yellow, remain open through the day which is not true of all South African annuals.

Species cultivated *U. anethoides* (syn. *Sphenogyne anethoides*), 1–2 feet, flowers bright orange-yellow with a central zone of deep purple, July to September; the cultivar 'Aurora' is bright orange with conspicuous crimson-red base. *U. versicolor* (syn. *U. pulchra*), 9 inches, flowers orange with dark centre, summer; the cultivar 'Golden Bedder' is light orange with deeper orange centre.

Cultivation These brightly coloured daisy-like plants require a light well-drained soil and full sun. They associate well with arctotis, as in the wild in Cape Province. Sow the seed under glass in late March and plant out in mid-May, or when the danger of frost is past.

Venidio-arctotis
(ven-id-ee-o-ark-to-tis)

A bigeneric hybrid (between the genera *Venidium* and *Arctotis*) which originated in England; slightly tender, with daisy-like flowers like *Arctotis*, in shades of orange, yellow, bronze, rose-pink, mahogany-crimson and ivory white. The flowers are borne erect on stems 1½–2 feet high and open during sunny periods only. The individual flowers are short lived but are produced in succession from June to October.

Cultivation The hybrid is sterile and has no seed, and must be propagated by cuttings, the stock plants being lifted and over-wintered in a frost-free greenhouse or frame. Cuttings taken in the autumn or spring may be rooted in sandy soil in a propagating frame and planted out in a sunny bed in well-drained soil in late May or early June or used as pot plants for a cool greenhouse.

Venidium (ven-id-e-um)

Possibly from the Latin *vena*, a vein, referring to the ribbed fruits (*Compositae*). A genus of up to 30 species of South African half-hardy annuals and perennials.

Species cultivated *V. decurrens*, 1½ feet, flowers orange-yellow with a paler zone around a dark disc, July to October, perennial, best treated as a half-hardy annual. *V. fastuosum*, Namaqualand daisy, 2–3 feet, flowers orange, to 5 inches across, with a dark purple zone around a shining black central disc, June to September, annual; the strain 'Dwarf Hybrids', 15 inches, is available in shades of cream, ivory, yellow and orange with black centres and maroon markings at the base of the petals.

Cultivation Sow seed in a cool greenhouse in April, and prick off into small pots and plant out in late May or early June, in a sunny position in a soil that is not too rich. Seed may also be sown in the open in late April where plants are to flower. Germination is often erratic.

Verbena (ver-be-na)

Possibly from the Latin *verbenae*, the sacred branches of laurel, myrtle or olive, or a corruption of the Celtic name *fervain* for *V. officinalis* (*Verbenaceae*). A genus of 250 species of half-hardy perennials and annuals, widely distributed, notable for the bright colouring of the flowers. Those described are from South America.

Species cultivated *V. bonariensis*, perennial, 3–6 feet, flowers purple-lilac, July to October. *V. corymbosa*, perennial, 3 feet, flowers heliotrope-blue in dense, terminal heads, late summer. *V.* × *hybrida*, florist's verbena, to 1 foot, hybrid, summer bedding plant, many cultivars with flowers in shades of blue, red, pink, many with white eyes, also pure white. *V. peruviana* (syn. *V. chamaedrifolia*), half-hardy perennial, semi-prostrate, flowers brilliant scarlet,

1 Venidio-arctotis is a slightly tender bigeneric hybrid.
2 Venidium fastuosum, the Namaqualand Daisy, has large orange daisy-like blooms with a dark zone around their central discs.
3 Venidium decurrens is a South African perennial best treated as a half-hardy annual.

July to October, bedding plant. *V. rigida* (syn. *V. venosa*), perennial, 1½–2 feet, flowers claret-purple to violet, July to October; cultivars include: 'Amethyst', 1 foot, blue; 'Blaze', 9 inches, scarlet; 'Compliment' 1 foot, pink with yellow eye; 'Miss Susie Double', 9 inches, salmon pink, double; 'Olympia Strain', 9 inches, various colours; 'Ellen Wilmott', 1 foot, salmon-pink with white eye; 'Rose Queen', 1 foot; 'Royal Blue', 1 foot, blue with white eye; 'Scarlet Queen', 1 foot, scarlet with white eye; 'Snow Queen', 1 foot, white eye. *V. tenera*, trailing, South America; var.

maonettii, reddish-violet and white, summer. *V. tenuisecta*, moss verbena, trailing, flowers in shades of blue, summer.

Cultivation Plant in spring in ordinary well-drained soil in a sunny position. In cold districts *V. bonariensis*, *V. corymbosa* and *V. rigida*, should be lifted and over-wintered in boxes of ordinary soil in a frost-free place. In March they should be started into growth in a temperature of 55°F (13°C) and the roots divided when new growth begins. Pot these and plant out in late May. Cuttings of *V. peruviana* should be rooted in late summer in boxes of sandy soil and over-wintered in a frost-free place. *V. bonariensis* is raised from seed sown outdoors in spring. Seed of half-hardy annual hybrids should be sown under glass in February; after the seedlings have been hardened off, plant them out in mid-May.

Verbesina (ver-be-see-na)

Possibly referring to the verbena-like foliage of some species (*Compositae*). A

genus of 150 species of hardy and half-hardy annuals and perennials, from the warmer parts of the Americas.

Species cultivated *V. encelioides* (syn. *Ximenesia encelioides*), tender annual, 2–3 feet, greyish, hairy foliage, flowers yellow, August. *V. virginica*, hardy perennial, 2 feet, leaves downy, flowers white, August.

Cultivation These plants do well in a rich loamy soil. Propagation is by seed, or by division of the perennials.

Xeranthemum (zer-an-them-um)

From the Greek, *xeros*, dry, and *anthos*, a flower (*Compositae*). A genus of six species of hardy annuals with dry, daisy-like 'everlasting' flowers, found from the Mediterranean area to south-western Asia. The only species to be cultivated is *X. annuum*, 2 feet tall, flowers purple, summer; vars. *ligulosum*, flowers semi-double; *perligulosum* (syn. *X. superbissimum*), flowers very double. Seed is usually obtainable of single and double flowering kinds in various colours. They are very suitable for winter decoration.

Cultivation These annuals will grow in ordinary soil in a sunny position. Seeds should be sown in light soil in the greenhouse in a temperature of 50–55°F (10–13°C) and the seedlings planted out in June; or seed may be sown in the open ground at the end of April. It is best to thin to about 6–8 inches apart and some support with short hazel twigs is an advantage. As soon as the flowers are fully expanded they may be gathered for winter decoration.

Zea (zee-a)

An old Greek name, possibly from *Zea*, a kind of corn (*Gramineae*). A genus of a single species, *Z. mays*, maize, Indian corn, mealies, etc., a grass of great economic importance in many parts of the world. It is treated as a half-hardy annual and certain varieties are grown for ornamental purposes. These include vars. *gracillima*, 3 feet, leaves narrow; *gracillima variegata*, leaves striped white; *japonica*, 4 feet, leaves striped white; *japonica tricolor*, 5 feet, leaves striped white, yellow and rose.

Zinnia (zi-nee-a)

Commemorating Johann Gottfried Zinn (1727–59), a German professor of botany (*Compositae*). A genus of 20 species of half-hardy annuals and perennials with beautiful flowers of various colours, natives of the southern United States to Brazil and Chile.

Species cultivated *Z. elegans*, 2–3 feet, flowers of various colours, summer; cultivars and strains are numerous; they include 'Aztec', bright orange; 'Big Snowman', white; 'Envy', green; 'Ice Cream', pure white; 'Chrysanthemum-flowered Hybrids', various colours; 'Giant Dahlia-flowered Strain', various colours; 'Mammoth', various colours;

'Polynesian', pink; 'Scabious-flowered Strain', various colours; 'Peppermint Stick', various striped colours. *Z. haageana*, 1 foot, flowers orange-scarlet, summer; 'Persian Carpet' is a double-flowered strain in various colours. *Z. linearis*, 9–12 inches, flowers golden-yellow, summer. *Z. pauciflora*, 1 foot, flowers yellow or purple, summer. *Z.*

1 Verbena rigida has claret-purple blooms in summer and autumn and is a good plant for mild climates.
2 Verbena peruviana is a half-hardy bedding plant with brilliant red flowers.
3 Verbesina encelioides is a tender greenhouse annual with daisy-like blooms and leaves similar to those of verbena.
4 Xeranthemum annuum produces everlasting purple flowers in summer.

tenuiflora (syn. *Z. multiflora*), 2 feet, flowers scarlet, summer. Other strains and cultivars include 'Button-flowered Mixed', 1½ feet; 'Pink Buttons', 1 foot, salmon-pink; 'Red Buttons', 1 foot, bright scarlet; 'Thumbelina', 6 inches, flowers semi-double or double in various colours.

Cultivation Zinnias do best in deep, loamy soil with decayed manure added, in sunny beds and borders. Sow seed in early April $\frac{1}{16}$ inch deep in light soil in a greenhouse, in a temperature of 55°F (13°C) and transplant the seedlings when the third leaf forms, 2 inches

1

2

3

4

apart in shallow boxes. When established they should be removed to a cooler house and then planted out in early May, 4 inches apart in a cold frame, gradually hardened off and finally planted out in early June, 8–12 inches apart. Seed may be sown directly out of doors in May and this has the advantage that the seedlings can grow undisturbed. Rapid changes of temperature should be avoided and the plants should be freely watered in dry weather. The taller species may be staked in windy conditions, as the blooms produced are often double and very big. When flowering starts the application of stimulants is helpful to the blooms.

Zinnias, bright-coloured flowers of summer named to commemorate a German professor of botany, are available in a wide variety of colours.
1 Zinnia 'Old Mexico' is a small, two-coloured double form.
2 Zinnia 'Early Wonder Serenata' has small blooms.
3 Zinnia haageana 'Persian Carpet' produces double flowers in various colours.
4 Zea gracillima, variegated Maize, grown chiefly for its foliage, is grouped with Tagetes, the African Marigold, and mixed antirrhinum tetra to make an excellent summer bedding collection. The Maize grows to about 3 feet in height and makes a pleasing foil for the flower colours.

A Selection of Hardy Annuals

Botanical Name	Common Name	Height inches	Colour
Althaea	Annual Hollyhock	48–60	various
Anagallis linifolia	Pimpernel	6	blue, red
Argemone	Prickly Poppy	24	yellow, orange, white
Calendula officinalis	Pot Marigold	24	orange, yellow
Centaurea cyanus	Cornflower	12–30	various
Centaurea moschata	Sweet Sultan	18–24	various
Chrysanthemum carinatum	Tricoloured Chrysanthemum	24	various
Chrysanthemum coronarium	Crown Daisy	12–24	various
Clarkia elegans	Clarkia	18–24	various
Collinsia	—	12–15	various
Convolvulus tricolor	Annual Convolvulus	12–18	various
Delphinium ajacis	Larkspur	24–36	pink, red, blue, white
Dianthus sinensis	Indian Pink	6–9	various
Eschscholzia	Californian Poppy	12	various
Gilia × hybrids	—	3–6	various
Godetia	Godetia	6–30	pink, crimson, white
Gypsophila elegans	Annual Gypsophila	18	white, pink, carmine
Helianthus annuus	Sunflower	36–96	yellow, bronze, brown
Helipterum	Everlasting	12	white, pink, yellow
Lathyrus odoratus	Sweet Pea	cl	various
Laverata trimestris	Mallow	24–36	white, pink
Leptosyne stillmanii	—	18	golden-yellow
Limnanthes douglasii	Butter and Eggs	6	white and yellow
Linaria maroccana	Annual Toadflax	9–15	various
Linum grandiflorum	Annual Flax	15–18	red, blue, pink, white
Lobularia	Sweet Alison	3–12	white, pink, lilac
Lupinus hartwegii	Annual Lupine	12–36	various
Malcolmia maritima	Virginia Stock	6–12	various
Malope grandiflorum	Mallow	24–36	pink, crimson, white
Matthiola bicornis	Night-scented Stock	12	lilac
Mentzelia lindleyi	Blazing Star	18	yellow
Nemophila menziesii	Baby Blue-eyes	tr	blue
Nigella damascena	Love-in-a-mist	18	blue, pink, white
Papaver rhoeas	Shirley Poppy	18–24	various
Papaver somniferum	Opium Poppy	18–36	various
Phacelia campanularia	—	9	blue
Reseda odorata	Mignonette	12–18	red, yellow, white
Rhodanthe manglesii	Everlasting	12	rose and white
Salvia horminum	—	18	blue
Saponaria vaccaria	Annual Soapwort	30	pink, white
Scabiosa atropurpurea	Sweet Scabious	18–36	various
Silene pendula	Annual Catchfly	6	various
Thelesperma burridgeanum	—	18	yellow, red-brown
Tropaeolum majus	Nasturtium	6 & tr	oranges, yellow, red
Tropaeolum peregrinum	Canary Creeper	cl	yellow
Viscaria oculata	Catchfly	6–12	various

Hardy Annuals to Sow in the Autumn

Botanical Name	Common Name	Height inches	Colour
Calendula officinalis	Pot Marigold	24	orange yellow
Centaurea cyanus	Cornflower	12–30	various
Cladanthus arabicus	—	30	yellow
Clarkia elegans	Clarkia	18–24	various
Delphinium ajacis	Larkspur	24–36	pink, red, blue, white
Eschscholzia	Californian Poppy	12	various
Godetia	Godetia	6–30	pink, crimson, white
Gypsophila elegans	Annual Gypsophila	18	white, pink, carmine
Iberis	Candytuft	6–15	various
Lathyrus odoratus	Sweet Pea	cl	various
Limnanthes douglasii	Butter and Eggs	6	white and yellow
Lobularia maritima	Sweet Alison	12	white, pink, lilac
Lychnis githago (syn. Agrostemma githago)	Corn-cockle	24–36	pale lilac
Malcolmia maritima	Virginia Stock	6–12	various
Nigella damascena	Love-in-a-mist	18	blue, pink, white
Oenthera biennis	Evening Primrose	30	yellow
Papaver rhoeas	Shirley Poppy	18–24	various
Saponaria vaccaria	Annual Soap-wort	30	pink, white
Scabiosa atropurpurea	Sweet Scabious	18–36	various
Specularia speculum-veneris	Venus's Looking Glass	9	blue
Viscaria	Catchfly	6–12	various

A Selection of Half-Hardy Annuals

Botanical Name	Common Name	Height inches	Colour
Ageratum	Ageratum, Floss Flower	6–18	blue
Amaranthus caudatus	Love-lies-bleeding	24	reddish-purple
Antirrhinum	Snapdragon	9–36	various
Arctotis hybrids	African Daisy	12–18	various
Begonia semperflorens	Begonia	6–9	white, pink, crimson
Brachycome iberidifolia	Swan River Daisy	15	white, pink, blue
Callistephus	Annual or China Aster	9–30	various
Celosia cristata	Cockscomb	12–18	yellow, scarlet
*Cobaea scandens	Cups and Saucers	cl	purple and green
Cosmos bipinnatus	—	36–48	various
Cosmos sulphureus	—	18	orange
Dimorphotheca aurantiaca	Cape Marigold, Star of the Veldt	12–18	orange, buff, salmon, white
Eccremocarpus scaber	Chilean Glory Flower	cl	orange-scarlet
Ipomoea purpurea	Morning Glory	cl	various
Kochia scoparia trichophila	Summer Cypress	12–36	foliage scarlet in autumn
Limonium bonduellii	Annual Statice	12–18	yellow
Limonium suworowii	Annual Statice	18–24	bright rose-pink
Lobelia erinus	Lobelia	6	blue, red, white
Matthiola incana	Ten-week Stock	12–15	various
Mesembryanthemum criniflorum	Livingstone Daisy	tr	various
Mimulus tigrinus	Annual Musk	12	various
Nemesia strumosa	—	9–12	various
Nicotiana	Flowering Tobacco	15–36	white, reds
Petunia	Petunia	9–18	various
Phlox drummondii	Annual Phlox	9–12	various
Portulaca grandiflora	Sun Plant	3	various
Rudbeckia Tetra Gloriosa	Gloriosa Daisy	36	various
Salpiglossis sinuata	Salpiglossis	12–30	various
Salvia splendens	Scarlet Salvia	9–15	scarlet
Tagetes	French and African Marigolds	6–36	various
Ursinia	—	9–18	various
Venidio-arctotis	—	18–24	various
Venidium fastuosum	—	30	various
Verbena hybrids	—	12	various
Zinnia	Zinnia	9–30	various

Annuals for Cutting

Botanical Name	Common Name	Height inches	Colour
Amaranthus caudatus	Love-lies-bleeding	24	reddish-purple
Arctotis hybrids	African Daisy	12–18	various
Calendula officinalis	Pot Marigold	24	orange yellow
Callistephus	Annual or China Aster	9–30	various
Centaurea cyanus	Cornflower	12–30	various
Chrysanthemum carinatum	Tricoloured Chrysanthemum	24	various
Chrysanthemum coronarium	Crown Daisy	12–24	various
Clarkia elegans	Clarkia	18–24	various
Cosmos bipinnatus	Cosmos	36–48	various
Cosmos sulphureus	Cosmos	18	orange
Delphinium ajacis	Larkspur	24–36	various
Dimorphotheca	Cape Marigold	12–18	orange, salmon
Gypsophila elegans	Annual Gypsophila	18	white, pink, carmine
Helichrysum bracteatum	Everlasting	24	various
Lathyrus odoratus	Sweet Pea	cl	various
Matthiola	Stocks	12–15	various
Limonium	Annual Statice	12–14	various
Moluccella laevis	Bells of Ireland	18–30	green and white
Nigella damascena	Love-in-a-mist	18	blue
Phlox drummondii	Annual Phlox	9–12	various
Scabiosa atropurpurea	Pincushion Flower, Sweet Scabious	18–36	various
Tagetes	African and French Marigolds	6–36	various
Tropaeolum majus	Nasturtium	6 & tr	oranges, yellow, red
Zinnia elegans	Zinnia	9–30	various

A Selection of Annuals for the Greenhouse

Botanical Name	Common Name	Height inches	Colour
Ageratum	Ageratum, Floss Flower	6–18	blue
Alonsoa	Mask Flower	12–24	scarlet, pink
Calendula officinalis	Pot Marigold	24	orange, yellow
Celosia cristata	Cockscomb	12–18	yellow, scarlet
Clarkia elegans	Clarkia	18–24	various
Exacum affine	—	12–15	violet, blue
Felicia bergeriana	Kingfisher Daisy	6–9	blue and yellow
Impatiens balsamina	Balsam	24	rose, scarlet, white
Ipomoea purpurea	Morning Glory	cl	various
Mimulus tigrinus	Annual Musk	12	various
Nemesia strumosa	Nemesia	9–12	various
Nicotiana affinis	Flowering Tobacco	15–36	white, reds
Primula malacoides	—	12–18	mauves, pinks
Salpiglossis sinuata	Salpiglossis	12–30	various
Schizanthus	Poor Man's Orchid, Butterfly Flower	12–24	various
Senecio cineraria	Cineraria	18–24	various

cl=climbing   tr=trailing.   *= perennials usually treated as annuals

The tiny yellow dwarf *Tagetes signata pumila*, a compact variety of the French or African Marigold, combines attractively with Nicotiana 'Crimson Bedder' in an annual border.

EVERLASTING FLOWERS

1

The natural everlasting flowers are those with papery petals, often called immortelles, that can be dried and kept for indoor arrangements during the winter. The most common are helichrysums and other members of the daisy family including helipterum, ammobium, anaphalis and xeranthemum, all yellow, bronze, gold, pink and white and a packet of seeds can produce a lovely selection. The sea lavenders, too, are popular. They are often called statice, but belong to the genus *Limonium*, and they include the two annuals, *L. sinuatum*, in various colours and *L. suworowii*, bright rose, and the perennial *L. latifolium*, with tiny blue flowers. If they are kept free from dust they will last for years. The latter is sometimes dyed because the blue flowers tend to lose their colour and the gold, red and bright green flowers sold by florists in Christmas decorations were originally blue.

Cultivation and harvesting All these plants revel in a hot dry summer and last much better after a good season. Sow them in the greenhouse in March to get an early start, planting them out in May. Or sow in the open ground in the sunniest spot in the garden in late April and May, thinning the seedlings to 6 inches apart, and hope for a dry summer. Be prepared to sacrifice garden decoration for winter display because these flowers for drying need to be cut just as they come to maturity. If they are left two or three days too long the petals are less closely folded over one another and they soon shatter once they are completely dry. Cut them all with stems as long as possible, except perhaps the helichrysums, which often have lateral flower buds. These can be snipped off just behind the head and later given false stems. Tie them loosely in small bunches and suspend them from a cord or wire stretched across a garage or spare room or spread them out on wire mesh frames where there is no dampness and no direct sun. The former will encourage rotting and the latter will bleach the colour away from the flowers. The stems of many flowers bend and are not strong enough to hold the heads. False stems can be made with florist's wire, straws, pipe cleaners or twigs.

Other plants which will dry There are other plants which will retain their colour and shape well after drying and which associate happily in arrangements with the true immortelles. *Achillea filipendulina* 'Gold Plate', and 'Coronation Gold', sea holly (*Eryngium*), thistles, teasels, the lanterns of *Physalis franchetii*, *Moluccella laevis*, (bells of

Ireland), echinops, ferns, grasses, gourds, montbretias, cornflowers, heathers, astrantias, lavenders, edelweiss and hops can all be preserved and used, provided they are cut just at the point of maturity and not left too long. Most of these can be dried in the same way as the true everlasting flowers, or laid on sheets of newspaper away from the sun, dampness or heat for a week or two until they are thoroughly dehydrated. Ferns benefit from pressing between sheets of paper under the carpet, or between sheets of blotting paper under a cool iron.

Drying leaves Leaves to accompany this material can be either copper beech, gathered just before they begin to dry, or green beech once it has assumed its golden autumn colour. Put the sprays of leaves into a tall container filled with a mixture of half water and half

2

3

1 A selection of everlasting Helichrysums provides many gaily-coloured flowers for winter use.
2 Moluccella laevis, Bells of Ireland, is a striking everlasting flower.
3 Limonium sinuatum is a useful annual to grow for dried flower arrangements.

1

2

3

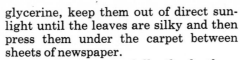

4

5

glycerine, keep them out of direct sunlight until the leaves are silky and then press them under the carpet between sheets of newspaper.

Some leaves, especially the leathery ones such as holly, magnolia, rubber plant (*Ficus elastica*) and camellia, can be skeletonised by leaving them in a tub of rainwater until the outer parts of the leaves become slimy and can be rubbed away, leaving the framework of the leaf. This needs washing in clean water and drying on paper and can be encouraged to curl without breaking once it is quite dry.

All this material, together with the seed-heads of such plants as nigella, columbines, larkspurs, poppies, *Iris foetidissima*, (the gladdon iris) with its brilliant orange fruits, honesty (*Lunaria*) which needs to have the outer coats gently removed to reveal the silvery 'moons' between, the fluffy seed-heads of clematis, the cones of conifers, acorns, nuts and the old female catkins of the alder and other hedgerow or garden material, provides endless scope for dried arrangements for indoor decoration. Materials should be stored in boxes once they have been dried, until they are needed, otherwise they will gather dust and lose their fresh look.

True everlastings

True Everlastings or Immortelles are those flowers grown specifically to be dried. They are annuals and grow best in a sunny place.

Acroclinium roseum *syn*. *Helipterum roseum* is a well-known straw daisy with petals softer than those of its near relative *Helichrysum bracteatum*. It grows to about 2 feet tall and has daisy-like pink or white flowers of papery texture. In a good summer it should flower six weeks after it has been sown, so you can grow and dry it in the same year.

Ammobium alatum grandiflorum (everlasting sand flower) has silvery-white petals and a domed yellow centre. It does grow to 2 feet tall but its stems are short in proportion to its flower-heads and you may need to lengthen them when you come to arrange them.

Gomphrena globosa (globe aramanth or batchelor's buttons) was a favourite in Elizabethan gardens. It grows 12–18 inches high, has white, red or purple globular flowers and is half-hardy.

Perhaps the best known of all the everlastings is **Helichrysum bracteatum** (the straw flower) which include both 3–4 feet tall and shorter dwarf varieties. It has flowers rather like those of a stiff, shiny-petalled double daisy in an assortment of colours—orange, wine-red, apricot, yellow, gold and white.

1 Anaphalis nubigena has silvery-white foliage and chaffy flowers.
2 The everlasting flowers of Ammobium alatum are silver and yellow.
3 Catananche caerula is a perennial everlasting for summer colour outdoors and winter decoration indoors.
4 Lonas annua is a South African Daisy with clustered papery flowers of yellow.
5 Dipsacus sylvestris, the native Common Teasel, grows up to 6 feet in height.

The flowers should be picked as soon as they begin to open.

Helipterum manglesii, also known as *Rhondanthe manglesii*, grows 12–18 inches tall and has tiny daisy flowers in clusters of florets—white, pink, or rose; both double and single blooms.

Statice (Limonium) sinuatum (sea lavender) grows 1–2 feet high and has papery flowers in blue, mauve, or white. Its perennial cousins are *Statice (Limonium) latifolium* which has mauve flowers—this is somewhat taller, reaching 2–3 feet—and *Limonium bonduellii* which has yellow flowers and grows to 1–2 feet. Both of these dry equally well.

Xeranthemum is another everlasting with silvery pink, mauve or white flowers. It grows to 2 feet tall and must be sown where it is to flower as it resents being moved.

Other flowers you can dry

There are also many perennials easily bought as plants or grown from seed which—although not true everlastings —have flowers, pods or seed heads which can be dried successfully. (Perennials are sown in summer for flowering the following year, or bought as plants and planted in spring or autumn.) With a little luck and a reasonable amount of care the most unexpected flowers can be dried—golden rod, cornflower, delphiniums, and double sunflowers.

Acanthus mollis (bear's breeches) with its tall spikes of white and purple flowers and large, jagged leaves grows to 3–4 feet and should be gathered when its lower florets are at their best. If you wait until these begin to fade the whole flower will fade and lose its colour.

Achillea is a yarrow which is found in many varieties from a few inches up to

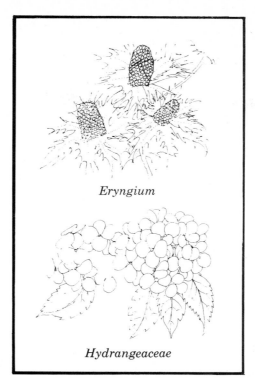

Eryngium

Hydrangeaceae

5 feet tall. It has flat white or yellow heads made up of a mass of tiny flowers and feathery grey-green leaves. This dries very well, and keeps its colour.

The silver-grey foliaged **Anaphalis** (pearl everlasting) has clusters of tiny everlasting-type daisy flowers and grows to 1–2 feet.

Catananche (blue cupidone or cupid's dart) has large blue daisy-like flowers and grows to 2–3 feet tall. It is one of the few which should be gathered when it is fully developed.

The prickly thistle family includes the superb silver-green and blue **Eryngiums** (sea holly) and the steely, blue metallic balls of **Echinops** (globe thistle). The thistle family as a whole provides a lot of interesting material in various sizes, all of which dry well and provide a bold contrast to the more fragile daisies.

Hydrangeaceae (hydrangea) is dried most successfully if it is arranged in fresh water and then just forgotten and left. Pick it when it is just changing colour, from blue to green and pink to red. For some inexplicable reason one or two blooms usually fail to dry well— remove these and keep the rest.

Grasses

Ornamental grasses are annuals and absolutely gorgeous for dried decorations. They flower in late summer and are sown and dried in the same way as flowers. (But the darker the place you dry them in the better; given a little light they turn pale and brittle.) Many of these set seed easily so grow them by themselves—they can be a nuisance in a mixed border.

Most reputable seedsmen sell good selections of grasses and below are listed just a few of those growable from seed. There are many more, some perennial,

from the common-or-garden wheat, barley, oats and millet right up to the giant 10 feet tall **Cortaderia argentea** (pampas grass) with its silvery plumes. They can be used on their own or mixed with dried flowers and look enchanting growing in rows or patches with their heads fluffy, furry, cloudy, wheat-like or woolly.

Agrostis nebulosa (cloud grass) grows to 1½ feet and has a charming head like a cloud of tiny flowers.

Briza maxima (pearl grass) and **Briza media** (quaking grass) have little hanging pendants or lanterns nodding in the breeze. They grow to 1–1½ feet and dry very well.

Coix lacryma-jobi (Job's tears) reaches 2–3 feet and has pea-sized seeds of pearly grey-green (which can be strung as beads) and thick leaves like maize.

Eragrostis elegans (love grass) has beautiful panicles (loose irregular arrangement of flowerheads) of cloudy florets, and grows to 2–3 feet.

Festuca ovina glauca (sheep's fescue) is a blue tufted grass with pretty small spikes of flower. This is one of the shorter grasses, rarely exceeding a height of 6 inches.

Hordeum jubatum (squirreltail grass) grows up to 2 feet and has feathery silver-grey flower heads on spiky wiry stems. Cut this young or the tails will disintegrate.

Lagurus ovatus (hare's tail) with its strong stems and fluffy, silky soft heads can be used fresh or dry.

Triticum spelta (ornamental wheat) is very decorative with a name that speaks for itself.

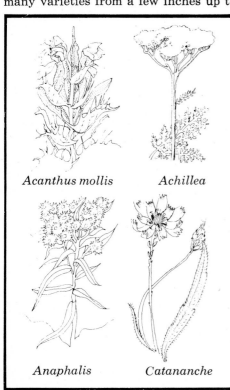

Acanthus mollis   *Achillea*

Anaphalis   *Catananche*

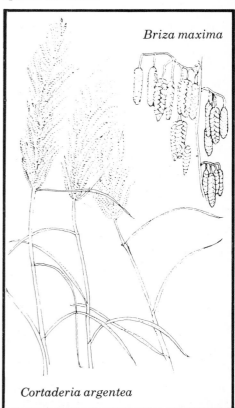

Briza maxima

Cortaderia argentea

CUT FLOWERS

One of the greatest joys of a garden is that with a little planning the gardener can have plenty of flowers and foliage for indoor decoration at all times of the year.

Even when done carefully, repeated cutting from the borders robs the garden of much of its decorative value. It is wise to grow plants just for cutting and any odd corner of the garden can be used for this but the best plan is to grow them in rows in the vegetable garden where they will get plenty of light, and the hoe can be worked around them when the vegetables are hoed. Annuals, perennials, ornamental gourds, grasses and even wild plants can be grown to provide material.

How to grow suitable material. Sow annuals in April or May in rows 9 inches apart and thin them to 6–8 inches apart according to the size of the ultimate plant. The thinnings can always be transplanted, either to some

other part of the garden or to make another row for cutting. The hardy annuals, such as asters and sweet peas, and perennials treated as annuals, such as antirrhinums, which need special treatment, should not be forgotten.

Biennials are grown from seed sown in rows in May and thinned in the same way as annuals, but later in the year the plants are best if they are transplanted. This makes them stockier plants, less likely to run to early flower, although the flower arranger might enjoy having Siberian wallflowers or honesty in September.

Plant perennials 2–3 feet apart to allow the plants to develop well and divide the clumps when they get either too congested or bare in the middle. In general they benefit from a spring mulch of compost.

What to grow Try to vary the annuals, biennials and vegetable material and plants for drying each year so that there can be a constant change of design in flower arrangement from year to year as well as from season to season. Seedmen's catalogues provide many ideas and recommendations and usually indicate the new strains of annual flowers which are always worth trying for a colour break or better constitution.

If some perennials fail, try others better suited to the position or if pyrethrums, especially the double varieties, give disappointing results, change to another variety because some of them seem to be very fussy about their surroundings.

Foliage is probably more important than anything else, and plants with leaves of interesting shape, texture or colour need to be included. Quite often these can be taken from the hedgerows, greenhouse or the rest of the garden, but consider planting in the cutting border some of the hostas for the value of their ribbed and undulating leaves, grey and silver-leaved plants, for example the senecios and artemisias, the purple-leaved *Phormium tenax purpureum* and the spotted pulmonaria or *Polygonum cuspidatum variegatum*. Grasses, some of them annuals, are always useful and do not overlook those plants that dry well and provide material for winter use. Several plants can be used after pressing under the carpet in sheets of newspaper or blotting

2

3

4

Many kinds of flowers are grown specifically for cutting.
1 'Serenade' is one of the Russell Lupins, useful for unusual and sophisticated flower arrangements.
2 Border pinks are useful for less formal cottage arrangements.
3 Erigeron 'Merstham Glory' is a semi-double flower for cutting in summer.
4 Papaver orientale, the Oriental Poppy, of which there are several varieties, both single and double, flowers for cutting in late spring and early summer.

1

2

3

paper. The flattened flower spikes of *montbretia* and many ferns can be preserved in this way.

Cutting It is the treatment the plant material receives at the time of cutting that determines whether it is going to last as long as possible or not in water. Naturally, some flowers do not last well whatever treatment is given and almost no material lasts quite as long once it has been cut as it would if left on the plant.

Always make a good clean cut when taking material from the plant, using scissors, secateurs or a sharp knife. In a very few instances, for example bergenia and heuchera, the stems should be pulled from the plant. There are special flower cutting scissors which have double blades, the one cutting the stem and the other gripping it at the base. These are extremely useful when one hand is holding aside other plants, for with the one hand the stem can be cut from the plant and carried back to the box or basket in which material is being collected without the bloom falling and getting bruised.

If the weather is particularly warm, it is worth taking a bucket of water to the plants and plunging the stems into this as soon as they are cut. This is essential for plants such as bergamot and calthas. Hollow-stemmed plants such as delphiniums should have their stems blocked by the thumb the moment they are cut and the hand not removed until it is below the water in the bucket. Further, delphinium spikes once cut can be turned upside down and the stems filled with water from a jug, plugged with cotton wool and then put into the bucket of water.

When to cut A general rule is not to cut material during the heat of the day but to collect it in the early morning or evening. Evening is perhaps the better time, when the flowers can be given a long drink in a cool place overnight and arranged the following day. Some material such as *Achillea millefolium* will flag when cut during the warm part of the day.

Most flowers need to be cut in bud if they are to last. This applies particularly to tulips, daffodils, paeonies, poppies, iris, roses, and most annuals. Kniphofias (red hot pokers), lupins and antirrhinums need cutting before the flowers at the bottom of the spike begin to fade. They will then curl a little in water and continue to be attractive until all the flowers are open, frequently dropping the older flowers; but the flower dropping is considerably reduced if the spikes are taken from the plant early enough.

The range of flowering plants that last well when cut is large and varied.
1 Delphiniums
2 Herbaceous paeonies
3 Crocosmis masonorum

Nicotiana 'Lime Green'

Salvia horminum 'Blue Bird'

PERENNIALS

This term is used to describe a plant which does not die after flowering, but persists for a number of years, in contrast with an annual which flowers once and then dies after setting seed, and a biennial which completes its life-cycle in two years. The term 'perennial' may properly be applied to shrubs and trees but is more often used in conjunction with the term 'hardy herbaceous' to describe the plants which form the mainstay of herbaceous borders, though they are often grown in other parts of the garden, either in company with other plants or as isolated specimens. Though the term is applied to plants which live for more than 2 years, many perennials live for many years and such plants as herbaceous paeonias and the oriental poppy (*Papaver orientale*) are particularly long lived. By contrast some perennial plants, for instance lupins, may have a life-span of only five or six years.

Planting perennials   With herbaceous plants, one of the problems is not so much *how* to plant them as *when*. The vast majority of border plants are pretty tough and perennials such as Michaelmas or Shasta daisies will quickly take root and establish themselves even if they are left lying on the soil surface. Most border plants, too, can be planted, weather and soil conditions permitting, at any time from September to March. But there is an important minority which planted in autumn, seem unable to survive their first winter. Catmint (*Nepeta* × *faasenii*) is one of the classic examples of this characteristic, a characteristic that is shared by other grey and silver-leaved perennials. Reputable nurserymen will automatically defer delivery of this kind of plant until early spring.

The actual operation of planting perennials is simple and straightforward. Planting with the new season's dormant shoots a few inches below soil level will be satisfactory for most of the better-known and more widely-grown border plants. Where established clumps are being divided up, it is the younger and more vigorous outside shoots that should be planted.

Herbaceous paeonies require very shallow planting; putting them in too deep is one of the main causes of delay in flowering and poor crops of bloom. The dormant eyes, which are easy to distinguish, since they are crimson in colour, should not be more than an inch below soil level.

Bearded irises are another group of border plants that require the shallowest of planting. Ideally the rhizomes should actually be resting on the soil with their upper surfaces above ground level, though on light soils, particularly, they may be planted so that the rhizomes are just covered with soil. This covering will gradually be washed away by rain, by which time their roots will have taken hold. They are rather tricky to plant and are easily disturbed by subsequent weeding or cultivating until the fleshy anchoring roots have had a chance to take hold. It is better to keep the hoe or fork well away from them during their first season and carry out any necessary weeding operations by hand.

Herbaceous borders

The herbaceous border, which is a comparative newcomer to the garden scene, is still one of its most popular features. Introduced at the turn of the century by Gertrude Jekyll as a protest against the monotonous formality of Victorian garden design, its popularity has steadily increased until today there are few gardens without some kind of perennial border to enhance their beauty throughout the months of summer and autumn.

Restricted originally to plants of purely perennial habit—in the main, those whose growth begins afresh from ground level each year—the terms of reference have gradually been extended so that today we find included not only spring and summer bulbs and corms but also small shrubby plants and those curious in-betweens whose woody top growth persists throughout the winter, but which otherwise display most of the characteristics of true perennials. These are the sub-shrubs, of which plants such as the plumbago-flowered *Ceratostigma willmottianum, Caryopteris clandonensis,* and the Russian sage, *Perovskia atriplicifolia* are typical examples.

Preparing the site   Preliminary preparation of the site for a herbaceous border is of paramount importance. Much of its subsequent success or failure will depend on the thoroughness with which it is carried out. Some soils, of course, are a good deal more difficult to prepare than others, but whether you garden on heavy, back-breaking clay or easily managed, well-drained sandy loam there must be sufficient supplies of humus in the soil if the plants are to give of their best.

Deep digging and thorough cultivation are two further essentials. Most of the occupants of the border will remain in the same positions for at least three years, while other more permanent specimens such as paeonies, hellebores, romneyas and hemerocallis can stay put almost indefinitely, without the necessity for division or replanting.

To make sure that such conditions are fulfilled it may be necessary to double dig the whole of the projected plot. This will result in a thorough breaking up of both the surface and second spits of soil. As far as medium to light well-drained loams are concerned, bastard trenching, which leaves the lower spit *in situ* but broken up with a fork, is probably just as effective, but it is better to give wet, heavy soils the full treatment.

Humus   Thorough digging, however, is not sufficient to create the soil conditions in which perennials thrive best. To provide them, plentiful supplies of humus or humus-forming material must be present in the soil, enough, in fact, to satisfy much of the plants' needs for several seasons, as normally the border will be due for a complete overhaul only once in every three to four years.

Humus can be provided by a variety of materials, the best of which, of course, is the almost impossible to obtain stable or farmyard manure. Most of us, however, will have to settle for alternatives. Compost, properly made and well rotted down, heads the list of these but supplies of this are quickly exhausted unless we supplement our garden and domestic waste with straw, sawdust, or other similar materials brought in from outside.

Leafmould is excellent, but expensive unless you are lucky enough to have access to natural sources of supply. Oak and beech leaves are the richest in plant foods, while bracken rots down to a material of peat-like consistency, good for stepping up the humus content of the soil but otherwise lacking in plant foods. Young bracken shoots, on the other hand, are rich in plant foods and minerals and make a valuable contribution to the compost heap.

For the town gardener and for those who cannot readily obtain the materials mentioned above, peat is the best soil conditioner. It is clean both to store and handle, and can hold many times its own bulk of moisture.

Spent hops are another first-rate humus-forming material. If you can obtain supplies in bulk from a local brewery, they will be relatively cheap. The so-called hop manures with added organic fertilizers are a convenient but expensive method of supplying humus to the border.

These, or any other similar materials, are best worked into the upper spit as

digging progresses. Alternatively they can be forked into the soil a few weeks before the plants are put in.

Fortunately, the vast majority of the more widely-grown herbaceous perennials are very accommodating. They will thrive in most types of soil although characteristics such as height, vigour and rate of increase will vary considerably between, for example, light, sandy loams and heavy, sticky clays. It is a good rule never to coddle temperamental plants. There is neither time nor room for them in the herbaceous border, where plants are grown more for their effect in the mass than as individuals.

Weeds The best time of the year to prepare the site for planting is late summer or early autumn. This will give the winter frosts a chance to break up heavy clods to a fine planting tilth. This, of course, is not so important with light sandy soils which can be cultivated at almost any season of the year. As digging progresses, it is imperative to remove every possible vestige of perennial weeds; the aim should be to start with a site that is completely weed-free, although when fresh ground is being taken over this can be no more than a counsel of perfection.

Watch particularly for the roots of bindweed, ground elder and couch grass. Any of these can soon stage a rapid comeback even if only a few pieces remain in the soil.

Couch grass, or 'twitch' as it is sometimes called, is easily recognizable; the narrow leaf blades are coarse, with serrated edges; leaves and underground runners are sectional, like miniature bamboo shoots, with nodules at the joints. Ground elder has leaves similar to those of its shrub namesake and quite attractive

flowers. It is easily identified by the pungent aroma of its bruised leaves and stems. Bindweed, also known as bellbind in some parts of the country, has attractive white trumpet-shaped flowers and a twining habit that can strangle any plant that is the object of its attentions.

Any of these weeds are anathema in the border and once established will prove well-nigh impossible to eradicate without a complete overhaul. Other perennial weeds—not quite as difficult but still a nuisance—include docks, thistles, clover and creeping buttercup. In acid soils sorrel, too, can be troublesome.

If annual weeds multiply alarmingly, and they will in very wet summers, there is no need for undue despondency. Regular sessions with a hand fork or a lady's border fork will keep them in check. Vigorous low-growing perennials will act as their own ground cover.

In autumn, and in early spring if possible, the border should have a thorough forking over, removing and burning all perennial weeds. Any clumps of plants that show signs of weed infestation should be dug up. After shaking or washing their roots free of soil, offending weed roots or runners that have penetrated the latter should be carefully teased out and removed. The clumps can then be replanted *in situ*, or if their size warrants it, be split up and re-grouped. If the replanting is carried out without delay the plants will not suffer any check. In fact, very vigorous growers such as Michaelmas

Weeds are anathema in the border.
1 Trifolium pratense, perennial Clover.
2 Bellis perennis, a wild Daisy.
3 Plantago media, the tenacious Plantain.

daisies, *Campanula lactiflora* and *Chrysanthemum maximum* will benefit from this procedure.

It follows from the foregoing that new stocks received from the nursery or from generous fellow-gardeners should have their roots carefully examined for invading weeds before they are put in. We may not be able to suppress entirely the weeds that are present in the soil, but there is no point in deliberately planting trouble.

Supplementary dressings Unless farmyard manure has been available in generous quantities it will be advisable to give a booster of some kind of fertilizer a few weeks before the border is planted.

Bonemeal and fish manure, which are both organic and slow-acting, will give good results, applied at a rate of 2–3 oz to the square yard. As an alternative, a good general fertilizer can be used at the rate recommended by the manufacturers.

A good way of distributing this supplementary plant food is to rake it into the soil when the final preparations for planting are being made. Alternatively, it can be pricked lightly into the surface with a fork. An established border will benefit from a similar dressing when growth starts in spring.

Siting Most of the more widely-grown perennials are sun-lovers, so that a position facing south or west will be the most suitable for the border. But since this feature is seen at its best when viewed lengthwise, it may be necessary if we plan to enjoy its beauty from some fixed vantage point such as a terrace or the living room windows, to effect some sort of compromise where aspect is concerned.

Generally speaking, any position except a sunless north-facing one, or one

1

2

3

where the plants suffer shade and drip from overhanging trees, will be quite satisfactory.

Background Just as a fine picture deserves an appropriate frame, so the herbaceous border needs a proper setting for its beauty. In the past this has usually been supplied by a background wall or hedge, but nowadays double-sided and island borders are becoming popular, where the only background is provided by the adjacent grass or paving. Nothing, however, makes a more suitable backcloth than a well-kept evergreen hedge—yew, holly, cypress, beech, or hornbeam. Mellowed brick or stone wall, too, can act as a pleasing accompaniment, and even wattle hurdles or a wooden fence, when discreetly covered by climbing plants, can provide an attractive setting.

Plants grown against walls or fences will require additional attention where staking and tying are concerned. In rough weather strong gusts and eddies develop at their base which can have disastrous results unless the plants are strongly secured.

Hedges, beautiful though they may be as backgrounds, also have their disadvantages. Most hedging plants are notorious soil robbers. Some, such as privet, are much worse than others and should be avoided if a new planting is to be made. The roots of an established hedge can be kept in check by taking out a trench a foot or so away from the base of the plants and chopping back all the fibrous roots with a sharp spade. This operation, which should be carried out while the hedge is dormant, could very well coincide with the periodic overhaul and replanting of the border.

If space permits, it is a good plan to leave a gap of 2–3 feet between the foot of the hedge and the rear rank border plants This, incidentally, will also provide useful access to the back of the border for maintenance work.

Yew, of course, is the best plant for a background hedge. Slow and compact in growth, it requires a minimum of attention—one 'short back and sides' trim annually will suffice, and its foliage of sombre green is the perfect foil for the bright colours of the border plants.

Planning Planning the border can be fun. With squared paper and a sheaf of nursery catalogues there could be few pleasanter ways of spending a winter's evening by the fire. Ready-made collections complete with planting plans are useful for the complete novice and can form the nucleus of a wider collection, but it is a good deal more interesting to work out your own colour schemes and to see the plans coming to fruition in the garden.

There is such a wide choice of herbaceous plants that the permutations and combinations of colour, form and texture are infinite in number. Individual tastes vary and so do fashions in flower colours. The pastel shades, popular for

so many years, are giving place to the stronger reds, yellows and blues of the Victorian era.

A border composed entirely of any one of these primary colours would be striking in its effect, but the planning would need very careful handling and a thorough knowledge of plant characteristics. If you lack experience, you would be well advised to use a mixture of colours, grouped according to your individual taste.

As a general rule, in a border of mixed colours the paler shades should be at each end, with the brighter, more vivid ones grouped mainly at the centre. For example, the pure whites of *Phlox paniculata alba, Achillea ptarmica* 'The Pearl', and *Gypsophila* 'Bristol Fairy' could melt almost imperceptibly into the cool primrose yellows of *Achillea taygetea* and *Verbascum bombyciferum* (syn. *broussa*), flanked by the deeper yellows of *Hemerocallis* 'Hyperion', one of the best of the free-flowering day lilies, and *Lysimachia punctata*, the yellow loose-strife.

The middle of the border could explode into brilliant colour with scarlet *Lychnis chalcedonica, Lobelia fulgens, Potentilla* 'Gibson's Scarlet', and the garnet-red *Astilbe* 'Fanal'. Once past its climax, the border could progress to white once more through the blues of delphiniums, sea holly (*Eryngium maritimum*) whose leaves, as well as the flowers, are metallic blue, and the stately *Echinops ritro,* with thistle-like dark green foliage and drumstick flower heads of steely blue. Other suitable blue perennials include the attractive indigo-blue monkshood, *Aconitum* 'Bressingham Spire' and the curious balloon flower, *Platycodon grandiflorum.*

These could be followed by the soft pinks of *Geranium endressii, Sidalcea* 'Sussex Beauty', the long flowering *Veronica spicata*—'Pavane' and 'Minuet' are both good varieties—and the later-blooming ice plant, *Sedum spectabile* 'Brilliant'.

And so back to white again, this time represented by Japanese anemones, *Anemone hupehensis* 'Honorine Jobert', *Lysimachia clethroides, Potentilla alba* and a good garden form of the sweetly scented meadow sweet, *Filipendula ulmaria plena.*

This, of course, would not constitute a complete planting plan, but is merely suggestion that could form the framework of an attractive herbaceous border. Colour, though it may take pride of place in the overall display, is not everything where the successful herbaceous border is concerned. The form and leaf texture of the plants, as well as the manner in which they are grouped, all play a part that is vitally important to the ultimate effect.

It is important to plant in relatively large groups, each restricted to one kind or variety, the size depending on the

1 Planning a new border carefully is important. Lay out irregularly shaped groups of plants with adequate space between to allow for growth.
2 Put the plants into the ground firmly with fine soil around the roots.
3 Firm the soil carefully by treading close to the plant, pushing the earth both downward and inward towards the plant.

103

overall dimensions of the border. Blocks of three plants should, as a general rule, be the minimum, while, for smaller edging and carpeting plants, six would be a reasonable number if spottiness is to be avoided.

Although the general trend should be towards 'shortest in the front, tallest in the rear', this is a rule that should not be too rigidly adhered to. Some of the taller plants should be allowed to wander to the middle or even, at certain points, to the front of the border while the lower marginal plants can be permitted to flow unobtrusively inwards to make small pools and rivulets of contrasting height and colour among their taller neighbours.

A number of perennials are grown as much for the beauty of their foliage as for the decorative quality of their flowers. Outstanding among these are the hostas, or plantain lilies with their outsize ribbed leaves; acanthus, whose sculptured foliage formed the classic model for the Corinthian capitals of Ancient Greek architecture, hemerocallis, *Iris sibirica* and kniphofias for the contrasting effect of their sword-like leaves, the variety of rue known as *Ruta graveolens* 'Jackman's Blue' and

An established and carefully planned herbaceous border gives an air of permanence to a garden.

others.

Other plants are cultivated for their attractive seed heads. These include the fascinating but invasive Chinese lanterns (*Physalis*), the silvery tasselled *Pulsatilla vulgaris* or Pasque flower, *Baptisia australis* with its soot-like seed pods and the magnificent *Heracleum mantegazzianum,* a garden plant resembling a giant cow parsley whose outsize flat seed heads are borne on stems, 10 feet or more tall.

Planting The great majority of perennial border plants can be planted with safety between the end of September and the last week of March. In fact, the planting of late-flowering specimens such as Michaelmas daisies and border chrysanthemums could very well be delayed until April.

Planting holes should be of sufficient depth and breadth to accommodate the roots of the plants without bunching or overcrowding. Small plants can be firmed in by hand, but for large clumps the heel of the boot will be required. Although firm planting is desirable,

this should not entail embedding the roots in a pocket of sticky 'goo'. In heavy clay soils, planting will have to be delayed until the soil condition improves or, better still, the holes can be filled with sifted compost or a mixture of dry soil and peat that has been kept under cover for this purpose.

With the more vigorous perennials such as golden rod, Shasta daisies, achilleas and campanulas, it is not necessary, if time presses, to be too fussy over planting procedure, provided that the soil has been properly prepared and is in good heart. Others, however, such as paeonies, alstroemerias and hellebores will need more careful attention. Paeonies, for example, should never be planted with their dormant growth buds more than approximately 2 inches below the surface; planting too deeply is one of the commonest causes of failure to bloom satisfactorily. The planting or division of catmint is better delayed until spring. Autumn-planted specimens frequently fail to survive. This is a rule that might well be applied to all grey-leaved border plants. Once established they can tolerate severe weather conditions but in their first winter they often succumb to severe frosts if they are planted in autumn.

For the newcomer to gardening, the importance of dealing only with reputable nurseries cannot be overstressed. Their catalogues, in addition to lists and descriptions of plants, will often contain a wealth of information regarding their likes and dislikes. Plants, too, will be delivered at the most appropriate time of year for planting out.

Choice of plants Anyone starting an herbaceous border from scratch would be well advised to take advantage of the many new plants and modern varieties of older favourites that require little or no staking and tying. By this means, one of the major summer chores in the border can be considerable reduced.

Many of these new-style border plants are entirely self-supporting; others need only a few twiggy sticks pushed in among them to keep them in order.

Plants such as tall delphiniums will, of course, have to have each individual flower secured to a stake or stout cane. If space permits, it is better to segregate these and other similar top-heavy plants; they do better where they are more easy to get at for maintenance.

Not all the taller border plants suffer from this shortcoming; *Artemisia lactiflora,* for example, is a plant whose 6 foot stems of feathery milk-white flowers, smelling like meadowsweet, will stand up to a howling gale without turning a hair, while others, for example the moon daisies and taller perennial asters, will collapse and sprawl at the first hint of rough weather, if they are not securely staked.

Careful and judicious selection at the planning stage, therefore, can make

the border practically trouble-free where staking and tying are concerned.

Double-sided or 'island' borders achieve similar results in a different way. Plants grown in an open situation are sturdier and more compact than those grown against a wall or hedge which tends to cause them to be drawn both upwards and outwards. This sturdier habit makes them less liable to damage by heavy winds and rough weather, and, in addition, access at both sides of the border makes routine maintenance a good deal easier. The idea of a double-sided border is not new. Formerly, in large gardens, they were commonly used as a decorative edging in the kitchen garden where they served the dual purpose of screening the vegetable crops and providing flowers for cutting.

Island borders, however, are a more recent innovation, for whose introduction we have largely to thank an Englishman, Mr Alan Bloom, whose display borders attract a host of admirers each year. One of their attractions, in addition to ease of maintenance, lies in the fact that they can be viewed from above as well as along their length and from the front. For this reason, the height of the plants should not exceed 3 or 4 feet in order that the kaleidoscope colour effects of the plant groupings can be seen to their best advantage.

Prolonging the display One of the main disadvantages of the herbaceous border as a garden feature is the comparatively short period during which it makes a major contribution to the garden display. Normally, it is only in early or mid-June that it really starts to make its colour impact, with lupins, oriental poppies, irises, anchusa, aquilegias and other June-flowering perennials.

Reaching its peak in July and August, it continues to delight in early autumn and retires in a blaze of Michaelmas daisies, red hot pokers, perennial sunflowers and border chrysanthemums, which carry it through, in most districts, until mid-October.

For the other seven months of the year, however, the border can lack colour and interest, unless steps are taken to extend its scope by supplementing the orthodox planting materials with others that flower both early and late.

Spring bulbs, such as daffodils, tulips, hyacinths, chionodoxas, scillas and grape hyacinths, all make first-class curtain raisers and will fill the spaces between perennials with bright spring colour. A little later, wallflowers, polyanthus, forget-me-nots and other spring bedding plants can be used as gap-fillers.

There are quite a few true herbaceous plants, beginning in January with the hellebores, that will considerably extend the border's period of interest and relieve the monotony of bare brown earth and dead stems. *Helleborus niger,* the Christmas rose, seldom fulfils the

Island borders, which can be viewed from all sides, are an up-to-date idea.

promise of its name unless it has the protection of cloches or a cold greenhouse, but it can be relied on to open its pure white chalices by the middle or end of January, although even then it will still appreciate a little protection to save its immaculate petals from damage by wind and rain.

Following close on its heels comes the Lenten rose, *Helleborus orientalis* and other delightful species that include the stately *H. argutifolius* (syn. *H. corsicus*) and the native *H. foetidus,* whose green flower clusters are a good deal smaller than those of the Corsican species.

In February and March, too, there will be the pink and carmine flower trusses of the bergenias, among the finest of flowering perennials. These useful plants, that used to be called megaseas, are outsize members of the saxifrage family and most species are evergreen so that their handsome fleshy leaves, bronze or reddish in winter, as well as their striking flowers, make a valuable contribution to the winter border. 'Ballawley Hybrid', a relatively new introduction from Ireland, is one of the most outstanding examples of the group. Other good forms and species include *B. cordifolia* with rounded crinkly leaves, *B. crassifolia,* probably the most commonly-seen, whose leaves are more spoon-shaped than round and *B. schmidtii,* an unusual species the leaves of which have hairy margins and whose loose sprays of clear pink flowers are the earliest to appear.

Blue flowers are always attractive and there are several perennials to provide them once winter is over. The so-called giant forget-me-not, *Brunnera macrophylla* (syn. *Anchusa myosotidiflora*) is one of these, as are the lungworts or pulmonarias. Both of these

have foliage that stays attractive throughout the remainder of the season.

There are several species of pulmonaria, the most striking of which is *P. angustifolia azurea,* with clear gentian-blue flowers. It looks superb in conjunction with the yellow daisy flowers of the leopard's bane, *Doronicum* 'Harpur Crewe'. *P. angustifolia rubra* has coral-red blossoms, those of *P. saccharata* are pinkish-purple turning to blue; the multi-coloured appearance is responsible for its nickname of soldiers and sailors, while its strikingly-mottled leaves have earned it the popular title of spotted dog. Incidentally, the foliage of all the lungworts, which remains tidy throughout the summer, acts as an excellent weed-cover.

In the shadier parts of the border *Hepatica triloba* with its leathery, ivy-like leaves and true-blue flowers, together with primulas and polyanthus will all make pools of colour in April and May. The golden flower of *Alyssum saxatile flore pleno* will shine even more brightly in association with the white flowers of the perennial candytuft *Iberis sempervirens* 'Snowflake', in sunny spots at the edge of the border.

Heucheras and heucherellas will enliven the early summer scene with their spikes of brilliant coral and clear pink miniature bells. The latter is an interesting hybrid between heuchera and tiarella, the foam flower, which is useful both for its decorative value at this time and as an evergreen carpeting plant later in the season. All these will do well in partial shade.

A complete contrast both in flowers and its ferny foliage is *Dicentra spectabilis,* the lyre flower, better known to cottagers as bleeding heart, lady's locket or Dutchman's breeches. This plant prefers partial shade and blooms in late spring, at the same time as the graceful Solomon's seal, *Polygonatum multiflorum,* with its hanging bells of

greenish white.

To provide colour continuity from late summer onwards there are, in addition to the indispensable Michaelmas daisies, various other perennial and bulbous plants. The grey-leaved *Anaphalis triplinervis* is one of these. Its papery 'everlasting' white star-like flowers, which first appear in July, will still be immaculate in October. The Japanese anemone, *Anemone hupehensis*, of which there are now many lovely named varieties, will start to put up clusters of chalice-like blossoms from early August until the first heavy frosts arrive. The single forms, both pink and white, are still firm favourites, but if you are looking for something out-of-the-ordinary you might like to try 'Margarete', a double pink, with rows of ruff-like petals. 'Prince Henry', sometimes listed as 'Profusion', is one of the most striking singles, its colour much richer than those of the other pinks.

In sheltered bays in the border from August onwards two closely-allied South African bulbous plants will make a welcome splash of colour. The blue African lily, agapanthus—the species *A. campanulatus* is perfectly hardy in the south of England — has drumstick heads of powder-blue flowers, while those of *Nerine bowdenii* are similar, but less tightly packed with pink florets. 'Fenwick's Variety', an attractive pink, is the best form for out-of-doors.

And so the year goes by in the herbaceous border, with the first Christmas

1 Pyrethrum 'Eileen May Robinson' flowers in May.
2 Gaillardia 'Wirral Flame' is one of the most reliable cultivars.
3 Ligularia, with its large, rather floppy leaves, is a dramatic plant for a moist spot or the back of a border.
4 Thalictrum aquilegifolium, a soft and dainty flowering plant for the border, blooms in late summer and early autumn.

roses plumping up their buds as the last lingering flowers of the border chrysanthemums shrivel and fade. In the well-planned perennial border there need never be a dull moment.

Winter work Apart from the periodic division, replanting and occasional re-planning of the border, winter maintenance will consist mainly of tidying-up and light forking between the plants. There are two schools of thought where the former operation is concerned. Some gardeners prefer to leave the tidying of the border until spring—the dead leaves and stems, they claim, protect the crowns of the plants in really severe weather. Others, who cannot stand the sight of so much dead untidy vegetation cut down the dead stems at the earliest opportunity.

There is a lot to be said for the former point of view, but a lot will depend on how the border is sited. If it is in full view of the house windows, the sooner it is made ship-shape the better. Only a very small number of popular herbaceous perennials are delicate enough to suffer irreparable damage, even in the severest winter. Plants such as eremurus and

Lobelia fulgens, which may be damaged by frosts, can be protected by covering their crowns with weathered ashes or bracken.

Where the border is more remotely situated, clearing up operations can take their place in the queue of urgent garden tasks that make their heaviest demands during the winter months.

Other uses of herbaceous plants Perennials have become so closely associated in our minds with the herbaceous border that we tend to overlook their many other uses in the garden. For example, bedding schemes employing perennials can be just as attractive as those in which the more orthodox hardy and half-hardy annuals are used. What is more important, management and upkeep will be be simplified and costs will be less where these versatile plants are utilized.

Perennials as bedding plants For bedding purposes, it will be necessary to choose perennials with a relatively long flowering season and/or attractive foliage, plus a solid and compact habit of growth. Among those fulfilling such requirements are *Brunnera macrophylla* (syn. *Anchusa myosotidiflora*), the so-called giant forget-me-not, *Anemone hupehensis,* the Japanese anemone, *Armeria maritima*, thrift, the medium and dwarf Michaelmas daisies and dwarf delphiniums, for example *D. ruysii* or *D. chinensis*. The two last-named, in common with a number of other perennials, have the added advantage of being easy to grow from seed.

Segregation of groups and species Another good way of making the best use of certain groups and species is to grow them in beds restricted to the one type of perennial. By growing them in this way, it is easy to make satisfactory provision for their special requirements in the way of feeding, staking, tying and general cultivation.

This works well for herbaceous plants such as lupins, flag irises, paeonies, oriental poppies and the taller delphiniums. A further point in favour of this method is that it avoids the bare patches that tend to appear in the border when such early-flowering perennials form part of the general scheme.

Other herbaceous perennials that will benefit from this method of culture are the Michaelmas daisies. Where sufficient space is available, a representative collection, grown in a bed or border devoted to them would make a far greater impact than they would dotted about in groups in the mixed border.

Waterside planting Although the great majority of perennials will thrive in a wide range of garden soils and situations, there are some that prefer shade and moisture, conditions that cannot always be easily provided in the herbaceous border. These make excellent plants for the waterside—by the banks of streams or artificial watercourses or at the edge of a garden

Geranium pratense is a floriferous plant which makes good full clumps quickly.

pool.

Primulas, astilbes, *Iris sibirica* and *Iris kaempferi*, kingcups (*Caltha palustris*) and the globe flower (*Trollius* species) are just a few plants that will grow better in damp, shady positions.

Cut flowers Satisfying the demands for flowers for the house in summer, when they fade so quickly, sometimes results in the display in the border being spoiled by too lavish cutting. A satisfactory way of avoiding this is to grow perennials especially for the purpose, either in rows in the kitchen garden or bordering the vegetable plot. For this, it is only commonsense to choose those that will not only cut and last well, but will also need minimum attention where staking and tying are concerned. The list *(right)* is representative, but far from exhaustive.

It should be obvious, from the foregoing, that the uses of perennials are many and varied. We are doing ourselves a great disservice if we restrict them solely to the herbaceous border.

Monocarpic plants Although the literal meaning is 'once-fruiting', as far as gardeners are concerned, plants which take an indefinite period to reach their flowering age and die immediately afterwards are said to be monocarpic. They represent only a small number of plants, but examples familiar to many gardeners include some meconopsis species, *Saxifraga longifolia*, *Saxifraga* 'Tumbling Waters', houseleeks (sempervivums), most bromeliads, and the so-called century plant, *Agave americana*, which, although it does not take a hundred years to flower and then die, may well take over fifty years. Annuals and biennials differ from monocarpic plants in that their life cycles are limited to one year in annuals and two years in biennials.

A selection of herbaceous plants

Name	Height in feet	Colour	Season
Acanthus	4–5	lilac-pink	July–Aug
Achillea spp & vars	1–4	white, yellow	June–Aug
Alchemilla	1–1½	yellow-green	June–July
Anaphalis	1–2	white	July–Sept
Aquilegia hybs	1–3	various	May–June
Armeria	1	pinks	June–July
Artemisia	3–5	grey foliage	Aug–Sept
Aster spp & vars	1–5	various	Aug–Oct
Astrantia	2–3	green-pink	June
Bergenia	1–1½	pinks, white	March–April
Campanula	1–4	blues, white	June–Aug
Centaurea	2–5	blues, yellow	June–Oct
Cimicifuga	2–4	creamy-white	July–Sept
Coreopsis	2–3	golden-yellow	June–Sept
Corydalis	1	yellow	May–Oct
Delphinium	3–8	blues, mauves	June–July
Dianthus	½–1½	various	May–June
Dicentra	1–2	pink	April–May
Doronicum	1–2½	yellow	March–April
Echinacea	2–3	purple-red	Aug–Sept
Echinops	2–5	steely blue	July–Aug
Erigeron hybs	1–2	blue, pink	June–Sept
Eryngium	2–4	glaucous blue	July–Aug
Euphorbia	1–3	yellow	April–June
Gaillardia hybs	2	yellow, orange	July–Aug
Galega	2–4	mauve	June–July
Gentiana	1–2	blues	July–Aug
Geranium	1–2½	pinks, mauves	June–Aug
Helenium	3–5	yellows, copper	July–Sept
Hemerocallis	2–3	yellow, orange	July–Sept
Heuchera hybs	1–2½	pinks, reds	May–Aug
Iris	1–5	various	May–June
Kniphofia	1½–4	yellow, orange	July–Sept
Lupin hybs	2–4	various	June
Lythrum	2–4	purple-red	June–Sept
Lysimachia	2–4	yellow, white	July–Sept
Macleaya	5–8	apricot pink	July–Sept
Malva	2–4	mauves, pinks	July
Monarda	2–4	various	June–Aug
Nepeta	1–2	blue	May–Sept
Paeonia spp & hybs	2–4	pink, red, white	May–June
Phlox	2–4	various	July–Sept
Pyrethrum	1–3	various	May–June
Salvia spp	2–5	mauves	June–Sept
Sidalcea hybs	2½–5	pinks	June–Aug
Verbascum	3–8	yellow, pink	July–Oct
Veronica spp & vars	1–3	blues, mauves	July–Oct

Perennials for cutting

Name	Height in feet	Colour	Season
Acanthus mollis	4–5	lilac-pink	July–Aug
Achillea 'Moonshine'	2	sulphur-yellow	June–July
Alchemilla mollis	1–1½	yellowish-green	June–July
Anaphalis triplinervis	¾	white 'everlasting'	July–Aug
Aquilegia hybrids	up to 3	various	May–June
Aster (perennial)	up to 5	white, pinks, purples	Aug–Oct
Astrantia	2–3	greenish-white, pink	June
Coreopsis grandiflora	2–3	golden-yellow	June–Sep
Dianthus	½–1	various	May–June
Heuchera spp & varieties	2	pinks, reds	June–July
Iris germanica	up to 3	various	May–June
Phlox decussata	up to 3	various	July–Sep
Pyrethrum varieties	2	various	May–June
Trollius	2	yellow, gold	May–June

Acanthus (ak-an-thus)

From the Greek *akanthos*, a spine (*Acanthaceae*). Bear's breech. Handsome hardy perennials known to the Greeks and Romans, who used the leaf form of *Acanthus mollis* for the decoration of the Corinthian column.

Species cultivated *A. caroli-alexandri*, 1–1½ feet, white or rose flowers in July. *A. longifolius*, up to 3–4 feet, purple flowers in June. *A. mollis*, the best-known species, 3–4 feet, with white, pink or mauve flowers and great bold leaves 2 feet long; vars. *latifolius* with wider leaves and white flowers, *nigrum*, with glossy, spineless leaves and lilac-white flowers. *A. spinosus*, 4 feet, very prickly deeply divided leaves, a handsome plant with purple, green and white flowers in July and August.

Cultivation Excellent as specimen plants where their form and character can be appreciated, acanthus stand erect without support. Tenacious because of their stout roots, they can withstand both drought and wind. The foliage of the young plants is less pointed and not as deeply cut as that of mature plants, and root cuttings taken from young plants will produce plants of less jagged leaf shape. Grow them in well-drained loam, preferably, but not necessarily, in a sunny position. Propagate by seed sown in gentle heat in spring, or root cuttings in winter or spring, or division in autumn or spring.

Achillea (ak-ill-e-a)

Named after Achilles, who is said to have used it as a treatment for his wounds (*Compositae*). Yarrow, milfoil. Hardy perennials, for the border or border rock garden.

1 Kniphofia 'Royal Standard', the Red Hot Poker, is just one of the many beautiful and unusual kinds of perennials.
2 Acanthus spinosus is the Bear's Breech, used decoratively by the early Greeks and Romans.
3 Achillea filipendulina 'Gold Plate' is effectively used in dried arrangements.

Species cultivated: Border *A. filipendulina*, large, plate-like heads of yellow flowers in summer; cultivars include 'Gold Plate', 4–5 feet, 'Flowers of Sulphur', 2½ feet, soft sulphur yellow flowers and powdered leaves, and 'Canary Bird', 1½–2 feet. *A. millefolium*, form of the native 'Old Man's Pepper'; cultivars are 'Cerise Queen', 2 feet, with rose-cerise flowers in July in a loose head, 'Crimson Beauty', 2½ feet, and 'Fire King', 2–2½ feet (probably the best). *A. ptarmica* (sneezewort), 2 feet, a white-flowered native, has several good cultivars of which 'The Pearl', 2½ feet, with small, tightly double flowers is the best. *A. sibirica*, 1½ feet, white flowers; 'Perry's White', 2–3 feet, is a fine variety.

Rock Garden *A. ageratifolia*, 4 inches, grey-white leaves and white flowers. *A. chrysocoma*, mats of grey leaves, flowers yellow on 4–6 inch stems. *A. huteri*, silvery tufts, short-stemmed white flowers. *A.* 'King Edward' (syn. *A. × lewsii*) 4 inches, grey-green leaves, buff-yellow flowers all summer. *A. portae*, 4 inches, grey leaves, white flowers. *A. prichardii* 4 inches, grey mats, white flowers. *A. rupestris*, 4–6 inches, foliage creeping, sprays of white flowers, May. *A. tomentosa*, 9 inches, leaves grey, flowers golden-yellow; needs protection from winter dampness; var. *aurea* flowers deeper yellow.

Cultivation Achilleas flourish in almost any soil, provided it is not sour or water-logged, and revel in sunshine. They prefer lime but are quite tolerant of acid conditions. They have tiny or double daisy-like flowers collected in loose clusters or flat heads and bloom in summer. Foliage is fern-like, stems stiff and unbreakable and the fragrance somewhat pungent. Some varieties are recommended for winter arrangements of dried flowers, the best being *A. filipendula*, 'Gold Plate', and if the heads are stored in powdered alum until quite dry, they last well and retain all their colour. Plant in autumn or spring or divide the plants at this time. Sow seed ¼ inch deep in early summer. Border kinds should be lifted and divided every three or four years and the shoots cut down in winter.

Alchemilla (al-kem-il-a)

From *alkemelych*, an Arabic word, indicating the plant's use in alchemy (*Rosaceae*). Lady's mantle. Hardy herbaceous low-growing plants suitable for use on rock gardens or at the fronts of

2

3

blotches; vars. *amabilis* (leaves orange-scarlet), *rosea* and *spectabilis*. *A. bettickiana*, 3–4 inches, leaves blotched with shades of yellow and red. Has given rise to most popularly grown forms: *aurea*, golden yellow leaves; *magnifica*, leaves similar to, though brighter than the species; *paronychioides,* leaves basically orange-red with olive green tints, red tips on young foliage; *spathulata*, 6–8 inches, stems and leaves red, underneath bronzy overtones. *A. versicolor*, 3–4 inches, leaves coppery red.

Cultivation An ordinary ,garden soil is suitable and a sunny position should be chosen. Plant 2 inches apart for massed effect. Set the plants out in May and lift in September after the first frost, when they are trimmed to 3–4 inches. Store for winter on the dry side in a temperature of 60–65°F (16–18°C). Propagate by division of stored plants in spring, rooted offsets being grown on. Cuttings can be taken in August, rooted with heat in winter and potted in spring.

Althaea (al-the-a)

Referring to its medicinal use, from the Greek *althaea*, to cure (*Malvaceae*). A genus of easily grown plants comprising annuals, biennials and perennials.

Biennial species cultivated *A. ficifolia* (fig-leaved or Antwerp hollyhock), to 6 feet, single or double flowers in spikes of mostly yellow, June. *A. rosea*, hollyhock, erect-growing, to 9 feet or sometimes a good deal more. Tall spikes of single or double flowers, sometimes 3 inches or more across, in shades of red, pink, yellow and white, July. This is strictly a perennial but is often treated as a biennial.

Perennial species cultivated *A. cannabina*, 5–6 feet, rose flowers, June; var. *narbonensis*, red flowers. *A. officinalis* (marsh mallow), 4 feet, blush-coloured flowers, July, native to British marshes.

Cultivars of hollyhocks 'Chater's Improved', fully double flowers, mixed colours. 'Apple Blossom', apple-blossom pink. 'Carmine Rose', double cherry-red flowers; and other separate colours. 'Allegheny Mammoth', mixed colours, single and semi-double. 'Begonia Flowered', fringed petals with central rosette, mixed. Annual hollyhock: 'Triumph Supreme', to 4 feet, compact growing.

Cultivation Hollyhocks will succeed in most soils, but prefer the heavier kinds, especially if they are enriched. They need plenty of water in dry periods and should be firmly staked with stout stakes 7 feet or more long, driven well into the ground, to prevent wind damage, particularly in exposed gardens. Stems should be cut down to within about 6 inches of the ground after flowering is over.

Anaphalis (an-af-a-lis)

Said to be an old Greek name for a simi-

borders. The flowers are in clusters, in shades of green or yellow, in July.

Species cultivated *A. alpina*, 6 inches, handsome foliage, grey green above, silvery below, flowers pale greenish-yellow. When grown on the rock garden, it is best planted in crevices between rocks. *A. mollis*, 12 inches. attractive, with kidney-shaped, wavy-edged, softly hairy leaves and greenish-yellow flowers, good for cutting. Contrasts well when grown in association with *Campanula poscharskyana*. Inclined to be invasive when established, but well worth growing, especially as ground cover in shady or semi-shady places, such as under trees.

Cultivation Drainage must not be impaired for alchemillas to thrive well; otherwise any ordinary garden soil suits them. They are best transplanted in autumn or spring. As they are spreading

Alchemilla mollis, Lady's Mantle, is a good, delicately-flowered cover for shady situations.

plants, division is a simple means of propagation and they set seed freely. This may be collected with the aid of polythene bags, placed over the faded flower heads, and sown in spring.

Alternanthera (al-tern-an-the-ra)

Alluding to the fact that alternate anthers are usually infertile (*Amaranthaceae*). Joy weed. Used in the main for foliage effect, these half-hardy shrubby perennials have brightly coloured foliage. The flowers are insignificant and are not usually allowed to develop.

Species cultivated *A. amoena*, 3 inches, leaves, green veined with orange-red

lar plant (*Compositae*). Hardy perennials with white woolly foliage and flowers which can be cut before maturity and dried for use as 'everlastings', sometimes being dyed.

Species cultivated *A. margaritacea* (pearly everlasting), 1 foot, white throughout, flowering June–August. *A. nubigena*, 6–9 inches, silvery white foliage, flowers white, summer. *A. triplinervis*, 12–18 inches, soft woolly silver foliage, pearly-white flowers, June–August. *A. yedoensis*, 2 feet, leaves grey above, white below, flowers white, summer.

Cultivation Anaphalis are suitable for the rock garden or for borders, according to size. An ordinary garden soil and a sunny position suits them. They do well on chalky soils. Plant out in autumn or spring. Established plants may be increased by division at the same seasons. New plants may also be raised from seed sown outside in April.

Anchusa (an-chu-sa)

The name originates from the Greek *anchousa*, a cosmetic paint (*Boraginaceae*). Alkanet, bugloss. Cultivated species are usually perennials or biennials, noteworthy for their blue flowers. The plant long known as *Anchusa myosotidiflora* is now correctly known as *Brunnera macrophylla*.

Biennial species cultivated *A. capensis*, 18 inches, flowers in panicles at tips of stems, July. *A. officinalis*, 1–2 feet, flowers sometimes purple in double spikes, May; var. *incarnata*, flowers pale pink.

Perennial species cultivated *A. azurea* (syn. *A. italica*), 3–5 feet, bright blue flowers summer. *A. barrelieri,* 2 feet, flowers, blue and white, yellow throats, May. *A. caespitosa* (syn. *A. angustissima*), 12–15 inches, tufted plant with gentian-blue flowers from May to July, rock garden or alpine house. *A. sempervirens*, 1½–2 feet, rich blue flowers, May; var. *variegata*, foliage cream and green.

Cultivars *A. azurea*—'Dropmore', 'Loddon Royalist', 'Morning Glory', 'Opal', 'Pride of Dover', 'Suttons Bright Blue' 'Suttons Royal Blue' *A. capensis*—'Blue Bird'.

Cultivation Sunny borders in ordinary soil. Plant out in autumn or spring. Perennials may be raised from seed, from root cuttings taken in February, or by dividing established plants in October. Biennials are raised from seed sown in April.

Aquilegia (ak-wil-e-je-a)

The flower form resembles an eagle's claw, hence the probable origin of this name from *aquila* the Latin for eagle (*Ranunculaceae*). Columbine. Hardy herbaceous perennials for the herbaceous border and rock garden. The flowers and leaves are very dainty. Unfortunately they are inclined to be short lived in heavy wet soils, but they are easily increased by seed. The flowers appear in May and June in a wide range of colours from yellows and creams to blues and reds and purples. The garden hybrids have been raised from various species, e.g. the long-spurred hybrids from *A. longissima*. 'Mrs Scott Elliott's' is a well-known strain, and more recently there are the McKana Giant hybrids, with larger flowers and long spurs.

Species cultivated *A. alpina*, 1 foot, flowers blue, white centre. *A. atrata*, 9 inches, purple-red flowers. *A. bertolonii*, 6 inches, flowers deep violet-blue. *A. caerulea*, 1½–2½ feet, flowers pale blue and white; various named forms, such as 'Blue King', 'Crimson Star', *candidissima* ('Snow Queen'), pure white, *cuprea* ('Copper Queen') coppery, 'Dragon Fly' a dwarf strain in various colours. *A. canadensis*, 1½ feet, pale yellow. *A. chrysantha*, 2–4 feet, golden-yellow. *A. clematiflora hybrida*, 1½ feet, spurless flowers in pink and blue shades. *A. discolor*, 3 inches, blue and white flowers. *A. flabellata*, 9 inches, white, tinged pink; var. *nana alba*, 6 inches, flowers white. *A. formosa*, 1½ feet, yellow or yellow and red flowers; var. *truncata*, smaller flowers. *A. fragrans*, 1½–2 feet, white or purple fragrant; needs a sunny sheltered position. *A. glandulosa*, 1 foot, lilac and white flowers. *A. helenae*, 1½ feet, blue and white. *A. longissima*, 2 feet, long-spurred yellow flowers. *A. skinneri*, 2 feet, crimson flowers. *A. viridiflora*, 9 inches, green and brown, fragrant. *A. vulgaris*, the common columbine, 1½–2½ feet, various colours and forms including the very double *flore pleno*, sometimes known as Granny Bonnets.

Cultivation The requirements are sun or partial shade and a loamy soil enriched with leafmould and not too heavy or dry. Dwarf species, grown on the rock garden, need well-drained soil and full sun. Plants do well on chalky soils. Seed is sown in May or June in the open, in August in a frame or the plants may be divided in spring or autumn.

Armeria (ar-meer-e-a)

This genus has retained the old Latin name for pink although it is not related to the true pink, a species of dianthus (*Plumbaginaceae*). Perennials mainly for the rock garden though the taller kinds are sometimes used at the front of the herbaceous border. They all need well-drained, sunny positions and grow well in seaside gardens; the common thrift, in fact, grows wild in extensive colonies on cliffs by the sea.

Species cultivated *A. caespitosa*, 2 inches, a true alpine so it must have good drain-

1 Althaea rosea, the well-known Hollyhock, one of the tallest of hardy perennials, is available in a wide range of colours.
2 Anaphalis nubigena is an everlasting flower with silvery-white foliage.

age, flowers pale lilac in early summer, a good plant for the alpine house; vars. *alba*, flowers white; *rubra*, ruby-red. *A. corsica*, 6 inches, brick-red. *A. maritima*, the common thrift or sea pink, 6 inches, flowers pink in early summer. There are good varieties of this species such as *laucheana*, 9 inches, bright red flowers; *nana alba*, with large, white flowers in May and June; 'Merlin', rich pink, and 'Vindictive', masses of reddish-pink flowers. *A. pseudoarmeria*, sea pink, thrift, 1 foot, a handsome plant for the herbaceous border; the bright rose-coloured flowers appear in June. The cultivar 'Bees Ruby' was developed from this species and is taller, at 2 feet, and bears rounded heads of deep rose flowers in early summer. *A. splendens*, 3–4 inches, pale pink, summer.

Cultivation Any good, sandy loam suits these plants which must have well-drained positions either in the herbaceous border or on the rock garden. Propagate by division of roots in autumn or spring when they should also be planted. Seeds can be sown in spring in sandy soil.

Artemisia (ar-tem-ees-e-a)

Named after Artemis the Greek goddess (*Compositae*). A large genus, widely distributed over the world, of shrubs, sub-shrubs, herbaceous perennials and annuals, grown mainly for their dainty, aromatic foliage which is very finely cut in some species. The genus shows a great diversity of habit and leaf shape: the flowers are very small and are seldom of much account, though they are often borne in large panicles or plumes. The tarragon herb used for flavourings and vinegar is a member of this family. Most of the artemisias are sun lovers, but *A. lactiflora*, with its sprays of creamy white flowers, will grow in semi-shade and is a useful plant for the herbaceous border.

Annual species cultivated *A. sacrorum viridis*, summer fire, 4 feet, strictly a sub-shrub but grown as an annual.

Herbaceous and sub-shrubs *A. absinthium*, wormwood, 1½ feet, flowers yellow, summer. There is a good form, 'Lambrook Silver' useful for the grey border. *A. baumgartenii*, 9 inches, silvery leaves, yellow flowers, late summer. *A. canescens*, 1 foot, makes a dome of silvery leaves and is suitable for the rock garden. *A. dracunculus*, tarragon, 2 feet, whitish-green. *A. filifolia*, dwarf carpeting plant with bright silvery foliage. *A. glacialis*, 3–6 inches, silvery leaves, yellow flowerheads. A plant for a scree in the rock garden or for the alpine house. *A. gnaphalodes*, 2 feet, foliage grey-white. *A. lactiflora*, 4 feet, creamy-white flowers in plumes, late summer. *A. lanata*, 4–6 inches, silvery leaves, yellow flowers.

Rock Garden *A. ludoviciana*, 3 feet, silvery leaves, yellow flowers, summer. *A. maritima*, sea wormwood, 1–1½ feet, silvery-white leaves, yellowish to reddish flowers, summer. *A. nutans*, 1½–2 feet,

1 *Anchusa azurea is a delicate border plant.*
2 *Armeria pseudoarmeria is the summer-blooming Sea Pink.*
3 *Dainty Aquilegia is the well-loved Columbine.*

finely cut silver-grey leaves. *A. pedemontana*, 6 inches, silvery leaves, rock garden. *A. pontica*, 1–2 feet, grey foliage, whitish-yellow flowers, late summer. *A. stelleriana*, 2–3 feet, silvery leaves, yellow flowers. *A. purshiana*, 2½ feet, white leaves, used as a foliage plant. *A. vulgaris*, mugwort, 2–4 feet, purplish or yellow flowers, autumn, a native plant.

Shrubs *A. abrotanum*, 3–4 feet, the well-known old man, southernwood, or lad's love, fragrant, grey, filigree foliage. *A. arborescens*, 3 feet, silvery foliage retained throughout the year. The flowers of both these shrubs, when produced, are insignificant. They are grown for their foliage.

Cultivation Plant in autumn or spring in sunny borders in ordinary soil. Propagate shrubby species by summer cuttings and herbaceous by cuttings or division. Seeds may be sown in spring of annual and herbaceous species.

Aster (as-ter)

From the Greek *aster*, star, describing the flower shape (*Compositae*). Michaelmas daisy. Among the most useful herbaceous perennials, most of the asters flower in late summer right into the autumn and are extremely hardy and easy

1 Artemisia gnaphalodes with its whitish leaves makes a good border plant.
2 and 3 Pink 'Beechwood' is a summer-flowering Aster alpinus.

to grow. They increase so rapidly, in fact, that many of them have to be lifted and divided about every second year. There are a great many cultivars suitable for the back of the herbaceous border, growing to about 6 feet in height, derived from *A. novi-belgii* and *A. novae-angliae* but there are also shorter, bushier cultivars, up to 3 feet in height that have been raised from *A. amellus* and *A. frikhartii*. These dwarfer varieties are also earlier flowering than the taller kinds. The really dwarf cultivars, from 9–15 inches tall, are excellent plants for the front of a border, as they are compact and very free flowering.

There are asters, too, for the rock garden, such as *A. subcaeruleus*, which flowers in June; the bright violet-blue flowers are produced on 9 inch stems and stand up above the foliage which makes small clumps as it spreads.

The two groups, *A. novi-belgii* and *A. novae-anglaie* are very similar, but the foliage in the *novi-belgii* group is smooth, whereas that of *novae-angliae* is downy.

A great deal of hybridizing has been carried out with Michaelmas daisies, the largest variations are to be seen in the *novi-belgii* group where the colours range from white, pinks, mauves, to deep rose-pink and purple. There are double and single flowers, and some of the varieties are short and bushy, more like the *amellus* group. In the *nova-angliae* group the colours are confined to deep pinks and purples and the flowers have an unfortunate habit of closing at sundown.

Species cultivated A. *acris*, 3 feet, masses of lavender-blue flowers in midsummer. A. *alpinus*, 6 inches, purple flowers in midsummer; 'Beechwood' is a fine cultivar. A. *amellus*, 2 feet, purple flowers in midsummer. A. *cordifolius*, 2 feet, mauve flowers on arching stems in summer. A. *ericoides*, 2–3 feet, abundant white flowers in autumn, angular branching habit: 'Perfection', 4 feet, white and 'Ringdove', 4 feet, rosy mauve, are two cultivars. A. *farreri*, 1½ feet, flowers long rayed, violet-blue in summer. A. × *frikartii*, 3 feet, flowers lavender-blue, in midsummer; 'Wonder of Staff', lavender-blue, is a popular cultivar. A. *linosyris*, goldilocks, 1½ feet, a native with showy golden-yellow flowers in late summer. A. *novae-angliae*, 5–6 feet, autumn-flowering, purple flowers. A. *novi-belgii*, 4 feet, blue flowers in autumn. A. *pappei*, 1 foot, bright blue flowers throughout summer and early autumn. Not reliably hardy except in milder places. A. *subcaeruleus*, 9 inches, violet-blue flowers on 9 inch stems above the foliage; 'Wendy', 1½ feet, pale blue with orange centre, a fine cultivar. A. *thomsonii*, 15 inches, pale blue, a parent, with A. *amellus*, of the hybrid A. × *frikartii*. A. *tradescantii*, 4 feet, white flowers in autumn. A. *yunnanensis*, 1 foot, lilac-blue flowers in summer; 'Napsbury' has larger flowers of heliotrope-blue.

Cultivars Named varieties of the major groups are numerous and new ones seem to appear each year and it is worth visit-

1 *The Astilbe hybrid 'White Queen' is an excellent plant for moist soils, bog gardens and the sides of streams or ponds.*
2 *The unspectacular flowers of Astrantia major repay close examination.*

ing a nursery or consulting an up-to-date catalogue before ordering plants. Among the best are the following:

Amellus 'Blue King', 2½ feet, bright blue. 'King George', 2½ feet, bright blue; an old favourite. 'Sonia', 2 feet, clear pink.

Novae-angliae 'Barr's Pink', 4 feet, 'Harrington's Pink', 4½ feet, clear pink, both old varieties. 'Lye End Beauty', 4 feet, pale plum and 'September Glow', 5 feet, ruby, are both newer varieties.

Novi-belgii 'Apple Blossom', 3 feet, cream, overlaid pink. 'Blue Radiance', 3 feet, large flowers, soft blue. 'Crimson Brocade', 3 feet, bright red, double. 'Little Pink Boy', 2 feet, deep pink. 'Marie Ballard', 3 feet, mid-blue, large fully double. 'My Smokey', 6 feet, deep mulberry, vigorous. 'Orlando', 3½ feet, clear pink, single. 'Peerless', 4 feet, soft heliotrope, semi-double. 'Sailing Light', 3 feet, deep rose. 'Sweet Seventeen', 4 feet, lavender-pink, fully double. 'The Cardinal', 5 feet, rose-red. 'The Rector', 3½ feet, claret. 'White Lady', 5–6 feet, pure white. 'Winston Churchill', 2½ feet, ruby-crimson.

Dwarf 'Audrey', 15 inches, large, pale blue. 'Lilac Time', 1 foot, soft lilac. 'Pink Lace', 15 inches, double pink. 'Professor A. Kippenburg', 15 inches, light blue, semi-double. 'Snow Cushion', 10 inches, white. 'Victor', 9 inches, light blue.

Cultivation Their cultivation is simple: plant in the autumn or spring except the *amellus* group which dislike autumn planting and so must be planted and divided in the spring. They like a sunny position but will tolerate a little shade, and though they will repay good cultivation they are not fussy about soil. They are readily increased by division. Attacks by powdery mildew often whiten the leaves and make them unsightly.

Spraying in summer with dilute lime-sulphur (1 part in 80 parts of water) will check this trouble.

Astilbe (as-til-be)

Many of the older species had colourless flowers which may be the origin of the name, from the Greek *a*, no, *stilbe*, rightness (*Saxifragaceae*). A small genus of herbaceous perennials with feathery plumes composed of myriads of minute flowers in white, many in shades of pink and deep crimson. They are delightful waterside plants but they will grow in the herbaceous border if given a good, rich, moist soil. They will grow well in partial shade and there are dwarf species suitable for the rock garden.

Species cultivated A. *chinensis pumila*, 1 foot, rose-lilac flowers in late summer. A. *crispa*, 6 inches, salmon-pink flowers, summer. A. *davidii*, 4–5 feet, rose pink flowers in late summer. A. *japonica*, 2 feet, white flowers in spring. A. *simplicifolia erecta*, 9 inches, pink flowers in arching sprays in summer. A. *thunbergii*, 1–2 feet, white flowers in May.

Cultivars 'Amethyst', 3 feet, lilac-purple. 'Cattleya', 3 feet, orchid-pink. 'Fanal', 2 feet, garnet red. 'Feuer', crimson with deep crimson foliage. 'Granat', 3 feet, rose-crimson. 'Professor Van der Weilan', 3 feet, white. 'Red Sentinel', 2 feet, brick red. 'Rhineland', 2½ feet, rich rose pink. 'Venus', 3 feet, deep pink. 'White Queen', 2½ feet. All these are known as A. × *arendsii* hybrids and are of complex parentage. Others will be found in nurserymen's lists.

Cultivation Plant in autumn or spring and water well in dry weather. Propagate by division or seeds. Astilbes may also be grown as early-flowering greenhouse plants. They should be potted up in the early autumn in a compost of loam, leafmould and sand. Pots should be kept plunged outdoors until December when they may be brought into the greenhouse and forced into early flower

in a temperature of 55–60°F (13–16°C). After flowering is over the plants should be hardened off, after which they may be planted outdoors again in May.

Astrantia (as-tran-te-a)
Starlike flowers, hence the name from the Greek *aster*, a star (*Umbelliferae*). Masterwort. Summer-flowering perennials with fascinating papery-looking flowers in shades of green, white and pink. The actual flowers are insignificant but they are surrounded by parchment-like bracts that give them colour. They make excellent and unusual cut flowers.

Species cultivated *A. biebersteinii*, 2 feet, flowers light lilac. *A. carinthiaca*, 1–2 feet, very similar to *A. major* with which it is often confused, flowers fragrant of marzipan. *A. carniolica*, 2 feet, white or bluish-pink flowers; var. *rubra*, reddish. *A. major*, 2 feet, pink, suffused with green. *A. maxima*, 2 feet, pink flowers, leaves bright green. *A. minor*, 9 inches, pale purple flowers, tinted green.

Cultivation Plant astrantias in the autumn or spring in ordinary soil in a shady position in the border or woodland garden. They will grow in more open positions provided they are not hot or dry. Propagate by division at planting time or grow from seeds sown in sandy loam in April in a cold frame.

Bellis (bel-lis)
From the Latin *bellus*, pretty, handsome (*Compositae*). The double daisy, a garden variety of one of our commonest wild plants, was cultivated in Elizabethan gardens side by side with double forms of the native buttercup. The original name was 'day's eye' as the little plant opened or closed according to the light.

Species cultivated *B. perennis*, the common daisy, 3–6 inches, white, April onwards. A native plant also widely distributed throughout Europe and Asia Minor. A weed, but the parent of many cultivated forms. *B. rotundifolia caerulescens*,

1 Bellis perennis florepleno, the Double Daisy, is a useful carpeting plant for spring. 2 Bergenia cordifolia flowers in March, one of the earliest perennials to bloom.

3 inches, a tiny white daisy tinted with pale blue, a native of Algeria. *B. sylvestris*, 4–6 inches, daisies with yellow discs and bright red surrounding florets, Mediterranean area.

Cultivated double daisies include many named forms of the double daisy, *Bellis perennis flore pleno*. At least a dozen forms or strains are obtainable with more or less of crimson in their colouring and varying also in size and doubling of the flowers and petal formation. In most of these the golden 'eye' is eliminated. All grow about 6 inches tall and their neatness and ability to produce large quantities of flowers makes them most useful in spring-bedding schemes. An uncommon but interesting form is the 'Hen and Chickens Daisy' which has secondary flower heads surrounding the main one.

Cultivation The double forms of *B. perennis* are very hardy herbaceous perennials which do not demand special soil or garden aspect. They may be raised from seed sown in a frame in March, or old plants may be divided in June, the pieces quickly making new plants if placed in a shaded bed of prepared soil.

Both *B. rotundifolia caerulescens* and *B. sylvestris* are suitable for the rock garden where they must have a sheltered position and a free draining soil. The former may need winter protection.

Bergenia (ber-gen-i-a)
Named for Karl August von Bergen, 1704–60, German botanist (*Saxifragaceae*). These hardy perennial herbaceous plants with large evergreen leaves were at one time called *megasea*, and were at another time included with the saxifrages. The flowers which come in early spring are showy in white, pink or red-purple, borne in large heads on long

stems. The large leathery, glossy leaves are also decorative, especially as in some kinds the foliage is suffused with reddish colour in winter.

Species cultivated *B. cordifolia*, 1 foot, pink, spring; var. *purpurea*, flowers purplish-pink. *B. crassifolia*, 1 foot, pink, spring. *B. delavayi*, 9 inches, leaves turn crimson in winter, flowers purplish-rose, March. *B. ligulata*, 1 foot, white or pink, January or February onwards. *B.* × *schmidtii*, 1 foot, flowers pink spring. *B. stracheyi*, 1 foot, pink, April.

Cultivars 'Ballawley Hybrid', 1½ feet, crimson flowers, dark purplish leaves in winter. 'Delbees', 1 foot, leaves turn red in winter, flowers rosy, March–April. 'Evening Glow', 15–18 inches, dark purple flowers, reddish-bronze foliage. 'Silberlicht', ('Silver Light'), 1 foot, flowers white flushed pink, spring. Others are available and more are likely to be seen in cultivation as time goes on.

Cultivation These members of the saxifrage family are in no way difficult, thriving in any soil, in sun or shade. However, to get full colour in the winter leaves (and this can be very fine), it will be necessary to give the bergenias full sun exposure; and under those conditions they will also produce their flowers somewhat earlier.

Callirrhoe (kal-ir-ho-ee)
Named after Callirhoe, one of the Greek goddesses (*Malvaceae*). Poppy mallow. This North American genus has both annual and perennial species. The flowers are saucer shaped and of red hues, which are brilliant in sunshine. They need an open, sunny position.

Species cultivated *C. involucrata*, the Buffalo rose, 9 inches, flowers crimson, 2 inches across.

Cultivation *C. involucrata* likes a dry sunny spot, the hotter the better, but requires plenty of space to spread. Plant in November. Propagation is by seed sown out of doors in a nursery bed in April, the young

1 *Campanula trachelium, the nettle-leaved Bell Flower, is an easy-to-grow autumn-flowering perennial that will flourish in the wild garden.*
2 *Campanula fragilis is a tufted form for the rock garden, which blooms in mid-summer.*

plants transplanted later to their permanent position, or by cuttings of young growths taken in spring, and put in sandy compost under a handlight or in a cold frame.

Campanula (kam-pan-u-la)

From the Latin *campanula*, a little bell, hence the common name, Bellflower (*Campanulaceae*). A large genus of annuals, biennials and perennials for growing in the border, wild garden, rock garden and greenhouse; widely distributed over the Northern Hemisphere.

Border species cultivated *C.* × *burghaltii*, 2½ feet, large lavender bells, June and July, sandy soil. *C. carpatica*, 9 inches, edging plant, also rock garden, flowers blue, July and August, plant in the autumn before leaves die down, avoiding dormant season; vars. 'Ditton Blue', 6 inches, indigo; 'Harvest Moon', violet-blue; 'Queen of Somerville', 15 inches, pale blue; *turbinata*, 6 inches, purple-blue; *turbinata pallida*, 6 inches, china-blue; 'White Star', 1 foot. *C. grandis* (syn. *C. latiloba*), 3 feet, sturdy, rather stiff growth, flowers close-set in spikes, open flat, blue, June and July, creeping root-stock, lift every third year, grows in shade. *C. lactiflora*, the finest of the bellflowers, 4–5 feet, establishes well in good moist soil, stem erect, covered with foliage, branching to trusses of lavender flowers, July and August; vars. 'Loddon Anna', pale pink; 'Pritchard's Variety', deep blue; 'Pouffe', 1 foot, dwarf variety, light blue. *C. latifolia*, 2½ feet, blue, June to August, easy to grow, tolerates shade; vars. *alba*, white flowers; 'Brantwood', 4 feet, violet-purple; *macrantha*, deep violet flowers, this species sometimes attracts blackfly. *C. persicifolia*, the peach-leaved bellflower, 2½–3 feet, best species to grow in the shade, sends out stolons and forms rosettes of leaves from which the wiry flowering stem grows, producing lavender flowers in June and July; vars. 'Fleur de Neige', 2 feet, semi-double white; 'Snowdrift', single white; 'Telham Beauty', large, single, lavender-blue; 'Wedgwood Blue'; 'Wirral Belle', good double deep blue; also mixed 'Giant Hybrids'. *C. rotundifolia*, 3–4 inches, the English harebell and Scottish bluebell, well-known on chalk and light soils, bears single nodding delicate flowers, July and August; var. *olympica*, 9 inches, lavender-blue, June to September. *C. sarmatica*, 1½ feet, spikes of pale blue flowers, July, greyish leaves.

Rock garden These are mainly dwarf species which require a gritty, well-drained soil and an open, sunny position, except where noted. All are summer-flowering unless otherwise stated. *C. abietina*, 6 inches, violet. *C. alliariaefolia*, 2 feet, white. *C. arvatica*, 3 inches, deep violet, needs scree conditions; var. *alba*, white. *C. aucheri*, 4–6 inches, tufted habit, deep purple, early. *C. bellidifolia*, 4 inches, purplish blue. *C. calaminthifolia*, prostrate, grey leaves, soft blue

flowers, alpine house. *C. carpatica* (as border species). *C. cochlearifolia* (syn. *C. pusilla*), 3 inches, bright blue; vars. *alba*, white; 'Jewel' 4 inches, large, blue; *pallida*, pale blue. *C. elatines*, 6 inches, purple blue. *C. formaneckiana*, 15 inches, silver-grey leaves, pale blue or white flowers, monocarpic, best in the alpine house. *C. garganica*, 4 inches, blue, good wall plant; vars. *hirsuta*, light blue, hairy leaves, May onwards; 'W. H. Paine', dark blue, white centres. *C. hallii*, 4 inches, white. *C. herzegovinensis nana*, 1 inch, deep blue. *C. jenkinsae*, 6 inches, white. *C. kemmulariae*, 9–12 inches, mauve-blue. *C. linifolia*, 9 inches, purple. *C. nitida* (syn. *C. planiflora*), 9 inches, blue; var. *alba*, 6 inches, white. *C. portenschlagiana* (syn. *C. muralis*) 6 inches, trailing, purple, good wall plant. *C. poscharskyana*, 6 inches, powder blue, walls or banks; var. *lilacina*, lilac. *C. pulla*, 4 inches, violet, likes limy soil. *C. raddeana*, 1 foot, deep violet. *C. raineri*, 1 inch, china-blue, scree plant. *C. sarmatica*, 9 inches, grey-blue leaves and flowers. *C. saxifraga*, 4 inches, deep purple. *C. speciosa*, 9 inches, purple blue. *C. stansfieldii*, 4 inches, violet. *C. tridentata*, 4–6 inches, deep blue. *C. valdensis*, 6 inches, grey leaves, violet flowers. *C. warleyensis*, 3 inches, blue, double.

Rock garden cultivars 'Birch Hybrid' (*C. portenschlagiana* × *C. poscharskyana*), 9 inches, purple blue; 'G. F. Wilson', 4 inches, violet-blue; 'Patience Bell', 3–4 inches, rich blue; 'Profusion', 4–5 inches, blue; 'R. B. Loder', semi-double, mid-blue.

Wild garden The growth of these is too rampant for the border. *C. barbata*, 1 foot, clear pale blue flowers. *C. glomerata*, native plant, 1½ feet, head of closely-packed deep purple flowers, June to August; vars. *acaulis*, 6 inches, violet-blue flowers; *dahurica*, 1 foot, violet; *superba*, 1 foot, purple. *C. rapunculoides*, 5 feet, drooping flowers, deep blue, spreads rapidly. *C. thyrsoides*, 1 foot, yellow bells in closely-packed spike, summer, monocarpic. *C. trachelium*, 2 feet, purple-blue flowers on erect stems June and July.

Greenhouse *C. pyramidalis*, the chimney bellflower, a biennial, 4–5 feet, spectacular, covered with white or lavender flowers. *C. isophylla*, a trailing plant for hanging baskets or edge of greenhouse staging, lilac-blue flowers, summer; vars. *alba*, white flowers, *mayi*, woolly variegated leaves.

Biennial *C. medium*, Canterbury bell, 2½ feet, in shades of pink and blue, and also white forms; vars. *calycanthema*, the cup-and-saucer type; *flore pleno*, double, 3 feet, with white, blue or pink flowers. Cultivars include 'Dean's Hybrids' with single or double flowers.

Annual *C. ramosissima*, 6–12 inches, pale blue to violet, this is not often grown but may be used to fill gaps in borders. Sow seed in early April and thin seedlings to 4–6 inches apart.

Cultivation: Border Many of the border campanulas may be grown in partial

shade; most like a well-cultivated soil. Plant in spring or autumn. Stake tall species. They are propagated by seed sown in pans in very fine compost, with no covering of soil, put in a shaded frame. Prick out seedlings and harden them off before planting out. Propagate plants with creeping roots by division in autumn.

Rock garden Propagate these kinds by seed sown in March in frames, by division in spring, or by cuttings after flowering.

Wild garden Plant out kinds suitable for the wild garden in spring or autumn, in sun or partial shade. Propagate them by seed or division as for border kinds.

Biennial Seed of *C. pyramidalis* is sown in pans in a cold frame in May and the seedlings potted up singly. Pot on until they are finally in 8-inch pots. Grow them in cool conditions, giving them ample ventilation. Plants may also be used out-of-doors in the border. Canterbury bells (*C. medium*) are raised in a shady site from seed sown in May or June. The bed should have a very fine tilth, and seed drills should be shallow; or sow in boxes in finely sieved soil and put the boxes in a frame, transplant seedlings to a nursery bed 6 inches apart. Set out in autumn where the plants are to flower, having added lime to the soil. *C. isophylla* and its varieties are propagated by cuttings taken in early summer and rooted in a greenhouse propagating frame. Potting compost is a suitable growing medium; the plant does best in a cold greenhouse or conservatory as it is nearly hardy and, indeed, may survive out of doors in sheltered gardens. It may be used for planting up hanging baskets intended for outdoor decoration in summer.

Catananche (kat-an-an-kee)
From the Greek *katananke,* a strong incentive, referring to its use in love potions (*Compositae*). A small genus of annuals or perennials of which *C. caerulea* is the only species likely to be found in cultivation. This is commonly known as Cupid's dart or blue cupidone and was introduced in 1596. It is a hardy perennial, $2\frac{1}{2}$ feet tall, somewhat similar to a cornflower in habit of growth with grey-green leaves and light blue flowers surrounded by papery, silver-coloured bracts. It is a good border plant and is also an excellent cut-flower, fresh or dried for winter decoration. It flowers from July to September. Improved forms are *major* and 'Wisley Variety'; var. *bicolor* has blue and white flowers; var. *alba,* a plant of very vigorous growth has large white flowers; 'Perry's White' is the best white variety, 'Snow White' is another excellent white kind.

Cultivation This perennial likes well-drained soil and is not averse to lime. It should be given an open sunny position. Plant in October or March and provide adequate staking when plants are in full growth. It survives the winter best if a proportion of the flower stems are

Campanula latifolia alba is a white, summer-flowering perennial that tolerates shade and is a tall, effective border plant.

removed at the end of August. Propagation is by division in March or by seed sown during April in a cold frame.

Celsia (sel-se-a)
Commemorating the famous theologian and botanist Olaf Celsius of Upsala (*Scrophulariaceae*). A genus of perennials and biennials treated as half-hardy annuals. They have tall spikes of yellow flowers in summer and look not unlike mulleins (verbascums).

Species cultivated: Greenhouse *C. arcturus,* 3 feet, perennial, flowers large, yellow with purple anthers, a good pot plant, Crete.

Hardy *C. cretica,* the Cretan mullein, 4 feet, biennial, fragrant golden-yellow flowers marked with brown, July and August, Mediterranean area.

Cultivation Seed of *C. arcturus* is sown in March, seedlings are potted on singly in potting compost and flowered in 8-inch pots. Seed of *C. cretica* is sown in the frame or in the cool greenhouse in March, the seedlings are pricked out and planted out at the end of May. Plants require staking. *C. cretica* may also be treated as a greenhouse biennial. Seed is sown in August to flower the following summer. Ample ventilation should be given.

Centaurea (sen-taw-re-a)
From the classical myths of Greece; the plant is said to have healed a wound in the foot of Chiron, one of the Centaurs (*Compositae*). A genus of annual and perennial plants with flowers not unlike those of a thistle in structure. The annuals (cornflowers and sweet sultana) are good for cutting; some species of perennials are used as foliage plants for the silvery-white leaves.

Perennial species cultivated *C. argentea,* semi-erect, fernlike silvery leaves, pale yellow flowers, half-hardy. *C. dealbata,* 3 feet, lobed leaves, silvery white beneath, pinkish-purple flowers, summer; var. *steenbergii,* flowers rosy-crimson. *C. glastifolia,* 5 feet, upright branching stems, pale yellow flowers, June and July. *C. gymnocarpa,* $1\frac{1}{2}$ feet, sub shrub, much lobed white leaves, half-hardy. *C. jacea,* $3-3\frac{1}{2}$ feet, narrow leaves, rosy-purple flowers, summer. *C. macrocephala,* 2–3 feet, large yellow flowers, June to August, a good border plant. *C. maculosa,* $2\frac{1}{2}$ feet, mauve flowers, summer. *C. montana,* 2 feet, deep blue flowers, April to June, easy to grow, one of the most popular; vars. *alba,* white; *rosea,* pink; *rubra,* rosy-red. *C. pulcherrima,* $2\frac{1}{2}$ feet, narrow leaves, grey beneath, flowers bright rose pink, May to July. *C. ruthenica,* 4 feet, finely cut leaves, graceful plant, yellow flowers on long stems, summer. *C. rutifolia,* 3 feet, silver foliage, yellow

flowers, summer. *C. simplicicaulis*, 1 foot.

Cultivation Plant in November or March in fairly light soil including chalky soils. Propagation is by division in spring.

Centranthus (ken-tran-thus)

From the Greek *kentron*, a spur, *anthos*, a flower, alluding to the shape of the flower (*Valerianaceae*). A small genus of annuals and perennials, natives of Europe and the Mediterranean area. The hardy herbaceous perennial, *C. ruber*, the red valerian is almost a weed on cliffs, railway embankments, and old walls. The name is sometimes spelt Kentranthus.

Species cultivated *C. macrosiphon*, 2 feet, annual, flowers tubular, rose-pink, summer. *C. ruber*, red valerian, 2½ feet, reddish-pink flowers, June and July; vars. *alba*, white; *atro-coccineus*, deep red. All are handsome plants.

Chrysanthemum (kris-an-the-mum)

From the Greek *chrysos*, gold, *anthemon*, flower (*Compositae*). A genus of over 100 species of annuals, herbaceous perennials and sub-shrubs, distributed over Africa, America, Asia and Europe, including Britain. The well-known greenhouse and early-flowering (outdoor) chrysanthemums are descended from *C. indicum*, found in China and Japan, and *C. morifolium* (syn. *C. sinense*), from

1 *Celsia arcturus is a half-hardy shrubby perennial for the greenhouse.*
2 *Centaurea macrocephala is a hardy summer-flowering plant native to the Caucasus.*
3 *Chrysanthemum rubellum is a hardy perennial variety. It has many good forms, including 'Clara Curtis', deep pink; 'Duchess of Edinburgh', fiery red; 'Mary Stoker', soft yellow and 'Paul Boissier', orange bronze.*

China, two closely related, variable plants.

Hardy perennials *C. alpinum* (syn. *Leucanthemum alpinum*) 3–6 inches, white flowers, summer, Pyrenees, Carpathians, scree in rock garden. *C. argenteum* (syns. *Matricaria argentea*, *Pyrethrum argenteum*, *Tanacetum argenteum*), 6 inches, sub-shrubby, grey-white stems and leaves, solitary white flowers, summer. *C. cinerariifolium*, 1–2 feet, white flowers, July and August. This is the species which produces pyrethrum insecticidal powder and is widely cultivated for this purpose in Japan and Kenya. *C. coccineum* (syn. *Pyrethrum roseum*), 2–3 feet, the pyrethrum of gardens, variable in colour; the origin of the garden pyrethrum (see Pyrethrum). *C. haradjanii*, 6 inches, silvery leaves, rock garden foliage plant. *C. leucanthemum*, oxeye daisy, 2–3 feet, white flowers, summer, Europe including Britain and North

118

*1 Convolvulus mauritanicus is a prostrate twining plant useful for hanging baskets.
2 Coreopsis verticillata is a hardy Tickseed reaching 2 feet in height.*

America, a good cut flower. *C. maximum*, Shasta daisy, 1½–3 feet, white flowers, summer, Pyrenees; vars. 'Beauté Nivelloise', fringed petals; 'Esther Read' double, the most popular; 'Horace Read', creamy-white, double; 'Ian Murray', anemone-centred; 'Jennifer Read', later flowering; 'Mount Everest', large flowered; 'Thomas Killin', large anemone-centred; 'Wirral Pride', double, lemon-centred when first open; 'Wirral Supreme', large, double. Many others are to be found in catalogues and new varieties appear from time to time. *C. nipponicum*, 12–15 inches, white flowers, summer, Japan. *C. parthenium*, feverfew, 2 feet, pungent stems and leaves, white flowers, summer, Europe including Britain, best in its double form; var. *aureum*, golden feather, dwarf, yellow leaves, used in bedding. Flower-heads should be removed when they appear. *C. praeteritum*, 9 inches, sub-shrubby, grey, finely divided aromatic foliage; foliage plant. *C. ptarmicaefolium*, 1 foot, silvery-white, much divided foliage, white flowers, summer, Canary Islands. *C. rubellum*, 2–3 feet, single flowers, in shades of lilac and pink, September and October, of unknown origin; var. 'Clara Curtis'. clear pink. *C. sibiricum* (syns. *C. coreanum* and *Leucanthemum sibiricum*), Korean chrysanthemum, 2–3 feet, variously coloured flowers, single and double, September and October, Korea. *C. uliginosum*, giant daisy, moon daisy, 5 feet, single white flowers, autumn, good for cutting, eastern Europe.

Cultivation The taller hardy perennials are useful border plants which will grow in any ordinary soil and sunny position. They may be planted in spring or autumn and clumps should be lifted, divided and replanted every third year. The dwarf kinds are suitable for sunny rock gardens. All are propagated either by division in March or by seeds sown in the greenhouse at the same time.

Convolvulus (kon-volvu-lus)

From the Latin *convolvo*, to entwine, as some of the species do (*Convolvulaceae*). A valuable race of plants both annual and perennial, herbaceous or sub-shrubby. Flowers are bell-shaped throughout and highly attractive.

Hardy perennial species cultivated *C. althaeoides*, 1–2 feet, pink flowers, summer. *C. cantabrica*, 1 foot, pink flowers, mid to late summer. *C. cneorum*, 1–2 feet, silvery leaves, pinkish-white flowers, summer, sub-shrubby, a little tender. *C. incanus*, 6 inches, trailing, silvery leaves, bluish-white flowers, summer. *C. mauritanicus*, trailing, with blue flowers, summer, hardy in warm places, otherwise a fine plant for a greenhouse hanging basket. *C. tenuissimus*, 6 inches, silvery-grey leaves, bright pink flowers, late summer.

Cultivation These convolvulus can be grown in beds and borders and appreciate good soil and sun. Trailing species may be provided with support if preferred. A sunny, sheltered rock garden is especially suitable for *C. cneorum, C. mauritanicus* and other

dwarf and trailing species. Propagation of hardier kinds is by seed sown out of doors in spring. Strike cuttings of *C. cneorum and C. mauritanicus* in sandy soil in a frame in July and August. Bottom heat is an advantage.

Coreopsis (kor-e-op-sis)

From the Greek *koris*, a bug or tick, *opsis*, like, a reference to the appearance of the seeds (*Compositae*). Tickseed. The annual species are often catalogued under *Calliopsis*. Hardy perennials and annuals with showy flowers, excellent for borders.

Perennial species cultivated *C. grandiflora*, 2–3 feet, yellow flowers, summer; var. *flore pleno*, double. Cultivars include 'Baden Gold', large golden yellow flowers; 'Mayfield Giant', orange-yellow; 'Sunburst', double yellow; 'Perry's Variety' semi-double, clear yellow; 'Baby Sun', 1½ feet, golden-yellow. *C. lanceolata*, 2–3 feet, yellow flowers, summer; var. *grandiflora*, large-flowered form. *C. major*, 2–3 feet, yellow flowers, mid to late summer. *C. palmata*, 1½–3 feet, orange-yellow flowers, mid to late sum-

Dahlias are among the most colourful flowers of late summer and early autumn, and they provide a wealth of material for cutting until the start of the cold frosty winter nights.

1 'Worton Jane' is a small-flowered decorative Dahlia.

2 The blooms of Dahlia 'Amethyst Piper', a small-flowered decorative, may be as wide as 6 inches in diameter.

3 'Schweiz' is a medium decorative Dahlia.

4 'Harmari Girl' is a giant decorative Dahlia.

5 'Ruwenzori' is a popular and unusual Dahlia of the collarette type.

6 Dahlia 'Grand Prix' is a giant decorative.

7 'Beauty of Baarn' is a medium semi-cactus type of Dahlia, growing to 3½ feet in height, which holds its blooms high above the foliage.

mer. *C. pubescens* (syn. *C. auriculata superba*), 2 feet, yellow and crimson flowers, summer. *C. rosea.* 9 inches–2 feet, pink flowers, summer. *C. verticillata,* 1½ feet, yellow flowers, summer; var. *grandiflora,* 2 feet, larger flowers.

Cultivation Coreopsis do well in ordinary well-drained garden soil and in sunny positions. Plant perennials during autumn and spring. Propagate single perennial species from cuttings in April, or seed sown a month later; double forms by cuttings in April. Split large clumps in autumn. The annuals are raised from seed sown out of doors during spring and early summer, where they are intended to flower, thinning the seedlings to 9 inches. Alternatively, seed may be sown under glass in a temperature of 65°F (18°C) in March.

Corydalis (kor-e-day-lis)

From the Greek *korydalis,* a crested lark, a reference to the shape of the flowers (*Fumariaceae*). Hardy annuals and perennials, widely distributed throughout the temperate regions of the northern hemisphere.

Perennial species cultivated *C allenii,* 3–4 inches, pink and white flowers, spring. *C. cashmeriana,* 6 inches, blue flowers, spring. *C. cheilanthifolia,* 10 inches, yellow flowers, summer. *C. halleri* (syn. *C. solida*), 6 inches, purple flowers, spring, tuberous-rooted, native plant. *C. lutea,* 1 foot, yellow flowers, spring to autumn, native plant. *C.*

nobilis, 1 foot, yellow flowers, early summer. *C. thalictrifolia,* 1 foot, yellow flowers, summer. *C. wilsonii,* 9 inches, yellow flowers, early summer.

Annual *C. sempervirens* (syn. *C. glauca*), 1½ feet, pale pink to purple flowers, summer.

Cultivation These plants thrive in ordinary soil in well-drained, sunny positions. Ledges, nooks and crannies in rock gardens and walls are very suitable, as well as borders. Plant perennials in March. Propagate annual species by seed sown *in situ* during April; perennials by seed at the same period, or by division after flowering; tuberous rooted species by offsets in March.

Dahlia (day-le-a or dah-le-a)

Commemorating Andreas Dahl, a Swedish botanist who was a pupil of Linnaeus (*Compositae*). Half-hardy, tuberous-rooted perennials from Mexico, first introduced into Britain in 1789 by Lord Bute.

Species cultivated (Few of the following original species are available, although they may occasionally be seen in botanic gardens and the like). *D. coccinea;* 4 feet, scarlet, September, the parent of the single dahlia. *D. coronata,* 4 feet, fragrant scarlet flowers on long stems, autumn. *D. excelsa,* 15–20 feet, purplish-pink flowers, summer. *D. gracilis,* 5 feet, scarlet-orange flowers, September. *D. juarezii,* 3 feet, parent of the cactus dahlias, flowers scarlet, late August and

September. *D. merckii,* 3 feet, lilac and yellow flowers, October (together with *D. variabilis* the parent of most modern double dahlias). *D variabilis,* 4 feet, (syns. *D. pinnata, D. rosea, D. superflua*), variable flower colours, even a green form was suspected at the end of the nineteenth century. The parent of show, fancy and pompon dahlias.

Cultivation Nowadays dahlias are comparatively easy to grow. They tolerate all soils between the moderately acid and alkaline and for ordinary garden purposes need little or no specialized attention, yet will flower profusely. In their evolution they have produced multiple types and hundreds of thousands of varieties simply because they are a cross-pollinated plant. This means that it is possible to produce unusual and original cultivars by raising plants from seeds, which is an additional asset. Furthermore, with correct culture, plants will flower continuously from July until the first autumn frosts, providing a colourful display over a range of several months.

Soil preparation This begins in winter or early spring by digging of the site, at the same time incorporating plenty of bulky organic materials such as peat, leaf-mould, spent hops, vegetable compost, or well-rotted horse, pig or cow manure, but not poultry manure which encourages too much growth at the expense of flowers. Put any of these into the top foot of soil, because dahlias make a mass of fibrous roots in this region. The organic materials can be mixed into the planting holes if only a few tubers or plants are grown, or if dahlias follow spring bedding plants, but generally it is better to dig them in the ground overall.

A fortnight before planting, topdress the ground with a general granular fertilizer containing a higher amount of potash in comparison with the nitrogen and phosphate content Root crop fertilizers have this analysis, and potato fertilizers are very good for the purpose. This application will provide the extra plant food needed during growth, the organic materials previously supplied mainly providing humus for improving the soil conditions and water retention.

Type of stock The choice of stock will depend on the purpose which the plants are to fulfil. Dormant tubers are best for a generaly garden display, for they flower earlier than dahlia plants and produce more flowers over the season as a whole. If you want extremely early flowers, for instance blooming in May, you can plant tubers in pots, or even in the greenhouse border, in February. If you have cloches, you can plant tubers out of doors in April and they will start to flower during early July. Remove the cloches in mid-June. In both these instances the best flowers will be over before the growing season has finished. For the best results over the whole

7

season, plant dormant tubers during the first half of May out of doors. They will not usually need protection, because by the time the shoots emerge above ground level it is likely that the threat of any late spring frosts will be past. Nevertheless keep sacks, pots, polythene bags or other materials handy in case of occasional night frost at this time. Flowering will start in late July and early August.

There are two types of tuber, one being the ground root, a large bulky root resulting from growing a dahlia out of doors without restricting the roots. If replanted from year to year, the number of tubers tends to increase to excess, too many poor quality flowers result, and vigour and tuber formation decrease. Division every second year into several portions is advisable; each portion containing several growth buds, or eyes, and having at least one complete healthy tuber to start them into growth. (At this point, it may be noted that, unlike the potato, dahlia eyes are not on each individual tuber, but are congregated at the base of the old stems). An easy way to judge how many portions a root can be divided into is to put it in the greenhouse for a fortnight or three weeks. Spray overhead with water every second day until the shoots are about ½ inch long. Do not bury the tuber in any material as this will encourage unwanted root growth. With a small hacksaw cut the root into portions according to where the emerging shoots are grouped, or lever it apart with an old screwdriver.

The other type of dahlia tuber, the pot-grown or pot tuber, is often sold in general garden shops and multiple stores in the spring. It is produced from cuttings struck in early spring and grown in pots all through the season so that the roots are restricted and the tuber forms into a neat rounded mass. Although pot tubers are easy to store and transport, forming very good stock for the garden, they are not so good as ground roots for producing cuttings, generally having insufficient bulk to be divided. Pot tubers become ground roots after a season of growth out of doors and their planting times are the same as for ground roots. Before actual planting, chip away some of the wax coating if present to allow moisture to swell the tuber. All tubers can be planted until mid-June.

The dahlia plant itself, which provides a type of stock commonly sold by dahlia nurseries, is formed by rooting dahlia cuttings. Plants grown from cuttings flower later than those grown from tubers, though if you need early flowers before mid-August, it is a good idea to specify on the order sheet 'April Delivery'. If you have a greenhouse or frame, you can then pot the plants into 5 inch pots and they will grow into fine bushy specimens by planting out time. This is standard technique for large and giant-flowered varieties.

1

2

6

10

It is not difficult to keep Dahlias from one year to the next if simple precautions are observed. The Dahlia is a native of the warm Mexican climate: therefore, in cooler areas the tubers must be lifted in the autumn, dried and stored in a dry, frost-free place.

1 Dahlia foliage is very sensitive to frost and will be blackened by the first frost.

2 Immediately after this occurs, cut down the plants to within 9 inches of ground level.

3 Remove the tops and lift the plants with a fork, taking care not to spear the tubers in the process.

4 Shake off the soil and stand the tubers upside-down in a dry, airy place to drain away the surplus sap.

5 Once the tubers are thoroughly dry, they can be stored in any dry frost-free place.

6 Storing them in a bit of dry peat is not necessary, but it will help to exclude frost and absorb excess moisture.

7 Tubers can be stored outside in a deep frame, if they are close together against a sheltered wall and protected with leaves and mats against frost.

8 Dahlias are usually propagated from cuttings made from shoots that arise from the old stems. These arise from the tubers, which are stood close together on a greenhouse bench and covered lightly with soil or peat to retain moisture.

9 Maintain a temperature of 60°F (16°C) and take cuttings when the shoots are 2 to 3 inches long.

10 With a sharp knife, remove lower leaves.

11 Make a basal cut below a joint.

12 Insert the cuttings firmly with a dibber around the edge of a 3½ inch pot of sandy compost.

13 Each cutting should be clearly labelled with the name of the variety and watered in. Then stand the pots in a close frame in the propagating house. Hormone rooting powders usually increase the number of cuttings that root while reducing the time. The inclusion of a fungicide helps reduce loss.

1

2

3

4

1 *Pot-grown Dahlias, raised from cuttings the previous spring, are sometimes sold for planting out. Grown in the open in pots throughout the season, the tubers develop*

into a neat rounded mass.
2 They should be cut down after the first frost, 3 dug up and dried off, and 4 stored in the normal way for re-planting.

Moreover, arranging the stakes in a desired pattern can be a useful guide to design.

Summer Care The main requirement is copious watering, not a lot of feeding. Provided that you have prepared the soil as suggested, all that will be needed during the growing period will be two topdressings of sulphate of potash, each at the rate of $\frac{1}{4}$ oz per square yard. One should be given at the first sign of the petal colour opening from the bud, to improve stem strength and flower colour; the other during early September to improve tuber formation. Monthly feeds of liquid manures made from seaweed extracts are also very good and give excellent results even if used for foliar feeding. The dahlia makes a lot of leaves in August and even in very wet weather the soil may remain dry round the roots. The need to water very frequently can be largely avoided even in the hottest weather if a thick mulch of straw is provided at the roots in mid-July. This keeps down weeds as well as encouraging better root growth.

Tubers will need at least one strong stake, but dahlia plants are better if they are supported by a triangle of three canes or stakes. Such plants have to carry all the weight of stems, leaves and flowers on one main stem or 'leg', so are very prone to wind damage. Tubers on the other hand, push out rigid shoots from below soil level and are much less likely to be broken by the wind in the early stages of growth. These shoots should be tied to the stake every 18 inches, whereas the dahlia plant needs tying every 6 inches for additional protection. A good average length for dahlia supports is 5 feet; these are knocked in to the ground to a depth of 1 foot. Avoid having the stakes higher than the blooms because the wind will knock the flowers against them.

Ground tubers can be left to produce flowers on the tips of their main stems. Allow about eight main stems per division to emerge, and cut off any others below soil level carefully with a knife. Large and giant-flowered varieties should be allowed to produce about five stems only.

Pot tubers, unless they produce sufficient main shoots from below soil level, will have to be treated like green plants. The leading growth tip of the plant is pinched out, or 'stopped', about a month after planting out, usually when about six pairs of leaves have developed. This encourages sideshoots to be produced so plenty of flowers come into bloom as a start; otherwise, if not stopped in advance, dahlia plants produce one central flower only at first. Take notice which are the strongest emerging sideshoots after stopping, and when they are 3 inches long, remove the excess ones by snapping them out from their joints with the main stem. Retain five shoots only, however, with large and

You cannot plant unprotected dahlia plants out of doors until late May, or even safer, the first ten days in June. With cloches or in sheltered situations, free from late spring frosts, you can plant out in late April or early May. In the north and in Scotland, mid-June.

Planting Out This stage is best tackled by taking out a hole in the ground with a small spade. Stakes should be inserted at this time to avoid damage to the tubers which would occur if they were put in later. The hole should be wide enough to prevent cramping and deep enough to allow the upper surfaces of the tubers to be about 2 inches below ground level. Replace the earth on top, shaking the tuber to settle it round the root as you proceed, firming it in by gentle treading. This applies to both ground and pot tubers. Planting distances are 2 feet apart for pompons, $2\frac{1}{2}$ feet for ball dahlias and all others, except the large and giant decoratives, such as cactus

and semi-cactus, which should be 3 feet apart.

Keep the soil watered periodically to swell the tubers and to start the shoots into growth. Shoots should emerge above the soil within five weeks; if not, dig up the tuber and inspect it for decay and slug damage. Slug pellets applied above soil level round the root when planting both tubers and plants are an advisable precaution. Dahlia plants are placed in a hole taken out with a trowel and their roots set so that the potting soil is just below ground level. Bituminised paper, or fibre pots, should be carefully removed from the plants before planting out. (With peat pots especially, make sure to keep the soil moist enough to encourage the roots to penetrate into the open ground, since failure to do this is a frequent cause of stunted, poorly growing plants). Again, it is important to plant to a stake, previously driven in, thus avoiding damage to the roots.

Rooted cuttings are potted up singly into 3 inch pots. When these are full of roots, plants should be transplanted into 5 inch pots.

1 Place a crock over the drainage hole.
2 Cover with leaves or compost fibre.
3 Remove the plant gently.
4 Cover it gently but firmly with the soil mixture.
5 Leave room in the pot for watering.
6 Firm evenly and level off, keeping the plant covered until it is established.

giant-flowered varieties. The technique with the pot tuber is to select initially the strongest main shoot, similar to that of the dahlia plant as the central growing stem, removing the others. This main shoot will be stopped and the sideshoots selected in exactly the same way. A ground tuber is not usually stopped, the flowers being borne on the terminal, or crown buds of each stem. It can, however, be treated like a pot tuber or green plant as far as shoot growth is concerned, but by stopping and selecting one main stem, the flowers, through having to be produced on sideshoots, will be about three weeks later than on the tips of the main stems. Pompon varieties need no de-shooting or disbudding.

Disbudding should be done to all other types when the flower buds are about the size of a pea. Allow the main, centrally placed, largest bud to remain and flower on each shoot, removing the others, together with the fresh secondary shoots which will emerge from each leaf joint on the stem as the flowers mature. Leave just one, fairly low down, on each stem to produce the successive flower, again disbudding and de-shooting. This technique is adopted throughout the flowering period and is the only way to achieve a long flowering season combined with good quality flowers with long stems for cutting.

Left to their own devices, dahlias produce a mass of buds and flowers and soon become uncontrollable, their very tiny, poor blossoms often becoming single by the end of the season. If you need small-flowered dahlias, grow special small-flowered varieties.

Lifting and Storing Ideally this is done once frost has blackened the foliage. If, however, the autumn continues without frost, it does no harm to lift dahlias in late October and early November. Only in the mildest of places, in very sheltered situations or during unusually gentle winters can dahlias be left out of doors in the ground all winter. They can be put into a clamp in the same way as potatoes, but the disadvantage here is that they may be killed if the weather becomes very severe. Furthermore, you cannot examine them for signs of rotting or put them in the greenhouse to take cuttings.

To lift dahlia roots, first cut off the stems just above soil level. Then lift by prising in a circle with a broad-tined fork, working well away from the stems. After lifting the roots clear of the soil, pick off as much adhering earth as possible. Then place the roots upside down in a well-ventilated greenhouse, frame or shed for at least a fortnight. During this period they will lose excess moisture and by the time the remaining soil becomes dust dry, they will be ready to be put into winter storage. There they should be covered with sacks or straw at night if frost threatens. Only in very wet autumns should artificial heat be used,

never exceeding 70°F (21°C).

Before placing them in store, retrim the stems as low as possible, without actually cutting into the tubers. Retie the labels on one of the tubers, because in store the stems will become paper dry and will actually drop off. Most dahlia roots need no covering in store, and in fact, a frequent cause of loss during the winter is covering them up, putting them away in a cupboard and forgetting about them until the spring. Lay them on racks in a frost-proof shed, cellar, or in a greenhouse which can be kept frost free. Straw bales provide good frost protection.

Very tiny tubers, however, should be covered in boxes or pots with material such as garden soil or sand. During the winter, sprinkle the surface with water very occasionally if it gets dust dry, but avoid giving sufficient water to start the tubers into growth. A good temperature to aim at in store is 40–50°F (4–10°C); failing that, it should never fall below 34°F (1°C) nor exceed 50°F (10°C). If you have to store them in a warm place, shrivelling is likely, so all tubers must then be covered with sand or soil in boxes, but keep the boxes separated and put only one layer of tubers in each box. Avoid any store that is subject to drips or draughts, or is so airtight that it encourages fungus rot.

Every month inspect the tubers and if any parts are rotting, cut them out with a sharp knife. Dry the surfaces left with a rag and smear on captan or zineb to prevent further rot. Occasionally fumigate with smoke pellets to deal with aphids which may have hatched out in store or bulb flies which sometimes attack the roots.

Pests and diseases As a general precaution, always spray dahlias with insecticides every three weeks during the season of growth, including those growing in the greenhouse and frame.

Sometimes the soil becomes infected with verticillium wilt, when the stock must be burnt and a fresh growing site found. Cauliflower-like outgrowths, due to crown gall, also mean that affected stock must be destroyed, but it is slow to spread and healthy stock can still be grown in the same ground.

A common leaf disease, especially in humid summers, is dahlia leaf spot, causing light green ringed spots which later turn brown. In this event, treat the leaves with zineb.

Plants are sometimes attacked by virus diseases, of which light green patches or yellowing bands up the veins

and perhaps dark green blisters on the leaves are symptoms. A more certain sign is dwarfing of the plant, which becomes very close-jointed and bushy, producing small flowers. Burn stock affected in this way, for there is no cure at present.

Common pests are blackflies in early summer, often migrating from broad beans, greenflies during summer and autumn, thrips and capsid bugs from time to time.

A difficult pest to control is the red spider mite which may attack some plants in dry seasons, causing yellow mottling. Frequent syringeing under the leaves with water and spraying with malathion every ten days is the control routine to follow.

Earwigs are often a nuisance, eating holes in leaves and flowers. These can be controlled if you provide upturned pots, loosely filled with woodwool, straw, hay, etc., and placed on top of the canes or stakes; these should be emptied into boiling water or paraffin. Also puff DDT on to young flower buds.

Wasps sometimes make damaging attacks on dahlia flower stems and it is usually necessary to destroy the nest completely.

Propagation The preparation for growing from seed is a simple matter. Remove the petals as they fade and take the seed pods indoors before the frost, later extracting the seed and placing it in envelopes. The seed is sown in boxes in mid-March, and the seedlings are potted off in May and planted out in June. The best breeding, however, is done by crossing selected varieties by hand, and covering the blooms with old nylon stockings to prevent chance pollination by bees and other insects. It should be remembered that dahlias do not come true to type or variety from seed, though dwarf bedding types, such as 'Coltness Gem' or 'Unwins Hybrids' are commonly grown in this way as they come reasonably true.

Years ago dahlia shoots were grafted on to tubers to produce plants, but only research into virus control now employs this technique. Nowadays dahlias are commonly propagated from cuttings. Tubers are packed close together in boxes of soil in February, put on the greenhouse bench with bottom heat of about 60°F (16°C) and watered. When the shoots, produced after some three weeks, are about 2½ inches long, they are cut off close to the tuber just below a leaf joint, and after removing the lower leaves, they are inserted into holes round the edge of 3 inch pots. The holes are made by inserting a pencil-sized dibber 1½ inches deep into the rooting medium in the pots, commonly sand or a mixture of equal parts of peat and sand. Five cuttings are placed in each pot. The pots are then placed over bottom heat from soil-warming wires, boiler pipes, or paraffin or electrical heating. The temp-

1 Before planting Dahlias in the open, water thoroughly and take out a hole large enough to hold the rootball.
2 Knock the plant out carefully.
3 Position the roots just below the level of the soil.
4 Fill in the hole, firm evenly and leave a shallow depression for watering.

erature should be about 60°F (16°C) round the pots. Cover the pots by suspending polythene sheeting above them in the daytime, plus brown paper if the sun shines, and spray them gently with water morning and night, removing the covers over night. Do not make the mistake of overwatering the pots during the rooting period, or rotting may take place. Add water to the pot only when the sand surface dries out and then dip it in a bucket of water with a finger over the drainage hole until bubbles cease to rise. Otherwise, rely on overhead spraying on the cuttings themselves.

After two or three weeks, when new tip growth is evident, the cuttings will have rooted and can be potted off individually in ordinary potting compost. For the first ten days afterwards, keep them in a warm part of the greenhouse, but for the rest of the time until planting out they grow much better if kept cool. Certainly they should be ready to be put into a cold frame three weeks after potting off.

The division of tubers described earlier is the other method of propagation.

Types of dahlias On January 1st 1966, a new system of dahlia classification came into being. As far as Britain is concerned the National Dahlia Society is the authority for domestic classification. Periodically the society issues a classified list of varieties showing the type or size to which any named variety belongs.

1 To encourage a bushy plant, take out the growing point when there are six pairs of leaves.
2 Three or four 'breaks' or side shoots will soon appear.
3 Old tubers may produce too many shoots, some of which may be removed.
4 Mulching with peat or compost retains moisture and controls weeds.

There are now ten main groups, some being subdivided into sizes according to flower diameter. These include single-flowered, anemone-flowered, collerette, paeony-flowered and miscellaneous (containing such types as orchid-flowered). As far as the gardener is concerned the most popular groups are the decorative dahlia, with flat broad petals; the cactus

dahlia with petals that roll backwards to form a quill; semi-cactus dahlias, which have part only of their petal length rolled; pompon dahlias, like drumsticks, their flowers having blunt, tubular petals, under 2 inches in diameter; and the new group of ball dahlias which comprise all the previously known groups of medium and

1 Dahlias require support from an early age, and a stout stake should be put in at planting time to avoid root injury.
2 Canes connected by string can be used to enclose the plant as it grows.
3 Large plants can be tied up in a circle of stakes.
4 Cut Dahlias early in the morning.

large pompons and the similar, but larger, double show varieties, plus any globular shaped varieties which were previously small or miniature decoratives.

Size groups are: pompons one size only; ball dahlias are divided into miniature balls, 2–4 inches, and balls over 4 inches, decorative, cactus and semi-cactus dahlias are each divided into five groups; miniature, under 4 inches, small, 4–6 inches, medium 6–8 inches, large-flowered 8–10 inches, giant-flowered over 10 inches. Bedding dahlias are put where their flower shape designates them.

Exhibiting Cultural technique varies little from that described. Cuttings are

mostly used for propagation purposes; they flower during late August and the first half of September when most dahlia shows are held. Tubers of the large-flowered and giant varieties are started into growth in the greenhouse in mid-January, cuttings being taken for rooting during early March; plants, when put in the frame, later on, should be put into 5 inch pots by early May. All other varieties are started off in mid-February, the best plants being obtained from cuttings rooted during the end of March and the first three weeks in April. Those taken before this period will usually flower much too early for the shows. For show work, it is much better to grow at least six plants of each good variety, so

1

2

3

4

restricting the number of varieties to the capacity of the outdoor space available to grow them in. When garden plants are grown for display, distances should be 2 feet apart for pompons, 2½ feet apart for ball dahlias and all others, except the large and giant decoratives, cactus and semi-cactus which should be placed 3 feet apart. Many exhibitors mulch the giant varieties with manure in July; for the others, a straw mulch is used. During flowering it is common practice to protect the flowers of the large and giant varieties either with cones of builder's bituminized brown paper, or even by erecting metal uprights to support a roof made of corrugated vinyl clear plastic sheeting, giving the effect of an open-sided greenhouse.

Always cut the flowers the evening before and stand them in a cool, dark place in water over night. Large and giant blooms must have a 2-foot cane tied along the stem when it is cut to prevent the bloom toppling over in transit. Common methods of transport include oil or distemper drums with holes drilled round the edge to which the individual blooms can be tied; milk crates with one bloom in each corner resting in a water-filled bottle, or old butcher's liver tins especially for pompons. It is always advisable to carry flowers to a show in water.

The best way to pick up showing techniques is to join a dahlia society if there is one in your locality, or if not, to contact the National Dahlia Society.

Delphinium (del-fin-e-um)

From the Greek *delphin*, a dolphin, the flowerbuds having some resemblance to that sea creature (*Ranunculaceae*). Larkspur. The genus consists of annual, biennial and herbaceous perennial plants, mostly hardy and showy plants for border cultivation, with some dwarf species suitable for the rock garden.

Perennial *D. brunonianum*, 1–1½ feet, light purple, June and July, western China. *D. cardinale*, 2–3 feet, bright red, July and August, California, somewhat tender. *D. denudatum*, 2½ feet, yellow and blue, summer, Himalaya. *D. elatum*, 2–3 feet, blue, June, Alps to Pyrenees eastwards, the plant from which most garden delphiniums have been derived. *D. formosum*, 3 feet, purple-blue, August, Caucasus, Asia Minor. *D. grandiflorum* (syn. *D. chinense*), 1–3 feet, violet-blue or white, long spurred, summer, Siberia. *D. nudicaule*, 1–1½ feet, red and yellow, April to June, California. *D. speciosum* (syn. *D. caucasicum*), 6 inches–2 feet, blue and purple, summer, Himalaya. *D. tatsienense*, 1½ feet, violet-blue, July, Szechwan. *D. vestitum*, 2 feet, pale and deep blue, summer, northern India. *D. zalil* (syn. *D. sulphureum*), 1–2½ feet, lemon-yellow, summer, Persia, requires a well-drained soil.

1 Dahlia 'Lady Tweedsmuir' is a small-flowered decorative.

2 Dahlia 'Coltness Gem' is a brightly coloured flower of the collarette type.

1 Delphiniums are easily propagated from cuttings taken from the emerging basal shoots.

2 Each shoot is removed with a sharp knife.

3 Up to six cuttings can be taken from one strong crown. Make a slanting basal cut below a leaf joint and remove the lower leaves.

4 Insert the cuttings firmly into sandy compost and place in a cold frame.

5 Porous vermiculite is a good rooting medium.

6 The cuttings should root quickly.

7 When ready, plant them out and protect them with a small cloche until set.

8 and 9 Caterpillars of the tortrix moth may attack the growing points.

10 Take precautions against damage.

11 Slugs and snails are also very partial to the new shoots of delphiniums.

Cultivation Sow annual varieties in a sunny, open border in April where they are to flower, or in boxes of light soil under glass in March in a temperature of 55°F (13°C). Prick out seedlings when large enough to handle and transplant in the open in May. Perennials should be planted out in the spring or autumn in beds of rich, deeply cultivated soil; dwarf varieties are suitable for rock gardens. Feed with liquid manure in the early summer. Lift and replant every third year. Propagation of perennial varieties is by means of cuttings of young shoots in early spring, inserted in sandy soil in pots in a shaded propagating frame, or by seeds sown in the open ground in late spring or under glass in spring.

Cultivation of modern hybrid delphiniums

Fast-growing plants, delphiniums require a deeply-dug, rich soil with adequate drainage. A medium loam is preferable to a light sandy soil. Where the soil is light dig in deeply plenty of compost or old farmyard manure before planting and during the summer a mulch of garden compost is excellent. Nitrogenous fertilisers should be used with care as they may only result in producing weak stems. If the stems are cut back immediately after flowering a second crop of spikes may be produced, but these should only be encouraged with strong-growing varieties. Adequate moisture will be required to produce this second crop during what may be hot, summer weather. Slugs can be a menace with the tender young delphinium shoots, especially in the early spring,

so precautions should be taken with slug pellets or other repellents. Varieties that grow to about 4–5 feet in height are more suitable for small gardens than those that tower to 7 feet or more, and they are less liable to damage by summer gales. Pea sticks, brushwood or twigs can be used to support the young growths but these should be put in position around the plants in good time so that the stems grow up through them. This is often left too late with the result that the tender stems get broken when the sticks are being pushed into the soil. Staking for exhibition spikes must be carefully done, using one stout cane to each spike. When growing the large flowering varieties it is usual to restrict one-year-old plants to one spike and two-year-old plants to two or three

spikes. Pea sticks, however, provide adequate support for the lighter, less tall graceful belladonna types of delphinium, with their branching stems, which are also so attractive for floral arrangement. Exhibition spikes should be straight, tapering and well filled with large circular florets but not overcrowded, and bearing few laterals. The foliage should be clean, healthy and undamaged. Immediately spikes are cut they should be placed in deep containers filled with water and stood in a cool, but not draughty place. There they should remain for some hours or overnight. Each stem should be wrapped in a large sheet of tissue paper (30×40 inches) before being taken to the show. A further step to ensure that the spike does not flag is to turn it upside down, immedi-

ately before final staging, fill the hollow stem with cold water and plug with cotton wool.

As they are easily raised from seed the delphinium has been of much interest to the plant breeder who has produced many stately varieties. The era of immense spikes has passed its zenith and the trend is to develop a range of hybrids not exceeding about 4½ feet in height. These are of much more general use in gardens which are ever becoming smaller, but more numerous. From the glorious shades of blue the colour range has been extended from white and cream through pink, carmine, mauve, lavender, purple and violet. Now, thanks to the work done by Dr Legro, the celebrated Dutch hybridist, the range includes shades of cerise, orange,

peach and tomato-red. Our garden hybrids have been mainly derived from *Delphinium elatum,* a natural tetraploid species, but Dr Legro succeeded in overcoming the sterility barrier when he made a number of species crosses at diploid level, tetraploided the resulting plants and then successfully married them to hybrid elatums (see Plant breeding). The rediscovery of the white African species, *D. leroyi,* which has a freesia-like fragrance, also opens up pleasing possiblities. First crosses at diploid level have shown that this quality is not recessive, so hopes are high, but all this work takes time. In this country Dr B. J. Langdon has also been working on these problems and during the next few years we should see a truly remarkable range of hybrid delphiniums.

Recommended tall varieties 'Alice Artindale', light blue, 6 feet; 'Ann Page', deep cornflower blue, 5½ feet; 'Bridesmaid', silvery-mauve, white eye, 7 feet; 'Charles F. Langdon', mid-blue, black eye, 6½ feet; 'Daily Express', bright sky-blue, black eye, 6 feet; 'Janet Wort', pure white, 6½ feet; 'Jennifer Langdon', pale blue and mauve, 5½ feet; 'Mogul', rosy-purple, 6½ feet; 'Purple Ruffles', deep purple, overlaid royal blue, 5 feet; 'Royalist', deep blue, 6 feet; 'Silver

1 *Delphinium 'Daily Express'.*
2 *Delphinium 'Silver Moon' is one of the finest cultivars ever raised.*

Moon', silvery-mauve, white eye, 5½ feet; 'Swanlake', pure white, black eye, 5 feet.

Shorter-growing varieties 'Blue Bees', pale blue, 4 feet; 'Blue Tit', indigo blue, black eye, 3½ feet; 'Blue Jade', pastel blue, dark brown eye, 4 feet; 'Cliveden Beauty', pale blue, 4 feet; 'Naples', bright blue, 4 feet; 'Peter Pan', deep blue, 3½ feet; 'Wendy', gentian-blue, 4–5 feet, the most popular of the belladonna type.

The Pacific Hybrids raised in America, growing 4–6 feet tall, include 'Astolat', lilac and pink; 'Black Knight' series, shades of violet; 'Blue Jay', mid-blue; 'Cameliard' series, lavender shades; 'Elaine', rose-pink; 'Galahad' series, whites; 'Guinevere' series, shades of

132

1

2

*1 The dwarf Dianthus 'La Bourboulle' is
a low-growing plant only 3 inches high for
the rock garden.
2 Dianthus 'Martinhoe' is happiest when
planted in alkaline soil and exposed to full
sun.*

lavender-pink; 'King Arthur' series,
shades of violet-purple; 'Lancelot' series,
shades of lilac; 'Percival', white with a
black eye; 'Round Table', including
various colours as above; 'Summer
Skies', good true blues.

Dianthus (di-an-thus)

From the Greek *dios,* a god or divine,
anthos, a flower, divine flower, flower of
Jupiter or Zeus (*Caryophyllaceae*). A
large genus of hardy annual, biennial
and perennial plants, which falls into
three main groups: pinks, carnations and
dianthus proper. The greatest number of
species come from the Balkans and Asia
Minor, some from the Iberian Peninsula
and North Africa, a few from China and
Japan and two are natives of the British
Isles. Many plants in the genus are very
fragrant with a unique perfume, pre-
dominantly clove, strongest among the
pinks and carnations. Many of the dwarf
kinds are excellent rock garden plants;
the taller kinds are suitable for the front
of sunny borders, banks or other places.

Species cultivated (All are perennials unless otherwise stated) *D.* × *allwoodii*, 6 inches–2½ feet, very variable in colour, single and double, summer, hybrid. *D. alpinus*, 3 inches, rose-red, May and June, *D. arvernensis*, 4–6 inches, clear pink, May and June. *D. barbatus*, Sweet William, 6 inches – 1½ feet, perennial usually grown as a biennial, variable in colour, summer. *D.* × *boydii*, 3–6 inches, rose-pink, May and July. *D. carthusianorum*, 1–1½ feet, rose-purple, June to August. *D. caryophyllus*, carnation, clove pink, picotee, 9 inches–3 feet, red, but very variable in cultivation, parent, with *D. chinensis*, of annual carnations and Chinese and Indian pinks. *D. chinensis* (syn. *D. sinensis*), Chinese or Indian pink, 9 inches, annual, variable in colour, summer. *D. deltoides*, maiden pink, 6 inches, purple to crimson, spotted and striped, summer, native; vars. *albus*, white; *erectus*, rich red. *D. fragrans*, 1–1½ feet, white, summer, *D. gratianopolitanus* (syn. *D. caesius*), Cheddar pink, 1 foot, pink, May and June; vars. *albus*, white; *flore-pleno*, double or semi-double. *D. haematocalyx*, 4–6 inches, bright pink, July. *D. knappii*, 1 foot, pure yellow, July and August. *D. microlepis*, 2–3 inches, pink, flowers small, spring, scree plant. *D. monspessulanus*, 6–12 inches, pink, summer. *D. musalae*, 2 inches, bright pink, spring, scree. *D. myrtinervis*, 2–3 inches, pink, small, spring. *D. neglectus*, 3 inches, rose-red, June, dislikes lime. *D. nitidus*, 6 inches–2 feet, rose-pink, July and August. *D. noeanus*, 6–8 inches, white, July and

Dicentra spectabilis, the Bleeding Heart or Lyre Flower, is a summer-flowering hardy perennial for the sun or shade. Its pendant flowers resemble lanterns hung along a cord.

August. *D. petraeus* (syn. *D. kitaibelii*), 8–12 inches, pink, June; var. *albus*, 6 inches, double white. *D. pindicola*, 2 inches, deep pink, summer, scree. *D. plumarius*, pink, Scotch pink, 1 foot, variable in colour, May to July. Parent of the garden pinks. *D. squarrosus*, 1 foot, white, summer. *D. sternbergii*, 6 inches, rose-red, June, *D. strictus*, 6 inches, white, June and July. *D. subacaulis*, 3 inches, rose-pink, June to August.

Cultivars are numerous. Those of species described above include 'Ariel' ('Crossways'), 4–6 inches, cherry-red, July and August; 'Baker's Variety', 6 inches, large, deep pink, June and July; *D. deltoides* 'Brilliant', 6 inches, crimson, summer, and 'Huntsman', 6 inches, bright red, June and July; 'Charles Musgrave', 9 inches, white with green eye, summer; 'Cherry Ripe', 6–9 inches, rose-red, summer; *D. gratianopolitanus* 'Prichard's Variety', 4–6 inches, rose pink; 'La Bourboulle', 3 inches, deep pink, summer, and 'Double Ruby', 9 inches, summer; 'F. C. Stern', 6 inches, rosy-red, June to September; 'Fusilier', 3 inches, shining crimson, summer; 'F. W. Millward', 9 inches, double pink, summer; 'Highland Queen', 1 foot, deep rose, summer; 'Holmsted', 6 inches, soft pink, summer; 'Inchmery', 1 foot, soft pink, double, summer; 'Isolde', 9 inches,

pink and white, double, summer; 'Len Hutton', 1 foot, claret-red, edge laced white, summer; 'Little Jock', 4 inches, rose-pink with darker eye, semi-double, summer; 'Little Jock Hybrids', various colours; 'Margaret Curtis', 1 foot, white, crimson zone, summer; 'Mars', 4 inches, rich red, double; 'Spencer Bickham', 4 inches, deep pink, summer; 'Sweet Wivelsfield' (*D.* × *allwoodii* × *D. barbatus*), 18 inches, half-hardy annuals in many bright colours, summer; 'Windward Rose', 6 inches, light rose, summer.

Cultivation Sharp drainage and preferably a limy soil in a sunny position is needed for most dianthus, except perhaps *D. alpinus* which likes less sun and tolerates an acid soil fairly well, and *D. neglectus* which dislikes lime. All do well in sandy loam. When the alpine species are grown in pots in the alpine house a compost ensuring brisk drainage but at the same time sufficiently retentive of moisture is needed. Make it up of 2 parts of coarse sand or crushed gravel, 2 parts of leafmould or spent hops, 1 part of loam and a scattering of bonemeal. Cover the surface of the pots with limestone chippings for attractiveness, to present the plant as a perfect cushion and to guarantee surface drainage. Propagation is from seed for annual and biennial kinds and those species that set seed, or by pipings and cuttings taken immediately flowering ends, and inserted in pure sand round the edges of a pot and protected until rooting has taken place.

Dicentra (di-sen-tra)

From the Greek *di*, two, *kentron*, a spur, referring to the two spurs on the petals (*Fumariaceae*). Hardy herbaceous perennials formerly known as *Dielytra*. Fibrous and tuberous rooted, they generally transplant badly because the roots are as brittle as glass. The flowers are pendant from arching stems, like lanterns hung along a cord.

Species cultivated *D. cucullaria*, Dutchman's breeches, 6 inches, very divided pale green foliage, flowers pearl white, tipped yellow, May and June. *D. eximia*, 1–1½ feet, reddish-purple flowers, May and September and intermittently between; var. *alba*, white flowers. *D. formosa*, 1–1½ feet, pink or light red, long flowering period; 'Bountiful' is a larger-flowered cultivar, with deep pink flowers. *D. oregana*, 6 inches, flowers creamy-pink, tipped purple, May and June. *D. peregrina* (syn. *D. pusilla*), 3 inches, rose-pink flowers in June and July, a good plant for a scree in the rock garden. *D. spectabilis*, Chinaman's breeches, bleeding-heart, lyre flower, 1½–2 feet, flowers rose-red, May and June; var. *alba*, white, a garden hybrid (*D. eximia* × *D. formosa*), 9–12 inches has deep red flowers.

Cultivation Dicentras will grow in light shade or full sun provided the soil does not dry out the roots. A rich loam is best with shelter from cold winds. Some

protection may be needed in winter. Propagation is by root cuttings in March or April raised in a temperature of about 55°F (13°C). Division of plants is possible in spring, but difficult because the roots are very brittle. *D. spectabilis* is sometimes grown in pots and forced in a compost of equal parts of loam, peat and sand. The plants are kept frost free all winter and taken into a temperature of 55–65°F (13–18°C) during February and started into growth. Water, and feed moderately with a liquid feed once the buds begin to show. Forced plants should be planted out in the open ground after they have flowered.

Dichorisandra (di-kore-iss-and-ra)

From the Greek *dis*, twice, *chorizo*, to part, *aner*, anther, referring to the 2-valved anthers (*Commelinaceae*). A genus of herbaceous perennial plants from tropical America, grown mainly for their ornamental foliage, though some also have showy flowers. They need warm greenhouse treatment in cooler areas.

Species cultivated *D. mosaica*, 2 feet, leaves green with white veins and other marks, reddish-purple on the undersides, flowers bright blue, autumn, Peru. *D. pubescens*, 2 feet, flowers blue; var. *taeniensis*, leaves striped with white, flowers blue and white, Brazil. *D. thyrsiflora*, 4 feet or more, leaves dark green, flowers dark blue in a 6 inch long spike, summer to autumn, Brazil. *D. vittata*, 6–12 inches, leaves purplish-green with white stripes, Brazil.

Cultivation These plants are potted up in March in a compost consisting of loam, leafmould and peat in equal parts, plus a little silver sand. The pots should be in the warmest part of the greenhouse, where a winter temperature of 55–65°F (13–18°C) can be maintained, rising in summer to 75–85°F (24–29°C), when shading from sunlight should be provided. Water freely from spring to autumn, moderately only in winter and avoid draughts at all times. Propagation is by seeds sown in heat in spring, by division of the plants in March or by cuttings taken at almost any time, rooted in a propagating case with bottom heat.

Dipsacus (dip-sa-kus)

From the Greek *dipsao*, to thirst, a reference to the water-holding cavity formed by the leaves united round the stem (*Dipsaceae*). Teasel. Biennial or perennial herbs, stiff, erect, rough plants with spiny or prickly stems and fruits, some of which can be found wild in Great Britain. The heads have long been used to tease wool and raise the pile on cloth. They are also useful for use in dried flower arrangements for winter decoration.

Species cultivated *D. fullonum*, fuller's teasel, 3–6 feet, flowers delicate mauve in conical heads from June to August,

1

biennial. *D. sylvestris*, common teasel, 5–6 feet, flowers pale lilac, summer, a native biennial plant.

Cultivation Chalky, well-drained soils in open sunny situations are best. Propagation is from seed sown in the open in May or June. The seedlings are thinned and transplanted to their permanent positions in September to flower the following year. No staking is required, but the plants need plenty of room and should be set not less than 2 feet apart. The flower heads should be cut with long stems any time in the late autumn and stored, wrapped in paper or polythene to keep them dust free, in a dry place until required. They can be gilded or silvered for indoor or Christmas decoration. Left unpainted they dry to a pleasant autumnal brown.

Doronicum (dor-on-ik-um)

From the Arabic name *doronigi* (*Compositae*). Leopard's bane. Hardy herbaceous perennials, natives of Europe and Asia, early-flowering, with long-stemmed, daisy-like yellow flowers. The sap from the root of *D. pardalianches* is said to be poisonous. Doronicums last well as cut-flowers.

Species cultivated *D. austriacum*, 18 inches, golden-yellow, spring. *D. car-*

2

1 Dichorisandra thyrsiflora is a summer-flowering native of Brazil.
2 Dipsacus sylvestris, the Teasel, is an attractive everlasting perennial.

perennial plants.

Species cultivated *E. angustifolia* (syn. *Rudbeckia angustifolia*), 2–3 feet, purplish red, summer. *E. purpurea* (syn. *Rudbeckia purpurea*), purple coneflower, 3–4 feet, purplish-red, August. The crimson cultivar 'The King', 6 feet tall, is outstanding, with flowers 5 inches across from August to October. 'Robert Bloom', is a newer cultivar, 3 feet tall, with large, carmine-purple flowers in July and August. Other named cultivars appear from time to time in nurserymen's lists.

Cultivation Plant in autumn or spring in a deep, rich, light loamy soil and in a sunny position. Propagation is by division in spring; by root cuttings in February, or by seed sown in boxes of light soil in March in a temperature of about 55°F (13°C), or sown out of doors in a sunny position in April.

Echinops (ek-in-ops)

From the Greek *echinos*, a hedgehog, *opsis*, like, referring to the spiky appearance of the flower heads which resemble

1 Doronicum plantagineum excelsum, sometimes called 'Harpur Crewe's Variety', is a tall hardy perennial.
2 Erigeron 'Foerster's Liebling' is a semi-double form.
3 Echinacea purpurea, the Purple Cone-flower, is a fine border plant.

petanum. 2 feet, yellow. May and June. *D. caucasicum*, 1 foot, yellow, April and May; var. *magnificum*, flowers larger. *D. clusii*, 1 foot, yellow, May and June. *D. cordatum*, 6–9 inches, deep yellow, April and May. *D. orientale*, 1 foot, yellow, April, *D. plantagineum*, 2–3 feet, yellow, spring; var. *excelsum* (syn. 'Harpur Crewe') larger, bright yellow flowers, April to June. Other good named varieties will be found in nurserymen's catalogues. The new German hybrid 'Fruhlingspracht', or 'Spring Splendour', 1 foot, is an interesting introduction with double yellow flowers during April and May.

Cultivation Plant in the autumn or spring in ordinary garden soil in sun or partial shade. Propagation is by division of the roots in October or March. Doronicums are adaptable plants which may be moved or divided without damage even when they are in bud, provided this is done in moist weather.

Echinacea (ek-in-ay-se-a)

From the Greek *echinos*, hedgehog, referring to the whorl of prickly, pointed bracts close beneath the flower head (*Compositae*). A genus of two North American species of hardy herbaceous

a rolled-up hedgehog (*Compositae*). Globe thistle. Hardy herbaceous perennial and biennial plants for the border.

Species cultivated (All perennial) *E. bannaticus*, 2–3 feet, violet-blue globular heads of flowers, summer, Hungary. *E. humilis*, 3–5 feet, large blue heads, September, Asia; var. *nivalis*, white. The cultivar 'Taplow Blue' has bright blue heads in summer. *E. ritro*, 3–4 feet, steel-blue, summer, southern Europe. *E. sphaerocephalus*, 6 feet, flowers silvery-grey, summer, Europe and western Asia.

Cultivation Plant in autumn or spring in ordinary soil, in sun or partial shade. Echinops are trouble-free plants for a large border or for a wild garden. The metallic lustre of the flower heads keeps them decorative for a long time when dried. The species *E. ritro* is probably the best for this purpose. Propagation is by root cuttings or division in October or March, or by seed sown in the open in a sunny position in April.

Erigeron (er-ij-er-on)

From the Greek *eri*, early or *ear*, spring, *geron*, old, possibly referring to the hoary leaves of some species (*Compositae*). Fleabane. Hardy herbaceous, daisy-flowered perennials some of which continue to flower intermittently throughout the summer.

Species cultivated *E. alpinus*, 9 inches, purple and yellow, August, northern Alps. *E. aurantiacus*, orange daisy, 12–18 inches,

orange, summer, Turkestan. *E. aureus*, 4 inches, bright gold, spring onwards, North America. *E. compositus*, 3 inches, purple, summer, North America. *E. glaucus*, 6–12 inches, purple to pink, summer, North America. *E. coulteri*, 15 inches, white or pale mauve, summer, North America. *E. leiomerus*, 4 inches, small, lavender-blue, North America. *E. macranthus* (syn. *E. mesa-grande*), 2 feet, violet, yellow centres, summer, North Africa. *E. mucronatus*, 9 inches, white, deep and pale pink, summer and autumn, Mexico, a useful wall plant. *E. philadelphus*, 2 feet, lilac-pink, summer, North America. *E. speciosus*, 18 inches, violet-blue, summer, North America. *E. trifidus*, 2 inches, pale lavender, summer, North America. *E. uniflorus*, 4 inches, white or purplish, summer, North America.

Cultivars include: 'B. Ladhams', 1½ feet, bright rose; 'Bressingham Strain', (*E. aurantiacus*), 1–1½ feet, orange to yellow shades, May to July; 'Charity', 2 feet, pale pink; 'Darkest of All', 2 feet, deep violet; 'Dignity', 2 feet, mauve-blue; 'Felicity', 1½–2 feet, deep pink, large; 'Foerster's Liebling', 1½ feet, deep pink, semi-double; 'Gartenmeister Walther', 2 feet, soft pink; 'Merstham Glory', 2 feet, deep lavender-blue, semi-double; 'Prosperity', 2 feet, deep blue; 'Quakeress', 2

1 Erodium corsicum forms a mat of summer flowers.
2 Eryngium maritimum, the Sea Holly, is an everlasting hardy perennial.

feet, pale blue overlaid silvery pink; 'Quakeress White', 2 feet, white; 'Unity', 2 feet, bright pink; 'Vanity', 3 feet, clear pink, late flowering; 'Wupperthal', 2 feet, pale blue.

Cultivation Plant in the autumn or early spring in a sunny position in ordinary soil on a rock garden, or towards the front of the border for the taller varieties. *E. mucronatus* is a good plant for paved areas or steps, where it can seed itself between the cracks. Cut down stems after flowering. Named varieties are propagated by division of the clumps in the autumn or spring, the species by seed sown in the open in light soil in a shady position from April to June.

Erodium (er-o-de-um)

From the Greek *erodios*, a heron; the style and ovaries resemble the head and beak of a heron (*Geraniaceae*). Heron's bill. Hardy perennials, closely related to the hardy geraniums, or crane's bills. There are dwarf species suitable for the rock garden and taller border plants.

Species cultivated *E. absinthoides*, 1 foot or more, violet, pink or white, summer, south-east Europe, Asia Minor; var. *amanum*, 6 inches, white, leaves hairy white. *E. chamaedryoides* (syn. *E. reichardii*), 2 inches, white, veined pink, June, Majorca; var. *roseum*, deep pink. *E. chrysanthum*, 6 inches, soft yellow flowers, summer, grey-green, ferny leaves, Greece. *E. corsicum*, mat-forming, rosy-pink with

ber, a hybrid. *E. pandanifolium*, 6–10 feet, narrow, spiny leaves up to 6 feet in length, purple-brown flowers, late summer, Uruguay, hardy in the south and west. *E. planum*, 2 feet, small, deep blue flowers, July and August, eastern Europe. *E. serra*, 6 feet, leaves up to 5 feet long, narrow, with spiny teeth, flowers white to pale green, autumn, Brazil. *E. spinalba*, 1–2 feet, small bluish-white flowers, summer, Europe. *E. tripartitum*, 2–2½ feet, steel blue, with long bracts, summer, possibly a hybrid, origin unknown. *E. variifolium*, 1½–2 feet, leaves white veined, flowers whitish-green, summer, Europe. Cultivars include 'Blue Dwarf', 2 feet; 'Violetta', 2½ feet, violet-blue, both flowering in late summer.
Cultivation Plant in the autumn or in the spring, preferably in light sandy soil, although these plants are not particular, so long as the drainage is good. They like a sunny site and dislike cold, wet soil in winter. The thong-like roots require the soil to be deeply-cultivated. Generally speaking, eryngiums from South America are half-hardy or hardy in warmer areas only. They are, however, striking plants where they can be grown. Propagation is by seed sown in boxes and placed in a cold frame in April or May; by division of the plants in October or April, or by root cuttings.

Erysimum (er-is-im-um)
From the Greek *erus*, to draw up; some species are said to produce blisters (*Cruciferae*). Alpine wallflower. Hardy annual, biennial and perennial plants, closely related to *Cheiranthus*. Some are rather weedy, but others make good edging plants for a perennial border, or on gravelly banks and retaining walls.
Annual species cultivated *E. perofskianum*, 1 foot, reddish-orange, summer, Afghanistan.
Biennial *E. allionii* see *Cheiranthus allionii*, *E. arkansanum*, 1½–2 feet, golden-yellow, July to October, Arkansas and Texas. *E. asperum*, 1 foot, vivid orange, early summer, North America. *E. linifolium* (syn. *Cheiranthus linifolius*), 1–1½ feet, rosy-lilac, early summer, Spain.
Perennial *E. dubium* (syn. *E. ochroleucum*), 1 foot, pale yellow, April to July, Europe. *E. rupestre*, 1 foot, sulphur-yellow spring, Asia Minor.
Cultivation The alpine wallflowers like ordinary soil in dryish, sunny beds or in the rock garden. Propagation of annuals is by seed sown in April where the plants are to flower; biennials by seed sown out of doors in June in a sunny place, transplanting the seedlings to their flowering positions in August; perennials by seed sown in a similar manner or by division in March or April, or by cuttings inserted in sandy soil in August in a cold propagating frame.

Euphorbia (u-for-be-a)
Named after Euphorbus, physician to

deeper veins, summer, Corsica; vars. *album*, white, *rubrum*, clear red. *E. × kolbianum*, 3 inches, white to pink, summer, hybrid. *E. loderi*, 4–6 inches, white or pale pink, summer. *E. macradenum*, 6 inches, violet, blotched purple at base, summer, Pyrenees. *E. manescavii*, up to 2 feet, wine-red, summer, Pyrenees. *E. pelargoniflorum*, 1 foot, white, marked purple, summer, Anatolia. *E. supracanum*, 4 inches, white, veined pink, summer, Pyrenees.
Cultivation Plant out the taller varieties in March or April in ordinary soil and in a sunny position. These plants dislike acid soils. They very seldom need transplanting, although pot grown alpine species should be repotted in April every year, in a compost of equal parts of loam, leafmould, and sharp sand. Propagation is by seed sown in March or April for the taller species in a temperature of 55°F (13°C) and in July or August in a cold frame for the alpine species. Plants may be divided in April, and cuttings of dwarf species for the rock garden may be taken in May. The cuttings should then be rooted in a sandy soil, in a frame.

Eryngium (er-in-je-um)
From the ancient Greek name *eryngeon*, the meaning of which is obscure (*Umbelliferae*). A genus of over 200 species of hardy and nearly hardy perennial herbaceous plants, some with thistle-like

Erysimum rupestre is a spring-flowering rock garden perennial.

leaves. Some species are seaside plants in the wild. All are more or less spiny and in some species a feature is the glistening, metallic bluish sheen that covers the stem, the inflorescence, and the floral bracts. If the stems are cut and allowed to dry slowly they retain their colour and sheen, thus providing useful winter decorations.
Species cultivated *E. agavifolium*, 5–6 feet, narrow spiny leaves up to 5 feet in length, flowers green, hardy in milder counties, Argentine. *E. alpinum*, 1–1½ feet, upper parts tinged blue, summer, Europe. *E. amethystinum*, up to 2½ feet, deep blue shiny flower-heads and upper stems, July to September, Europe. *E. bourgatii*, 1½–2 feet, leaves marked grey-white, flowers light blue on spreading branches, June to August, Pyrenees. *E. bromeliifolium*, 3–4 feet, long, slender leaves, flowers pale green to white, July hardy in the south and west, Mexico. *E. dichotomum*, 1–2 feet, blue, July and August, southern Europe. *E. giganteum*, up to 4 feet, rounded blue heads, July and August, Caucasus. *E. heldreichii*, 1–2 feet, bluish, summer, Syria. *E. leavenworthii*, 3 feet, purple, summer, North America. *E. maritimum*, sea holly, 1–1½ feet, pale blue, summer to autumn, Europe, including Britain. *E. × oliverienum*, 3–4 feet, teasel-like, metallic blue flowers, July to Septem-

King Juba of Mauritania (*Euphorbia-ceae*). A genus of about a thousand species, widely distributed, mainly in temperate regions, showing immense diversity of form and requirements. They include annual, biennial and perennial herbaceous plants, shrubs and trees and succulent plants. The decorative parts are really bracts, often colourful, round the small and inconspicuous flowers. Some are warm greenhouse plants; others are hardy. The succulent species are mainly from Africa, most of them from South and West Africa. Many of those resemble cacti in appearance. For the purposes of this article the succulent species are dealt with separately. All euphorbias exude a poisonous milky latex when the stems are cut, which can burn the skin and eyes and which, in some species, is poisonous if taken internally.

Greenhouse species cultivated (all non-succulent), *E. fulgens* (syn. *E. jacquinae-flora*), 2–3 feet, small leafy shrub, scarlet bracts carried on the upper side of young shoots, autumn and winter, Mexico. *E. pulcherrima* (syn. *Poinsettia pulcherrima*), poinsettia, 3–6 feet, brilliant scarlet showy bracts in winter, Mexico. The modern Ecke hybrids are increasing in popularity. They include 'Barbara Ecke', fluorescent carmine bracts; 'Pink Ecke', coral pink and 'White Ecke', white. Some have variegated foliage. Even more popular now is the Mikkelsen strain, introduced in 1964. These, with shorter stems and with bracts in scarlet, pink or white, are a good deal 'hardier' in that they will withstand lower temperatures and fluctuating temperatures, yet will retain their bracts and remain colourful for 5–6 weeks.

Hardy *E. biglandulosa*, 2 feet, yellow, February and March, Greece. *E. cypa-rissias*, cypress spurge, ploughman's mignonette, 1–2 feet, small narrow leaves, small greenish-yellow flowers and yellow, heart-shaped bracts, May, Europe. *E. epithymoides* (syn. *E. polychroma*), cushion spurge, 1–1½ feet, rounded heads of golden-

1 Euphorbia epithymoides makes a colourful spring bedding plant.
2 Euphorbia obesa is distinguished by unusual plaid-like markings.

yellow bracts, early April to late May, Europe. *E. griffithii*, 1½–2 feet, reddish-orange flowers and bracts, April and early May; the cultivar 'Fireglow' has redder flower-heads, Himalaya. *E. heterophylla*, Mexican fire plant, annual poinsettia, 2 feet, scarlet bracts, annual, North and South America. *E. lathyrus*, caper spurge, 3 feet, large green bracts, biennial, Europe. *E. marginata*, snow-on-the-mountain, 2 feet, leaves banded white, bracts white, annual, North America. *E. myrsinites*, trailing, good when sprouting between stones of a dry wall, fleshy stems, blue-grey foliage, bright yellow flower-heads, late winter and spring, southern Europe. *E. pilosa*, 18 inches, usually grown in its form *major*, with yellow foliage, turning bronze in autumn, Europe, north Asia. *E. portlandica*, 9 inches, blue-green leaves, yellow bracts, British native. *E. robbiae*, 1½ feet, rosettes of dark green leaves, bracts yellow, good ground cover plant for shade. *E. sikkimensis*, 2–3 feet, young shoots bright red, bracts yellow-green, summer, India. *E. veneta* (syn. *E. wulfenii*), to 4 feet, nearly 3 feet across, very hand-some almost sub-shrubby plant, grey-green foliage, yellow-green flower-heads with black 'eyes', spring to summer, Europe. Other species and varieties of hardy spurges may be found in nurserymen's catalogues.

Succulent There are very many species in cultivation: some of the following are some of the more popular ones, *E. alci-cornis*, to 2 feet, leafless, spiny shrub, stem five-angled, Madagascar. *E. bupleur-ifolia*, dwarf, thick stem like a tight fir cone, large deciduous leaves growing from the top, pale green flowers, Cape Province. *E. canariensis*, shrub with small yellow flowers, many erect stems, 4–6 ribbed, short spines on edges, Canary Isles. *E. caput-medusae*, dwarf, thick main stem,

making a large head from which radiate many thin branches a foot or more long, small yellow flowers. There is a cristate or monstrous form with thin, flattened branches, Cape Province. *E. echinus*, shrub with erect stem and many branches, 5–8 angled, stems similar in shape to the cactus, *Cereus eburneus*, south Morocco. *E. obesa*, one of the most popular euphorbias, plants round when young, coloured like plaid, becoming columnar, closely resembling the cactus, *Astrophytum asterias*; this plant does not make offsets so must be grown from seed, Cape Province. *E. splendens*, crown of thorns, 2–3 feet, succulent, spiny, few-leaved shrub, pairs of round scarlet bracts, mainly in spring, Madagascar.

Cultivation: Greenhouse (non-succulent) species A good compost is 4 parts of fibrous loam, I part of decayed cow manure and a half part of silver sand. Young plants should be potted into 6- or 8-inch pots in summer and kept in a cold house or frame until September. Then feed regularly with a liquid feed and bring into a temperature of 60–65°F (16–18°C) to bring the plants into flower in December. After flowering, reduce watering and temperature until the soil is quite dry. In April cut back to two buds and start to water. Repot in May when the young shoots are about 1 inch long. Pot on as required; in high summer the pots can be stood out of doors or kept in a cold frame and brought in again in September. Propagation is from cuttings of young shoots taken in summer and inserted in sand in a temperature of 70°F (21°C).

Hardy species Any good garden soil suits them. *E. veneta* (*E. wulfenii*) prefers a slightly sheltered position, but the others should be given sunny places. The dwarf kinds are suitable for the rock garden, although *E. cyparissias* tends to ramp, spreading by underground rhizomes. Propagation of perennial kinds is by division of the plants in spring or autumn but *E. veneta* (*E. wulfenii*) is best increased

from seed or soft cuttings taken in early spring and inserted in a sandy compost out of doors or under a cloche. The annuals and the biennial, *E. lathyrus*, are easily raised from seed sown out of doors in April where the plants are to flower, thinning the seedlings later. *E. lathyrus* seeds itself freely.

Succulent species Most of these plants like a richer soil than some succulents but it must be porous. The compost should be made up from a good potting compost with a fifth part added of sharp sand, grit or broken brick. Repot in March every two years or when the plants become pot-bound; water well from April to September, keep fairly dry from October to March. Temperatures should be 65°F (18°C), in the growing period, 45–50°F (7–10°C) in winter. Plants should be given a light sunny place in the greenhouse or on a window sill. Propagation is by seed sown in early spring in pans of seed compost. Cover the seed with its own depth of soil, keep moist at temperature of 70°F (21°C), shade from sun but give light when seedlings appear. Large seeds should be washed well before sowing. Plants may also be propagated by cuttings which should be dusted with powdered charcoal to prevent bleeding, then dried and rooted in sharp sand and peat in equal

Gaillardia 'Goblin' with its crimson centre bordered with yellow is, like others of its kind, a gay and colourful border plant for late summer effect.

parts. Pot up the cuttings when they have rooted in compost.

Gaillardia (gal-ar-de-a)

Commemorating M. Gaillard de Marentonneau, a French patron of botany (*Compositae*). Blanket flower. A small genus of annuals and perennials, natives of America, with a long flowering period, useful for cut flowers. Somewhat untidy in habit, the long stalks fall about in wind and rain. Gaillardias need some twiggy stakes to help to keep the flowers clean and in full view.

Annual species cultivated *G. amblyodon*, 2–3 feet, maroon-red flowers, autumn. *G. pulchella*, 2–3 feet, crimson and yellow flowers, late summer and autumn, best treated as a half-hardy annual; vars. *brenziana*, double flowers in reds and yellows; *picta*, larger flower-heads. 'Indian Chief' with coppery-scarlet flowers is a named cultivar. In addition seedsmen usually offer mixed annual types under such names as 'Choice Double Mixed', 'Special Mixture', and 'Double Fireball'.

Perennial species cultivated All garden varieties originate from *G. aristata* (syn. *G. grandiflora*) and comprise a great range of colour from pale primrose-yellow to crimson and bold orange, all flowering from June to October. Named cultivars include 'Burgundy', 2 feet, rich wine red with a narrow yellow frill along the outer edges of the petals; 'Copper Beauty', 2 feet, smaller flowers of orange-yellow suffused with brown; 'Dazzler', 2 feet, yellow with brown-red central zone; 'Firebird', 2 feet, a vigorous variety with flame-orange flowers; 'Goblin', 1 foot, dwarf, yellow with red zone; 'Ipswich Beauty', 2½–3 feet, large deep yellow flowers touched with reddish-brown; 'Monarch Strain', 2½ feet, mixed colours; 'Nana Nieski', 1–1½ feet, red and yellow flowers on shorter stems; 'The Prince', 2½ feet, very large flowers up to 4 inches across, deep yellow tinged reddish-brown at the centre; 'Tokaj', 2 feet, wine-red and tangerine; 'Wirral Flame', 2½ feet, a strong growing variety, tangerine flowers tipped yellow; 'Yellow Queen', 2 feet, golden-yellow.

Cultivation A sunny border in a moderately light soil is ideal and the drainage should be good. The annual kinds are raised from seed sown in March in gentle heat and gradually hardened off and

planted in the border in late May to flower for the remainder of the season.

Twiggy stakes are needed for good effects, and bold planting repays in garden decoration. The perennial kinds prefer drier soils. Autumn and winter damp is their enemy, and if they do not survive, it is probably because of dampness. On the other hand, a sun-baked soil stunts the plants, so a mulch of leaf-mould or decayed manure in summer is helpful. Liquid feeds can be given to good advantage when the plants are coming into flower. Named varieties are best propagated from root cuttings taken at any time between February and April and put in a sandy box in the frame or greenhouse. Those that are taken early and do well may flower the first year. Alternatively basal cuttings taken from August to October, put into a sandy compost in a cold frame or under a cloche will soon get away. The plants can be divided in either October or March and any roots left in the ground at this time will sprout again.

Galega (gal-ee-ga)

From the Greek *gala*, milk, *ago*, to lead; the plant was used as fodder for cattle and goats and was thought to stimulate the flow of milk (*Leguminosae*). Goat's rue. A small genus of hardy herbaceous plants with pinnate leaves, useful for the border. The only species likely to be found in cultivation is *G. officinalis*, 3–5 feet tall with spikes of bluish sweet-pea-

shaped flowers in summer and autumn. It is variable in flower colour and has several varieties, including *alba*, white flowers, and *hartlandii* with larger flowers of a better lilac than the type. Cultivars include 'Duchess of Bedford', mauve and white; 'Her Majesty', clear lilac; 'Lady Wilson', blue and white flushed with pink.
Cultivation In the border, put the galegas well to the back or towards the middle in an island border so that their tendency towards untidiness can be masked by other plants. Light twiggy stakes thrust in early in the season so that the leaf growth can hide the support and at the same time use it, are the best. Ordinary garden soil is all that is required and the plant does well on poor chalky soils. It remains fairly compact, so does not need dividing too often. Propagate by division of roots in October or March or from seed sown in April out of doors in a sunny position, thinned and later transplanted. Self-sown seedlings usually appear in large numbers.

Gazania (gaz-ay-ne-a)

Commemorating Theodore of Gaza, fifteenth-century translator of the botanical works of Theophrastus (*Compositae*). Treasure flower. Half-hardy perennials from South Africa, with showy

1 Gazania splendens is a showy flower.
2 The Gazania and its hybrids, such as the one shown here, are half-hardy.

flowers, which open in the sun and close about 3 p.m. The species hybridize freely and gazanias have been much improved in recent years; seed is offered in red and orange shades and pink and cream shades, both groups coming true from seed. The ray petals are frequently beautifully marked with zones of contrasting colours. All flower from June to September.
Species cultivated *G. longiscapa*, 6 inches, golden-yellow. *G. pavonia*, 1 foot yellow and brown. *G. rigens*, 1 foot, orange. *G. splendens*, 1 foot, orange, black and white. This, which is probably the showiest species, will thrive out of doors in very favoured districts. Cultivars include 'Bridget', orange with black centre; 'Freddie', yellow with green centre; 'Roger', citron-yellow with a purple feathering at the centre; 'Sunshine', deep yellow with a brown ring dotted white. In addition, under the name *G. hybrida*, seedsmen offer seed in mixed colours, including shades of yellow, pink, red, brown orange and white, variously marked.
Cultivation Treat the gazanias as half-hardy annuals, sowing seed in gentle heat in February and hardening off and planting out in May. They are not fussy about soil and will do well on chalk, but must be given the sunniest possible positions. *G. splendens* can be propagated from cuttings in August, rooted in a cold frame. The rooted cuttings should be taken into a frost-proof greenhouse for the winter unless the frame can be made frost proof.

spring. *G. cachemirica*, 4–6 inches, pale blue, August. *G. clusii*, 1–4 inches, deep blue, spring. *G. dahurica*, 6 inches, dark blue, August. *G. farreri*, 4 inches, Cambridge blue flowers, August and September. *G. fetisowii*, 6 inches, purplish-blue, August. *G. gracilipes*, 6 inches, deep blue, summer; var. *alba*, white. *G. freyniana*, 4 inches, pale blue, July to September. *G. grombezewskii*, 9 inches, pale yellow, August. *G. hascombensis*, 1 foot, blue, summer. *G.* × *hexa-farreri*, 3–4 inches, deep blue, August, hybrid. *G. hexaphylla*, 3 inches, pale blue flowers heavily marked on the outside with darker bars, July and August. *G.* × 'Inverleith', prostrate, clear blue, August and September, hybrid. *G. lagodechiana*, 9 inches, blue, white spotted, August and September. *G. lutea*, 4–6 feet, pale yellow in tall, unbranched spikes, June to August, bog garden. *G.* × *macaulayi*, 4 inches, deep blue, September and October, hybrid. *G. pneumonanthe*, 6–9 inches, heather gentian, bog gentian or marsh gentian, a native, deep blue, heavily speckled outside with bands of greenish spots, August and September; var. *depressa*, shorter, more prostrate; 'Styrian Blue' is upright (1½ feet) with larger, paler flowers. *G. saxosa*, 4 inches, ivory-white, summer. *G. septemfida*, 6–12 inches, bright blue, July. *G. sino-ornata*, 3 inches, deep blue, September. *G. stragulata*, 2–3 inches, deep purplish-blue, August. *G. verna*, 3 inches, deep blue, April and May.

Cultivation It is impossible to generalize about the cultivation of gentians. Some, such as *G. cachemerica, hexa-farreri, hexaphylla*, 'Inverleith', *macaulayi, pneumonanthe, saxosa, sino-ornata* and *stragulata*, will not tolerate lime. Most require a well-drained, gritty soil containing leafmould or peat, but both *G. lutea* and *G. pneumonanthe* are bog garden plants. These two, together with *G. asclepiadea,* will grow in partial shade. Others require sunny positions and although they like ample moisture in summer, they dislike winter wet, hence the need for good drainage. All should be planted firmly. Propagation is by seed sown in March in a cold frame or in pans in a frost-free greenhouse. Seed sometimes takes a year or so to germinate so the compost must be kept moist. *G. sino-ornata* and *G. acaulis* can be divided in spring, but many other species resent this kind of disturbance.

By potting these up in spring, as an alternative to planting them out of doors, in a compost of 2 parts of loam to 1 part of peat and 1 part of sand, they will make fine greenhouse flowering plants in early summer.

1 Gentiana acaulis has deep-blue trumpet-shaped flowers in spring.
2 Gentiana lagodechiana flowers in late summer.
3 Gentiana sino-ornata is an effective bedding plant.

Gentiana (jen-te-a-na)
Named after Gentius, King of Illyria who first used the plant medicinally (*Gentianaceae*). Gentian. A large genus of hardy perennials. Most of those in cultivation are dwarf plants suitable for the rock garden, but a few are more at home in the border. Some of them are lime-haters.

Species cultivated *G. acaulis* (now con-sidered to be a hybrid), gentianella, 4 inches, glossy green tufts of pointed leaves, stemless, deep blue trumpet flowers, spring; vars. *alba*, white; *alpina*, compact form; *coelistina*, pale blue; *dinarica*, short-stemmed, clear blue flowers. *G. angulosa*, 2–5 inches, deep lilac, May and June. *G. asclepiadea*, 2–3 feet, willow gentian, dark blue flowers, July and August; var. *alba*, white. *G. brachyphylla*, 2 inches, deep blue flowers,

Geranium (jer-ay-ne-um)
From the Greek *geranos*, a crane, because the seed pod resembles a crane's head and beak (*Geraniaceae*). Crane's-bill. A genus of hardy herbaceous summer-flowering perennials with lobed or cut leaves, widely distributed over the temperate regions of the world. They are easily cultivated, free flowering, and some are useful rock garden plants, others good border plants.

Species cultivated *G. aconitifolium*, 15–18 inches, leaves finely divided, flowers white

with black veins, May and June. *G. anemonifolium*, 1–2 feet, pale purple, May and June, may need winter protection. *G. argenteum*, 4 inches, clear pink, summer, scree plant. *G. atlanticum*, 9 inches, purple, red-veined, summer. *G. candidum*, 1 foot, spreading, sprawling habit, white, crimson-centred, cup-shaped flowers, summer. *G. celticum*, 4 inches, white, all summer. *G. cinereum*, 6 inches, pale pink, June to August; vars. *album*, white; *subcaulescens*, cerise, dark-centred, May to October. *G. collinum*, 9–12 inches, red to purplish-violet, May and June. *G. dalmaticum*, 6–9 inches, pink, summer; var. *album*, white. *G. delavayi*, 1 foot, crimson, summer. *G. endressii*, 9–18 inches, light rose, June to October or later; cultivars include 'A. T. Johnson', silvery-pink; 'Rose Clair' salmon, veined purple; 'Wargrave Variety', deeper pink. *G. grandiflorum*, 1–1½ feet, blue, red-veined, spring to autumn; var. *alpinum*, 9–12 inches, deeper blue, larger flowered. *G. ibericum*, 1 foot, violet-purple, all summer. *G. kotschyi*, 9 inches, soft purple, darker veined, early summer. *G. macrorrhizum*, 18 inches, red to purple, all summer; var. *album*, white. 'Ingwersen's Variety', 9–12

True geraniums should not be confused with the Zonal Pelargoniums or Bedding Geraniums.

1 The summer-flowering Geranium atlanticum grows to 9 inches in height.

2 The long-lasting Geranium endressi blooms from June until October.

3 Geranium cinereum subcaulescens.

inches, rose-pink, is a fine cultivar. *G. napuligerum* (syn. *G. farreri*), 4 inches, soft pink, May and June, scree plant. *G. phaeum*, mourning widow, 18 inches, dark purple, May and June. *G. platypetalum*, 2 feet, deep violet, red-veined, June and July. *G. pratense*, meadow crane's-bill, 2 feet, blue, May to September, native; vars. *album*, white; *flore-pleno*, double blue; *roseum*, 1½ feet, rose-pink. *G. psilostemon* (syn. *G. armenum*), 2 feet, magenta-crimson, dark-centred, May and June. *G. pylzowianum*, 3–4 inches, clear pink, early summer. *G. renardii*, 9 inches, white, purple centred, summer. *G. sanguineum*, bloody crane's-bill, 6–24 inches, blood-red, summer, native; vars. *album*, white; *lancastriense*, 4 inches, pink; *prostratum*, 6 inches, rosy-pink. *G. sessiliflorum*, prostrate, white and purple, summer; var.

nigricans, dark leaves. *G. stapfianum* var. *roseum*, 4 inches, crimson-purple flowers. summer, richly coloured autumn foliage. *G. striatum*, 15 inches, pale pink, reddish veins, May to October. *G. sylvaticum*, 18 inches, purple-blue, summer, native; vars. *album*, white; *roseum*, rose-pink. *G. tuberosum*, 9 inches, purplish, May; var. *charlesii*, pink. *G. wallichianum*, 1 foot, purple, August and September; 'Buxton's Blue', deep blue with a white eye, is the cultivar usually offered. *G. yunnanense*, 12–15 inches, white, purple-veined, summer.

Cultivation In general the crane's-bills are easy to grow, although, as noted above, some of the dwarf species need scree conditions in the rock garden. The others will grow in any kind of soil; most of them do best in a sunny position although *G. endressii*, one of the finest, as it produces its pink flowers over a very long period, will tolerate a good deal of shade, as will *G. aconitifolium*, *G. macrorrhizum* and *G. phaeum*. The taller species are apt to look a little untidy after they have flowered, and benefit from a trim over, just above the leaves to remove the spent flower stems. This will often result in a second

Geum 'Lady Stratheden' is a popular double-flowered cultivar which is a useful addition to the border.

flush of flowers being produced, especially if it is done before the seeds ripen. Most species form clumps (a few are tap-rooted) and these are very easily propagated by division in autumn or spring. With those that form vigorous, wide-spreading clumps, such as *G. endressii* and *G. grandiflorum*, it is not even necessary to dig up the clumps in order to divide them; it is sufficient to cut away pieces from around the clump and replant these. Seeds may also be sown, either under glass in the cold frame or greenhouse, or out of doors, in March or April.

Geum (jee-um)

From the Greek *geno*, to impart an agreeable flavour, referring to the aromatic roots of some species (*Rosaceae*). Avens. A genus of hardy herbaceous perennials, some of which are useful border plants, the dwarf species good rock garden plants. Several are natives of the British Isles but those valued for gardens are from Europe, South America and the Near East.

Species cultivated *G.* × *borisii*, 1 foot, vivid orange flowers, May to August, hybrid. *G. bulgaricum*, 1–1½ feet, yellow flowers, summer. *G. chiloense* (syn. *G. coccineum* in some catalogues), 2 feet, scarlet flowers, summer. The species itself is rarely cultivated, but from it many cultivars, mostly with double flowers, have been produced. They include 'Dolly North', orange; 'Fire Opal', single orange overlaid with red; 'Lady Stratheden', golden-yellow; 'Prince of Orange', bright orange; 'Princess Juliana', golden-orange; 'Mrs Bradshaw', pillarbox red; 'Red Wings', semi-double, bright scarlet, late flowering. *G.* × *heldreichii* 9–12 inches, orange-red, summer, hybrid. *G. montanum*, 6–12 inches, yellow flowers, May. *G. reptans*, 6 inches, yellow, late summer. *G. rivale*, water avens, 1 foot, reddish, May and June, a native; 'Leonard's Variety', with pink and orange flowers, is a cultivar. *G. triflorum*, 9–12 inches, soft pink, July.

Cultivation Geums are easily grown in any good, well-drained garden soil. They appreciate sunshine, but the border kinds are tolerant of shade and damp conditions. Propagation is by division in spring or autumn or from seed sown out of doors in April or May, or in a cold frame or greenhouse in March or April.

Gypsophila (jip-sof-ill-a)

From the Greek *gypsos*, chalk, *phileo*, to love; the plants prefer chalky soils (*Caryophyllaceae*). Hardy annuals and perennials of great value in both the border and rock garden; the dwarf kinds also look well in pans in the alpine house. They are mainly natives of the eastern Mediterranean region.

Perennial species cultivated *G. aretioides*, 1 inch, a cushion plant for a sunny scree, with white, stemless flowers, spring. *G. cerastioides*, 3 inches, leaves in dense flat mats, white flowers much veined with purple, spring; var. *flore-pleno*, double flowers. There are various garden forms. *G. dubia*, mat-like dark green foliage, white, pink-flushed flowers, spring, good for walls or crevices. *G. pacifica* (syn. *G. oldhamiana*), 3–4 feet, dark leaves, pink flowers in cloudy sprays, August and September. *G. paniculata*, baby's breath, chalk plant, 2½–3 feet, light sprays of white flowers occasionally pinkish, June to August; vars. *compacta*, 1½ feet, *flore-pleno*, double flowers, a better form. Cultivars include 'Bristol Fairy', 3 feet, 'Rosy Veil' (sometimes called 'Rosenchleirer'), 9 inches, 'Flamingo', 2½ feet, large double pink flowers. *G. repens*, 6 inches, white flowers June to August; vars. *fratensis*, compact form, pink flowers. *rosea* 9 inches, rose-pink. 'Letchworth Rose', 9 inches, is a named cultivar.

Cultivation Plant both rock garden and border kinds in autumn or spring, the rock garden sorts in pockets containing a large amount of mortar rubble or limestone chippings. Although the border kinds like limy soil, they are tolerant of other soils but need a sunny spot with good drainage. They provide useful cut flower material when well grown. Propagation of the annual species and *G. repens* and *G. pacifica* is from seed. *G. paniculata* itself comes true from seed but cuttings of the varieties should be taken in June. These should be of young growth with a heel, 2 inches long, inserted in silver sand with gentle bottom heat. Commercially named forms are propagated by root grafting. Trailing species can be increased by cuttings or by division in spring.

Helenium (hel-ee-knee-um)

After Helen of Troy; according to legend the flowers sprang from her tears (*Compositae*). Sneezeweed. Hardy herbaceous perennials from North America, good for cutting and popularly grown for their late summer flowers. The disc of the flower head is very prominent, a characteristic of the entire genus.

Species cultivated *H. autumnale*, 3–5 feet, yellow flowers, July to October; var. *pumilum magnificum*, 3½ feet, golden-yellow. *H. bigelovii*, 4 feet, yellow and brown, July to September. *H. hoopesii*, 2 feet, yellow flowers, June onwards. There are many fine cultivars including 'Bruno', 3–3½ feet, bronze-red; 'Butterpat', 3–3½

feet, rich yellow. 'Chipperfield Orange', 4–5 feet, yellow streaked and splashed crimson; 'Copper Spray'. 3½ feet, copper-red; 'Crimson Beauty', 2 feet, bronze-crimson; 'Goldlackzwerg', 2½–3 feet, gold and copper-red; 'July Sun', 3 feet, golden-bronze; 'Moerheim Beauty', 3–3½ feet, glowing bronze-red; 'Riverton Beauty', 4½ feet, yellow; 'Riverton Gem', 4½ feet, crimson streaked yellow; 'The Bishop', 3 feet, buttercup-yellow; 'Wyndley', 2–2½ feet, chestnut and orange.

Cultivation Almost any garden soil is suitable, but a stiff loam is ideal. Plant in autumn or spring, the lower growing kinds towards the front of the border in clumps and taller growing varieties towards the back. Propagate by division or by seed.

Helianthemum (hel-ee-an-them-um)

From the Greek *helios*, the sun, and *anthemon*. a flower (*Cistaceae*). Sun Rose. A genus of evergreen and semi-evergreen shrubs, sub-shrubs, perennial plants and annuals, very free flowering. Numerous named varieties and hybrids are grown and four species are native plants.

Species cultivated *H. alpestre*, 1 foot, a tufted alpine, yellow flowers, summer, European alps. *H. apenninum*, 1 foot, spreading plant, grey leaves, white flowers, June, short-lived sub-shrub, Europe, southwest England and Asia Minor. *H. lunulatum*, 6–9 inches, sub-

shrub, yellow, summer, Italy. *H. nummularium* (syn. *H. vulgare*, *H. chamaecistus*), common sun rose, 6–12 inches trailing, yellow, June, July, Europe (including England). There are many cultivars including 'Beech Park Scarlet', 'Ben Attow', primrose yellow, deeper centre; 'Ben Hope', carmine shading to orange; 'Ben Ledi', dark red; 'Butterball', clear yellow, double; 'Jubilee', double yellow; 'Lemon Queen', lemon yellow; 'Mrs C. W. Earle', scarlet, double; 'Rose of Leeswood', rich pink, large double; 'The Bride', white; 'Watergate Rose', deep carmine, foliage grey-green; 'Wisley Pink', clear pink. *H. tuberaria*, 9 inches, herbaceous perennial forming tufts of brownish leaves with yellow flowers, July, south Europe.

Cultivation As the name implies, a sunny spot is essential for the sun roses. Ordinary soil is suitable and they are excellent plants for dry walls, rock gardens and sunny banks. Most are not very long-lived and need replacing in preference to cutting hard back to encourage new growth. Propagate from cuttings of young shoots in July or August, inserted in sandy compost. Once these are rooted they should be potted singly

1 Gypsophila paniculata flore-pleno is the double-flowered form.
2 The yellow-orange Helenium 'Wyndley' combines well with crimson 'Moerheim Beauty'.

into small pots and over-wintered thus. Because they do not transplant well, it is common practice to put them into their permanent positions from these pots, planting out in April.

Helianthus (hel-ee-an-thus)

From the Greek *helios*, the sun, *anthos*, a flower. (*Compositae*). Sunflower. A genus of tall, coarse-growing plants, annuals and perennials, gross feeders which dominate the border in which they are planted. *H. annuus*, the common sunflower, is a plant of some economic importance, as the seeds are fed to fowl and produce an edible oil, and the flowers yield a yellow dye.

Perennial species cultivated *H atrorubens* (syn. *H. sparsifolius*), 6–8 feet, golden-yellow, September, 'The Monarch', with flowers 6 inches across is a good cultivar. *H. decapetalus*, 4–6 feet, tough, sharply toothed leaves, sulphur-yellow flowers, August to October. Cultivars include 'Capenoch Star', lemon yellow, single, good for cutting; 'Capenoch Supreme', large, single, pure yellow 'Loddon Gold', double, rich yellow; 'Soleil d'Or', double, sulphur-yellow, quilled petals. *H. laetiflorus* (syn. *H. rigidus*), 5–7 feet, yellow, September and October. 'Miss Mellish', orange-yellow, is the best cultivar of this, but both are very rampant plants. *H. salicifolius* (syn. *H. orgyalis*), 6 feet, small yellow flowers. September and October.

willow-like leaves. *H. tuberosus*, Jerusalem artichoke, 6–8 feet, yellow, October.
Cultivation The best plants are grown in a stiff loam in full sun. Seeds of annual kinds can be sown *in situ* in April. To get the largest flowerheads, water and give liquid feeds occasionally up to flowering time. The perennials can be divided in autumn or spring. *H. laetiflorus* needs constant checking to prevent it from dominating the surrounding area and is best planted in rough corners where it will provide useful flowers for cutting.

Helichrysum (hel-ee-kry-sum)

From the Greek *helios*, the sun, *chrysos*, gold, referring to the yellow flowers of some species. (*Compositae*). Everlasting flower, Immortelle flower. A large genus of plants ranging from alpines to shrubs, bearing daisy-like flowers. Some are commonly dried as everlasting flowers. Not all are hardy.

Perennial species cultivated *H. arenarium*, yellow everlasting 6–12 inches, bright yellow bracts, summer, Europe. *H. frigidum*, mat-forming, silvery leaves, rather moss-like, white flowers, May and June, suitable for scree or alpine house, Corsica. *H. marginatum* (syn. *H. milfordae*), 3 inches, forming hummocks of silvery rosettes, white, spring. *H. orientale*, 9 inches, yellow, August, southeast Europe. *H. plicatum*, 1–3½ feet, silvery foliage, small yellow flowers, needs warm position, southeast Europe. Shrubby and sub-shrubby *H. angustifolium*, 1 foot, yellow, summer, southern Europe. *H. bellidoides*, mat-forming, white flowers, summer, useful rock garden plant, New Zealand. *H. fontanesii*, 1 foot, narrow, silvery leaves, yellow flowers in loose sprays, summer, rock garden. *H. lanatum*, 1 foot, leaves white of a flannel-like texture, yellow flowers, summer, useful for bedding, South Africa. *H. petiolatum*, 12–15 inches, white, summer. *H. rosmarinifolium* (syn. *Ozothamnus rosmarinifolius*), 6–9 feet, branches and leaves sticky, flowers white, small, produced very freely, June, Tasmania; var. *purpurescens*, 4 feet, purple. *H. selago*, 9 inches, white, summer, New Zealand. *H. splendidum*, 2–5 feet, shoots and leaves grey-white, flowers bright yellow, summer, South Africa. *H. stoechas*, goldilocks, 1–2 feet, leaves silvery-white, flowers yellow in heads to 2 inches across, summer, southern Europe. *H. virgineum*, 9 inches, cream, summer.
Cultivation Treat the annuals as half-hardy, sowing in gentle heat in March, gradually hardening off and planting out in May. Late sowings can be made out of doors in early May. The rock garden kinds all like dry sunny, spots with sharp

1 Helianthus 'Colour Fashion' is a cultivar with enormous blooms.
2 Helianthus 'Italian White' is a single-flowered form with white flowers and a yellow central zone.
3 Helichrysum virgineum has papery yellow flowers in summer.

drainage, and make good scree plants. The shrubby kinds are rather tender and need wall protection in all except mild localities. Plant in April and fasten the main branches to a trellis or wire support. Prune away unwanted branches early in April. They may be grown as attractive greenhouse shrubs in a gritty compost of sand, peat and loam. Propagation of the perennial species is by division in April or by cuttings in a cold frame in spring, and of the shrubby kinds from cuttings of half-ripened wood in August, inserted round the edges of a pot of sandy soil and put in a cold frame.

Heliopsis (he-le-op-sis)

From the Greek *helios*, the sun, *opsis*, like,

referring to the flowers (*Compositae*). Orange sunflower. Hardy herbaceous perennials resembling sunflowers, good border plants, especially since the more recent introduction of several good forms; useful for cutting from July onwards.

Species cultivated *H. helianthoides* (syn. *H. laevis*), North American ox-eye, 3–6 feet, rich yellow flowers. *H. scabra*, 3–4 feet, golden-yellow flowers; vars. *incomparabilis*, 3 feet, rich orange-yellow, semi-double; *patula*, 3½ feet, large-flowered semi-double, golden-orange; *zinniiflora*, 2½ feet, orange, double, zinnia-like flowers. *H. vitellina*, 3 feet, double golden-yellow. Cultivars include 'Golden Plume', double; 'Gold-greenheart', double, yellow with greenish centre; 'Light of Loddon',

branched growth. single. butter-yellow flowers; Orange King, bright orange; 'Sonnenschild,' 4 feet, golden-yellow; 'Summer Sun', clear orange-yellow.

Cultivation Plant in autumn or spring in sunny well-drained borders but never let the plants suffer from drought. An occasional liquid feed when the buds are swelling will help, or a mulch of compost or leaf-mould in May once the soil has warmed up is advantageous. Propagation is by division in spring.

Helleborus (hel-le-bor-us)

From the Greek *helein*, to kill, *bora*, food; some species are poisonous (*Ranunculaceae*). Hellebore. Hardy perennials, often retaining their leaves through the winter, with thick fibrous roots. All flower early in the year and the flowers are long lasting. Most of them have handsome, leathery, divided leaves, sometimes spiny. They are natives of southern Europe and western Asia.

Species cultivated *H. abchasicus*, 1 foot, flowers purplish-green, January to March; vars. *coccineus*, wine red, *venousus*, rosy-purple with dark veins. *H. argutifolius* (syn. *H. corsicus*), 2–3 feet, apple-green flowers in February and March which persist until mid-summer. *H. foetidus*, stinking hellebore, 2–3 feet, pale green flowers, the petals tipped purple, February and March, native plant. *H. guttatus*, 1½ feet, white flowers, heavily spotted with crimson inside, January to April, the parent of most spotted hybrids in cultivation. *H. lividus*, 3 feet, green flowers soon turning brown; doubtfully hardy. *H. niger*, 1½–2 feet; Christmas rose, 1 foot, white, saucer-shaped flowers with a boss of golden-yellow anthers; vars. *altifolius*

1 Heliopsis 'Light of Loddon' is an anemone-centred Sunflower, butter-yellow in colour and double.
2 Heliopsis 'Golden Plume' is a fully-double cultivar with long-lasting flowers of bright gold.

and *macranthus*, longer stems. 'Potters Wheel' is a fine cultivar. *H. × nigricors*, (*H. niger × H. corsicus*), 1½ feet, pale green, February, hybrid. *H. odorus*, fragrant hellebore, 1½ feet, greenish-yellow flowers with faint elderflower scent, March. *H. orientalis*, Lenten rose, 2 feet, variable flowers, purple, pink or almost black and often spotted with other shades, February to May. 'Albion Otto' is a white, purple-spotted cultivar. *H. torquatus*, 1½ feet, flowers purple inside and blue-purple outside, February to March, rather shy-flowering, leaves die down in summer. *H. viridis*, green hellebore, 1–1½ feet, pale green flowers, February.

Cultivation A well-drained, rich soil is best and although a shaded position is usually recommended, this is not essential, although partial shade is preferable to full sun. Once established, the plants like to be left undisturbed, although they quickly settle down if they are moved in winter with plenty of soil round their roots. In December, protect the flowers of the Christmas rose by a cloche or by mulching with peat to prevent the short-stemmed flowers from being splashed by soil. Plant in October or November, or March, 15 inches apart in groups, preparing the site well and incorporating some manure.

Plants can be forced in pots by lifting and potting up in October and maintaining a temperature of 40–50°F (4–10°C). Replant out of doors in April.

3 Helleborus x nigricors, a pale green hybrid, is slightly perfumed.
4 Helleborus niger is the well-loved Christmas Rose.

Propagate from seed or by division of roots after flowering.

Helxine (helks-in-e)

Derivation uncertain. Possibly from the ancient Greek name for pellitory, a related plant, or from the Latin *helix*, ivy, since the plant creeps (*Urticaceae*). Baby's tears. A genus of a single species from Corsica, *H. soleirolii*, a nearly hardy creeping perennial with insignificant flowers, grown for its attractive tiny, bright green leaves. It is quick growing and useful for dry walls and among paving stones in mild districts; it can become invasive but is easily blackened by frost; however, usually not all the plant is killed. It is particularly useful in cold greenhouses as an edging to staging or in pots or hanging baskets for conservatories. The plant grows about 2–3 inches tall. The varieties 'Silver Queen', with silver variegated foliage, and 'Golden Queen' with yellow variegation, are also attractive.

Cultivation Ordinary garden soil to which a little leafmould has been added at planting time is suitable. Dry banks, rock work, dry walls in sun or shade are all suitable positions. It makes a good pot plant for patios, conservatories or cold greenhouses in a compost of 1 part of loam and 1 part of leafmould. Pot in spring and water moderately. Propagation is easy by division in spring.

Hemerocallis (hem-er-o-kal-lis)

From the Greek *hemero*, a day, and *kallos*, beauty, referring to the life of the flowers (*Liliaceae*). Day lily. Hardy perennials from temperate E. Asia and S. Europe, very adaptable, flowering for many weeks, but with the individual funnel-shaped flowers lasting only for one day. There have been a bewildering number of cultivars both from America and from England and continental Europe with the result that the species have been somewhat neglected.

Species cultivated *H. aurantiaca*, Japanese day lily, 3 feet, orange-yellow flowers, July. *H. citrina*, 3½ feet, lemon-yellow, slightly fragrant flowers, July to September; var. *baronii*, larger flowers, citron-yellow. *H. flava*, 2–3 feet, orange-yellow flowers, June and July. *H. fulva*, 3 feet, vigorous, orange-brown, June to August; vars. *flore pleno*, double, *kwanso flore pleno*, double flowers and variegated striped foliage. *H. × luteola*, 3 feet, large, light yellow, June and July, hybrid. *H. middendorffi*, 1–1½ feet, rich yellow, fragrant, June. *H. minor*, 9 inches, clear yellow, reddish-brown on outside, June. *H. thunbergii*, 2–3 feet, light yellow, fragrant, July to September. There are many cultivars such as 'Ambassador', currant red, rich yellow centre; 'Apollo' bright apricot-yellow; 'Bagette', dark brown; 'Ballet Dancer', soft pink; 'Black Prince', purple-red; 'Bonanza', soft golden-yellow, dwarf; 'Display', bright red; 'Golden Chimes', golden-yellow, a miniature with well-branched growth; 'Hyperion', canary yellow; 'Morocco Beauty', very dark

purple with golden throat; 'Norma Borland', copper; 'Pink Prelude', flesh pink, yellow throat; 'Rajah', late flowering, orange, shaded mahogany and violet; 'Red Torch', cardinal red; 'Viscountess Byng', orange flushed rose, long flowering season. New ones appear each year; nurserymen's catalogues should be consulted for the latest varieties.

Cultivation Day lilies are most accommodating as to soil and position, provided they are not planted in full shade. They do not, however, give of their best in poor, chalky soils. Plant in autumn or spring, incorporating some compost or old manure. The plants will survive for many years unattended except for an occasional early summer mulch and a regular dressing of slug repellent.

Hepatica (he-pat-ik-a)

From the Greek *hepar*, liver, from a supposed resemblance of the leaves to that organ (*Ranunculaceae*). A genus of three or four species of low-growing hardy perennials, sometimes included in the genus *Anemone* and growing wild in woodlands over the whole of the north temperate zone.

Species cultivated *H. americana* (syns. *H. triloba*, *Anemone hepatica*), 6 inches, almost stemless deep lavender-blue flowers,

1 *Hemerocallis 'Orange Beauty' has clear bright yellow flowers.*
2 *Hemerocallis 'Black Prince' is a striking Day Lily.*

148

March; vars. *alba*, white, *rubra flore pleno*, double pink. *H. media*, 9 inches, offered in its var. *ballardii*, large clear blue flowers, spring. *H. transsilvanica* (syns. *Anemone transsilvanica*, *A. angulosa*), 3–5 inches, lavender-blue, slightly larger flowers than *H. americana*, spring. A pink form is sometimes offered.

Cultivation The leaves appear after the flowers and form good green tufts for the remainder of the summer and throughout the winter. Shady rock gardens or shrub borders in moist soil suit them best. They will tolerate lime in the soil. Propagation is from seed sown in pans of sandy compost in autumn or by division of the roots.

Heracleum (her-ak-le-um)
Named after Hercules who is said to have discovered the plant's medicinal uses, or after *heracles*, a plant dedicated to Hercules (*Umbelliferae*). Cow parsnip. Vigorous and coarse-growing hardy perennials suitable for the wilder parts of the garden. Two species are natives of Great Britain.

Species cultivated *H. mantegazzianum*, 7–9 feet, small white flowers in summer carried on enormous umbels, up to 4½ feet across, stems coarse and thick, ridged and bearing very large leaves, individually about 3 feet long, together making a tuft 10–12 feet across. *H. villosum* (syn. *H. giganteum*), cartwheel flower, 10–14 feet, white flowers carried in great flattened

1 *Hemerocallis fulva 'Kwanso' is a double-flowered Day Lily with orange blooms.*
2 *Heracleum villosum is a coarse-growing plant for the wild garden.*
3 *Hesperis matronalis, the Sweet Rocket or Dame's Violet, bears fragrant white to pale lilac blooms in early summer.*

umbels, rough stout stems and enormous deeply cut leaves.

Cultivation These plants thrive in any soil, but attain their best proportions in deeply-dug, manured ground. Plant in the autumn in the wild garden or on the margins of lakes and streams. If they are required for foliage effect, remove the flowering shoots once they appear in June because better foliage is produced if the plant is prevented from flowering. Propagation is from seed sown in March out of doors or from division of established plants in either October or March.

Hesperis (hes-per-is)
From the Greek *hesperos*, evening, when the flowers of some species become fragrant (*Cruciferae*). A genus of hardy plants including biennial and perennial species. Similar in form to *Matthiola* and *Cheiranthus*, and native to Europe and W. and N. Asia.

Perennial species cultivated *H. matronalis*, sweet rocket, dame's violet, dame's rocket, 2–3 feet, flowers fragrant in evenings, variable between white and lilac, May to July; vars. *candissima*, 15 inches,

pure white, *purpurea*, purple. Double forms have appeared from time to time but are rare in cultivation.

Biennial *H. tristis*, 1–2 feet, flowers ranging from white through brick red to purple, fragrant at night, summer. *H. violacea*, 6–12 inches, violet flowers, June.

Cultivation *H. matronalis* and its forms will thrive in an ordinary soil with a regular moisture supply, in full sun. Plant in autumn or spring. Plants do best if fed by mulching with well-rotted manure in May. Remove spent flower stalks in autumn. Double varieties, when obtainable, benefit from occasional extra feeding with liquid manure during summer, and replanting in alternate years. Single varieties can be raised from seed sown $\frac{1}{4}$ inch deep in a warm spot outside in April. Transplant seedlings in June or July. Double varieties can be perpetuated only by cuttings, 3 inches long, taken from July to September, and inserted in a shaded position outdoors. Later cuttings, taken in September or October, require glass protection. Transplant in March. Established plants may be divided in autumn or spring. Biennial species are raised from seed sown direct in sunny flowering positions in July. Thin seedlings to 9 inches apart. *H. violacea* can be established on stone walls where a roothold permits.

Heuchera (hu-ker-a)

Named in honour of Professor J. H. Heucher, 1677–1747, German professor of medicine, and a botanist (*Saxifragaceae*). Alum-root. A genus of hardy perennials with dainty, small, bell-like flowers in loose panicles which are produced over a long period, blooming on and off from spring through to autumn. The leaves are evergreen and the flowers are attractive when cut for indoor use.

Species cultivated *H. americana*, 18 inches, red flowers, summer. *H. × brizoides*, 1 foot, pink flowers, hybrid. This name includes various hybrids, such as 'Coral Cloud', raised from crossing *H. americana* with *H. sanguinea*. *H. micrantha*, 2 feet, pale yellow flowers, summer. *H. pubescens*, 1 foot, flowers deep pink marked with yellow, summer, foliage mottled with brown. *H. sanguinea*, coral bells, 12–18 inches, red flowers, summer; vars. include *alba*, white, *atrosanguinea*, deep red, *grandiflora*, larger flowers, coral scarlet; *rosea*, rose-red; *splendens*, dark crimson. *H. villosa*, 1–3 feet, small pink flowers, late summer. Cultivars include 'Bressingham Blaze', 2 feet, coral flame; 'Bressingham Hybrids' a fine modern strain with flowers from crimson to pink in all shades. 'Carmen', 2 feet, intense carmine-pink; 'Edge Hall', 2 feet, bright rose; 'Oakington

1 *Heuchera 'Scintillation' is a cultivar that provides colour throughout the summer months.*
2 *The flowers of the half-hardy greenhouse perennial Impatiens, Busy Lizzie or Balsam, are attractively marked.*

Jewel', $2\frac{1}{2}$ feet, deep coral rose, coppery tinge; 'Pearl Drops', 2 feet, white; 'Pluie de Feu', $1\frac{1}{2}$ feet, bright red; 'Red Spangles', 20 inches, crimson scarlet, 'Rhapsody', 20 inches, glowing pink; 'Scintillation', 2 feet, bright pink, tipped carmine; 'Snowflake', 2 feet, white; 'Sparkler', 2 feet, carmine and scarlet; 'Splendour', $2\frac{1}{2}$ feet, salmon-scarlet.

Cultivation Heucheras do best in light but rich, well-drained soil or in ordinary soil with peat added in full sun or partial shade. Plants do not thrive in clay. Plant in autumn or spring. Increase by dividing plants from March to May or by sowing seeds in spring under glass protection in a light compost. Seedlings are best grown on in pots for planting out when a year old.

Impatiens (im-pa-she-ens)

From the Latin *impatiens* in reference to the way in which the seed pods of some species burst and scatter their seed when touched (*Balsaminaceae*). Balsam, busy lizzie. A genus of about 500 species of annuals, biennials and sub-shrubs mostly from the mountains of Asia and Africa. The succulent hollow stems are brittle and much-branched. Few species are now cultivated; those that are may be grown in flower borders or under glass, or in the home as house plants.

Species cultivated *I. balsamina*, $1\frac{1}{2}$ feet, rose, scarlet and white, summer, annual, greenhouse. *I. holstii*, 2–3 feet, scarlet,

almost continuous flowering, half-hardy, greenhouse perennial; var. Imp Series, F₁, low growing, brilliant mixed colours, in shade and sun. *I. petersiana*, 1 foot, reddish-bronze leaves and stems, red, almost continuous flowering, half-hardy, greenhouse perennial. *I. sultanii*, 1–2 feet, rose and carmine, almost continuous flowering, greenhouse perennial. *I. amphorata*, 5 feet, purple, August, annual. *I. roylei* (syn. *I. glandulifera*), 5 feet, purple or rose-crimson, spotted flowers in profusion, summer, annual.

Cultivation Greenhouse plants are potted in a mixture of equal parts loam, leaf-mould and sharp sand in well-drained pots, during February or March. They do best in well-lit conditions and require moderate watering March–September, but only occasionally otherwise. They require a temperature of 55–65°F (13–18°C) from October to March, 65–75°F (18–24°C) March to June, and about 65°F (18°C) for the rest of the time. Pinch back the tips to make them bushy during February. Hardy species do well in ordinary soil in a sunny position, about 6 inches apart. *I. holstii* can be grown as a bedding plant and prefers light shade out of doors; it will tolerate varied temperatures. Propagate by seed in spring, sown in heat for the greenhouse species, and out of doors where the plants are to grow, for the hardy species, or by cuttings taken March to August, and placed in sandy soil in a temperature of 75°F (24°C).

Incarvillea delavayi is an early-summer flowering herbaceous perennial.

Incarvillea (in-kar-vil-le-a)
Commemorating Pierre d'Incarville (1706–57), a French Jesuit missionary to China (*Bignoniaceae*). A genus of about 6 species of herbaceous perennials, first introduced in the mid-nineteenth century, hardy or nearly hardy in suitable conditions.

Species cultivated *I. delavayi*, 2 feet, rose-pink trumpet shaped flowers in May and June. *I. grandiflora*, 1½ feet, large, deep rose-red flowers with orange tube, and throat blotched white, June–July; var. *brevipes*, a variety with crimson flowers. *I. olgae*, 2–3 feet, somewhat shrubby, with clusters of pale pink flowers and finely divided foliage, summer.

Cultivation A light, well-drained warm soil in a sunny but sheltered border is essential. Cold, stagnant moisture is fatal. Plant in March or April, and protect the crowns with bracken in winter. Liquid manure applied occasionally during the summer is beneficial. Propagation is by division of large plants in autumn or by seed in heat in March, or in a cold frame in April, transplanting outdoors in June. Seedlings may take 3 years to reach flowering size.

Iris (eye-ris)
From the Greek *iris*, a rainbow (*Iridaceae*). A large genus of bulbous, creeping and tuberous rooted perennials, some of which are evergreen. They are natives of the north temperate zone from Portugal to Japan. Among the most varied and beautiful of flowers, irises have been compared to orchids by some gardeners who, without the required greenhouse facilities for orchids, have decided to specialize in this most interesting genus. They may be divided into six main sections: tall bearded, dwarf bearded, beardless, Japanese, cushion or regelia and bulbous-rooted.

Tall bearded These are known best as the flag or German irises, flowering in May and June, and suitable for growing in ordinary, well-drained borders, especially on chalk. *I. flavescens*, 2½ feet, pale lemon flowers, almost white, probably of garden origin. *I. florentina*, 2½ feet, white flowers tinged pale blue on the falls, May; grown near Florence for orris root. This iris is the fleur-de-lis of French heraldry. *I. germanica*, common iris, 2–3 feet, lilac-purple flowers, May. Other forms slightly differently coloured.

Dwarf bearded Growing requirements similar to those of the previous section. *I. chamaeiris* (syn. *I. lutescens*), 10 inches, blue, purple, yellow or white, tinged and veined brown, April–May, S. Europe. Most variable in colour and growth, and frequently confused with *I. pumila*. *I. pseudopumila*, 6–9 inches, purple, yellow or white, April, southern Italy. *I. pumila*, 4–5 inches, almost stemless and much variation in colour, April, Europe, Asia Minor.

Beardless Species suitable for moist soils, margins of pools or streams: *I. douglasiana*, 6–12 inches, very variable in colour, violet, reddish-purple, buff, yellow white, May, leaves evergreen and leathery, California. *I. fulva* (syn. *I. cuprea*), 2–3 feet, bright reddish-brown, June–July, southern United States; var. *violacea* is a violet form. *I. foetidissima*, gladwyn iris, 2 feet, lilac-blue flowers followed by an ornamental seed capsule with breaks to expose brilliant orange seeds in winter, Britain. *I. ochroleuca*, 4–5 feet, creamy-white, with orange blotch, June–July, western Asia Minor. *I. pseudacorus*, yellow flag or water flag, 2–3 feet, bright orange-yellow, May–June, Europe including Britain; *variegata*, with variegated leaves. *I. sibirica*, 2–3 feet, blue, purple, grey or occasionally white, June–July, invaluable for waterside or border planting, central Europe and Russia. *I. versicolor*, 2 feet, claret-purple, May–June, N. America.

Species requiring sunny borders: *I. chrysographes*, 1½ feet, deep violet with golden veins, for a moist place, June, Yunnan. *I. innominata*, 4–6 inches, golden-buff, veined light brown, and there are lavender, apricot and orange-yellow forms, Oregon; 'Golden River' is an attractive named variety. *I. japonica* (syn. *I. fimbriata*), 1–1½ feet, lilac, spotted yellow and white, evergreen, sage-green leaves, April, Japan, China. The form 'Ledger's Variety' is said to be

1

2

3

5

4

hardier than the type. *I. tectorum*, 1–1½ feet, bright lilac, flecked and mottled with deeper shades. There is a white form. Lift and divide after second year's flowering, May–June, Japan. *I. unguicularis* (syn. *I. stylosa*), 1 foot, lavender, blue, November–March, ideal in dry poor soil against south wall. One of the gems of winter. Japanese: These species thrive in 2–4 inches of water and do well in moist soil or on the margins of ponds. *I. kaempferi*, clematis iris, 2 feet, varying shades lilac, pink, blue and white, June and July. *I. laevigata*, 2 feet, deep blue, June and July.

Cushion or Regelia Very beautiful, easily grown hardy irises, doing best in a calcareous soil in a sunny sheltered site. *I. hoogiana*, 1½–2 feet, soft lavender-blue flowers, early May, Turkestan. *I. korolkowii*, 1–1½ feet, chocolate-brown markings on creamy-white ground, May, Turkestan.

Bulbous-rooted Other than the Spanish and English iris which may be planted on sunny borders, this section includes choice kinds which may be grown in pots in the alpine house or in the rock garden. *I. bucharica*, 1–1½ feet, golden-yellow falls and small white standards, April, Bokhara. *I. bakeriana*, 4–6 inches, deep violet, with a touch of yellow on the falls, January–February, Asia Minor.

I. danfordiae, short, bright yellow, January and February. A gem but rarely survives to flower a second year. *I. filifolia*, 1–1½ feet, deep purple, June, southern Spain. *I. graeberiana*, 6–8 inches, mauve falls marked cobalt-blue and whitish veins. For a sunny position, April, Turkestan. *I. histrioides*, short, dark blue, purple, January, Asia Minor. *I. reticulata*, 6 inches, violet, purple and yellow, February, Caucasus. *I. winogradowii*, 3–4 inches, light yellow, January–February, Caucasus. *I. xiphioides*, English iris, 1–2 feet, various colours, June–July, Pyrenees. *I. xiphium*,

1 The blue-flowered Iris unguicularis blooms in winter.
2 Iris douglasiana produces flowers in a wide range of colours.
3 Iris laevigata flowers in summer.
4 Iris xiphium is the Spanish Iris.
5 Iris longipetala.
6 Iris reticulata.
7 Iris histroides.
8 The deep blue form of Iris reticulata.
9 Divide clumps of Iris after they flower.
10 Cut the leaves back to about 9 inches, making 'fans'.
11 Set the plant into a hole, leaving the rhizome above ground to get the light.

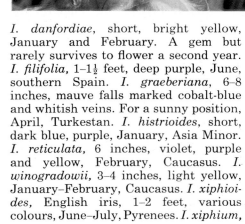

Spanish iris, 1–2 feet, various colours, white, yellow or blue, with orange patch on blade, May–June, south Europe and North Africa.

Miscellaneous *I. cristata*, 4–6 inches, pale lilac with deep yellow crest. A delightful miniature for a sink garden in full sun, May–June, eastern United States. *I. vicaria* (syn. *I. magnifica*), 2 feet, white, tinged pale blue, April, central Asia. Other species are offered by specialist nurseries.

Cultivation The most widely grown of this large and varied family are the tall bearded irises. These colourful hybrids have been developed by plant breeders from the long-cultivated, dark blue *Iris germanica*. This type of iris is one of the few plants that may be lifted, divided and replanted soon after it has finished flowering, preferably in July. By planting in July the fleshy rhizomes will soon make new roots in the warm soil and will be firmly established before the winter.

Choose a sunny well-drained site, and if planting in wet, heavy soil is unavoidable, build the bed up a few inches above the surrounding level. On light soil, add leafmould or peat, but manure should be used sparingly, for it will only induce soft growth. These irises like lime, so if the soil is deficient in this, work in some builder's rubble. Bonemeal and bonfire ash are both useful for feeding irises. It is important not to bury the rhizome when planting. In nature, it grows along the surface of the soil, and if the rhizome is planted too deep a year's flowering may be lost. On light soil it is necessary to plant somewhat deeper, otherwise the plants are liable to topple over. It is usual at planting time to cut back the sword-like leaves, but this can be overdone, for the plants do depend, to some extent, on the leaves to assist them in making new roots; drastic cutting back should be avoided. When planting, leave ample room between each variety so that the rhizomes will not require lifting and dividing for three years.

For those who do not know one variety from another the best way to start a collection is to buy 12 varieties in 12 different shades of colour from a specialist iris nursery. With some 300 different named varieties listed in iris catalogues it will be an easy matter to obtain individual varieties to increase the selection. Among outstanding modern hybrids are: 'Berkeley Gold', a handsome tall deep gold; 'Blue Shimmer', ivory-white dotted with clear blue; 'Caprilla', yellow-bronze falls and blue-lavender standards; 'Chivalry', a ruffled medium blue; 'Cliffs of Dover', creamy-white; 'Dancer's Vale', with pale violet dottings on a white ground; 'Desert Song', a ruffled cream and primrose; 'Enchanter's Violet', violet; 'Golden Alps', white and yellow; 'Green Spot'; 'Harriet Thoreau', a large orchid-pink self; 'Inca Chief', a ruffled bronze-gold; 'Jane Phillips', intense pale blue; 'Kangchenjunga', pure white; 'New Snow', pure white with bright yellow beard; 'Pegasus', a tall white: 'Party Dress', a ruffled flamingo-pink; 'Patterdale', a clear pale blue; 'Regal Gold', glowing yellow; 'South Pacific', a pale shimmering blue: 'Total Eclipse', almost black with a similar coloured beard, and many Benton hybrids raised in Suffolk by Sir Cedric Morris. Another amateur iris breeder in this country, the late Mr H. J. Randall, made crosses of many of the best American hybrids with remarkable success.

Waterside irises are charming beside a formal pool or in a wild garden. The June-flowering *I. sibirica* and its hybrids have long been appreciated. They thrive in boggy conditions, although they will grow in a border provided the soil is deeply dug, reasonably moist and in partial shade. In the bog garden they flower happily in full sun. Good hybrids include; 'Heavenly Blue', 'Perry's Blue' with china-blue flowers on 3-foot stems, and 'Eric the Red' with heavily veined wine-red flowers. The elegant *I. kaempferi*, of Japanese origin, is in all its glory

in July. The flowers are large and handsome, with blends of colour of great charm. There are both single and double varieties in shades of velvety purple, rosy-lilac, plum and white shaded blue, for instance, 'Morning Mist', purple, flecked grey, and a double white, 'Moonlight Waves'. They must have lime-free soil and, for that matter, lime-free water. They like a rich loam with ample moisture during the growing season but moderately dry roots during the rest of the year. Another handsome Japanese species, *I. laevigata*, is sometimes confused with the clematis-flowered *I. kaempferi*. The large, brilliant, violet-blue flowers of *I. laevigata* are borne on 2-foot stems at intervals from June to September, above a mass of deep green, arching foliage. It does well in a bog garden or in water up to 4 inches deep. The North American, claret-coloured water-flag, *I. versicolor,* is also a good waterside plant.

These waterside irises are best propagated by division of the roots in the spring, although it can be done in the autumn if necessary. They may also be raised from seed sown in a cold frame in the autumn in well-drained soil, covering them with $\frac{1}{2}$ an inch of sifted soil. They should germinate in the spring, but some may prove erratic, so do not discard the pans in too much of a hurry.

The bulbous irises are quite distinct from the tall bearded and waterside irises. They are admirable for the rock garden or in a sunny well-drained border containing plenty of sharp sand or grit. Plant the bulbs in September. The miniature varieties which flower in February and March may also be grown in pans in a cold greenhouse or frame—the violet-blue *I. reticulata*, and its pale blue variety 'Cantab', *I. histrioides major,* bright blue with yellow markings, and bright yellow *I. danfordiae,* are particularly suitable for this purpose. The taller growing Dutch, Spanish and English irises are easily grown in any reasonably good soil in the garden and are most useful for cutting. Plant the bulbs in October about 4 inches deep in a sunny position. The Dutch irises produced by crossing *I. xiphium* with other bulbous species, flower in June, followed a little later by the Spanish and then the English. The English irises prefer a cool moist position and should be left undisturbed for three or four years before being lifted and divided. Dutch and Spanish irises should be lifted every year after the foliage has died down and stored until planting time. There is a good selection of named varieties to be found in bulb catalogues.

By making a careful selection of the many different types of iris, including the April-flowering Juno species and hybrids which have brittle swollen roots needing careful handling, it is possible to have irises of one sort or another in flower for many months of the year.

1 Iris 'Caprilla'.
2 Iris 'Regal Gold'.
3 Iris 'Jane Phillips'.
4 Japanese Iris kaempferi.
5 Iris 'Patterdale'.
6 Iris 'Pegasus'.

Kniphofia (nif-of-e-a)

Commemorating a German professor of medicine, Johann Hieronymus Kniphof, 1704–63 (*Liliaceae*). Red-hot pokers. These herbaceous perennials from South and East Africa and Madagascar are tolerant of wind, but dislike badly-drained soil. They are often seen in seaside gardens where the milder climate suits them well, as they are not altogether hardy and need protection in the winter in colder districts. There are many good garden hybrids and and varieties of *K. uvaria* in colours ranging from pure yellow through to reds, some of them being shaded in the spikes. The leaves are strap-shaped.

Species cultivated *K. caulescens*, 4 feet, buff changing to red, autumn. *K. foliosa*, 3 feet, yellow tinged with red, late summer. *K. galpinii*, 2–3 feet, slender plant, orange-red flowers, late autumn. *K. macowanii*, 2 feet, slender plant, orange-red, late summer. *K. nelsonii*, 2 feet, bright scarlet tinged orange, autumn. *K. northiae*, 2 feet, foliage grey-green, flowers yellow at base changing to red up the spikes, October. *K. pumila*, 4 feet, grey-green foliage, orange-red flowers, to orange-yellow and finally yellowish-green. August. *K. uvaria*, 4 feet, coral red, late summer. A hardy species from which many hybrids and cultivars have been developed; they include 'Buttercup', 3½ feet, yellow; × *erecta*, 4 feet, orange-scarlet; 'Maid of Orleans', 4 feet, ivory-white; 'Mount Etna', 5 feet, large terra-cotta spikes; 'Royal Standard', 3 feet, deep gold; 'Yellow Hammer', 3 feet, yellow to orange.

Cultivation Plant in autumn or spring, choosing an open sunny position. Divide the clumps in spring as it becomes necessary. Kniphofias prefer a rich soil. Propagate by seed, but seedlings will not reach flowering size for about three years and then may not breed true.

Lathyrus (lath-eye-rus)

Lathyrus is the ancient Greek name for the pea (*Leguminaceae*). A genus of hardy

1 Kniphofia 'Springtime' is typical of the striking and attractive half-hardy Red Hot Pokers.
2 Kniphofias are especially effective when grown in sturdy clumps in the late summer garden.
3 Kniphofia uvaria 'Buttercup' is a fine, hardy cultivar with yellow flower spikes reaching 3½ feet in height.

annual and herbaceous perennial climbers, from temperate zones and tropical mountains.

Perennial species cultivated *L. grandiflorus*, 5 feet, rosy carmine, summer, southern Europe. *L. latifolius*, 10 feet, everlasting pea, bright carmine, August; var. *albus*, white flowers. *L. magellanicus*, 8 feet, bluish-purple, summer to early autumn, Straits of Magellan. *L. pubescens*, 5 feet, pale blue, mid to late summer, Chile. *L. rotundifolius*, 6 feet, pink, summer, Asia Minor. *L. splendens*, sub-shrub, 1 foot, carmine summer, California. *L. undulatus*, 3 feet, rosy-purple, early summer, Turkey. *L. vernus*, 1 foot, purple and blue, spring, Europe.

Cultivation Any good rich soil is suitable. Plant the perennials in the autumn or spring, choosing a sunny position where the plants can climb over a trellis, wall or other support. These plants need a lot of water in the growing season and they should be fed during the summer with liquid manure or a balanced fertilizer. In the autumn cut down the stems and top-dress with manure in the spring. The perennial species are propagated by seeds or by division of the roots in the spring.

Leptosyne (lep-to-sy-knee)
From the Greek *leptos*, slender, describing the growth of these plants (*Compositae*). A small genus of hardy annuals and perennials that deserve to be better known, as they are showy in the garden and good as cut flowers. They are very similar in appearance to *Coreopsis*, to which they are closely related, and are natives of America.

Species cultivated Annual: *L. calliopsidea*, 1½ feet, yellow, late summer. *L. douglasii*, 1 foot. *L. stillmanii*, 1½ feet, bright yellow autumn. Perennial: *L. maritima*, 1 foot, yellow, autumn.

Cultivation Any ordinary soil will suit these plants but they like an open, sunny position. Sow seeds of the annual species in the spring in the open ground where the plants are to flower, or sow them under glass and transplant the seedlings to their flowering positions in late May or early June. The perennial species can be planted in the autumn or spring and they are either raised from seed or from division of the plants in the autumn or spring. Cuttings of young growths can be taken and rooted in a frame.

Ligularia (li-gu-lair-ee-a)
From the Latin *ligula*, a strap, referring to the strap-shaped ray florets (*Compositae*). A genus of about 80 species of herbaceous perennials, formerly included in *Senecio* but now placed in their own genus. These handsome members of the

daisy family from the temperate zones of the Old World grow best in damp situations. In recent years they have been considerably hybridized and some striking varieties have been obtained.

Species cultivated *L. dentata* (syn. *L. clivorum*), 4–5 feet, orange-yellow, July–September, China; cultivars include 'Desdemona', large, heart-shaped leaves with a purple tinge, orange flowers: 'Gregynog Gold', 4 feet, large rounded leaves, orange-yellow flowers in pyramidal spikes; 'Othello', leaves veined purple, and large orange flowers. *L. × hessei*, 5 feet, flowers orange, August–September. *L. hodgsonii*, 1½ feet, rounded leaves, orange-yellow flowers. *L. japonica*, 3–5 feet, orange-yellow flowers, July, Japan. *L. przewalskii*, 3–4 feet, stems purple tinged, deeply cut leaves, tapering spikes of small yellow flowers, June and July; 'The Rocket', 5 feet, orange, August, is a cultivar. *L. tussilaginea*, 1–2 feet, softly

1 Lathyrus latifolius, the Everlasting Pea, and 2 Lathyrus undulatus are both excellent perennial climbers.

hairy stems, light yellow flowers, August, Japan. *L. veitchiana*, 4–6 feet, leaves large, roughly triangular, yellow flowers in long flat spikes, July and August. *L. wilsoniana*, 5–6 feet, similar to *L. veitchiana*, flower spikes more branched, June.

Cultivation These hardy perennials grow best in a good loamy soil, if possible fairly moist. They do well in slight shade; otherwise any position will suit them. *L. japonica* and *L. dentata* are most successful at the edge of a pool or stream. Mulching occasionally with rotted garden compost or similar material is beneficial. They are propagated by dividing the crowns in autumn or spring, by taking cuttings in spring or by sowing seed in spring in the cold greenhouse or out of doors in early summer.

Limonium (li-mo-nee-um)

From the Greek *leimon*, a meadow, because certain species are found growing in salt marshes (*Plumbaginaceae*). Sea lavender. A genus of annuals, perennial herbaceous plants and sub-shrubs, hardy, half-hardy and tender. Once known as *Statice*, these plants are natives of all parts of the world, particularly coasts and salt marshes. The numerous small flowers, usually borne in branched spikes, are easily dried and are much used for long-lasting flower arrangements. All flower in summer.

Species cultivated Perennial: *L. altaicum*, 15 inches, blue. *L. bellidifolium*, 9 inches, white or blue, Europe including Britain. *L. dumosum*, 2 feet, silvery-grey. *L. incanum*, 1½ feet, crimson, Siberia; vars. *album*, dwarf, white; *nanum*, 6 inches, dwarf; *roseum*, 6 inches, rosy-pink. *L. latifolium*, 2–3 feet, blue, south Russia. *L. minutum*, 6 inches, violet, Mediterranean area. *L. peticulum*, 4 inches, white. *L. puberulum*, 6 inches, violet to white, hardy in milder areas only, Canaries. *L. sinense*, 1 foot, yellow, China. *L. tataricum*, 1 foot, red and white, southeast Europe and Siberia. *L. vulgare*, 1 foot, purple-blue flowers, Europe including Britain.

Cultivation All the limoniums prefer well-drained, sandy loam and a sunny position. The outdoor species are suitable for borders, the dwarf kinds for rock gardens. Plant the hardy perennials in spring and the annuals in late May. Greenhouse species are potted in the spring and fed occasionally with a weak liquid fertilizer. They require a summer temperature of 55–65°F (13–18°C) and 40–50°F (4–10°C) in the winter. Propagation is by seeds sown in sandy soil in early spring, when the temperature should be 55–60°F (13–16°C). Root cuttings of the perennials can be taken in late winter or early spring and rooted in a cold frame.

1 Ligularia przewalskii bears spikes of yellow spikes of flowers with purplish stems and deeply cut leaves.
2 Limonium latifolium is the Sea Lavender.

Linum (li-num)

From the old Greek name, *linon*, used by Theophrastus (*Linaceae*). Flax. This important genus contains, besides the economically valuable annual which supplies flax and linseed oil, a number of very decorative garden plants. The flower colour which is characteristic of the genus is a fine pale blue, but there are a number of shrubs with yellow blossoms and a lovely scarlet annual. The genus is widely distributed in the temperate regions of the world.

Species cultivated Perennial: *L. alpinum*, 6 inches, blue, July–August, Alps. *L. campanulatum*, 1 foot, yellow, June–August, south Europe. *L. capitatum*, 9 inches, yellow, June–August, south Europe, Asia Minor. *L. flavum*, 1–1½ feet, yellow, June–August, Germany, Russia. *L. hirsutum*, 15 inches, blue with white eye, summer, south Europe, Asia Minor. *L. monogynum*, 2 feet, white, June–July, New Zealand. *L. narbonense*, 2 feet, blue, May–July, south Europe. *L. perenne*, 1½ feet, blue, June–July, Europe. *L. salsoloides*, 9 inches, pink, June–July, south Europe.

Cultivation The flaxes are not fussy about soil, provided it is well-drained, and will do very well on an alkaline medium. Most of the perennials and shrubby species will be happy and certainly look well on the rock garden in full sun. *L. arboreum* is not entirely hardy. Propagate by seed

1 The yellow-flowered Linum 'Gemmell's Hybrid' is a very floriferous plant.
2 Linum narbonense, a favourite garden plant, is a native of Europe.

sown in April outdoors, or by firm cuttings taken in summer and kept close until rooted.

Lobelia (lobe-ee-lee-a)

Commemorating Matthias de L'Obel, 1538–1616, a Fleming, botanist and physician to James I (*Campanulaceae*). A genus of some 200 species of annuals, herbaceous perennials or sub-shrubs, widely distributed over temperate and tropical regions of the world. All should be regarded as half-hardy, although the herbaceous perennials will survive out of doors in the milder parts of the temperate zone. Elsewhere, the bright red-flowered species from America may well be grown in the garden from June onwards, but usually need protection in winter, or should be lifted and over-wintered in a frame or in a frost-proof greenhouse, since prolonged frost will kill them. These red-flowered Lobelias have the additional charm of dark purple-bronze leaves.

Species cultivated *L. cardinalis*, cardinal flower, perennial, 3 feet, scarlet, late summer, North America; var. *alba*, white; 'Queen Victoria' is a cultivar with bronze foliage, deep scarlet flowers, *L. erinus*, annual, 6 inches, blue, summer, South Africa; cultivars include 'Blue Gown', dwarf, sky blue; 'Blue Stone', clear blue without eye; 'Crystal Palace', bronze foliage, intense blue flowers; 'Emperor William', compact, bright blue, very good for bedding; 'Prima Donna', wine; 'Rosamund', deep carmine-red with white eye. This is the lobelia much used for summer bedding. *L. fulgens*, perennial, 3 feet, scarlet, May–September, Mexico. *L. × gerarens*, perennial, 3–4 feet, pink to violet-purple, July, hybrid. *L. syphilitica*, perennial, 2 feet, blue, autumn, Eastern United States, nearly hardy. *L. tenuior*, annual, 1 foot, blue, September, western Australia, the Lobelia of trailing habit, used for hanging baskets. *L. tupa*, perennial, 6–8 feet, reddish-scarlet, autumn.

Cultivation The scarlet-flowered *L. cardinalis* and *L. fulgens* when planted in the border need frequent watering since in their native habitat they are streamside plants. They are otherwise not difficult and, except in the mildest localities, should be lifted and stored in October. Propagation of these is by seeds, sown in sandy compost in autumn in a cold frame, or in a temperature of 55°F (13°C) in March or by cuttings rooted in a warm propagating frame. Plants may also be divided in March. The bedding Lobelias with blue flowers may be grown from seed sown in February in the greenhouse, in the orthodox half-hardy annual method, but in September these plants may be lifted and stored in the greenhouse to provide cuttings for rooting in a heated propagating frame in March.

Lupinus (lu-py-nus)

From the Latin *lupus*, a wolf (destroyer), because it was thought that the plants depleted the fertility of the soil by sheer numbers (*Leguminosae*). Lupin. A genus of over 300 species of annuals, perennials and sub-shrubs, mainly from North America, though there are a few Mediterranean species which, since Roman times, have been used for green manuring. This is surprising, since the Roman farmers did not know that within the root nodules were colonies of bacteria capable of utilizing nitrogen to produce

1 Lobelia cardinalis, the Cardinal Flower, is a 3 foot high perennial.
2 The tall Lobelia tupa bears red flowers in autumn.
3 The yellow-flowered Lupinus arboreus is the short-lived Tree Lupin.
4 The bicolour Lupin 'Vogue' is a good cultivar.

valuable nitrates. The fine Russell hybrid lupins are among the most showy of herbaceous perennials and have a wide colour range embracing the three primary colours: red, yellow and blue. They do not, however, thrive on alkaline (chalky or limy) soils.

Perennial species cultivated L. *nootkatensis*, 1 foot, blue, purple and yellow, May–July, north-west America. L. *polyphyllus*, 4 feet, blue, white or pink, June–August, California.

Shrubby: L. *arboreus*, 6 feet, short-lived, yellow, white or violet, fragrant, summer, California. L. *excubicus*, 1–5 feet, blue, violet, summer, California; var. *hallii* (syn. L. *paynei*), larger flowers.

Russell hybrids These well-loved hybrids have developed from a cross made at the end of the last century between L. *arboreus* and L. *polyphyllus*. Some years later a seedling with rose-pink flowers appeared, L. *p. roseus*, and with the help of this, Mr George Russell was able to develop and select the superb colours and strong spikes that are available today in the now famous Russell strain.

Some good cultivars are: 'Betty Astell', 3 feet, deep pink; 'Blue Jacket', 3 feet, deep blue and white; 'Fireglow', 3 feet, orange and gold; 'George Russell', 4 feet, pink and cream; 'Gladys Cooper', 4½ feet, smoky blue; 'Joan of York', 4 feet, cerise and pink; 'Josephine', 4 feet, slate blue and yellow; 'Lady Diana Abdy', 3½ feet, blue and white; 'Lady Fayne', 3 feet, coral and rose; 'Lilac Time', 3½ feet, rosy-lilac; 'Mrs Micklethwaite', 3 feet, salmon-pink

and gold; 'Mrs Noel Terry', 3 feet, pink and cream; Thundercloud', 3 feet, blue and rose-mauve.

Cultivation The most popular section is that of the perennial species, which are easily grown in any sunny border that has not too much lime or chalk. Mulch with compost in spring and cut down the old flower stems in October.

The Russell lupins are now available from seed, though the named forms are still raised from cuttings of young growths in March. These are not among the longest-lived plants and it is wise to renew them from time to time. Since they are hardy they may be raised from seed sown in drills ¼ inch deep in April and put in their final places in the autumn. Many will flower during the following summer.

The tree lupin, L. *arboreus*, may be raised from seed with extreme ease. These shrubs make rapid growth, and will flower in their second season. They are, however, not long-lived, but generally manage to renew themselves by self-sown seedlings. The shrubby lupin, L. *excubicus*, makes a fine large plant, but needs some frost protection. Like most lupins, this has very fragrant flowers.

Lychnis (lik-nis)

From the Greek *lychnos*, a lamp, alluding to the brilliantly-coloured flowers (*Caryophyllaceae*). This small genus from the north temperate zone of the Old World contains some good herbaceous perennials and one good hardy annual. Two of our most impressive wild plants, the red and the white campion belong here, and, in fact, are worthy of garden cultivation, the white one in particular for its extreme fragrance in the evening. There is a natural hybrid between these two plants which has delicate pink flowers. The ragged robin, L. *flos-cuculi*, is also a native plant quite worth growing in the wild garden. It is interesting that L. *chalcedonica* gives us the brightest scarlet in the herbaceous garden, while L. *flos-jovis* (syn. *Agrostemma flos-jovis*, A. *coronaria flos-jovis*) gives us the most saturated magenta to accompany its greyish foliage.

Species cultivated L. *alba* (syn. *Melandrium album*), white campion, 3 feet, May to August, Europe. L. *alpina* (syn. *Viscaria alpina*), 6 inches, pink, summer, Europe. L. *arkwrightii*, 1½ feet, scarlet, summer, hybrid. L. *chalcedonica*, 3 feet, scarlet, summer, Russia. L. *coeli-rosa* (syn. *Silene coeli-rosa*), rose of heaven, 1 foot, purple and various other colours, annual, Levant; L. *coronaria*, 2½ feet, magenta, July and August, south Europe. L. *dioica* (*Melandrium rubrum*), the red campion, 3 feet,

159

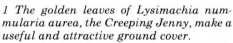

strong pink, summer, Britain. *L. flos-cuculi*, 1½ feet, ragged robin, rose-pink, May and June, Britain. *L. fulgens*, 9 inches, vermilion, May to September, Siberia. *L. grandiflora* (syn. *L. coronata*), 18 inches, salmon, summer, Japan. *L. × haageana*, 9 inches, very large scarlet flowers, hybrid. *L. lagascae* (syn. *Petrocoptis lagascae*), 9 inches, rose and white, summer, Pyrenees. *L. viscaria* (syn. *Viscaria vulgaris*), catchfly, 1 foot, reddish-purple, summer, Europe.

Cultivation Most lychnis are very easily grown in any kind of soil and can withstand dry conditions better than many other herbaceous plants. However, *L. alpina* and *L. lagascae* need rather richer soil. Some of these herbaceous plants are rather short-lived perennials—*L. alba* is almost biennial. All may be readily raised from seed sown in March in the open garden, as they are supremely hardy. The one annual species needs the standard hardy annual treatment.

Lysimachia (lis-e-mak-e-a)

Probably from either *Lysimachus*, King of Thracia, or from the Greek *luo*, to loose, and *mache*, strife, hence the common name of *L. vulgaris* (*Primulaceae*). This genus, of which most species in cultivation are hardy herbaceous perennials, has some species which have long been cultivated. There are about 120 species in all from temperate and sub-tropical regions of the world, three of them being British natives. The yellow loosestrife and creeping jenny are cultivated in gardens, the latter plant making an excellent specimen for a hanging basket with its neat leaves and abundance of yellow flowers.

Species cultivated *L. atropurpurea*, 2 feet, purple, summer, Greece. *L. clethroides*, 3 feet, white, summer, foliage brightly coloured in autumn, Japan. *L. ephemerum*, 3 feet, white, summer, Europe. *L. fortunei*, 3 feet, white, summer, China and Japan. *L. leschendultii*, 1 foot, rose-red, summer, India, does best in light, sandy soil. *L. nemorum*, creeping, yellow, summer, Britain. *L. nummularia*, creeping jenny, yellow, summer, Britain; var. *aurea*,

1 The golden leaves of Lysimachia num-mularia aurea, the Creeping Jenny, make a useful and attractive ground cover.
2 Lychnis chalcedonica is a brightly flowered herbaceous perennial.
3 Lychnis dioica, the Red Campion, is a native of Britain.
4 The yellow-flowered Lysimachia punctata reaches 3 feet and spreads quickly.
5 Lythrum salicaria, the Purple Loosestrife, has several cultivars such as 'Rose Queen', shown here.

golden leaves. *L. punctata* (syn. *L. verticillata*), 3 feet, yellow, summer, Europe. *L. thyrsiflora*, 3 feet, yellow, summer, north Europe. *L. vulgaris*, yellow loosestrife, 3 feet, yellow, summer, Britain.

Cultivation Rich moist soil is appreciated by these plants, and many species do best by the sides of pools or streams. They will tolerate some shade. The soil needed in hanging baskets or pots for *L. nummularia* consists of 1 part of leafmould and coconut-fibre and 1 part of sand. The baskets should be suspended in partial shade. This plant also makes useful ground-cover under trees etc., particularly in its golden-leaved form. Propagation is by division of plants in spring or autumn.

Lythrum (lith-rum)

From the Greek *lythron*, black blood, in reference to the colour of the flowers of some species (*Lythraceae*). Loosestrife. This is a small genus, mainly consisting of hardy herbaceous and shrubby perennials from temperate regions. One of them, *L. salicaria*, makes the banks of many streams beautiful, and it grows abundantly in wet meadows, its long flower spikes coming in late summer when flowering wild plants are beginning to be scarce.

Species cultivated *L. alatum*, 3 feet, crimson-purple, July to October, North America. *L. salicaria*, purple loosestrife, 3 feet, crimson-purple, July, Britain; cultivars include 'Brightness', rose; 'Prichard', rose-pink; 'The Beacon', deep crimson. *L. virgatum*, 2–3 feet, crimson-purple, summer, Taurus; 'Rose Queen', rosy-red, is a less tall cultivar.

Cultivation These are ideal plants for the borders of ponds and streams. However, provided the soil is moist, these loosestrifes will grow in any border. It is as well to lift and divide the plants periodically, and this is, in fact, the best method of propagation. It is best carried out in October or April.

Macleaya (mac-lay-a)

Commemorating Alexander Macleay, 1767–1848, Secretary of the Linnean Society (*Papaveraceae*). This genus, sometimes listed under the synonym *Bocconia*, consists of two Chinese species of perennial herbaceous plants very valuable in the garden. Their most outstanding virtue is their great height (8 feet or more) which lifts their large airy heads of tiny petalless flowers and unusual rounded and lobed leaves above less statuesque plants. Because of their bold and dignified appearance they are useful specimen plants to stand as isolated eye-catchers, although a group of them is even more impressive.

Species cultivated *M. cordata* (syn. *Bocconia cordata*), plume poppy, tree celandine, 8–12 feet high, leaves 8 inches across, white beneath and containing an orange-coloured sap which oozes out of any cut or broken surface, buff flowers in graceful panicles, summer. *M. microcarpa* (syn. *Bocconia microcarpa*), similar to the former, but the flower plumes are somewhat yellower in colour, and the plant is somewhat less tall; 'Kelway's Coral Plume' is a cultivar with coral-pink buds.

Cultivation Rich soils suit these plants, which should also have full sun. They do very well on well-drained chalky soils. They should not require staking, except in very exposed situations, as they have stout hollow stems. Since they sucker rather freely, detachment of suckers in early summer provides the most suitable method of propagation. If a clump is being dug up for transplanting it is essential to remove every piece of root, otherwise new plants will eventually appear even from quite small pieces of

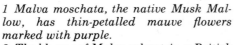

1 *Malva moschata*, the native Musk Mallow, has thin-petalled mauve flowers marked with purple.
2 The blooms of *Malva sylvestris*, a British native, are foxglove-purple.
3 *Macleaya cordata*, the Plume Poppy, reaches 8–12 feet and bears filmy summer flowers of pale coral.

root left in the soil.

Malva (mal-va)

From the Greek *malakos*, soft or soothing, probably in reference to an emollient yielded by the seeds (*Malvaceae*). A genus of hardy herbaceous perennial and annual plants. *M. moschata*, the musk mallow, is one of the most decorative of wild flowers, quite suitable for the herbaceous border. It is even more lovely in its white variety. All parts of the musk mallow are said to give off a musky odour when taken

indoors, especially in warm dry weather. It is unfortunate that in some areas all malvaceous plants are afflicted by *Puccinia malvacearum*, the hollyhock rust.

Species cultivated *M. alcea*, 4 feet, rosy-purple, summer, hardy perennial, often grown as annual, Europe; var. *fastigiata*, flowers red, July to October. *M. crispa*, 5 feet, purple and white, summer, annual, Europe. *M. moschata*, 3 feet, rose or white, summer, perennial, Europe including Britain; var. *alba*, white. *M. sylvestris*, 3 feet, purple, summer, biennial, Europe including Britain.

Cultivation In general, these plants will grow in any kind of soil and in most

aspects, though the annuals need sunny conditions to give their best. All can be easily raised from seeds sown in sandy soil in spring under glass in a temperature of 55 °F (13°C). The perennials will flower in their second season.

Meconopsis (mek-on-op-sis)

From the Greek *mekon*, a poppy, and *opsis*, like (*Papaveraceae*). This genus of poppy-like and very showy annual, biennial and perennial plants generally attracts much attention in those fortunate gardens which provide the necessary conditions for their cultivation. Most of the showy Chinese and Himalayan species need light woodland conditions and a moist soil or climate. Very many of these plants are monocarpic, that is, they will die when they attain flowering age whether it be in one, two, three or more years' time. It is probably the bright blue species which are most admired, though some of the delicate yellow ones are extremely fine.

One species, *M. cambrica*, the Welsh poppy, is a British native which, with its golden-yellow or orange flowers will brighten sunny or shady places in the garden and will successfully seed itself, often in such inhospitable places as

1 The white-flowered Meconopsis superba has a central boss of golden anthers which enhances the bloom.
2 Meconopsis regia, a native of Nepal, is attractive summer and winter, as a basal rosette of silvery leaves remains after the plant has finished flowering.
3 Meconopsis grandis, with its delicate, deep blue summer flowers, is a native of Sikkim.

between the cracks in paving stones or even between the bricks in old walls where the pointing has decayed.

Species cultivated (monocarpic unless otherwise noted) *M. aculeata*, 15 inches–2 feet, pale blue-violet, summer, western Himalaya. *M. betonicifolia* (syn. *M. baileyi*), blue poppy, blue Himalayan poppy, 4 feet, azure blue, June to July, Himalaya. *M. cambrica*, 1½ feet, yellow, summer, Europe including Britain, perennial; vars. *aurantiaca*, flowers orange; *plena*, flowers double, orange or yellow. *M. delavayi*, 6 inches, violet, summer, western China. *M. dhwojii*, 2½ feet, primrose-yellow, summer, Nepal. *M. grandis*, 3 feet, blue, June, Sikkim, perennial; 'Branklyn' is a form with large, rich blue flowers. *M. horridula*, 3½ feet, blue, red or white, Asia. *M. integrifolia*, 6 inches, violet, Central Asia. *M. napaulen-*

sis, 5 feet, pale mauve and pink, June, Himalaya. *M. paniculata*, 5 feet, yellow, July to August, Western China. *M. punicea*, 1½ feet, crimson, autumn, Tibet. *M. quintuplinervia*, 1½ feet, lavender-blue, Tibet. *M. sarsonii*, 2–3 feet, sulphur-yellow, summer, hybrid. *M. simplicifolia*, 2 feet, purple to sky blue, summer, Himalaya. *M. sinuata*, 2 feet, pale blue, May to June, east Himalaya. *M. superba*, 4 feet, pure white, May and June, Tibet, Bhutan. *M. villosa*, 2 feet, buttercup-yellow, July, Himalaya, perennial.

Cultivation A woodland soil containing leafmould is most suitable, and some light overhead shade during part of the day is appreciated. It is best to sow the seeds as soon as they are available in autumn, but if you get your seeds from a commercial source they will not be available until the spring. A few species, such as *M. quintuplinervia* may be propagated by division; others, for example *M. grandis*, may be increased by removing and rooting side-shoots. Many of the species, especially those with rosettes of silvery leaves, are suited to the lower stratum of the rock garden. Water generously in summer but keep dry in winter. In general the meconopsis do better in moist conditions.

Mimulus (mim-u-lus)

From the Greek *mimo*, ape; the flowers were thought to look like a mask or monkey's face (*Scrophulariaceae*). Monkey flower, monkey musk, musk. A genus of

1 Mimulus cardinalis, the Cardinal Flower, is a summer-flowering perennial with red and yellow flowers.
2 The perennial Mimulus guttatus, Monkey Musk, has yellow flowers sploched with red in summer.

hardy annual, half-hardy perennial and hardy perennial plants, grown for their showy flowers. They are found in many temperate parts of the world, particularly in North America.

Species cultivated Annual *M. brevipes*, to 2 feet, yellow flowers, summer. *M. fremontii*, 6–8 inches, crimson flowers, summer. Hardy perennial *M. × burnetii*, 1 foot, yellow, spotted bronze; var. *duplex* flowers double. *M. cardinalis*, cardinal monkey flower, 1–2 feet, red or red and yellow flowers, summer. *M. cupreus*, 8–12 inches, flowers yellow to copper-red, summer; cultivars include 'Monarch Strain', 1 foot, various colours; 'Red Emperor', 6 inches, scarlet flowers; 'Whitecroft Scarlet', 4 inches, bright orange-scarlet flowers. *M. guttatus* (syn. *M. langsdorfii*), 1–1½ feet, yellow, red spotted flowers, summer. *M. lewisii*, 1–1½ feet, red or white flowers, late summer. *M. luteus*, 1½ feet, yellow flowers, summer. *M. moschatus*, monkey musk, 9 inches, yellow flowers, summer. *M. primuloides*, 2–3 inches, creeping habit, yellow, June and July. *M. ringens*, 2 feet, violet to white flowers, summer. *M. variegatus*, 1 foot, blotched flowers, summer, best grown as a half-hardy annual. Cultivars include 'Bonfire', 9 inches, orange-scarlet flowers;

'Queen's Prize', 9 inches, white, cream and yellow, blotched red flowers.

Cultivation Annual species do best in moist, shady positions, though they will grow in sunny places provided the soil is sufficiently moist. Propagation is by seed sown under glass in a temperature of 55–65°F (13–18°C) in spring. The seedlings are pricked out, and gradually hardened off, finally in a cold frame, before being planted out at the end of May or the beginning of June. The hardy perennials grow well in sun or shade, provided the soil is moist. They should be planted from spring to early summer. Propagation is by seed sown from spring to early summer in a temperature of 55–60°F (13–16°C), by cuttings of young growths inserted in sandy soil at almost any time, in a temperature of 55–65°F (13–16°C) or by division of established plants in spring.

Monarda (mon-ar-da)

Named after a sixteenth-century Spanish physician and botanist, Nicholas Monardes (*Labiatae*). A small genus of annual and perennial herbs from North America, with fragrant leaves and flowers, related to *Salvia*. The leaves are nettle-like and the flowers have a spiky appearance and are clustered together in whorls: the colour ranges from white through pink, mauve and purple to red.

Species cultivated *M. didyma*, bee balm, oswego tea, 2–3 feet, scarlet flowers, sometimes in twin whorls, late summer; cultivators include 'Adam', 2½ feet, cerise;

'Beauty of Cobham', purple leaves, pink flowers; 'Cambridge Scarlet', crimson-scarlet; 'Croftway Pink', soft pink; 'Dark Ponticum', dark lilac; 'Melissa', soft pink; Pale Ponticum', lavender; 'Pillar Box', bright red; 'Sunset', 4 feet, purple-red. *M. fistulosa*, wild bergamot, 4–5 feet, purple flowers, summer, not as showy as *M. didyma;* var. *violacea* (*Violacea superba*), deep violet-purple. *M. menthae-folia*, similar to *M. fistulosa*, with mint-like foliage.

Cultivation Any ordinary garden soil will suit these plants but there must be plenty of moisture and good drainage. They will grow in sun or partial shade. They can be planted in the autumn or spring and need top-dressing. Propagation is by division in February or March, or they can be raised from seed sown out of doors in a semi-shaded position in spring or in boxes placed in the greenhouse or cold frame in March. Seeds germinate easily, but the plants will need rogueing and any drab coloured varieties discarded.

Nepeta (nep-ee-ta)

An early Latin name, probably taken from an Italian place name Nepi *(Labiatae).* A genus of about 150 species of hardy herbaceous perennials and annuals, a few of which are grown partly for their aromatic foliage. Some were once used for their remedial properties. One, grown commonly under the name of *N. mussinii*, often used for edging, is of hybrid origin and is more correctly called *N. × faassenii.* Creeping kinds can be usefully grown as ground cover in shady places.

Species cultivated *N. × faassenii* (syn. *N. mussinii* of gardens), 1–1½ feet, silvery foliage, flower spikes formed by whorls of soft lavender-blue flowers with darker spots, May to September, hybrid. *N. cataria*, catmint, catnip, catnep, 2–3 feet, flowers whitish–purple in whorls on upright stems, summer. *N. macrantha* (syn. *Dracocephalum sibiricum*), 3 feet, blue flowers clustered on stems, summer. *N. nervosa*, 1–2 feet, light blue flowers in dense spikes, July-September. Cultivars include 'Six Hills Giant', 2½ feet, light violet flowers, summer; 'Souvenir d'André Chaudron', 1 foot, rich lavender-blue

1 Nepeta x faassenii is a silvery-lavender summer-flowering perennial frequently used as an edging plant in bedding schemes.
2 Oenothera biennis, the very fragrant Evening Primrose, is a native of North America and the West Indies.
3 Oenothera fruticosa 'Yellow River' is a good, free-flowering herbaceous perennial for the border.

flowers, July–September.

Cultivation The nepetas will do well in ordinary well-drained soil in sunny borders, grouped or as edging plants. As growth is vigorous and sprawling, it is inadvisable to plant nepetas too near smaller plants which may easily be smothered. Plant in autumn or spring. Cutting back of dead autumn growth should be delayed until the spring when the new growth begins. Then the plants should be trimmed over to remove the dead stems. Propagation is by seed sown in spring, division in spring or cuttings taken from new growth made from base of plants cut back in summer after flowering. Young shoots root readily in sandy compost in a cold frame and can be planted out in the following spring.

Oenothera (ee-noth-er-a)

From the Greek *oinos*, wine, and *thera*, pursuing or imbibing, the roots of one plant being thought to induce a thirst for wine *(Onagraceae).* A genus of 80 species of annuals, biennials and numerous good herbaceous and shrubby perennials for the herbaceous border and rock garden, natives of America and the West Indies, but now widely naturalized in many parts of the world. The flowers, fragrant in many species, are fragile in appearance, carried in racemes or singly in the leaf axils and generally yellow but there are white, pink and red forms. The common name, Evening Primrose, relates to *O. biennis* in particular, the flowers opening in the evening.

Species cultivated *O. acaulis*, trailer, flowers white, ageing to rose, spring to autumn, hardy perennial. *O. biennis,* biennial, 3 feet, yellow, very fragrant, June–October. *O. erythrosepala* (syn. *O. lamarckiana*), 4 feet, flowers yellow, ageing to reddish, to 3½ inches across, summer to autumn, probably of garden origin. *O. fruticosa*, about 2 feet, lemon-yellow flowers, July and August, one of the best of the herbaceous perennials. *O. glaber*, 1½ feet, foliage bronze-green, flowers golden-yellow, summer. *O. missouriensis*, about 9 inches, trailing and spreading in habit, bright, light yellow flowers, July, perennial. *O. odorata*, to 1½ feet, flowers yellow, turning red, to 2½ inches across, opening in the evening, April to June, perennial; var. *sulphurea*, taller, later flowering, leaves, buds and stems tinted red. *O. perennis* (syn. *O. pumila*), 1 foot, flowers yellow, opening in daylight, July, perennial. *O. speciosa*, 2 feet, white flowers, scented at night, appearing throughout the summer and early autumn, perennial, United States, Mexico. *O. tetragona* (syn. *O. youngii*), 2 feet, flowers yellow, to 1½ inches across, opening by day, summer; var. *riparia*, 1½ feet, flowers larger. Cultivars: 'Fireworks', 1½ feet, bright red buds opening to yellow flowers, makes a very good plant for the front of the border; 'Yellow River', 1–1½ feet, canary yellow, very free-flowering.

Cultivation These plants are sun lovers; they do well in any ordinary soils, including those that contain much chalk. The trailing kinds are suitable for the rock garden, taller kinds for sunny borders. They can be propagated by division in spring or they may be grown from seed. Seed of the biennial species is best sown in May or June where the plants are

required to flower, the flowers being produced the following year in July and August. Cuttings can also be taken of the perennial species in May and rooted in a sandy compost.

Paeonia (pe-o-ne-a)

Commemorating *Paeon*, an ancient Greek physician, said to have first used *P. officinalis* medicinally. Although the genus has long been considered a member of the buttercup family, *Ranunculaceae*, some modern botanists now place it in a family of its own, *Paeoniaceae*. A genus of 33 species of hardy herbaceous and shrubby perennials and a few shrubs, among the noblest and most decorative plants for a sunny or shaded border. The main division of the genus is between the herbaceous and the tree paeony, but botanically the matter is much more complex. Stern's monograph, *A Study of the Genus Paeonia*, published by the Royal Horticultural Society in 1946, deals with the whole classification. The wild herbaceous species are single-flowered and vary in height from about 1 foot up to 3 or 4 feet. The double varieties have been developed by breeding and selection. The tree paeonies, although woody shrubs, are deciduous and are often grown in association with other hardy perennial plants. They enjoy a sunny position but are liable to be broken by summer gales so should be planted in a reasonably sheltered place. Long established specimens—they live many years—may attain a height of 7 feet or more with a considerable spread. Accordingly it is necessary to allow ample space when planting tree paeonies for no paeony likes being moved once it has been planted. Tree paeonies are often grafted on to the rootstock of *P. officinalis*, the common garden paeony, and when planting, care should be taken to bury the point of the union between the stock and the scion 3 inches below the surface. It is at this point that a young specimen may get broken in rough weather. If possible choose a site that does not get the early morning sun because tree paeonies come into growth earlier than herbaceous varieties and the young shoots may be damaged by late spring frosts.

Species cultivated *P. anomala*, 1–1½ feet, foliage finely cut, flowers bright crimson, May, Russia, central Asia. *P. bakeri*, 2 feet, flowers purplish-red, May, possibly of garden origin. *P. broteri*, 1–1½ feet, purplish-red, May, Spain and

1 Paeonia mlokosewitschii, a native of the Caucasus, bears single yellow spring flowers held high above the grey-green foliage.
2 Paeonia 'Sarah Bernhardt' is a beautiful fully double hybrid whose pale pink petals are tipped with silver.
3 The hybrid Paeonia x 'Esperance', the result of a cross between Paeonia lutea and Paeonia suffruticosa, has large yellow semi-double flowers.

Portugal. *P. cambessedesii,* 1½ feet, deep rose-pink, April–May, Balearic Isles, liable to damage by spring frost. *P. clusii* (syn. *P. cretica*), 1 foot, white, May, Crete. *P. coriacea,* 1½–2 feet, rose, April, Spain, Morocco. *P. delavayi,* up to 5 feet, shrubby, dark red, May, China; var. *angustiloba,* leaves finely divided. *P. emodi,* 1–3 feet, white, May, Himalaya. *P. humilis,* 15 inches, distinct small leaflets, dark pink to red, May, southern France, Spain. *P. lactiflora* (syns. *P. albiflora, P. edulis*), up to 2 feet, white, fragrant, June, Siberia, northern China, Mongolia. *P. lutea,* shrubby, up to 4½ feet, yellow, June,

China, Tibet. *P.* × *lemoinei (P. lutea* × *P. suffruticosa),* shrubby, 4–5 feet, flowers large, yellow, May–June, hybrid race. *P. mascula* (syn. *P. corallina*), 2–3 feet, deep rose, May, Europe, naturalised in Britain. *P. mlokosewitschii,* 1½ feet, foliage, grey-green, flowers yellow, coral stamens, April, Caucasus. *P. officinalis,* up to 2 feet, red, May, southern Europe; vars. *albo-plena,* the old double white paeony; *rosea plena,* the old double rose paeony; *rubra plena,* the old double crimson paeony. *P. peregrina* (syns. *P. decora, P. lobata*), up to 3 feet, deep maroon-red, May, southern Europe, Asia Minor. *P. pota-*

ninii (syn. *P. delavayi angustiloba*), shrubby, up to 5 feet, deep maroon, May, western China. *P. suffruticosa* (syn. *P. moutan*), tree paeony, up to 6 feet, rose-pink, May, China, Tibet. *P. tenuifolia,* 1–2 feet, leaves finely dissected, fern-like, flowers deep crimson, May, Transylvania, Caucasus. *P. veitchii,* 1–2 feet, purplish-red, June, China. *P. wittmanniana,* up to 3 feet, yellowish, April, Caucasus.

Hybrid Double Paeonies (a selection) 'Adolphe Rousseau', 3 feet, maroon, golden anthers, large, June. 'Alice Harding', 2½ feet, pale pink, cream within, fragrant, excellent foliage on

strong stems, May and early June. 'Baroness Schroder', 3 feet, free flowering, white, with yellow centre, large globular blooms excellent for cutting, fragrant, late May and June. 'Claire Dubois', 3 feet, satiny pink and silver, June. 'Duchesse de Nemours', 3 feet, free flowering, white to pale sulphur-yellow, medium-size, incurved bloom, fragrant, May and June. 'Edulis Superba', 3 feet, old rose-pink, edged silver, fragrant. Early May onwards, much used as a commercial variety for cut bloom. 'Eugene Verdier', 3 feet, soft pink, silver-edged, free-flowering, a famous old variety, June. 'Felix

1 Paeonia 'Lady Alexandra' is a good summer-flowering rose pink specimen.
2 Paeonia 'Bowl of Beauty' is an outstanding cultivar with pink petals and cream petaloid stamens in the centre, giving the effect of a fine anemone-flowered bloom.
3 The single-flowered Paeonia 'White Wings' with its bright yellow central boss of stamens holds its flowers well above the foliage.
4 Paeonia delavayi is a shrubby type growing up to 5 feet in height with dark crimson summer flowers.
5 There are many named forms of the herbaceous Paeonia which appear in a wide range of colour.

Crousse', 2½ feet, bright deep carmine, large, a popular variety. 'Festiva Maxima', 3 feet, pure white, flecked crimson, fragrant, a splendid old variety, the name meaning the largest and gayest, May. 'Germaine Bigot', 2½ feet, semi-double, glistening white, shaded pale salmon, fragrant, June. 'Karl Rosenfeld', 2½ feet, bright crimson, June. 'Kelway's Glorious', 2½ feet, creamy-white, large, fragrant, among the best of the doubles, May–June. 'Sarah Bernhardt', 2½ feet, bright pink, tipped silver, large, June.

Hybrid Single Paeonies 'Eva', 2½ feet, deep salmon-pink, June. 'Lady Wolseley',

1

2

2½ feet, deep rose, large, June. 'Lord Kitchener', 3 feet, deep maroon-red, May. 'Pink Delight', 2 feet, pale pink, becoming white, May.

Cultivation Paeonies are easily grown in sun or partial shade and in deep fertile soil, preferably containing lime, where they can remain undisturbed for many years. Top dress with old manure or garden compost in February every two or three years. Named varieties of herbaceous and tree paeonies are increased by division in September or October, which gives the newly-planted pieces time to make fresh roots before the ground is frozen. Great care must be taken when lifting the clumps for division, as the thick root-stock is very brittle. Paeonies can be raised from seed, but it is a slow process and the seedlings may vary considerably

3

5

4

6

1 The pink flowers of Paeonia 'Queen Elizabeth', like most of the single kinds, have prominent golden yellow stamens.
2 The semi-double Paeonia 'Asian Jewel' is a deep mauve-pink rather loose in flower form.
3 Paeonia suffruticosa 'Rock's Variety' is a cultivar of Paeonia suffruticosa, the Moutan Paeony, better known as the Tree Paeony. The white bloom with deep purple blotches low on each petal appears in May.
4 Paeonia 'Souvenir de Maxime Cornu', a Paeonia lutea hybrid, has apricot-yellow double flowers.
5 The fragrant, summer-flowering Paeonia lactiflora is a native of Siberia and Mongolia. It has given rise to a number of garden cultivars known as Chinese Paeonies, among the easiest of all perennials to grow.
6 Paeonia lutea is a shrub, growing to 4 or 5 feet, with dark green leaves with a glaucous underside and cup-like blooms.

in colour and form. Seed should be sown about 2 inches deep in sandy loam in a cold frame in September. Newly gathered seed is best. With old seed the covering may be hard and the seed should be soaked in water for a few days before sowing. Some seeds may germinate the first spring, but the majority may take up to two years. Placing seed in a refrigerator for 48 hours or so before sowing sometimes accelerates germination. Seedlings may take five years or more to develop into plants large enough to produce mature blooms. One cannot assess accurately the quality of the blooms from those produced in the first and second year of flowering as they are not usually typical. Grafting in August is done by commercial growers, usually on to stock of *Paeonia albiflora*. Tree paeonies can also be layered, but it is a slow process, and air layering has been attempted on a small scale without great success.

Pansy

The pansy and the viola are very similar and belong to the same family (*Violaceae*). Pansies are used mainly for summer bedding, although they can be treated as perennials and increased by means of cuttings. This is, in fact, what is done to perpetuate outstanding varieties for show purposes. In most gardens, however, pansies are treated as biennial plants and discarded after flowering. There are a number of different colourful strains which have been produced by crossing *Viola tricolor* with selected varieties— 'Monarch Strain', 'Engelman's', 'Roggli' of Swiss origin, and 'Morel's'—or by hybridizing different strains. The work continues and there is no telling what splendid flowers will appear in the years to come. What is known as the Fancy Pansy is grown for exhibition purposes and has superseded the Show Pansy. For show work the flower should be large, circular in outline, with smooth, thick, velvety petals without serrations. The middle of the flower should be slightly convex with the petals gently reflexed. The colours should be harmonious, with a margin of uniform width, and the yellow eye large, bright and clearly defined. The flower should be not less than $2\frac{1}{2}$ inches in diameter.

Cultivation Pansies thrive in well-drained, deeply dug soil that has been enriched with bonemeal or well-rotted horse manure. Choose an open position, preferably with some shade from the midday sun. Where the soil is heavy, fork in gritty material—old weathered ashes, sharp sand, brick dust—or compost and a dressing of lime may help to break up the soil. With such a soil the bed should be raised about 6 inches above the surrounding level. On light soil dig in cow manure and garden compost some weeks before planting time.

Planting may be either in the autumn or in the spring, but this depends upon local conditions. Plants put out in the

1 Red is the rarest tint in the extensive range of colour to be found in the Pansy family.
2 There is a good range of bedding Pansies which bloom from late winter onwards.
3 The colourful display provided by Pansies in the herbaceous border can be prolonged by removing dead flower heads.
4 The attractive markings on the Pansy add variety to the numerous strains.

autumn will usually start to flower earlier than those bedded out in spring; however, on heavy soil it is wise to defer planting until the spring. Where plants are put out in the autumn, top-dress the bed or border with equal parts of loam, sedge peat or leafmould and sharp sand a week or two after planting. This will prove a useful protection to the roots during the winter. The plants are reasonably hardy but will not withstand excessive winter wet. When planting is done in the spring, this should be during the second half of March as long as there are no bitter east winds. Set out the plants about 10–12 inches apart and during dry weather water them freely in the evenings.

Propagation is by seed sown in light soil in boxes or pans in July or August and placed in a cold shady frame. Transplant the seedlings into their flowering positions in September or early October,

or prick out and overwinter in a cold frame. Outstanding plants may be increased by cuttings taken in August or September and inserted in sandy soil in a cold, shady frame, or by division in September or October. For exhibition purposes allow one bloom only to grow on each shoot, removing other buds at an early stage. Plants grown for exhibition should be fed with weak liquid fertilizer once a week throughout the growing season (see also Viola).

Strains and cultivars include 'Cardinal Giant', brilliant red. 'Chantreyland', apricot. 'Coronation Gold', yellow flushed orange. 'Early Flowering Giant', sky-blue. 'Engelmann's Giant', mixed colours. 'Felix' strain, large flowers, various colours, yellow centres. 'Feltham Triumph', various colours. 'Indigo Blue', blue with dark blotches. 'King of the Blacks'. 'Masquerade', various light

colour combinations. 'Pacific Toyland F_2 Hybrids', mixed colours. 'Paper White'. 'Roggli', mixed colours, very large flowers. 'St Knud', lower petals orange, upper apricot. 'Westland Giants', mixed colours, very large flowers.

Winter-flowering kinds (flowering from February onwards). These include 'Celestial Queen', sky-blue. 'Helios', golden-yellow. 'Ice King', white with dark spots. 'Jupiter', sky-blue with a purple blotch. 'March Beauty', velvety purple. 'Moonlight', primrose-yellow. 'Orion', golden-yellow. 'Winter Sun', golden-yellow with dark spots.

Pansy stem rot This is a disease usually referred to as pansy sickness, in which the stem base and roots rot and the plant turns yellow. It is now common among pansies and violas and it is necessary to plant in fresh ground and to sprinkle a little 4 per cent calomel dust in the planting holes. Do not plant too deeply. The fungus responsible for the stem rot is called *Myrothecium roridum*.

Papaver (pap-a-ver)

An ancient Latin plant name of doubtful origin, but possibly derived from the sound made in chewing the seed (*Papaveraceae*). Poppy. A widespread genus of 100 species of colourful hardy annual and perennial plants. Poppies like full sun, although some will flower reasonably well in partial shade. The newly unfolded petals have the appearance of crumpled satin and many varieties have a glistening sheen on the blooms. They produce seed freely and many hybrids have been raised which are very decorative and easily grown. When used as cut flowers they will last longer if the stems are burned when they are cut before putting them in water. This seals the milky sap in the stems.

Perennial species cultivated *P. alpinum*, 6 inches, bluish-green foliage in neat tufts, yellow, orange, salmon and white flowers, summer, Europe. *P. atlanticum*, 18 inches, orange flowers, summer, Morocco. *P. nudicaule*, Iceland poppy, yellow, white and orange flowers, summer, sub-arctic regions. *P. orientale*, Oriental poppy, 3 feet, orange-scarlet, June, Asia Minor. *P. pilosum*, 2 feet, leaves form a green hairy rosette, orange-buff flowers, summer, Asia Minor. *P. rupifragum*, Spanish poppy, 2 feet, soft terra-cotta pink flowers, summer, Spain.

Cultivars There are many delightful varieties of the poppies in many and diverse colours; the following is a selection from those currently available. The annual varieties include the Shirley poppies, derived from *P. rhoeas*, single, and one of the best of all annuals; the double 'Ryburgh' hybrids and the begonia-

Papaver orientale, the Oriental Poppy, a native of Asia Minor, usually has a dark blotch at the base of each petal. The petals themselves are inclined to flop.

flowered, also double in many colours and both also derived from *P. rhoeas*; from *P. somniferum* come the 'Daneborg' hybrids, scarlet with fringed petals and four white inner petals, the carnation-flowered also fringed, the paeony-flowered doubles, and 'Pink Beauty', 2½ feet, with grey leaves and double salmon-pink flowers. The perennial varieties include those from *P. nudicaule*, such as 'Coonara', salmon pink and rose; 'Golden Monarch', 'Kelmscott Strain', rich mixed colours; 'Red Cardinal', crimson-scarlet; 'Tangerine', brilliant large orange flowers. Also varieties of *P. orientale* such as 'Beauty of Livermere', scarlet frilled flowers; 'Grossfurst', crimson; 'Lord Lambourne', orange-scarlet; 'Princess Victoria Louise', cerise-pink; 'Olympia', light orange-scarlet, double early; 'Queen Alexandra', rose; 'Perry's White', white with dark blotches; 'Rembrandt', orange-scarlet; 'Salmon Glow', salmon-pink, double; 'Watermelon', single large, cherry-red.
Cultivation Sow annual varieties in April in patches where they are to flower. They prefer a sunny position and reasonably good soil. Thin the seedlings to 2 or 3 inches apart when quite small. Plant the perennial varieties in October or early spring in deeply dug, loamy soil in full sun, and top-dress with old manure or compost in March or April. Propagation of the perennials is by means of root cuttings in winter, by division of the roots in March or April or by seed sown in pans or boxes in a cold-frame in spring or on a finely broken-down seed bed out of doors in early summer, scarcely covering the fine seeds. *P. alpinum* and *P. nudicaule* are frequently grown as annuals

1 Papaver orientale has numerous forms.
2 Papaver 'Mrs Perry' is one of the best known and popularly grown of the cultivars of Papaver orientale.

or biennials (for the Welsh poppy see Meconopsis).

Pelargonium (pel-ar-go-knee-um)

From the Greek *pelargos*, a stork, referring to the resemblance between the beak of the fruit and that of a stork *(Geraniaceae)*. This is the correct name for the plant which is grown in public parks and our gardens and greenhouses. The zonal pelargoniums have in the past 70 years mostly been called 'Geraniums' which is a complete misnomer. The true Geraniums were described in an earlier article.

Within the past 10 years the horticultural public has been made aware of the misnomer, mainly by the efforts of the specialist societies throughout the world, and are now using the correct term for the zonal and regal pelargoniums in increasing numbers.

To help to sort out the confusion that has existed, it is worth stating that the cultivars of the genus *Pelargonium*, both regal and zonal types, have definitely been bred from the true *Pelargonium* species and not from the genus *Geranium*; this is the key to the correct definition.

In the genus *Pelargonium* there are over 300 recorded species; this does not include the sub-species and other varieties not recorded yet, of which there must be a considerable number.

The species are identified in one way by the fact that the plants breed true

from seed, although some have individual races within the species which also breed true from seed, and a lot of cross-pollination is done by insects on plants growing in their natural habitat, causing much confusion among taxonomists. Many of these natural hybrids are very closely identified with the original plant but may have slightly different leaves, form or flowers.

The species were mainly brought to Europe from many parts of Africa, although several places in other parts of the world such as Australia, New Zealand and Tasmania have also contributed during the last three centuries. They are not hardy in cooler zones and have to be protected during the winter months, although a wide range of species is grown out of doors in some places.

What is remarkable is that such a large number of colourful cultivated varieties could ever have been bred from plants that have only very small flowers. It shows the tenacity and enthusiasm of the breeders who performed this task, mainly during the last century, although this work has been carried on into the present era.

The species are fascinating to explore, and there is no doubt that they are more important than the cultivars in many ways, especially in their use for hybridizing purposes and also for experimentation and research.

There are many kinds of fantastic shapes and forms among the various kinds and a great number have perfume in their leaves. Although this scent is often clearly defined, it cannot be assessed absolutely in all varieties because so many factors

which contribute to the amount of volatile oil in the tissues have to be taken into consideration. Variations of this can be caused by environment, feeding, soil structure, age of plants, time or season of year, etc., all of which can vary from county to county and country to country. One of the main reasons why smells or perfumes seem to vary is because the sense of smell varies widely between one person and another.

The volatile oil is distilled from many of the species to be used in cosmetics and perfumes.

The scented-leaved kinds are listed here because they are mainly species and thus they are easy to classify.

The leaves of the pelargonium are edible and are used a great deal in cooking and can add at least ten different flavours to any cake or sweetmeat. It is, therefore, worthwhile growing certain species for this purpose alone.

The following is a list of the species most commonly known and grown and obtainable in Britain. If they do have a perfume this is described in terms which are generally accepted for the particular species. Except where stated all species are natives of South Africa, and, in general, they all flower in summer and normally grow to between 9 inches and 2½–3 feet in height.

Species cultivated *P. abrotanifolium*, flowers white or rose veined with purple, leaves fragrant of southernwood (*Artemisia abrotanum*). *P. acetosum*, leaves silvery-green, tasting of sorrel, single carmine flowers, can be used in cooking. *P. angulosum*, plant hairy, leaves 5-lobed, flowers purple, veined maroon. *P. australe*, flowers rose or whitish, spotted and striped carmine, Australia, New Zealand, Tasmania. *P. capitatum*, rose scent, pale mauve blooms. *P. crispum*, strong lemon scent, flowers pink or rose; vars. *major*, larger; *minor*, smaller; *variegatum*, lemon scent, grey-green leaves with cream edges, very elegant for floral display work. *P. cucullatum*, rose-scented cupped leaves, flowers red with darker veins, late summer, a parent of the regal pelargoniums and very good for outdoor pot plant growing. *P. denticulatum*, sticky leaves with strong undefined scent, flowers lilac or rosy-purple, best species with fern-like foliage. *P. echinatum*, sweetheart geranium, tuberous-rooted, stems spiny, leaves heart-shaped, lobed, flowers purple, pink or white, nearly hardy. *P. filicifolium* (syn. *P. denticulatum filicifolium*), fern-like leaves, very pungent scent, small rose flowers. *P. formosum*, salmon flowers, white-tipped, upright habit. *P. × fragrans*, nutmeg-scented geranium, small dark green leaves smelling of spice, flowers white, veined red; var. *variegata*, a minia-

1 *Pelargonium 'Carisbrooke' has soft rose-pink petals with darker markings.*
2 *The white flowers of Pelargonium 'Muriel Harris' are feathered with red.*
3 *Pelargonium 'Black Prince'.*

ture plant with a very pleasant scent, tiny light green leaves edged with cream, easily grown and propagated, should be in every collection. *P. frutetorum*, prostrate habit, salmon flowers. *P. gibbosum*, gouty pelargonium, so named because the joints are similar to those on elderly people so afflicted, flowers greenish-yellow, early summer. *P. graveolens*, rose-scented geranium, strong rose scent, flowers pink, upper petal with dark purple spot; much used in the distillation of perfume. *P. inquinans*, scarlet flowers, plain leaves, one parent of the zonal pelargoniums. *P. multibracteatum*, leaves heart-shaped, deeply lobed, with dark green zones, flowers white. *P. odoratissimum*, apple-scented geranium, leaves heart-shaped or kidney-shaped, fragrant of apples, flowers small, white. *P. peltatum*, ivy-leaved geranium, leaves fleshy, flowers pale rosy-mauve, a parent of the ivy-leaved cultivars. *P. quercifolium*, oak-leaved geranium, leaves roughly oak-leaf shape, grey-green, strongly scented, flowers mauve. *P. radula*, fern-like leaves, fragrant of verbena, flowers rose, upper petals blotched purplish-carmine, very attractive if grown out of doors during the summer when it grows into a small shrub. *P. saxifragioides*, very dainty plant with tiny leaves similar

1 *The flowers of Pelargonium 'Mrs Lawrence' are rose pink.*
2 *The double white flowers of Pelargonium 'Gonzale' make a compact head.*
3 *Pelargonium 'Salmon Irene' bears full heads of coral-pink blooms.*
4 *Pelargonium 'Harvester' produces a consistently rounded head.*

to some ivy-leaved kinds, flowers mauve, marked purple. *P. tetragonum*, often called the cactus-type pelargonium because of its four-sided stems; its growth should be controlled by stopping because of its vigorous habit, flowers small, white, single. *P. tomentosum*, strong peppermint scent, leaves grey-green, soft and spongy, sometimes difficult to keep during the winter period, flowers tiny, white. *P. tricolor*, foliage sage green, small tricolor flowers, lower petals white, upper petals magenta, with dark spots, a good plant for pots in the greenhouse, a prize collector's piece. *P. triste*, the sad geranium, tuberous rooted, long, much-divided leaves, flowers brownish-yellow with a pale border; sweetly scented in the evening. *P. zonale*, flowers single, mauve, pink or red, leaves lightly zoned. 'Lady Plymouth', foliage as *P. graveolens* except that the leaves are variegated green and

lemon. 'Mabel Grey', strong lemon scent, upright grower that needs frequent stopping. 'Prince of Orange', orange scented, small pale mauve flowers.

The 'Uniques' are another group that have sprung up in recent years and are stated to be *P. fulgidum* hybrids. *P. fulgidum*, a sub-shrubby species with bright red flowers, is prominent in their ancestry. They are best grown in pots and hanging baskets. There are many different perfumes in the leaves of the varieties listed below:
'Crimson Unique', red and black flowers; 'Scarlet Unique', lemon scent, red flowers, parent of 'Carefree' and 'Hula'; 'Paton's Unique', verbena scent, rose flowers; 'Purple Unique', peppermint scent, purple flowers; 'Rose Unique', rose scent, rose flowers; 'White Unique', white flowers with purple veins. Cultivars: one of the most important sections of the cultivars are the regal or domesticum Pelargoniums which have very beautiful flowers and green leaves, but recently some sports have been discovered with golden and green bicolor leaves which should make these beautiful plants much sought after if hybridizers are successful in breeding these coloured leaves into this section.

The main parents of the regals are *P*.

173

strawberry pink and white; 'Blythwood', purple and mauve; 'Caprice', pink; 'Carisbrooke', rose pink; 'Doris Frith', white; 'Grand Slam', red; 'Marie Rober', lavender; 'Muriel Hawkins', pink; 'Rapture', apricot; 'Rhodamine', purple and mauve; and the outstanding sport from 'Grand Slam', 'Lavender Grand Slam'.

The flowering season of the regals has been greatly lengthened within the last five years by the introduction of the new American cultivars.

A great advantage in growing plants in this section is that they are rarely troubled by disease. The worst pest is the greenhouse white fly which appears at all times and can spread rapidly. It can, however, easily be controlled by using a good insecticide.

The section which dominates the genus consists of the hortorums, usually referred to as zonals. These are divided into many groups which are classified as follows (selected cultivars are listed under each heading):

Single-flowered group (normally with not more than five petals):
'Barbara Hope', pink; 'Block', scarlet; 'Countess of Jersey', salmon; 'Doris Moore', cherry; 'Elizabeth Angus', rose; 'Eric Lee', magenta; 'Francis James', bi-color flowers; 'Golden Lion', orange; 'Highland Queen', pink; 'Maxim Kovaleski', orange; 'Mrs E. G. Hill', pink; 'Pandora', scarlet; 'Pride of the West', cerise; 'Victorious', scarlet; 'Victory', red.

Semi-doubles:
American Irenes of various shades and colours are extremely useful for bedding purposes; many named cultivars are very similar to each other. Other cultivated varieties include 'Dagata', pink; 'Genetrix', pink; 'Gustav Emich', scarlet; 'King of Denmark', pink; 'Pink Bouquet', pink; 'The Speaker', red.

Double-flowered group:
'Alpine Orange', orange; 'A. M. Maine', magenta; 'Blue Spring', red-purple; 'Double Henry Jacoby', crimson; 'Jewel', rose; 'Jean Oberle', pink; 'Lerchenmuller', cerise; 'Monsieur Emil David', purple; 'Maid of Perth', salmon; 'Mrs Lawrence', pink; 'Paul Reboux', red; 'Rubin' red; 'Schwarzwalderin', rose; 'Trautleib', pink.

Cactus group (single or double flowers with quilled petals):
'Attraction', salmon; 'Fire Dragon', red; 'Mrs Salter Bevis', pink; 'Noel', white; 'Spitfire', red with silver leaves; 'Tangerine', vermilion.

Rosebud group (flower buds tight and compact, centre petals remaining unopened, like small rosebuds):
'Apple Blossom Rosebud', pink; 'Red

cucullatum and *P. betulinum* which are indigenous to the coastal regions of South Africa. Hybridization started on the species mainly in England and France and also in central Europe well over a century ago. These plants should be grown under glass or in the house throughout the year in cool areas, although they may be grown out of doors in summer in exceptionally protected places. Two lovely cultivars have been produced that will grow well out of doors in all kinds of weather during the summer months. These are 'Hula' and 'Carefree' from America. These two are the result of crossing the cultivars back to the species. 'Hula' and 'Carefree' do not have flower umbels as large as the true regals but have the advantage of being able to stand up to bad conditions out of doors.

Some recommended cultivars are as follows (dominating colours only are mentioned): 'Annie Hawkins', pink; 'Applause', pink and white; 'Aztec',

1 The decorative uses of the Pelargonium are numerous if the plants are protected from frost, such as on this conservatory wall.
2 Pelargonium quercifolium is described by its common name, the Oak-leaved Geranium.

1 Take cuttings of Pelargoniums in mid-to-late summer from the tops of the lateral shoots about 3 inches in length. Remove the bottom leaves with a sharp knife.
2 Trim the cutting back to a node.
3 Using a dibber, insert the cutting in a 3-inch pot filled with a sterile rooting compost.
4 The cuttings need to be kept moist to encourage rooting, and as they progress, they can be potted on.

Rambler', red; 'Rosebud Supreme', red.
Miniature group:
'Alde', pink; 'Caligula', red; 'Cupid', pink; 'Goblin', red; 'Jenifer', carmine; 'Grace Wells', mauve; 'Mephistopheles', red; 'Mandy', cerise; 'Pauline', rose; 'Picca-ninny', red; 'Taurus', red; 'Timothy Clifford', salmon; 'Wendy', salmon; 'Waveney', red.
Dwarf group:
'Blakesdorf', red; 'Emma Hossler', pink; 'Fantasia', white; 'Miranda', carmine; 'Madam Everaarts', pink; 'Pixie', salmon.
Fancy-leaved group (the colours given are those of the flowers):
Silver leaves: 'Flower of Spring', red; 'Mrs Mappin', red; 'Mrs Parker', pink; 'Wilhelm Langguth' (syn. 'Caroline Schmidt'), red.
Golden leaves: 'Golden Crest'; 'Golden Orfe'; 'Verona'.
Butterfly leaves: 'A Happy Thought'; 'Crystal Palace Gem'; 'Madame Butterfly'.
Bronze bicolour leaves: 'Bronze Corrine'; 'Bronze Queen'; 'Gaiety Girl'; 'Dollar

Princess'; 'Maréchal MacMahon'; 'Mrs Quilter'.
Multi-coloured leaves: 'Dolly Varden'; 'Lass o' Gowrie'; 'Miss Burdett-Coutts', 'Henry Cox'; 'Mrs Pollock'; 'Sophie Dumaresque'. Ivy-leaved group:
One of the best in this group is *P. peltatum*, the original species from which this section has been derived. Cultivars are: 'Abel Carrière', magenta; 'Beatrice Cottington', purple; 'Galilee', pink; 'La

France', mauve; 'L'Elegante', leaves cream and green with purple markings; 'Madame Margot', white and green leaf; and two with green leaves and white veins, 'Crocodile' and 'White Mesh'.

In general the large-flowered cultivars described above will grow under normal garden and greenhouse conditions as will the coloured-leaved cultivars, which benefit from being left out of doors during the summer months to get full sunshine and rain.

The miniature and dwarf sections are best grown in the greenhouse in pots, or they are very useful plants to grow out of doors in containers such as window boxes or urns. They are especially good for hanging baskets when used in conjunction with ivy-leaved kinds.

Hanging baskets are very useful for enhancing a display out of doors, especially under porches. One of the best cultivars for this purpose is 'The Prostrate Boar', a newer introduction

which grows very quickly and produces an abundance of flowers throughout the summer. Make sure that you get the prostrate type and not the ordinary 'Boar' which does not grow so vigorously, nor flower so freely. 'The Boar', or *P. salmonia,* is inclined to grow vertically.

P. frutetorum has had in the past, and should have in the future, a great influence on the pelargonium genus because of its great vigour and its ability to influence the pigments in the leaves of the many cultivars crossed with it.

Hybridization merely consists in taking the pollen from one flower and transferring it on to the stigma of another compatible cultivar. This method will give some good results, but if you are going to go in for a proper breeding programme, you should isolate those plants intended for breeding purposes and keep clear records of each individual cross. This is very necessary should any of your seedlings turn out to be good ones and you wish to register them as new introductions. The miniatures and the dwarfs are very adaptable for cross-breeding, so it is advisable to work on these for primary experiments.

Cultivation In general pelargoniums grown in pots will do well in most good potting composts, though it is advisable

1 The dwarf Pelargoniums are well-suited to rock gardens.
2 The Ivy-leaved Pelargonium with its distinctively-shaped, fleshy foliage grows particularly well in hanging baskets out of doors.

to add a little extra lime to neutralize the acidity of the peat. Alternatively, particularly for potting on rooted cuttings, a suitable soil mixture consists of 2 parts of good loam, 1 part of sand, 1 part of peat, all parts by bulk, not weight, plus 1 pint of charcoal and 1 cupful of ground limestone per bushel of the mixture. The ingredients should be thoroughly mixed together and then watered with a liquid fertilizer with a high potash content. Some growers have been successful with the 'no-soil' composts (peat/sand mixtures plus balanced fertilizers), while others use ordinary good garden soil which has been cleared of worms and sterilized to kill harmful soil organisms.

Pelargoniums should never be overpotted. When repotting becomes necessary it is often possible, by removing old compost and slightly reducing the size of the root-ball, to repot into pots of the same size; otherwise the plants should be moved into pots one size larger only.

They should always be potted firmly.

Although plants should be watered freely during the growing period in spring and summer, they should never be overwatered and, in any case, the pots in which they are grown should be properly crocked and the soil mixture should be free-draining so that surplus moisture can get away quickly, otherwise various root-rots and stem-rots may be encouraged. In winter plants will need little water, though the soil in the pots should not be allowed to dry out.

Some shading will be required in the greenhouse from late April or early May onwards. A light application of 'Summer Cloud' or other proprietary shading compound to the glass will be sufficient.

In order to prevent damping-off of the flowers the atmosphere in the greenhouse should be kept as dry as possible during the summer. This means that proper use should be made of the ventilators and that every attempt should be made to keep the air circulating to avoid an over-humid stagnant atmosphere. During the winter, when it is equally important to keep the air dry but warm, good circulation can be provided by using an electrical blower heater.

To keep the plants growing freely and

to maintain good leaf colour it is necessary to feed them during the growing season. Regular weak applications of proprietary liquid fertiliser should be given from about a month after the plants are in their final pots, until September. It should be noted, however, that plants in the fancy-leaved group should either not be fed at all, or the feed they are given should not contain nitrogen. These kinds should, in any case, be given less water than others.

A number of zonal varieties can be induced to flower in winter, when blooms are always welcome. The method is to take cuttings in the spring, by normal propagation methods described below. The young plants are grown on steadily during the summer and all flower buds are removed until late September. Plants treated in this way should flower throughout the winter months. It is best to maintain a minimum temperature of 60°F (16°C) and the plants should be given as much light as possible. During the summer the plants may be placed in a sunny cold frame or the pots may be plunged in a sunny, sheltered place out of doors. They should be brought into the greenhouse in September.

Plants which are to be used for summer bedding purposes are raised from cuttings taken in August or September, rooting several in each 5-inch pot, or in boxes, spacing the cuttings 2 inches apart. In February the rooted cuttings are potted into individual 3-inch pots and kept in a temperature of 45–50°F (7–10°C) until April. They are then hardened off in a cold frame before planting them out of doors in late May or early June, when all danger of frost is over. Do not plant shallowly; it is best to take out a hole large enough and deep enough to take the plant up to its first pair of leaves. Leggy plants may be planted more deeply. Remove dead leaves and flowers as soon as they are seen and pinch out long, unwanted shoots from time to time to keep the plants bushy. Keep the plants well watered in dry weather. A gentle overhead spray in the evenings in hot weather is beneficial. In September, before the first frosts, the plants should be lifted and brought into the greenhouse for the winter. The shoots should be cut back, long roots trimmed and the plants potted into small pots. The minimum winter temperature in the greenhouse should be around 42°F (5°C).

Propagation of regal pelargoniums is by cuttings, which, like those of the other types, root easily. They should be about 3 inches long, taken from the top of the lateral shoots. They are trimmed back to a node and the bottom leaves are removed. They will root quickly in a sterile rooting compost, in pots or in a propagating frame in the greenhouse. Bottom heat is not required. Cuttings of this type are usually taken in July or August.

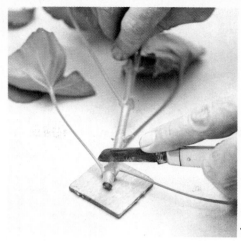

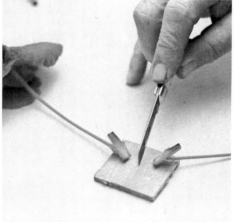

Propagation of the hortorums or zonal pelargoniums may be effected in several ways. Cuttings of the type described above may be taken and either rooted singly in 2½-inch pots or three cuttings may be inserted round the edge of a 3-inch pot. If large numbers are to be rooted they may be inserted in a suitable rooting compost in a frame, or 2 inches apart in shallow boxes. Cuttings are usually taken in June, July or August in this country, to enable them to form roots early. If they are taken later they may not root properly before the end of the season and thus may be lost. However, they may be rooted later in a propagating case in the greenhouse, and commercially they are rooted in quantity by mist propagation methods, using bottom heat.

The leaf-axil (or leaf-bud) method of taking cuttings has become popular in recent years. This consists in taking a

The leaf-axil method of propagating Pelargoniums is a popular way.
1 Cut the stem ¼ inch above and below the node.
2 Also cut the stem vertically through the centre.
3 Set the cutting in a pot of clean, damp rooting compost.
4 When inserting the cutting into the compost, allow it just to cover the bud.
5 Pelargonium 'Dolly Varden' is an attractive decorative variety.

leaf and ½ inch of stem from the parent plant, ¼ inch above and below the node or joint. The stem section is cut vertically through the centre of the stem. The cuttings thus formed are inserted in rooting compost in the normal way, just covering the buds. If some bud growth is seen in the leaf axils you are more certain of rooting the cuttings. Such cuttings are normally taken in the summer months.

Whichever method you adopt, make sure that you use clean stock only. Almost any piece of a zonal pelargonium containing stem and leaves can be used for propagation purposes, provided the conditions are right. It is quite normal to root stem cuttings of these plants out of doors during the summer months, in the open ground.

Plants may also be raised from seed obtained from a reliable source. It is unwise to buy unnamed seedlings as they may produce large plants with few flowers. Seeds should be sown 1/16 inch deep in light sandy soil, in pans or boxes, in the greenhouse, from February to April, in a temperature of 55–65°F (13–18°C).

Tuberous-rooted pelargonium species may be divided in spring for propagation purposes.

The principal pests of pelargoniums grown under glass are aphids and greenhouse white fly. These may be controlled by insecticidal sprays or by fumigation methods. The disease variously known as black leg, black rot, black stem rot or

1 The dark leaves contrast with the deep red flowers of Pelargonium 'Red Black Vesuvius'.
2 Pelargonium 'Decorator' has magenta blooms and attractive bicolour leaves.
3 Pelargoniums can be trained as standards by removing all lateral shoots.

pelargonium stem rot, is very liable to attack cuttings and sometimes mature plants. It first appears on the lower part of the stem, which turns black. It spreads rapidly up the stem and soon kills the plant. It seems to be encouraged by too much moisture in the compost and in over-humid conditions. Some control may be obtained by spraying or dusting plants with captan in the autumn. It is also important not to damage the skin of the stem when taking cuttings, otherwise disease spores may enter through the skin at this point. Always use a sharp sterile knife or razor blade when taking or trimming cuttings.

Grey mould (Botrytis cinerea) will attack plants under glass, especially in close, humid conditions. It appears as a grey furry mould on stems, leaves or flowers. Proprietary fungicides based on copper or thiram will control this disease, but it is more important to maintain the correct conditions in the greenhouse, with ample ventilation and a dry atmosphere. When plants are overwintered remove all dead, furry leaves, but make sure that the leaf is quite dead. When taking away discoloured leaves do this by removing the leaf only at first, leaving the stalk intact until the abscission layer has formed between stalk and stem, when the stalk may be removed easily. To attempt to remove it before the abscission layer has formed will result in the stem being damaged with the consequent risk of disease spores entering.

1 Penstemon hirsutus (syn. P. pubescens latifolius) is a summer-flowering North American native.
2 The unusual blooms of Penstemon 'George Home' appear in summer.
3 Penstemon rupicola is a native plant of northwestern North America.

colour range through pinks and reds to deep maroons and purples. *P. hetero-phyllus* is a fine sub-shrub with blue flowers which usually attracts interest when well grown. Another striking plant is the herbaceous *P. barbatus* (syn. *Chelone barbata*), a tall grower, to 3 feet, with bright vermilion-scarlet flowers.

Species cultivated *P. angustifolius*, 1 foot, soft blue, July, western United States. *P. antirrhinoides*, 3 feet, lemon-yellow, July, California. *P. azureus*, 1 foot, blue, August, North America. *P. barbatus*, 3 feet, scarlet, summer, Colorado. *P. barrettiae*, 1 foot, bright violet, May–June, western United States. *P. bridgesii*, 2 feet, scarlet, July to September, North America. *P. campanulatus*, 2 feet, rosy-purple, violet or white, June, Mexico and Guatemala. *P. centranthi-folius*, 3 feet, scarlet, summer, California and western Arizona. *P. cobaea*, 2 feet, purple or white, August, United States. *P. confertus*, 1 foot, purple and blue, summer, Rocky Mountains. *P. cordifolius*, 4 feet, scarlet, summer, partial climber, southern California. *P. davidsonii*, 1–2 inches, ruby-red, summer, spreads by underground stems, rock garden. California. *P. diffusus*, 2 feet, blue or purple, September, western North America. *P. fruticosus*, 9–12 inches, purple, summer, north-western United States; var. *crassifolius*, with minor leaf differences. *P.*

glaber, 2 feet, purple, July, United States. *P. glaucus*, 15 inches, purple, July, Rocky Mountains. *P. hartwegii*, 2 feet, scarlet, summer, Mexico. *P. heterophyllus*, 1–3 feet, sky blue, July, California. *P. hirsutus* (syn. *P. pubescens latifolius*), purple or violet, 1–3 feet, July, United States. *P. isophyllus*, sub-shrubby, 4–5 feet, crimson-scarlet, white within, late summer, Mexico. *P. laevigatus*, 3 feet, white or pink, summer, United States. *P. menziesii*, 6 inches, purple, June, northwestern America. *P. ovatus*, 2 feet, blue to purple, August to October, United States. *P. richardsonii*, 2 feet, violet, summer, United States. *P. rupicola*, 4 inches, ruby, north-western America. *P. scouleri*, 1½ feet, purple, May to June, United States. *P. spectabilis*, 4 feet, rosy-purple, summer, Mexico and southern California.

Cultivars

The following are some good modern varieties: 'Blue Gem', azure-blue, summer; 'Chester Scarlet', summer; 'Evelyn', pink, May–October; 'Garnet', wine-red; 'George Home', summer; 'Newberry Gem', pillar-box red; 'Six Hills Hybrid', rosy-lilac, May–June.

Cultivation A rich, slightly acid soil is most suitable or a compost mixture of 1 part of leafmould or peat and 2 parts of good loam. A sunny aspect is required. A weekly watering with a soluble fertilizer or liquid manure is needed by the summer bedding penstemons to keep them growing and flowering well. Seed is available for many species. This should be sown under glass in February or March in a temperature of 55–65°F (10–18°C) and the young plants are set out in May after they have been hardened off. But to get exactly similar plants of

Penstemon (pen-ste-mon)

From the Greek *pente*, five, and *stemon*, stamen, in reference to the five stamens (*Scrophulariaceae*). This genus of over 250 species of hardy and half-hardy herbaceous annuals, perennials and sub-shrubs is almost exclusively North American. The name is sometimes erroneously spelt *Pentstemon*. Though many are grown in British gardens, some of the species do not thrive and it seems likely that the continental climate, with its colder winters and hotter summers, is needed to make these plants really happy. The very popular late summer bedding penstemons were derived from an initial crossing of *P. cobaea* and *P. hartwegii*, and they have a fairly wide

hybrids it is necessary to take cuttings and raise them under glass in August. They should not be disturbed till the following April. Plants may also be divided in April.

Phlox (flocks)

From the Greek *phlego*, to burn, or *phlox*, a flame, referring to the bright colours of the flowers (*Polemoniaceae*). A genus of nearly 70 species of hardy, half-hardy, annual and perennial herbaceous plants all, with one exception, natives of North America and Mexico. Almost all the most important species are from the eastern United States, though the popular annual, *P. drummondii*, is from Texas and New Mexico. The fine herbaceous plants derived originally from *P. paniculata*, the garden forms of which may sometimes be listed as *P. × decussata*, have a most important part to play in the garden as they give colour at a time—July and August—when it very much needs their bright colours. They are extremely easy to grow and all have fragrant flowers. Our rock gardens would be much poorer if they lacked the various forms of either *P' douglasii* or *P. subulata* or their hybrids.

Herbaceous perennial species cultivated *P. carolina*, 2 feet, phlox-purple to pink and white, May and June, eastern United States. *P. glaberrima*, 2 feet, red, May and June, eastern North America in swamps. *P. maculata*, wild sweet william, 3 feet, violet and purple, summer, eastern North America. These three species are the parents of the early flowering taller phlox. *P. paniculata* (syn. *P. × decussata*), 1½–4 feet, violet purple, summer, eastern North America.

Alpine species cultivated *P. amoena*, 6–9 inches, rose, May to June, southeastern United States; var. *variegata*, leaves variegated with white. *P. bifida*, sand phlox, prostrate, tufted habit, spiny leaves, flowers pale violet to white, spring, eastern North America. *P. divaricata* (syn. *P. canadensis*), 6–15 inches, blue-lavender, May, eastern North America. *P. douglasii* 4 inches, lilac, May to August, western North America. *P. × frondosa*, pink, spring, hybrid. *P. kelyseyi*, 6 inches, flowers lilac, spring, eastern North America. *P. ovata*, 1 foot, rose, summer, eastern North America. *P. pilosa*, 10–20 inches, purplish-rose, summer, eastern North America. *P. × procumbens*, 6 inches, lilac-blue, June, a hybrid. *P. stellaria*, 6 inches, pale blue, April to May, hybrid. *P. stolonifera* (syn. *P. reptans*), 6–12 inches, stoloniferous habit, flowers violet to lavender, 1 inch across, April to May, eastern North America. *P. subulata*, moss phlox, 6 inches, purple or white, eastern United States.

Border cultivars *P. paniculata* is the border perennial phlox which has given rise to many good plants, flowering from July to October, sweet smelling, and very colourful. 'Antoine Mercie', deep mauve with white centre; 'Border Gem', deep violet; 'Brigadier', orange-red; 'Europe', white with red centre; 'Frau Antonin Buchner', white; 'Jules Sandeau', pure pink; 'Le Mahdi', rich purple; 'Leo Schlageter', dark red; 'Lofna', rose-pink; 'Mrs A. Jeans', silvery-pink; 'Rijnstroon', rose-pink; 'Starfine', red; 'Thor', salmon-red. Many more will be found in nurserymen's lists.

Alpine cultivars *P. douglasii*, 'Boothman's Variety', clear mauve; 'Eva', pink with deeper centres; 'May Snow', white; 'Rose Queen', silvery pink; 'Snow Queen', white; 'Supreme', lavender-blue. *P. kelseyi*, 'Rosette', stemless pink flowers. *P. stolonifera* 'Blue Ridge', soft blue. *P. subulata* 'Appleblossom', pink; 'Benita', lavender-blue; 'Brilliant', bright rose; 'Camla', clear pink; 'Fairy', mauve; 'G. F. Wilson', mid-blue; 'Model', rose; 'Pink Chintz', pink; 'Sensation', rose-red; 'Temiscaming', magenta-red; 'The Bride', white.

Cultivation The tall herbaceous phloxes need a moist loam, preferably on the heavy side. They do perfectly well on chalky soils, provided these are enriched. Though in the past shady positions have been given to phloxes and this does not actually kill them, they do better in sunny positions. Plant from October to March, and feed generously thereafter with manure or compost and inorganic fertilizers, as they are greedy feeders. Lift, divide and replant every three years.

1 Phlox 'Brigadier' is a magenta cultivar of Phlox paniculata.
2 Phlox maculata, the Wild Sweet William, is a fine summer-flowering herbaceous perennial.

They are readily raised from root cuttings and this has the advantage of providing plants free from the stem eelworm, by which the herbaceous phlox are all too often attacked.

Alpine phlox species also like a rich soil, and a sunny ledge on the rock garden or on top of a wall. Many of them may be easily increased by layering, or they may be divided into separate plants each possessing roots, and this is best done in March. A few of the more dwarf or less vigorous kinds may be given alpine house treatment. Winter wet is their bane.

Eelworm attack on phlox, by the eelworm species *Ditylenchus dipsaci*, causes bloated and wrinkled foliage, stunted, swollen and split stems and whiptail shoots. The same strain of eelworm will attack gypsophila, oenothera, gladiolus, potato, aubrieta, as well as a number of weeds such as mayweed and shepherd's purse. Hot water treatment of the dormant stools for one hour at a temperature of 110°F (43°C) controls the pest. The plants must be put back in uncontaminated soil and infected areas should be kept free of susceptible plants and weeds for at least three years. It is possible to propagate infested phlox without transmitting eelworm by means of seed or by true root cuttings.

Physalis (fy-sa-lis)
From the Greek *physa*, a bladder, an allusion to the inflated calyx (*Solana-*ceae). A genus of 100 or more species of which the two most well-known are *P. alkekengi*, the Bladder Cherry or Chinese Lantern Plant, with its brilliant, flame-coloured, air-filled calyces, and *P. peruviana*, the Cape Gooseberry, which is a greenhouse species. They are annual and perennial herbaceous plants, mostly from Mexico and North America.

Species cultivated *P. alkekengi* (syns. *P. alkekengi franchetii, P. bunyardii, P. franchetii*), bladder cherry, bladder herb, Chinese lantern plant, winter cherry, hardy perennial, 1–2 feet, flowers whitish, similar to those of the potato, summer, fruit a single scarlet berry enclosed in the much inflated showy calyx, up to 2 inches long, turning orange in autumn, southeastern Europe to Japan, naturalized in many other parts of the world; vars. *gigantea*, calyces larger; *pygmaea*, 9 inches, dwarf form. *P. ixocarpa*, tomatillo, half-hardy annual, 2 feet, flowers yellow, $\frac{3}{4}$ inch or more across, with black-brown blotches in the throat, fruit purple, sticky, almost filling the yellow, purple-veined calyx. The fruits are edible and may be stewed or used for jam making, Mexico, southern United States. *P. peruviana* (syns. *P. edulis. P. peruviana edulis*), Cape gooseberry, 3 feet,

1 Physalis alkekengi, the Bladder Cherry or Chinese Lantern, has papery, air-filled calyces of bright orange-red.
2 Pulmonaria angustifolia, the Blue Cowslip, lacks the identifying leaf spots found in other species of the genus.

flowers yellow, blotched purple, summer, fruit yellow, edible, South America, greenhouse. *P, pruinosa*, dwarf Cape gooseberry, strawberry-tomato, half-hardy annual, 2 feet, flowers bell-shaped yellowish, fruits yellow, edible, southern United States.

Cultivation The hardy species require a rich, well-drained soil in a sunny or partially shaded position and should be planted in the spring. The fruits, popularly called 'lanterns' (the inflated calyces) can be used for winter decorations and can be picked and dried in the autumn. If left out of doors, they become skeletonized. The tender species require a compost of loam, leafmould and a little sand and should be planted singly in 5–6 inch pots placed in a sunny position. Water freely during the summer and feed regularly with a liquid fertilizer. Pot up or plant in early spring. Propagate hardy species by division every three years, and greenhouse species from seed sown in sandy soil in heat in the spring or from cuttings placed in sandy soil in heat between January and April. *P. alkekengi* grows very vigorously and spreads by means of underground runners. It may be used as a deciduous ground cover plant in sun or semi-shade. Where it is suited it can become something of a nuisance, difficult to eradicate unless every piece of root is removed.

Pulmonaria (pul-mon-air-ee-a)
From the Latin *pulmo*, lung; derivation

1

2

uncertain; either because the spotted leaves bore a resemblance to diseased lungs, or because one species was regarded as providing a remedy for diseased lungs (*Boraginaceae*). Lungwort. This is a genus of 10 species of hardy herbaceous perennials, natives of Europe. *P. angustifolia*, a rare native, is an excellent garden plant. The charm of these early-flowering lungworts is in their flowers, which change from red to blue—they also have the name soldiers-and-sailors on this account—and in their hairy leaves which, in some species, are spotted with a much paler green or with white. The spotted leaves suggested to some herbalists the human lung, and it was thus in accordance with the 'doctrine of signatures' that the plant was used to dose unfortunate sufferers from lung complaints.

Species cultivated *P. angustifolia*, blue cowslip, to 1 foot, leaves lacking spots, flowers pink, changing to blue, spring, Europe including Britain; vars. *alba*, white; 'Mawson's Variety' is a selected garden form. *P. officinalis*, Jerusalem cowslip, spotted dog, to 1 foot, leaves spotted white, flowers pink then violet, spring, Europe. *P. rubra*, 1 foot, leaves usually lacking spots, flowers brick red, Transylvania. *P. saccharata*, to 1 foot, leaves blotched white, flowers pink, April to July, Europe.

Cultivation Any soil is suitable and the plants will grow in sun or shade. Quite the best companions for lungworts are other early spring flowering plants including bulbs, primroses and so on, interspersed with native ferns. Plant in autumn or spring and lift and divide the plants every four to five years. Propagation is by seed sown in a shady border out of doors in March or April or by division of the roots in spring or autumn.

Pulsatilla (pulse-a-til-a)

The name was first used by Pierandrea Mattioli, a sixteenth-century Italian botanist and physician, and possibly means 'shaking in the wind' (*Ranunculaceae*). This genus of 30 species, distinguished from *Anemone* only by minor botanical differences, includes some of the most beautiful of low-growing flowering plants, and one in particular, *P. vernalis*, which is so lovely that it must have converted many to the growing of alpine plants. The plants are very suitable for alpine house cultivation. One of their attractions is the feathery foliage, and another is the equally hairy and feathery seedheads. They are natives of the temperate regions of Europe and Asia.

Species cultivated *P. alpina,* 1 foot, blue

1 A red form of Pulsatilla vulgaris has more pronounced colour on the inside of the petals.
2 The outstanding purplish flowers of Pulsatilla vulgaris, the Pasque Flower, have bright orange centres.

182

buds opening white, May to June, European Alps; var. *sulphurea* with pale yellow flowers. *P. halleri,* 10 inches, flowers of deep violet, finely cut leaves, April to May, Swiss Alps and the Austrian Tyrol. *P. slavica* (syn. *P. vulgaris slavica*), 6 inches, flowers plum-purple with golden centres, April. *P. vernalis,* 6–9 inches, evergreen, finely cut foliage, hairy bronze-violet buds opening to a glistening crystalline white with a boss of golden stamens, April, high Alpine meadows. *P. vulgaris,* Pasque flower, 1 foot, rich purple flowers covered with shaggy fur, April, Europe including Britain; vars. *alba,* white; 'Budapest', large powder-blue flowers; red-flowered seedlings are offered by some nurserymen.

Cultivation A light open soil is suitable; *P. vulgaris* is found naturally on chalk and limestone formations. A well-drained rock garden suits most species, but they *must* be protected from wet during the winter. It is for this reason that they are so eminently suitable for the alpine house. Seed, sown as soon as it is ripe in July or August, in sandy soil in a cold frame, is quite the best method of propagation.

Pyrethrum (py-re-thrum)
From the Greek *pyr,* fire, probably with reference to fever, since the plant was used medicinally to assuage fever (*Compositae*). These hardy plants are admirable for a sunny border and last

1 Pyrethrum 'Eileen May Robinson', a clear pink, mixes well with the deep rose of Pyrethrum 'Kelway's Glorious'.
2 The purplish-red flowers of Pyrethrum 'Marjorie Robinson' are single with very prominent central discs.
3 Pyrethrum 'Radiant' is one of many hybrids of Pyrethrum roseum.

well as cut flowers. Long known as pyrethrum they are botanically classified under *Chrysanthemum.*

Species cultivated *P. roseum* (syn. *Chrysanthemum coccineum*), 1–2 feet, with large, daisy-like flowers in May and June. The colour is variable from red to white, occasionally tipped with yellow. The leaves are vivid green, graceful and feathery, Caucasus and Persia. There are many hybrids, both single and double. *Single* 2–2½ feet, 'Allurement', rich pink; 'Avalanche', pure white; 'Brenda', bright carmine; 'Bressingham Red', large crimson; 'Eileen May Robinson', clear pink; 'Kelway's Glorious', glowing scarlet; 'Salmon Beauty', bright salmon-rose. *Double* 2–2½ feet, 'Carl Vogt', pure white; 'Lord Rosebery', velvety red; 'Madeleine', lilac-pink; 'Yvonne Cayeux', pale sulphur-yellow. For the plant sometimes listed as *Pyrethrum parthenium,* the feverfew, see *Chrysanthemum parthenium.*

Cultivation A well-drained loamy soil and a sunny position suit pyrethrums best, though they will grow well on chalky soils. They require ample moisture when coming into bud and during the growing

season. Plant in March and leave them undisturbed for three or four years. If left longer the plants will deteriorate and the flowers become smaller and fewer. Lift and divide in March or after flowering in July, discarding the old, woody pieces. Each year cut the plants hard back after flowering. This often results in a second crop of blooms in late summer or autumn. Slugs and rabbits can be a menace but of course, weathered ashes are scattered around and over the crowns in the autumn this will deter them, as will slug pellets. The plants are somewhat floppy in habit so some light staking should be provided. Propagation is by division in March or after flowering in July, or by seed sown in a cool greenhouse or frame in spring. (See also Chrysanthemum, *C. coccineum*).

Romneya (rom-nee-a)

Named in honour of the Rev T. Romney Robinson (1792–1882), an Irish astronomer who discovered *Romneya coulteri* (*Papaveraceae*). A genus of two species of handsome, semi-shrubby perennials from southwestern California with extremely attractive poppy-like flowers, borne singly at the ends of the stems.

Species cultivated *R. coulteri*, Californian tree poppy, 6–8 feet, leaves and stems glaucous, flowers satiny white, fragrant, 4–5 inches across, petals frilled, with a prominent mass of golden stamens, throughout the summer. *R. trichocalyx* (syn. *R. coulteri trichocalyx*), similar, but with more erect growth and somewhat larger flowers with a dense covering of bristle-like hairs on the calyx. Hybrids are sometimes offered under the name *R. × hybrida* (syn. *R. vandedenii*).

Cultivation These beautiful plants should be planted in April or May in a deep, well-drained soil and a sheltered sunny position, preferably beneath a south-facing wall where they can spread. Once planted, the roots should be left undisturbed unless the underground stems or roots are required for propagation purposes. They are not suitable for exposed districts. Propagation is by root cuttings taken in March or April, about 2 inches long and inserted singly in small pots containing sandy soil and placed in a propagating frame with gentle bottom heat, or seed may be sown in pans of sandy soil in February or March in a temperature of 55°F (13°C). Whichever method of propagation is used, the plants should be grown on for a year or more in pots before they are planted out in their permanent positions.

Rudbeckia (rud-beck-ee-a)

Commemorating Olaf Rudbeck (1660–1740) Swedish professor of botany and counsellor of Linnaeus (*Compositae*). Cone flower. A genus of about 25 herbaceous plants, mostly perennial and hardy, natives of North America, related to

1

2

1 Romneya coulteri, the California Tree Poppy, is a semi-shrubby perennial from the southwestern United States.

2 The blooms of Romneya coulteri are satiny white, fragrant and large, measuring from 4 to 6 inches across.

Echinacea. The flowers are showy, daisy-like, often with drooping petals and conspicuous conical centres. Most of them are excellent herbaceous border plants and are valuable for late summer effect in the garden.

Species cultivated *R. bicolor*, 1–2 feet, half-hardy annual, yellow, ray petals yellow, sometimes with purplish bases, disk purplish, conical, July; var. *superba*, flowers 2 inches across, petals brown on the under-sides; cultivars include 'Golden Flame', golden-yellow; 'Kelvedon Star', 3 feet, golden-yellow with mahogany red zone; 'My Joy' ('Mon Plaisir'), dwarf habit, flowers golden-yellow. *R. fulgida deamii* (syn. *R. deamii*), 2–3 feet, a somewhat hairy plant of erect habit; flowers deep yellow, 2–3 inches across with purple-black centres, freely produced, July to September; var. *speciosa* (syns. *R. speciosa*, *R. newmanii*), 2½ feet, black-eyed Susan, similar but of laxer habit, an old favourite;

'Goldsturm', 2 feet, an excellent larger-flowered form of stiffer habit and less hairy, August–September, a good garden plant. 'Goldquelle', 2½–3 feet, a newer hybrid of erect growth with lemon-yellow flowers three or more inches across, August–September. 'Herbstsonne' (*R. laciniata* × *R. nitida*), 6–8 feet, a tall, erect-growing plant with large, deeply-cut leaves and golden-yellow flowers with green cones, September. *R. hirta hybrida*, 2 feet, usually grown from seed as an annual or biennial, a bristly-hairy plant, striking flowers in shades of gold, orange and mahogany, summer. *R. laciniata* 'Golden Glow', 6 feet, deeply-lobed green leaves and fully double yellow flowers, 3 inches across, August to September. *R. maxima*, 4–6 feet, a rather rare and very ornamental species with large handsome glaucous leaves and rich yellow flowers with dark centres, August–September, Texas. *R. purpurea* see *Echinacea purpurea*, *R. tetra* 'Gloriosa', Gloriosa daisy, 2–3 feet, half hardy annual, flowers to 7 inches across, colours various including yellow, mahogany-red, bronze, and bicolors; double-flowered forms are also offered.

Cultivation Most rudbeckias are easy to grow. A sunny or semi-shaded site with good but well-drained loamy soil is preferable, though the plants grow well on

chalk. Some of the taller species and their varieties prefer moister soils and are particularly useful when grown in groups among shrubs or in the wild garden where they provide an early autumn display. Hybrids or cultivars have now largely replaced many of the species in general cultivation. The perennial sorts do best if they are divided and replanted every third or fourth year. *R. hirta* is best treated as an annual and succeeds in a sunny position in well-drained soil. Seeds of the half-hardy annual kinds should be sown under glass in gentle heat in early spring. After they have been hardened off the seedlings should be planted out 9 inches apart in late May or early June, where they are to flower. *R. maxima* is rather slow to become established and requires a moist soil. Propagation of the perennials is easily effected by seed or by division in the spring.

Salvia (sal-vee-a)

From the Latin *salveo*, meaning save or heal, used by Pliny with reference to the medicinal qualities of some species (*Labiatae*). A large genus of over 700 species of hardy, half-hardy and tender annual, biennial, perennial plants and shrubs, some with aromatic leaves, widely distributed in the temperate and warmer

The daisy-like Rudbeckia are distinguished by prominent dark conical centres and showy, often droopy, petals.
1 Rudbeckia 'Bambi' has a red zone at the base of each petal.
2 Rudbeckia 'Herbstsonne' is a tall and very erect hybrid form with down-turned petals.
3 Rudbeckia 'Goldsturm' bears large thin-petalled flowers in late summer.

zones. It includes the common sage, *S. officinalis*, a valuable culinary plant, as well as many colourful summer and autumn flowering border plants.

Species cultivated *S. ambigens*, about 5 feet, perennial or sub-shrub, flowers deep sky-blue, September–October, South America, slightly tender. *S. argentea*, 2 feet, most decorative, leaves large, silvery-grey, felted, flowers white, small, in spikes, June and July, Mediterranean region; for a dry soil and a sunny position. *S. aurea*, shrub, leaves rounded, covered with fine hairs, flowers yellowish-brown, South Africa, hardy in mild areas. *S. azurea*, 4 feet, sub-shrub, flowers deep blue, autumn, North America, hardy; var. *grandiflora*, flower spikes denser. *S. fulgens*, Mexican red sage, 2–3 feet, shrub, flowers scarlet, in whorls, July, Mexico, tender. *S. ges–*

neraeflora, 2 feet, sub-shrub, flowers bright scarlet, summer, Colombia, tender. *S. grahamii,* shrub, to 4 feet, flowers deep crimson, July onwards, Mexico, somewhat tender. *S. greggii,* shrub, 3 feet, flowers scarlet, summer, Texas, Mexico, tender. *S. haematodes,* biennial, 3 feet, leaves large, wrinkled, heart-shaped, light blue flowers on branching stems from June to August, Greece. *S. interrupta,* 2–3 feet, sub-shrub, leaves 3-lobed, aromatic, flowers violet purple with white throat, May to July, Morocco, nearly hardy. *S. involucrata,* sub-shrub, 2–4 feet, flowers rose, summer and autumn, Mexico, not quite hardy; var. *bethelii,* flowers rosy crimson in longer spikes. *S. juriscii,* perennial, 1 foot, flowers violet, June, Serbia, hardy. *S. lavandulifolia,* perennial, 9–12 inches, leaves grey, flowers lavender, early summer, hardy. *S. mexicana minor,* sub-shrub, to 12 feet in nature, flowers violet-blue, February, Mexico, tender. *S. neurepia,* sub-shrub, 6–7 feet, flowers scarlet, late summer and autumn, Mexico, hardy in the milder counties. *S. officinalis,* common sage, sub-shrub, 2–3 feet, leaves wrinkled, aromatic, flowers variable purple, blue or white, June and July, southern Europe, hardy; vars. *purpurascens,* reddish-purple stems and leaves, strongly flavoured; *aurea,* leaves golden, flowers rarely produced. *S. pratense,* perennial, 2 feet, flowers bright blue, June to August, Europe, including Britain, hardy; var. *rosea,* flowers rosy-purple. *S. rutilans,* pineapple-scented sage, sub-shrub, 2–3 feet, flowers magenta-crimson, summer, tender. *S. sclarea,* clary, biennial or short-lived perennial, leaves and stems sticky, flowers pale mauve, bracts white and rose, conspicuous, June to September, Europe; various strains are offered; var. *turkestanica,* flowers white, bracts and stems pink. *S. splendens,* scarlet sage, sub-shrub, 3 feet, flowers scarlet, in spikes in summer, Brazil, usually grown as half-hardy annual; vars. for summer bedding: 'Blaze of Fire', 9–12 inches, scarlet; 'Fireball', 15 inches, rich scarlet; 'Harbinger', 15 inches, long scarlet spikes; 'Salmon Pygmy,' 6 inches. *S. × superba* (syn. *S. nemorosa*), 3 feet, bracts reddish, persistent, flowers violet-purple in spikes, July to September, hybrid, hardy; var. *lubeca,* identical but 1½ feet tall only. *S. uliginosa,* bog sage, 4–5 feet, leaves shiny green, deeply toothed, flowers azure-blue in spikes, August to October, eastern North America, hardy.

Cultivation Salvias are easily grown in ordinary, well-drained garden soil and in a sunny position. *S. argentea* particularly likes dry soil, as well as sun, and *S. officinalis* should be cut back in spring to encourage new bushy growth. *S. × superba* makes a particularly good border plant when planted in a bold group. *S. uliginosa* prefers moister conditions than the others, and its creeping rootstock should be given a

covering of bracken or dry peat in cold districts. Those described as tender will succeed in the milder counties, given the shelter of a warm wall, or they may be grown in the greenhouse in pots in a compost of loam and well-rotted manure or leafmould plus some sand to provide drainage. The pots may be placed out of doors in June and brought in again in September. Water freely form spring to autumn, moderately in winter. Maintain a temperature in winter of 45–55°F (7–10°C). Propagate the shrubs, subshrubs and hardy perennial kinds by division in the spring or by soft-wood cuttings, rooted in sandy soil in a

1 Some Salvia cultivars, such as the deep blue Salvia 'May Night', are tall, handsome plants.
2 Salvia horminum, with its wealth of coloured bracts, is useful for dried winter arrangements.
3 Salvia grahamii, a rather tender, shrubby native of 'Mexico, bears deep crimson flowers from mid-summer onwards.

propagating case in spring in a temperature of 65°F (18°C). *S. splendens* is increased by seed sown under glass in February or March in a temperature of 60°F (16°C) and planted out in late May or June.

Saxifraga (sax-ee-fra-ga)

From the Latin *saxum*, rock or stone, and *frango*, to break, alluding either to its ancient medicinal use for 'breaking' stones in the bladder or to the supposed ability of the roots to penetrate and assist the breakdown of rocks (*Saxifragaceae*). Saxifrage, rockfoil. A genus of some 370 species of mainly dwarf tufted perennial and annual plants inhabiting the mountain regions of the northern and southern temperate regions. The many species, varieties and cultivars are usually grown on the rock garden or in the alpine house.

For the convenience of classification, the genus is divided into 15 or 16 sections, largely on the basis of the characteristics of its foliage and habit. From the gardener's point of view, however, it is best divided as below into fewer larger groupings according to cultivational requirements.

Species cultivated *S. aizoides*, yellow mountain saxifrage, a loosely tufted mat-forming species with yellow, orange or red flowers and linear fleshy leaves. *S. aizoon* (see *S. paniculata*). *S. apiculata* (*S. marginata* × *S. sancta*), a cushion or Kabschia hybrid, forming wide mats of green, silver-tipped rosettes and primrose-yellow flowers on 3-inch stems. *S. × arco-valleyi* (*S. burseriana* × *S. lilacina*), a Kabschia hybrid with compact silvery cushions and soft pink flowers on 1-inch stems. *S. aretioides* produces hard, grey-green cushions and yellow flowers; a Kabschia that has given rise to many good hybrids easier to grow. *S. × assimilis* (probably *S. burseriana* × *S. tombeanensis*) has firm grey cushions and white flowers on 1–2-inch long stems. *S. biternata* is an ally of the meadow saxifrage from the Mediterranean area. It has tufts of hoary, kidney-shaped, divided leaves and large glistening white flowers on 6–8-inch long stems. *S. × borisii* (*S. ferdinandi-coburgii* × *S. marginata*) is a Kabschia hybrid with blue-grey cushions and large citron-yellow flowers on 3-inch stems. *S. boryi*, allied to *S. marginata*, but more compact in habit. *S. × burnatii* (*S. paniculata* × *S. cochlearis*) is a silver or encrusted hybrid showing a blend of the parental characteristics; white flowers in loose panicles are borne on reddish stems. *S. burseriana* is the finest of the Kabschias and a parent of many excellent hybrids and cultivars. The type plant forms large cushions of crowded, silver-grey rosettes composed of many narrow, somewhat spiny, leaves. Each rosette bears a 2-inch long reddish stem surmounted by one or more large glistening-white flowers in early spring. *S. b.* 'His Majesty' is a splendid form with the flowers flushed pink; *S. b.* 'Gloria' has larger flowers on redder stems; *S. b. sulphurea* may be a hybrid, but looks like the type plant with soft-yellow flowers. *S. cespitosa* (syn. *S. caespitosa*), tufted saxifrage, is one of the 'mossy' species and a rare native in Wales and Scotland. It makes dense cushions of somewhat glandular, hairy, deeply divided

leaves and bears small white flowers on short slender stems. *S. caucasica* is a green-leaved Kabschia with yellow flowers on 1-inch high stems. *S. cernua* may be likened to a mountain form of the meadow saxifrage (*S. granulata*) with a drooping inflorescence bearing both white flowers and red bulbils in the leaf axils. It is a very rare Scottish native. *S. cochlearis* is an encrusted species, with small spoon-shaped silver leaves forming the hummock-like plants, from which arise slender panicles of milk-white flowers on reddish glandular stems. *S. c. minor* and *major* are smaller and larger forms. *S. cortusifolia* belongs to the Diptera section, to which the better known *S. fortunei* belongs, and has rounded, deeply-cut leathery leaves on stiff 3-inch long stems and panicles of white flowers with irregularly-sized narrow petals. *S. cotyledon* is one of the largest encrusted species, with broad rosettes of wide strap-shaped leaves rimmed with silver and huge airy panicles of white flowers that may be 1½ feet or more long. *S. c. caterhamensis* and 'Southside Seedling' are superior forms with red-spotted flowers. *S. crustata*, also an encrusted sort, is smaller, the rosettes forming cushions or mats with off-white flowers on branched 6-inch stems. *S. cuneata* is a loose 'mossy' species with toothed, deeply-lobed, leathery leaves and open panicles of white flowers. *S. cuneifolia* belongs to the Robertsonia section

1 Saxifraga aizoides, the Yellow Mountain Saxifrage, forms loose golden mats.
2 Saxifraga fortunei has panicles of white flowers and kidney-shaped leaves.
3 Saxifraga apiculata is a mat-forming dwarf type.

whose chief representative in gardens is London pride (*S. umbrosa*). It is a small species with flat rosettes of leathery daisy-like leaves and flowering stems reminiscent of London pride in miniature. *S. cuscutiformis* is a smaller edition of mother of thousands (*S. stolonifera*) with the leaves prettily veined white. Abundantly produced red stolons, or runners, resemble the leafless stems of common dodder (*Cuscuta*). *S. cymbalaria* is an annual, with smooth shining kidney-shaped leaves and numerous starry yellow flowers. *S. decipiens* (see *S. rosacea*). *S. × engleri* (*S. crustata* × *S. hostii*) resembles the first parent, and has pink flowers on 3-inch stems. *S. exarata* is a distinctive 'mossy' saxifrage, with dark green, strongly-nerved, deeply-cleft leaves, and flowers that may be either white, yellow or purplish. *S. ferdinandi-coburgii* belongs to the encrusted group, forming neat mounds of silver-grey, spiny-leaved rosettes topped by 4-inch high stems bearing red buds and bright yellow flowers. *S. × florariensis* (*S. hostii* × *S. lingulata*) is an encrusted hybrid eventually forming mats of handsome 3-inch wide, silvered

187

rosettes that turn red in autumn, and have foot-long sprays of white flowers. *S. fortunei* is undoubtedly the finest member of the Diptera section, with large, glossy, thick-textured, kidney-shaped leaves which are often red beneath, and tall airy, elegant panicles of glistening white flowers, each with one or more extra long tail-like petals. The plant is completely deciduous after the first severe frost of late autumn. *S. × frederici-augusti* (probably *S. media × S. porophylla*) is a hybrid in the Engleria section, noteworthy for the flowering stems being clad in leafy often coloured bracts. This hybrid has silver-rimmed rosettes and flowers composed of a bell-shaped calyx covered with claret hairs below the small pink petals. *S. geum* (see *S. hirsuta*). *S. × godseffiana* (*S. burseriana × S. sancta*) produces mats of narrow spiny-leaved rosettes and lemon-yellow flowers on reddish stems. *S. granulata*, the meadow saxifrage of Britain and also known as fair maids of France, is a deciduous species, the kidney-shaped, rounded-toothed leaves dying away soon after the plant has flowered; milk-white flowers are borne on branched stems up to 1 foot tall; var. *plena* has double flowers. *S. grisebachii* belongs to the Engleria section, eventually forming humped mats of 3-inch wide grey rosettes set with leafy flowering spikes 9 inches tall. The bell-shaped calyces and bracts are set with deep red glandular hairs. *S. × haagii* (*S. ferdinandii-coburgii × S. sancta*) is a Kabschia with dark green rosettes in cushions and bears rich yellow flowers. *S. hederacea* rather resembles a small creeping *Linaria* or *Cymbalaria*, with small ivy-shaped leaves and starry white flowers. *S. hirculus* is placed in a section of the same name, and forms tufted mats of narrow leaves and branched stems set with quite large yellow flowers speckled with orange. It is a rare British native and known as yellow marsh saxifrage. *S. hirsuta*, probably better known as *S. geum*, is a Robertsonia saxifrage akin to London pride, but with longer leaf stalks and rounded leaves heart-shaped at the base, set with long hairs on both surfaces. The flower stems, covered with short hairs, support open panicles of small white blossoms, each petal bearing a yellow spot at its base. *S. hostii* is one of the finest encrusted species, forming wide mats of silvery rimmed rosettes set with creamy-white flowers in short corymbs. *S. huetiana* is a small bushy annual with starry yellow flowers freely produced. *S. hypnoides*, Dovedale moss, is a cushion or mat-forming mossy species native to Britain and most of the hilly regions of the northern temperate zone. It is very variable in habit, flower size and colour, the type being white; var. *condensata* is very compact with yellow flowers; var. *kingii* is close-growing, the leaves turning red in winter; var. *purpurea* has reddish flowers. *S. × irvingii* (probably *S. burseriana × S. lilacina*) was raised at Kew Gardens and is one of the

1 *Saxifraga x haagii*, a Kabschia Saxifrage, bears golden-yellow blooms.
2 *Saxifraga hypnoides*, the Dovedale Moss, looks most effective in winter when the flowers have died back.

free-blooming Kabschia hybrids with lilac-pink flowers. *S. × jenkinsae* is similar to the preceding and probably of the same parentage. *S. juniperifolia* has dark green, spine-tipped leaved rosettes in humped cushions, usually only sparingly set with small yellow flowers. *S. lilacina* produces wide dense mats of small green rosettes set with amethyst flowers on 1 to 2-inch tall stems. This distinctive Kabschia has entered into the parentage of many fine hybrids. *S. lingulata* should now be known as *S. callosa*. It is a very garden-worthy encrusted species with mats of large iron-grey rosettes and 1–1½ feet long, gracefully-arching panicles of pure white flowers; var. *catalaunica* has shorter broader leaves and shorter, stiffer flowering stems. *S. longifolia* is perhaps the finest of the large encrusted species with huge, densely leafy rosettes and elegant flowering stems up to 2 feet, long branched right to the base. *S. marginata* is another Kabschia that has contributed to some good hybrids; it forms mats or loose cushions of small green rosettes rimmed with silver and bearing short-branched stems set with large white flowers. *S. media* is another Engleria somewhat smaller than *S. grisebachii* and which has entered into the parentage

of many hybrids. *S. moschata* covers most of the common 'mossy' hybrids seen in gardens; it is similar to *S. decipiens* in appearance, but usually a little more dwarf and in various shades of red and pink, but sometimes yellow. *S. m.* 'Cloth of Gold', has golden-green foliage and white flowers; 'Mrs Piper' is a good bright red; 'Elf' is pink; 'James Bremner' is white; and var. *sanguinea superba* is scarlet. *S. oppositifolia* is the familiar purple saxifrage of the mountains of the northern temperate zone, extending down to sea-level in the more northern latitudes. This is a variable species as regards flower colour and leaf size, though always mat-forming with leafy interlacing stems and solitary terminal almost stemless purple flowers; var. *splendens* has large red-purple flowers; 'R. M. Prichard' is lilac-purple; *alba* is a poor form with white flowers, and *rudolphiana* is bright rose-purple. *S. paniculata* is still usually grown under the name of *S. aizoon*, a very variable encrusted species of great charm; var. *baldensis* (*minutifolia*) is very dwarf and compact-growing with small silvery-rimmed rosettes in low mounds and 4-inch stems of pure white flowers; var. *lutea* is similar to the type with mounds of stoloniferous rosettes and soft yellow flowers; var. *rosea* has clear pink flowers and reddish leaves; var. *orientalis* has green rosettes and milk white flowers on 4-inch stems. *S. porophylla* is akin to *S. media* and others of the Engleria group, but with purple calyces and small pink petals. *S. retusa* is akin to *S. oppositifolia* but with smaller foliage and the rose-purple flowers in short terminal clusters. *S. rosacea* is still better known as *S. decipiens* and is the main 'mossy' species in cultivation, often as one parent with *S. granulata*, *S. moschata* and others. Most of the cultivars form loose cushions or are mat-forming with divided leaves and a profusion of short-stemmed flowers in all shades of pink, red and white. Some of the cultivars listed under *moschata* may well belong here. *S. rotundifolia* belongs to the Miscopetalum section which is close to Robertsonia and London pride. It has rounded or kidney-shaped leaves in tufts and airy panicles of small starry flowers, white speckled pink; var. *heucherifolia* is smaller, more hairy and with flowers more heavily spotted. *S. sancta* forms wide carpets of small rosettes of dark green spine-tipped leaves and bears rich yellow flowers on 2-inch tall stems. It is one of the most frequently grown green-leaved Kabschias. *S. scardica* is a blue-grey Kabschia, forming hard mounds topped by 4-inch stems of large white flowers sometimes flushed pink. *S. spathularis*, St Patrick's cabbage, is an Irish native belonging to the Robertsonia section. It resembles a smaller edition of London pride with airy panicles of starry white flowers spotted with yellow and crimson. Crossed with *S. umbrosa* it gives the familiar London pride which thrives so well in shady town gardens.

S. stolonifera (syn. *S. sarmentosa*), mother of thousands, has long red, branched runners like those of a strawberry, large round marbled rather fleshy leaves and graceful panicles of white flowers spotted with yellow and red. Typical of the Diptera section, each flower has one or two extra elongated petals. *S. trifurcata* belongs among the 'mossy' species with deeply cut recurved leaves somewhat aromatic when bruised and 6-inch stems of large white flowers. *S. umbrosa* is akin to *S. spathularis* but with shorter, long-hairy leaf stalks and the leaf blades with a cartilaginous border. *S. valdensis* is similar to, but smaller and slower growing than, *S. cochlearis*, with stiff glandular stems surmounted by heads of round white flowers. Cultivars: 'Amitie' (*S. lilacina* × *S. scardica obtusa*) is a Kabschia with firm cushions of grey-green rosettes and lilac flowers on 1-inch stems. 'Apple Blossom' ('mossy' hybrid) has small pale pink flowers in profusion. 'Boston Spa' (Kabschia hybrid) bears deep yellow flowers with red buds over green cushions. 'Buttercup' (Kabschia) has rich yellow flowers on grey-green cushions. 'Cecil Davies' (*S. lingulata* × *S. longifolia*) has very compact mounds of silvered rosettes and elegant sprays of white flowers. 'Cranbourne' is probably the finest of the Kabschia hybrids with neat grey-green mounds of ½-inch wide rosettes and almost stemless large clear pink flowers. 'Dr Ramsay' (*S. cochlearis* × *S. longifolia*) is an encrusted cultivar with symmetrical silvered rosettes and sprays of white flowers on 1-foot stems. 'Edie Campbell' and 'Elf' are both 'mosses', the former with large pink flowers in profusion, the latter smaller and neater. 'Ester' (*S. paniculata lutea* × *S. cochlearis*) bears soft yellow flowers in short sprays over vigorous masses of silvered rosettes. 'Faldonside' (*S. aretioides* × *S. marginata*) is a first-rate Kabschia with citron-yellow flowers, the overlapping petals of which are charmingly crimped at the margins. 'Gem' (*S. burseriana* 'Gloria' × *S. irvingii*) is another good Kabschia with neat bluegrey spiny mounds and pale pink flowers with a ruby eye. 'Four Winds' is a rich red 'mossy' sport. 'Iris Pritchard' (*S.* × *godroniana* × *S. lilacina*) bears flowers of apricot-rose over neat grey hummocks. 'James Bremner' is one of the few good white-flowered 'mosses' and 'Kingscote White' is a larger flowered pure white 'mossy' variety. 'Kathleen Pinsent' (encrusted) may be a *S. ligulata* × *S. callosa* hybrid, with 1-foot long stems and sprays of yellow-eyed pink flowers. 'Myra' (Kabschia) is probably an *S. lilacina* hybrid, with compact, slow-growing mounds of silvery rosettes and deep pink blossoms. 'Mrs Piper' ('mossy') forms wide mats of soft green foliage studded freely with bright red flowers on 3-inch stems. 'Pearly King' is a similar 'mossy' with pearlywhite flowers. 'Pixie' is a compact growing 'mossy' with rose-red flowers. 'Riverslea' (*S. lilacina* × *S. porophylla*) is a Kabschia

Saxifraga x jenkinsae, growing in tufa, is a free-blooming Kabschia hybrid which forms a firm, pale-pink cushion of flowers.

× Engleria hybrid, with silvery rosettes in compact mounds and purple-rose flowers on 3-inch stems. 'Salomonii' (*S. burseriana* × *S. marginata*) produces freegrowing silvery mats and 3-inch stems bearing large vase-shaped white flowers that are pink in bud. 'Sir Douglas Haig' ('mossy') bears dark velvety-crimson flowers. 'Southside Seedling' is a comparatively new *S. cotyledon* hybrid with large silver-rimmed rosettes and long sprays of white, intensely red-spotted blossoms. 'Tumbling Waters' (*S. lingulata* × *S. longiflora*) is the finest large encrusted hybrid with huge silvered rosettes and magnificent 2-foot long plumes of white blossoms. 'Winston Churchill' ('mossy') bears soft pink flowers on 6-inch stems.

Cultivation With the exception of species in the section Hirculus, a few of the 'mossy' group, and *S. aizoides*, which need moist to wet conditions to thrive well, practically all saxifrages require a well-drained site either on the rock garden, dry wall, raised bed, moraine, or in pots and pans in the alpine house. The Robertsonia species, typified by London pride, the Miscopetalum section, and such species as *S. hederacea*, require a shady site, the first mentioned doing particularly well even in complete shade or in woodland. Kabschia species require

particularly good drainage and are best grown in a scree or raised bed. Flowering very early, they are ideally suited to alpine house culture where their delicate-looking flowers may be appreciated unsullied by heavy rain and mud splash. Most of the encrusted group are ideal for the open rock garden, in rock crevices or dry walls; *S. cotyledon* and *longifolia* should always be grown in the latter habitat if at all possible. All the popular mossy hybrids and some of the species are good all-rounders on the rock garden and are also suitable for paved areas and as ground cover for small bulbs. Generally speaking they will stand partial shade well and seem to thrive better if the site is not too sun drenched. Propagation is effected by seeds sown in pots or pans in early spring, stood in a cold frame, by division after flowering, or by offset rosettes inserted as cuttings in a sand frame from spring to late summer.

Scabiosa (skay-bee-o-sa)

From the Latin *scabies*, itch, for which some of these plants were used as remedies, or from the Latin *scabiosus*, rough or scurfy, referring to the grey felting on the leaves of some species (*Dipsacaceae*). Scabious. This genus of 100 species of hardy biennial and perennial herbaceous plants, mainly from the Mediterranean region, gives a number which are good decorative plants for the garden. The three species which are

British native plants, *Scabiosa arvensis*, *S. columbaria* and *S. succisa*, are among the prettiest-flowering wild plants and are quite suited to garden cultivation. *S. succisa*, the devil's bit, is especially good as it has flowers of a bright blue colour. In the plants in the *Dipsacaceae* family the so-called flower is made up of a large number of small florets gathered into a head, or *capitulum*, somewhat as in *Compositae*.

Perennial species cultivated *S. arvensis* (syn. *Knautia arvensis*), field scabious, 1 foot, flowers bluish-lilac, July–August, Europe (including Britain). *S. caucasica*, 1–1½ feet, flowers mauve, blue or white, June to October, Caucasus; vars. 'Clive Greaves', flowers mauve, large; 'Miss Willmott', large, white; 'Moonstone', large, lavender-blue. *S. columbaria*, 1–2 feet, lilac or blue-purple, July to September, Europe including Britain. *S. graminifolia*, 9 inches, leaves narrow, silvery-white, flowers pale mauve to rose, summer, southern Europe. *S. ochroleuca*, 2 feet, yellow, July to November, south-eastern Europe; var. *webbiana*, 6 inches, flowers creamy-white. *S. succisa* (syn. *Succisa pratensis*), devil's bit, 1–2 feet, blue-purple or white, July to October, Europe including Britain.

Cultivation These plants all do well in chalky or limy soil, which, however, should be enriched. *S. caucasica* is suitable for the herbaceous border, but may also be grown to supply cut flowers, for which purpose its long clean stems make it very suitable. These plants should be lifted and divided every three or four years, moving them in spring as disturbance in autumn can kill them. *S. craminifolia* and *S. ochroleuca webbiana* are suitable for the rock garden. *S. atropurpurea* can be raised from seed sown in February or March in a temperature of 60°F (16°C). Plant out the seedlings in May to flower as annuals, for later disturbance (July) will cause them to behave as biennials. In the latter case, over-winter them in a cold frame and plant out in April. They are good for cutting. Other species may be propagated by division of the clumps in March.

Sidalcea (sid-al-see-a)

A compound of two related genera, *Sida* and *Alcea*. The former comes from an ancient Greek name used by Theophrastus for the water-lily, the latter from *Althaea*, the generic name for hollyhock (*Malvaceae*). These hardy perennial herbaceous plants belong to the

1 The delicate blooms of Scabiosa caucasica are equally suitable for the herbaceous border or for use as cut flowers. Its blooms range from mauve and blue to pure white.
2 Sidalcea malvaeflora bears soft lilac blooms in mid-summer. A number of reliable cultivars are available in a variety of colours.

same family as the hollyhock and the mallow. Their flowers have delicate papery petals in varying shades of pink and purple. There are 25 species, all from western North America.

Species cultivated *S. candida*, 2–3 feet, flowers white, summer, Colorado. *S. malvaeflora*, 1½–3 feet, rather twiggy in habit, flowers lilac, summer, California; var. *listeri*, pink. *S. spicata*, 1–3 feet, rosy-purple flowers, July–September, western North America. Some good cultivars include 'Brilliant', crimson; 'Elsie Heugh', pink, fringed flowers; 'Interlaken', pink; 'Puck', large clear pink flowers; 'Rev Page Roberts', soft pink; 'Rose Queen', tall; 'William Smith', salmon-red.

Cultivation Ordinary, slightly sandy soil is suitable; the position should preferably be a sunny border. Plant in the autumn or spring, and lift and divide every three or four years. Propagation is by seeds sown in light soil in April, transplanting the seedlings in April or by division in October or March for the named varieties.

Silene (si-le-ne)

Probably from the Greek *sialon*, saliva, in reference to the gummy exudations on the stems which ward off insects (*Caryophyllaceae*). Catchfly. A genus of 100 species of annual, biennial and herbaceous perennials of the northern hemisphere and South Africa, having a wide range of colour through white, pink and red to purple. Some make good rock plants, but some can only be considered as weeds and should be banned from the garden.

Annual species cultivated *S. armeria*, 1–2 feet, flowers pink, summer, Europe. *S. pendula*, 12 inches, rose to white, summer, Europe.

Biennial species cultivated *S. compacta*, 1½ feet, flowers pink, summer, Russia, Asia Minor. *S. rupestris*, 4–6 inches, flowers white to pink, June to August, western Europe, Siberia.

Perennial species cultivated *S. acaulis*, cushion pink, moss campion, 2 inches, flowers pink, June, northern hemisphere. *S. alpestris* (syn. *Heliosperma alpestre*), 4 inches, white, summer, eastern Europe; var. *plena*, flowers double. *S. laciniata* (syn. *Melandrium laciniatum*), 8–10 inches, flowers scarlet, summer, United States. *S. maritima*, sea campion, 6 inches, flowers white, large, July to September, Europe including Britain; var. *plena*, flowers double. *S. saxifraga*, 6 inches, flowers white and brown, summer, Greece. *S. schafta*, 6–9 inches, flowers pink, summer and autumn, Caucasus. *S. virginica* (syn. *Melandrium virginicum*), fire pink, 1–1½ feet, flowers crimson, North America. *S. zawadskyi* (syn. *Melandrium zawadskyi*), 4–6 inches, flowers white, large, summer, Romania. Some good cultivars include *S. pendula compacta*, pink; *rubervina*, ruby red; 'Peach Blossom', single pink; 'Triumph', crimson-rose; 'Special Dwarf Mixture', double white through pink and lilac to crimson.

Cultivation The soil for annual and biennial species should be light and sandy, in a sunny bed or border. For perennials a sandy loam mixed with well-rotted organic material is suitable. *S. acaulis* requires equal parts of loam, peat and stones and prefers a sunny crack or shelf on a rock garden, as does *S. virginica*. Planting is carried out in the spring, and lifting and replanting should be undertaken only when absolutely essential. Propagation for annuals is by seed sown in September, transplanting the seedlings when they are 1 inch high, and then planting them in their permanent positions in March for spring flowering, or by seed sown in April, transplanting to flowering positions when 1-inch high for summer blooming, or by sowing seed where required to grow and thinning out in May. Perennials are propagated from seed sown in spring, in pans placed in cold frames, from cuttings and by division in spring.

Silphium (sil-fee-um)

The ancient Greek name referring to the resinous juice (*Compositae*). Rosinwood. A genus of 15 species of hardy perennial plants with the typical composite flower. The sap is resinous, and the plants were introduced from eastern North America.

Species cultivated *S. laciniatum*, the compass plant, so-called because the leaves often face north and south, 6–8 feet, flowers yellow, July to August. *S. perfoliatum*, the cup plant, so-called because the leaves are joined together and form a cup round the stem, 4–6 feet, flowers yellow, July.

Cultivation These plants are easily grown in ordinary soil in a sunny border or bed. Planting can be carried out between October and April, and every two or three years the plants should be lifted, divided and replanted. Propagation is by division of the roots, in October or March, or from seed sown in the spring.

Stachys (stak-is)

From the Greek *stachus*, a spike, alluding to the pointed inflorescences of this plant (*Labiatae*). A genus of 300 species of herbaceous perennials, annuals, subshrubs, with a few shrubby species, widely dispersed throughout the world. One tuberous-rooted species, *S. affinis*, is the

1 Silene maritima is the low-growing, white-flowered Sea Campion with a creeping habit.
2 Silene acaulis, the Moss Campion, forms a low pink cushion and prefers a sunny spot in the rock garden.
3 Silphium perfoliatum is called the Cup Plant because of its perfoliate leaves. It bears yellow daisy-like flowers in midsummer.

191

Chinese or Japanese artichoke or crosnes. Some species are also known as woundwort or betony; they are closely related to the deadnettles (*Lamium*).

Species cultivated *S. affinis* (syn. *S. sieboldii*, *S. tuberifera*), Chinese or Japanese artichoke, crosnes, 1–1½ feet, roots edible, flowers pink, rarely seen, summer, China, Japan. *S. coccinea*, 2 feet, flowers scarlet, summer, Central America. *S. corsica*, 1 inch, a good rock garden plant, forms carpets of small leaves, flowers pale pink, almost stemless, all summer, Mediterranean region. *S. lanata*, lamb's-ear, 1 foot, grey, densely woolly foliage, flowers small, purple, July, Caucasus to Persia. *S. lavandulifolia*, 6 inches, lavender-leaved, flowers purplish-rose, July to August, Armenia. *S. macrantha* (syns. *S. grandiflora*, *Betonica macrantha*), betony, 1 foot, violet, May to July, Caucasus. *S. officinalis*, bishop's wort, wood betony, to 3 feet, flowers purple, June to August, Europe.

Cultivation The hardy perennials thrive in ordinary soil in a warm sheltered border. The most attractive is *S. corsica*, which is a little tender and needs good drainage and sun. It is better under glass in winter. *S. lanata* is good for edgings to border or beds, and there is a form obtainable which does not flower. It should be planted in autumn or spring. Propagation is by division in autumn or spring.

1 Stachys macrantha, the Betony, is a summer-flowering native of the Caucasus. 2 Thalictrum aquilegiifolium has delicately textured foliage and fluffy pinkish flowers like tiny daisies.

Thalictrum (thal-ik-trum)

From the Greek *thaliktron*, a name used to describe a plant with divided leaves, possibly of the same family (*Ranunculaceae*). Meadow rue. A genus of 150 species of hardy perennials, herbaceous plants, mainly from north temperate regions but also represented in tropical South America, tropical Africa and South Africa. Those cultivated have elegant, fern-like foliage and dainty flowers. They are most effective when planted in bold groups.

Species cultivated *T. aquilegiifolium*, 3–4 feet, flowers pale purple in fluffy panicles, May to July, Europe, northern Asia. *T. chelidonii*, 2–3 feet, flowers large, mauve, July to August, Himalaya. *T. diffusiflorum*, 2–3 feet, finely cut, grey-green foliage, sprays of clear lilac flowers, July and August, Tibet; a difficult plant to establish. *T. dipterocarpum*, 3–5 feet, leaves dainty, blue-green, smooth, flowers deep lavender with prominent yellow anthers borne on slender stems, July and August, western China; vars. *album*, a graceful white form; 'Hewitt's Double', bright violet-mauve, fully double flowers,

freely produced. *T. flavum*, 2–3 feet, grey-green, glossy, finely cut foliage, soft yellow, feathery heads of flowers, July and August, Europe including Britain. *T. glaucum* (syn. *T. speciosissimum*), 5 feet, foliage glaucous, flowers yellow, summer, southern Europe, North Africa. *T. kuisianum*, 4 inches, foliage fern-like, flowers rosy-purple, spring, Japan, rock garden or alpine house. *T. minus* (syn. *T. adiantifolium*), 1½–2 feet, grown purely for its decorative, maidenhair fern-like foliage, borne on wiry stems which make it admirable for use with floral decorations, inconspicuous yellowish-green flowers in loose panicles, Europe (including Britain). *T. rocquebrunianum*, 4 feet, stems and leaf stalks purplish, flowers lavender-blue in large heads, summer.

Cultivation Thalictrums will grow in almost any soil, preferably of reasonable depth, but including those that contain much chalk, provided they do not bake dry. Plant them in full sun or dappled shade. Propagation is by seed or by division in the spring.

Tradescantia (trad-es-kan-tee-a)

Commemorating John Tradescant (died 1637), gardener to Charles I (*Commelinaceae*). A genus of 60 species of hardy perennial and greenhouse plants from

North America and tropical South America. The hardy varieties are commonly called spiderwort, flower of a day, Moses-in-the-bulrushes, or devil-in-the-pulpit. According to some botanists the garden plants grown under the name *T. virginiana* belonging to a hybrid group known as *T. × andersoniana*.

Species cultivated *T. albiflora,* wandering Jew, trailing, fast-growing greenhouse or house plant with shiny·stems, swollen at the nodes, leaves narrow, pointed, South America; several variegated forms are known with cream and yellow-striped leaves, green and white, or with faint red markings. *T. blossfeldiana,* creeping or trailing greenhouse or house plant, dark green leathery leaves, purple and whitely-hairy beneath, Argentine. *T. fluminensis,* wandering Jew, trailing greenhouse or house plant, often confused with *T. albiflora,* leaves slender-pointed, green, purplish-red beneath; several variegated forms, South America. *T. virginiana* (or *T. × andersoniana*) spiderwort, etc., hardy perennial, 1½–2 feet, flowers violet-blue from June to September, eastern United States; vars. *alba,* a white form; *coerulea,* bright blue; 'Iris Prichard', white, shaded violet at the centre; 'J. C. Weguelin', large azure-blue; 'Osprey', large, white,·with feathery blue stamens; *rosea,* pink, *rubra,* dark ruby-red.

Cultivation The tender species and varieties require a minimum winter temperature of 55°F (13°C), and should be potted in March or April, in ordinary potting soil. Avoid a rich compost which may cause the leaves to turn green and lose their variegations. Hardy varieties can be grown in ordinary garden soil in sun or partial shade. Lift and divide in autumn or spring every three or four years. Propagation of tender species is by cuttings taken from April to August and insert.d in pots of sandy soil in a warm propagating frame; they will root in four to six weeks. Hardy varieties may be increased by division in the spring.

Trollius (trol-lee-us)

From the German common name *trollblume,* or the Latin *trulleus,* a basin, referring to the flower shape (*Ranunculaceae*). Globe-flower. A genus of 25 species of hardy perennials with large buttercup-like blooms, and usually with palmately-lobed leaves. They are natives of northern temperate and arctic regions and are at their best beside a pool or stream.

Species cultivated *T. europaeus,* 1–2 feet, flowers lemon-yellow, May and June, Europe (including northern Britain and South Wales); vars. 'First Lancers', deep orange; 'Earliest of All', lemon-yellow, April–June; 'Goldquelle', orange-yellow, May; 'Helios', citron yellow; 'Orange Princess', bright orange-yellow. *T. ledebourii* (syn. *T. chinensis*), 2–3 feet, flowers deep orange with bright orange

1 *Verbascum dumulosum thrives in a hot, dry place.*
2 *Trollius europaeus 'The Globe' is one of many cultivars.*
3 *Tradescantia virginiana is a good herbaceous perennial for damp soil.*

stamens, June, northern China; a cultivar is 'Golden Queen', 2 feet, bright orange with conspicuous stamens. *T. pumilus,* 6–12 inches, buttercup-yellow, rock garden, June and July, Himalaya. *T. yunnanensis,* 1½–2 feet, flowers golden-yellow, western China.

Cultivation Plant in early autumn in semi-shade or in full sun, provided the soil is deep, moist and loamy. Every three or four years, lift and divide them in autumn. Seed may also be sown, preferably on ripening, in pans or boxes of a loamy compost in September or April and placed in a shaded cold frame or stood in the open in the shade.

Verbascum (ver-bas-kum)

Possibly from the Latin *barba,* a beard, many species having a hairy or downy look (*Scrophulariaceae*). Mullein. A genus of 300 species of hardy herbaceous plants, mostly biennials or short-lived perennials, from temperate parts of Europe and Asia.

Species cultivated *V. blattaria,* moth mullein, to 4 feet, flowers yellow·or cream, Europe, (including Britain). *V. bombyciferum* (syns. *V.* 'Broussa', *V.* 'Brusa'), biennial, 4–6 feet, stem and leaves covered in silvery hairs, flowers golden-yellow, embedded in silvery hairs, June–July, western Asia Minor. *V. chaixii* (syn. *V. vernale*), 3 feet, stems purple, leaves covered with whitish hairs, flowers yellow, June–August, Europe. *V. dumulosum,* 1 foot, perennial, leaves grey felted, flowers lemon-yellow, May–June, needs a hot, dry place or alpine house, Asia Minor. *V. nigrum* (syn. *V. vernale*), normally perennial, 2–3 feet, yellow, blotched reddish-brown, June to October, Europe including Britain. *V. olympicum,* peren-

nial, 5–6 feet, leaves grey felted, flowers golden, June to September, Bithynia; several cultivars in shades of amber, terracotta, purple and yellow. *V. phoeniceum,* purple mullein, 3–5 feet; hybrids available in pink, lilac, purple. *V. pulverulentum,* hoary mullein, leaves white hairy, flowers yellow, July, Europe including Britain. *V. thapsus,* Aaron's rod, hag taper, to 3 feet, very woolly, flowers yellow summer, Europe, Asia.

Cultivation Verbascums grow easily in sunny positions and ordinary or chalky soil. Propagation of species is by seed sown in light soil outdoors in April. Hybrids, some of which are sterile, are increased by root cuttings in autumn or winter.

Veronica (ver-on-ik-a)

Origin doubtful, possibly named after St Veronica (*Scrophulariaceae*). Speedwell. A genus of some 300 species of hardy perennials, annuals and sub-shrubs, mainly from northern temperate regions. Those described are hardy perennials, their flowers often borne in spikes. Dwarf kinds are suitable for the rock garden.

Species cultivated *V. agrestis,* procumbent speedwell, prostrate, flowers pink, annual weed, Europe including Britain. *V. chamaedrys,* germander speedwell, 1–1½ feet, bright blue, May onwards, Europe including Britain. *V. cinerea,* 6 inches, leaves grey, flowers pale blue, early summer. *V. exaltata,* 5 feet, mauve in tall spikes, late summer. *V. fruticans* (syn. *V. saxatilis*), rock speedwell, 3 inches, sub-shrub, deep blue with red eye, late summer. *V. gentianoides,* 2 feet, pale blue in slender spikes, May–June; vars. *nana,* 1 foot; *variegata,* leaves variegated, flowers deeper blue. *V. × guthrieana,* 3 inches, flowers large, blue, hybrid. *V. hederifolia,* ivy-leaved speedwell, similar to *V. agrestis,* Europe including Britain. *V. incana,* 1–2 feet, leaves grey, flowers dark blue, summer; var. *rosea,* pink. *V. longifolia,* 2–4 feet, lilac-blue, late summer; var. *subsessilis,* royal blue. *V. pectinata,* 3 inches, mat-forming, leaves grey, flowers deep blue with white eye, May; var. *rosea,* pink. *V. prostrata,* 6 inches, creeping, blue, summer; vars. 'Mrs Holt', pink; *rosea,* rosy-pink; 'Shirley Blue', deep blue; 'Trehane', leaves golden, flowers light blue. *V. spicata,* 2 feet, bright blue, late summer; vars. *alba,* white; many varieties in blue, purple, and pink. *V. scutellata,* marsh speedwell, creeping, flowers pale blue, pink or white, Europe, North America. *V. teucrium,* 1–2 feet, lavender-blue, late summer; vars. 'Blue Fountain', 2 feet, intense blue; 'Royal Blue', 1½ feet. *V. virginica,* 4–5 feet, light blue, late summer; var. *alba,* white. *V. whitleyi,* 3–4 inches, tufted, blue with white eye, June to August.

Cultivation Veronicas will grow in ordinary soil and a sunny position. Propagation is by division in August or in spring, or by seed sown in the open in spring in light soil and in part shade.

Viola (vi-o-la)

An old Latin name for violet (*Violaceae*). A genus of some 500 species of hardy perennials, mainly from northern temperate regions, including violas, pansies and violets of which there are many hybrids and strains.

Species cultivated *V. adunca,* hooked spur violet, to 4 inches, violet or lavender with white eye, spring, North America. *V. arvensis* field pansy, 6 inches, cream, Europe including Britain, Asia, annual weed. *V. cornuta,* horned violet, 9–12 inches, flowers violet, June to August, Pyrenees; cultivars, including the 'Violettas', derived mainly from this species, are available in shades of yellow, plum-purple, rosy-lilac, blue and white with a yellow eye. *V. cucullata,* 6 inches, white, veined lilac, April to June, North America. *V. × florairensis,* 4 inches, mauve and yellow, spring and summer, hybrid. *V. gracilis,* 4–6 inches, deep violet, April to August, Balkans, Asia Minor; vars. *alba,* white; 'Black Knight', purplish-black; *lutea,* golden-yellow;

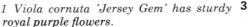

1 *Viola cornuta 'Jersey Gem' has sturdy royal purple flowers.*
2 *Viola tricolor hortensis 'Ardrossan Gem' is marked with yellow.*
3 *Viola odorata is the Sweet Violet.*
4 *Veronica teucrium 'Trehane' blooms in late summer.*
5 *Phlox paniculata (sometimes called Phlox decussata) 'Aurore'*

major, violet. *V. hispida,* Rouen pansy, to 8 inches, violet, summer, Europe. *V. labradorica,* 4–6 inches, porcelain-blue, summer, North America. *V. odorata,* see Violet. *V. palmata,* 6 inches, violet-purple, summer, North America. *V. rupestris,* Teesdale violet, to 2 inches, bluish-violet, Asia, Europe including Britain, North America. *V. saxatilis,* 4–8 inches, violet, summer, Europe, Asia Minor. *V. × wittrockiana,* see Pansy.

Cultivation Violas do best in a moist, well-drained soil and in light shade. Propagation of cultivars is by cuttings rooted in late summer in sandy soil in a cold, shaded frame. Species and strains are raised from seed sown in late summer in light soil in a cold, shaded frame.

Violet

Viola odorata, the sweet violet, is a hardy perennial, parent of the florist's violets, many of them sweetly scented. The soil should be rich and moist but well-drained. Plant the crowns in the open in a sheltered, shady position in April, or in September for winter flowering in a cold sunny frame. Propagation is by runners removed in April. Other runners that are produced during the summer months should be removed and discarded.

Named varieties include: 'Couer d'Alsace', pink; 'Czar', blue; 'De Parme', pale lavender, double; 'Governor Herrick', deep blue; 'Marie Louise', mauve, double, good for frame cultivation; 'La France', violet-blue; 'Princess of Wales', large violet-blue; 'Sulphurea', creamy-yellow; 'White Czar', single white.

Index